Debt and the
Less Developed Countries

Other Titles in This Series

Oil and Money and the World Economy, Yoon S. Park

The New International Economic Order, edited by Karl P. Sauvant and Hajo Hasenpflug

International Business in the Middle East: Case Studies, edited by Ashok Kapoor

The Sogo Shosa: *Japan's Multinational Trading Companies*, Alexander K. Young

Kuwait: Trade and Investment, Ragaei El Mallakh

Foreign Investments and the Management of Political Risk, Dan Haendel

U.S.-Mexico Economic Relations, edited by Barry M. Poulson and T. Noel Osborn

Extraterritorial Antitrust: The Sherman Act vs. the Market Entry Strategy of Selected Multinational Corporations, James B. Townsend, Jr.

International Trade and Agriculture: Theory and Policy, edited by Jimmye S. Hillman and Andrew Schmitz

Westview Special Studies in International Economics and Business

Debt and the Less Developed Countries
edited by Jonathan David Aronson

Scholars and practitioners from the fields of economics, political science, sociology, and government discuss the nature and importance of debt in the international system and question whether international debt is a necessary element of international development or a potential root of international economic collapse (and of the demise of the dollar as denominator of the monetary realm). They then turn specifically to the impact of external debt on developing countries, exploring the potential for both positive and negative effects. In the final section of the book they look at the interactions between debtors and creditors when loans begin to sour.

Jonathan David Aronson is assistant professor of international relations and director of the Mid-Career Master's Program at the School of International Relations, University of Southern California.

Debt and the
Less Developed Countries

edited by Jonathan David Aronson

Westview Press / Boulder, Colorado

Westview Special Studies in International Economics and Business

Copyright © 1979 by Westview Press, Inc.

Published in 1979 in the United States of America by
    Westview Press, Inc.
    5500 Central Avenue
    Boulder, Colorado 80301
    Frederick A. Praeger, Publisher

Library of Congress Cataloging in Publication Data
Main entry under title:
Debt and the less developed countries.
    (Westview special studies in international economics and business)
    Bibliography: p.
    1. Underdeveloped areas—Debts, External. 2. Debts, External. I. Aronson, Jonathan David. II. Series.
HG4517.D36   336.3'435'091724   79-569
ISBN 0-89158-370-X

Printed and bound in the United States of America

For Zieb

He lived with passion and elegance,
He cared for people and for justice,
And he had the courage to try to help

Contents

List of Tables and Figures xi
Introduction xv
The Contributors. xix

Part One
The Expansion of External Debt
within the Less Developed Countries

Introduction 3

1. Debt and Default in the International
Political Economy, *Susan Strange* 7

2. International Public Lending and American
Policy, *Brian G. Crowe* 27

3. Private Overseas Lending: Too Far, Too Fast?
Jane D'Arista. 57

4. Financial Interrelations, the Balance of
Payments, and the Dollar Crisis,
Hyman P. Minsky 103

Part Two
Debt and Development

Introduction 125

5. Bankers as Revolutionaries in the Process
of Development, *Clark W. Reynolds* 129

6. Debt, Indenture, and Development, *Arthur B. Laffer* 157

7. Brazil's Debt-Burdened Recession: Consequences of Short-Term Difficulties or of Structures of Production and Consumption? *W. Ladd Hollist*......171

8. Political Economy of International Debt: The Dynamics of Financial Capital, *R. Peter DeWitt and James F. Petras*..............191

Part Three
The Politics of International
Debt Renegotiations

Introduction 219

9. Peru and the U.S. Banks: Privatization of Financial Relations, *Barbara Stallings*...........225

10. The Politics of Debt Relief: Official Creditors and Brazil, Ghana, and Chile, *John S. Odell* 253

11. The Politics of Private Bank Lending and Debt Renegotiations, *Jonathan David Aronson* ..283

12. The IMF, Commercial Banks, and Third World Debts, *Charles Lipson*..............................317

Selected Bibliography, *William. E. Westermeyer*..........335
Index..347

Tables and Figures

Tables
Chapter 1
1. Gross Disbursements, Debt Service, and Net Transfers
   for 67 Non-Oil-Exporting LDCs, 1965 and 1973. 19
Chapter 2
1. World Payments Patterns—Balances on Goods, Services,
   and Private and Government Transfers 28
2. Non-Oil-Exporting Developing Country External Debt. . . .29
3. Breakdown of 1977 Debt Attributable to Non-Oil-
   Exporting Developing Countries .31
4. International Debt Rescheduling Exercises: 1956-1978 . . .38
5. Proportion of Non-Oil-Exporting Developing Country
   Debt Attributable to Private Sources. 47
Chapter 3
1. Ratios of Foreign Loans of U.S. Banks to Bank Capital . . .66
2. Ratios of Loans of U.S. Banks to Bank Capital for
   Selected Less Developed Countries 67
3. U.S. Bank Loans to Selected Foreign Governments:
   June 1977 and December 1977. .68
4. Maturity Structure of LDC Debt. 71
5. U.S. Bank Loans to Foreign Countries by Groups of
   Countries, Groups of Banks, and Types and Maturities
   of Loans 75
6. U.S. Bank Loans to Selected LDCs by Groups of Banks
   and Types and Maturities of Loans 77
7. Eurocurrency Market: Sources and Uses of Funds by
   Groups of Countries, December 1977 86

8. U.S. Capital Account Summary. .87
9. Claims (Liabilities) of U.S. Banks' Overseas Branches 90
Chapter 4
1. United States Balance of Payments 112
Chapter 7
1. Brazil's Real Output Growth Rates by Major Sector 173
2. Indexes of Brazil's Per Capita Production in Food
   and Manufactures: 1962-1974. .178
3. Changes in Brazil's Income Distribution 179
Chapter 8
1. Average Interest Rates on Loan Commitments,
   Selected Countries. 200
Chapter 9
1. Peruvian Debt and Debt Service, 1968-1978 230
Chapter 11
1. Publicly Announced Private Bank Lending to Zaire by
   the Largest 300 Banks in the World: 1973-1976 290
2. Publicly Announced Private Bank Lending to Indonesia
   by the Largest 300 Banks in the World: 1973-1976 294
3. Publicly Announced Private Bank Lending to Turkey by
   the Largest 300 Banks in the World: 1973-1976 298
4. Publicly Announced Private Bank Lending to Brazil by
   the Largest 300 Banks in the World: 1973-1976 301
5. Publicly Announced Private Bank Lending to Mexico by
   the Largest 300 Banks in the World: 1973-1976 302

Figures
Chapter 5
1. A Complete Sector Sources and Uses of Funds
   Statement 147
2. Flow of Funds Matrix for the Whole Economy. 149
3. A Resource Intensive Activity's Real and Financial
   Flows During the Raw Material Product Cycle 152
Chapter 8
1. Total, International and Domestic Earnings of 13
   Large U.S. Banks for 1972 and 1976. 193

It's a curious thing, this thing we call civilization. . . . We think it is an affair of epochs and of nations. It is really an affair of individuals.

—William Dean Howells
The Rise of Silas Lapham

Introduction

Debt's role in the transition from backwardness to dignity and appropriate development is subtle and complex. Too much debt or the inefficient use of borrowed funds can result in heightened dependence of less developed nations on their external creditors and to brutal and worsening inequity within those nations. Borrowed funds can also be used to build the structures needed to satisfy basic human needs and to make the dreams of people and nations a reality. Debt is neither inherently good nor bad. It is therefore desirable to examine the possibilities and the pitfalls that accompany the extension of debt to nations attempting to industrialize their economies and enter the modern world.

Debt and its relationship to less developed countries (LDCs) can be analyzed at several levels. Most straightforwardly, the magnitude of a single nation's or the world debt can be computed. Domestic and external debt can be compared and their relative rates of accumulation assessed. The sources and uses of funds can be categorized and the policies of official and private debtor and creditor institutions investigated. Past records of repayments and defaults can be noted and policies aimed to safeguard future debt servicing underscored. Such statistical and historical measures are the essential base from which political and economic analyses of debt and the developing countries must proceed.

A second level of analysis, too often ignored, focuses on the implications of expanding global debt, including LDC debt, for the stability of the world monetary system and for the growth and prosperity of the developed nations. The 1970s has been a decade of turmoil in the world monetary realm. The collapse of the Bretton Woods system has required a transition from fixed to flexible exchange rates. Inflation has become endemic throughout much of the world. The quadrupling of oil prices in the wake of the 1973 embargo sent bureaucrats scurrying to reconsider their overall growth strategies, created severe balance-of-payments discrepancies in many nations, and focused attention on the necessity of petrodollar recycling. Simultaneously, the Eurocurrency markets continued to expand, beyond the control of government regulators, at breakneck speed throughout the 1970s. Within this milieu, private banks became the major lenders to many of the wealthier non-oil developing countries, replacing governments and official institutions in this role. It is therefore important to consider the implications of debt for the stability of the entire monetary system and for creditors as well as for debtors.

A third perspective on debt and the LDCs requires a close study of the effectiveness of borrowed funds in helping achieve development objectives. Does the expansion of debt necessarily lead to fruitful improvements in the quality of life for the bulk of the population, or does debt exacerbate the divisions between the rich and poor in the dependent, developing nations? How could and should borrowed domestic and external funds be employed to improve the lot of people and nations? If debt is improving the welfare of the developing world, how might it be used more effectively and could more funds be efficiently used? If debt is creating growth without development, how might this situation be remedied? These questions are critical to understanding the role of official and private external debt in the process of development.

Finally, it is necessary to examine the past, present, and potential future interactions between creditors and debtors. What are the political and economic implications of these interactions? How have relations between official creditors and debtors developed? Does this differ importantly from the political interactions between private creditors and LDC debtors? Specifically, what impact might private actors have on the political and economic dealings between nations? In addition, what direct or mediating roles do the International Monetary Fund (IMF), the World Bank, and other international institutions play in the expansion and flows of global debt?

This volume explores these dimensions of debt. Part One looks at the history and statistical panorama that illuminates the growth of external LDC debt in the past decade. The final essay in the section explores the opportunities and ambushes facing the world monetary system as a result of the expansion of U.S. lending to the world system. Part Two examines the impact of external debt on the process of development. Part Three looks at the interactions between creditors and debtors in the light of recent fears that massive defaults, refinancings, and reschedulings could rock the stability of major financial institutions and of the world economic system.

One advantage of an edited volume such as this one is that it is possible to gather perspectives on the same question from different disciplines and ideological viewpoints. The present volume includes material by five political scientists, three economists, two sociologists, two practitioners (one from the executive and one from the legislative side), and one international political economist. Most of them will rankle somewhat at being so definitely classified since their interests in almost all cases extend beyond the formal boundaries of their own disciplines and encompass questions that fall into the gaps between fields.

Normative and ideological assumptions of the contributors also diverge widely. Some authors for this volume firmly believe that current development policies of the industrial world are cogent and sensible in their handling of debt and debt servicing and others see current debt practices as misguided at best and as disruptive, impoverishing, and neo-imperial at worst. Between these extremes are several fence sitters who see both hope and problems with current debt developments.

Thus, although this volume is designed to link together the most critical aspects of the international debt situation, it does not speak with a coherent voice. The object is to provoke thought and further concern, not to solve the problems surrounding international debt. Ambiguity and passion of the contributors remain. There are instances where direct clashes of prospects and outlooks are made explcit. Nonetheless, it is hoped that this systematic treatment of issues surrounding debt and the less developed countries will underscore the salience of these problems for development and for the management of global interdependence in the remaining years of this century.

Still, this collection does not deal with many critical areas involving international debt. Questions revolving around lending to the Soviet Union, China, and other socialist nations are not considered here. It also would have been possible to assemble entire volumes dealing with governmental, private, or international-organizational lending to LDCs. Although these distinctions are repeatedly emphasized, contributors tried to look beyond short-term problems and concentrate on continuing phenomena. The intention here is to clarify trends and relationships that will continue to haunt debtors and creditors in the world economy long after the individual cases cited here have faded from memory.

—J.D.A.

The Contributors

Jonathan David Aronson is an assistant professor of international relations at the University of Southern California and author of *Money and Power: Banks and the World Monetary System* (Sage Publishers, 1978).

Brian G. Crowe is a foreign service officer with the Department of State. He has worked with the Office of Monetary Affairs on issues related to developing country indebtedness since 1975.

Jane D'Arista is an analyst in the National Security and International Affairs Division of the Congressional Budget Office. She was previously on the staff of the House Banking, Finance, and Urban Affairs Committee and has written studies on the development of Federal Reserve open-market operations, foreign bank activities in the United States, and American bank operations overseas.

R. Peter DeWitt is an assistant professor in the School of Management at the State University of New York at Binghamton and author of *The Inter-American Development Bank and Political Influence* (Praeger, 1977).

W. Ladd Hollist is an assistant professor of international relations at the University of Southern California. His recent research focused on the empirical analysis of dependence relations, particularly within the United States–Latin American context. His work has appeared in the *Journal of Politics*, the *International Studies Quarterly*, the *American Journal of Political Science*, and elsewhere.

Arthur B. Laffer is professor of business economics in the

School of Business Administration at the University of Southern California. He is well known for his work on global monetarism and tax theory and particularly for his "Laffer curve."

Charles Lipson is an assistant professor of political science at the University of Chicago. He is the author of *Standing Guard: The Protection of Foreign Investment* (University of California Press, 1979). His work has appeared in *World Politics, International Organization,* and elsewhere.

Hyman P. Minsky is a professor of economics at Washington University. He is the author of *John Maynard Keynes* (Columbia University Press, 1975) and is well known for his work on financial fragility.

John S. Odell is an assistant professor of government and a research fellow of the Center for International Affairs at Harvard University. His work has concerned the formation of U.S. international monetary policy, U.S.-Latin American trade relations, and economic theories of imperialism.

James F. Petras is professor of sociology at the State University of New York at Binghamton. His numerous works on Latin America include *The United States and Chile* (Monthly Review Press, 1975), *The Nationalization of Venezuelan Oil* (Praeger, 1977), and *Critical Perspectives on Imperialism and Social Class in the Third World* (Monthly Review Press, 1978).

Clark W. Reynolds is a professor of economics at the Food Research Institute, Stanford University. His current research includes work on financial intermediation and development and on the impact of the U.S. economy on the economy of Mexico and its border regions. He is the author of *The Mexican Economy: Twentieth Century Structure and Growth* (Yale University Press, 1970), "The Use of Flow of Funds Analysis in the Study of Latin American Capital Market Development," *International Review of the History of Banking* (9:1974), and numerous other books and articles on Latin American economics.

Barbara Stallings is assistant professor of political science at the University of Wisconsin-Madison. She is the author of *Economic Dependency in Africa and Latin America* and *Class Conflict and Economic Development in Chile*. She is currently working on a book on private bank loans to Third World countries.

Susan Strange is the Montague Burton Professor of International Relations at the London School of Economics and Politics. Her works include *Sterling and British Policy* (Oxford University Press, 1971) and *International Monetary Relations,* which is the second volume of *International Economic Relations of the Western World 1959-1971,* edited by Andrew Shonfield (Oxford University Press, 1976).

William E. Westermeyer is a graduate student at the School of International Relations at the University of Southern California.

Part One

The Expansion of External Debt within the Less Developed Countries

Let us live in as small a circle as we will, we are either debtors or creditors before we have had time to look round.

—Goethe

Introduction

Individual debt dramas are pieces of an unassembled jigsaw puzzle. Viewed in isolation, they are blotches of color on a drab background. Only after a frame has been assembled around them do the pieces begin to become part of a larger whole. The initial section of this volume sets the context. We dash across the stage of history, indicating the links between the debt of nations today and the debt of preceding eras. At a more leisurely pace, the articles in Part One outline the dimensions of the current international debt situation. The extent and distribution of public debt are analyzed and the policies of the major public creditors toward their debtors are explained. The rapid growth of private external debt and its distribution throughout borrowing nations are also documented. Finally, the view of the role of debt is widened by examining the place of debt in the maintenance and management of a stable international monetary system. This frame-building of Part One will, it is hoped, make it possible to see the pieces examined in Parts Two and Three in better perspective.

Part One opens with Susan Strange's analysis of the broad sweep of international debt. She examines the role of debt in the process of economic development, paying particular attention to the role of external debt. She places international debt into a longer historical perspective and considers the relevance that past behavior of lenders and borrowers may have for their contemporary counterparts. She concludes that, despite inevitable setbacks, international debt (or credit creation) can serve the interests of both the international public and private lenders and the borrowers in developing countries.

Brian G. Crowe presents the data on official lending to developing countries in recent years and describes the creditor-club mechanism employed during official debt renegotiations. Moreover, he articulates the U.S. policy concerning the renegotiation of international debts and illustrates the process favored by the U.S. government in cases where international debt repayments fall into arrears. The assumptions underlying American policy directions are also explained.

Jane D'Arista's essay complements Brian Crowe's effort in the private lending realm. She has assembled a remarkable collection of information that paints the expansion of American international bank lending in the past decade in vivid detail. But her analysis extends far beyond the statistics she has assembled and treats the key problems of how much lending, from what sources, and at what rate of expansion makes sense for the banks, the borrowing countries, and the system itself. She examines the implications of debt for the banks' solvency and also for the stability of the Eurocurrency market in a time of massive growth and petrodollar recycling.

Hyman P. Minsky's thoughtful analysis of the implications of the proliferation of American dollars beyond the control of American authorities concludes the initial section. He is concerned with the constraints that the debt/credit process has placed on creditors and particularly on the nation that supplies the key currency for the operation of the international monetary system. He argues that, although currencies that are not used to denominate transactions and debts may depreciate without destabilizing the world economy, the same is not the case for the system's reserve currency. Professor Minsky chides the United States to accept its responsibility for the maintenance of the dollar not only to ensure the strength of the American economy but also to safeguard the monetary system. He suggests appropriate policies. Although dealing only indirectly with the developing countries, he shows how the expansion of debt to

those and other countries and entities has created significant
problems for the management of the global economic and
monetary system.

—J.D.A.

1
Debt and Default in the International Political Economy

Susan Strange

Indebtedness among developing countries generates fierce emotions. Anger, anxiety, fear, resentment, jealousy, disdain, and discontent—these are strong feelings often associated with debtors or creditors or (for different reasons) with both at once. Neither side in a debt situation finds it easy to keep cool, particularly when the debt is international, the debtor being of one nationality, the creditor another. All the more reason, then, for cool assessments that seek to ascertain the relevant facts, perceive the long-run interest of those concerned, and lay out for judgment the rational choice of policy options.

By way of introduction to the other, more specialized essays in this volume, this chapter will propose two ways of standing back a little from the immediate situation, in order to deal with it as rationally and prudently as possible. One is to consider the way in which the treatment of debts has evolved in most of the advanced market economies, how it has been managed politically as well as how it has contributed to economic development. The second is to put international debt into a longer historical perspective than just the past ten years or so, and to consider what conclusions may be drawn from past behavior of debtors and creditors.

Rather more than ten years ago, I tried to do this in an article published in *International Affairs*, the journal of the Royal Institute of International Affairs.[1] I began it by remarking that in the nineteenth century and in the pre-1914 period the problem of default on international debt was a recurrent one, to which the creditor countries especially gave much time and thought,

seeking to devise theories, policies, legal concepts, and adminis-
trative remedies to deal with it. The sense of surprise with
which the topic was rediscovered during the 1960s was possible
only because for the two decades before World War II and the
two decades after it the problem was suppressed rather than
solved. It was not really a new problem; it only seemed so.

Having blocked out the broad features of the subject from
these wider perspectives, it is necessary to ask if any major
changes—political or economic—have appeared in the last ten
years to modify conclusions reached in the mid-1960s. This
introductory paper, then, may suggest some broad hypotheses
about the role of debt in the development of international political economy which might be borne in mind while examining
in subsequent chapters specific aspects of the problem, or specific issues and situations.

1. Debt and Economic Growth

A political economy has two ways to grow: by direction and
by debt. Direction requires a central authority to use its political
power to preempt resources from immediate consumption and
to make sure that they are used for capital goods and for such
other long-term investments (in transport, education, "infrastructure" of all kinds) as will enhance the possibilities of future
consumption. This is the preferred path to growth of socialist
and other centrally planned economies. It is not a path open to
an international political economy in which political power is
dispersed among more than a hundred state governments. However weak some of them may be, they have enough power to
frustrate any overall plan for economic growth.[2] There remains
debt—or the creation of credit, which is the inseparable, mirror
image of debt, but without all the emotive associations of guilt,
dependence, or obligation.

Every one of the developed market economies has been able
to expand its productive capacity only by steadily increasing
the amount and complexity of debt—or conversely the amount
and complexity of credit—and by extending to new groups and
activities the necessary access to credit instruments and credit-
creating institutions, whether public or private. Every one of

them has also embarked on the path of credit creation with little idea of the political requirements of a credit-based economy. The lessons have usually been learned only by bitter experience—of bursting bubbles and collapsing banks, of fraudulent enterprises and imprudent risk-taking.

In almost all the national economic systems, the emphasis of political management was first put on the control of debtors, often by personal punishment used in the hope that it would also act as deterrent. It was strongly reinforced by social disapproval. Dickens's novels of English life in the mid-nineteenth century, for example, are full of the overhanging threat of the debtors' prison and the shame and hopelessness of those condemned to it, with the consequent loss of their best chance of repaying their debts. The Scottish novelist Sir Walter Scott wrote furiously for years primarily to repay his father's debts and thus to clear the family name and honor. But in most of the European countries, it was only a social minority that had access to credit on any scale and had the chance of falling into debt. For them, social status and family connections opened the doors to credit. The great majority had only the moneylender and the pawnshop, with its harsh requirements of negotiable collateral, to look to for temporary (and expensive) credit.

Even so, the punishment of debtors soon gave way in Europe and America to the regulation of creditors, or more precisely of credit creators, especially banks and insurance institutions. As the pyramid of created credit grew in each of the industrializing countries, so did the concern of governments with the regulation of financial markets and their operators. The managerial functions of the central bank, as watchdog, director, and lender of last resort to the major banks and credit institutions, everywhere became more vital for the stable management of the national economy.

Yet, paradoxically, as access to credit slowly opened up for new groups and classes and as the volume of debt outstanding in these national economies grew, the risks to the system from default did not seem to increase proportionately. It even seems as if the extension of credit over greater numbers actually reduced the risks incident on any one or two debt situations. It became commonplace for bankruptcies to be counted by millions of pounds or dollars and for individual banks or corporations to register very large defaulted debts without causing grave reverberations through the rest of the economy. By the 1920s, each of the major national systems could sustain the shock of quite substantial bankruptcies and defaults. It was usually external variables—as in 1929—that introduced new instability into national credit structures. Other times the credit-creating activities of governments on their own behalf brought on new strains. Admittedly, the supervision of credit systems by national monetary authorities has required (and still requires) eternal vigilance. The profits of credit creation are an invitation to the ingenious to find gaps in any set of restrictions. As recently as 1973, the Bank of England found itself unexpectedly enmeshed in a major crisis concerning the operations of secondary banks.[3] The U.S. authorities quite recently found that the restrictions on real-estate investment trusts (REITs) that were subsidiaries of banks were too loose for the latter's security.

Two parallel developments have accompanied the paradox of expanding debt and decreasing risk to the system. One is the spread of insurance, both for corporate enterprises and for individuals. The other is the extension of publicly financed welfare. Both have served to reduce the incidence of desperate debt. That is to say, there is less need to resort to further borrowing by a debtor already unable to service past debts out of current income—thus starting a vicious circle from which escape is very difficult. Welfare services provide a floor cushion between the debtor and total destitution. Insurance covers many of the risks which, when they come together, can make a debtor default. And, although the absolute cost of insurance against all the possible risks can increase quite sharply because of the capital involved in high-technology industry, the relative cost as a proportion of assets or of sales may still decline. Moreover, in advanced credit structures, the insurance principle works for the creditor as well as the debtor. Shops and other larger enterprises insure against bad debts as they do against shoplifting, pilfering, and other risks. The larger the turnover, the easier it is for the enterprise to absorb or even disregard such losses. On a larger scale, this is also true for national economies. The bigger the balloon, the more pinpricks it can bear without collapse.

To sum up, it seems as though economies growing through constant credit creation rather than by direction have been able to abandon the use of punishment as a means of controlling debtors and to take bigger and bigger risks by continually extending access to credit. The credit system has been shielded from the full impact of all these risks by the increasing provision of welfare and the increasing resort to insurance—a system of credit creation that differs from banking chiefly in that the credit is based on the debtor's own deposits rather than someone else's, but resembles banking in that the availability of credit based on insurance assets is far greater at any one time than the amount deposited.

2. The Historical Perspective

By the mid-1960s, certainly by 1966, the reemergence of international indebtedness as a generic issue in the international political economy was becoming acknowledged. By then, there had been enough debt crises and near crises for some sort of pattern to be perceived, and for discussion to be started on the general issue of debt rather than just on the problems of particular countries in difficulty with their international debts. Dragoslav Avromovic, a World Bank Staff economist, had published his seminal study, *Economic Growth and External Debt.*[4] The Economic Secretariat of the United Nations had collected data on the growth during the 1960s of export credits and published the findings in a report, *Export Credits and Development Financing.*[5] Also, the newly established United Nations Conference on Trade and Development (UNCTAD) had requested the World Bank to collect more detailed information on the use of suppliers' credit for exports to developing countries.[6] This sudden reawakening to an old problem was probably a result of the close coincidence of three quite serious debt crises, all in 1966: Ghana, Indonesia, and the United Arab Republic. The circumstances common to each of the three countries—heavy involvement in external borrowing, great ambitions for economic power never quite matched by economic performance, plus a measure of political instability—were not at all unusual

among developing countries. Others, it was realized, might soon
follow a similar path.

In retrospect, even then, this recognition of an endemic question seemed belated. International economic historians and international lawyers were familiar with the dilemma of creditors in
an anarchical political system: the need to choose between the
risks of political destabilization that might follow coercive intervention to collect the debts and the risks of economic loss,
possibly repeated elsewhere, if the debts went uncollected and
default took place with indemnity. But after World War II, the
dilemma was forgotten, or at least treated lightly, for a combination of political and economic reasons. The U.S. involvement
in fighting the Cold War in Western Europe had produced a
mammoth effort of credit creation in the shape of Marshall aid.
The American farsightedness in excluding the question of repayment, not only from Lend-Lease but also from the Marshall
Plan and putting (in effect) four-fifths of its $32 billion trade
surplus at the disposition of the European countries for their
postwar recovery, ensured that the damage and disruption
caused by the war was quickly repaired. Aided by the 1949
devaluations of almost all the European currencies except the
Swiss franc, Europe was consequently able, in its turn and by
the end of the 1950s, to join with the United States in extending credit to the less developed countries (LDCs).

Yet at the same time, the ten-year time lag between the war's
end and Europe's economic recovery affected the world economic debt situation in another way. It took ten years, or there-
abouts, for the American-European balance to be so restored
that currencies other than the dollar could become fully convertible. But until this happened, the private international credit
structure could not resume its business in earnest. This delay in
the revival of any significant international banking and borrowing meant that international lending in the 1950s was still on a
fairly modest scale. Much of it was either directly devoted to
financing trade or was in the shape of direct investment by
corporations, mainly U.S., in Canada, Europe, and Latin
America with some outflow also from Britain, primarily to the
old sterling area.[7] As the Reddaway report on British overseas
investment made very clear, this sort of capital flow created few

debt problems since companies could rarely expect much immediate return on their capital.[8]

Even so, indicators of coming debt instability and of the return of the creditors' old dilemma (and, conversely, of the debtors' old dependence) were already there by the late 1950s. The first two cases of near-default—by Brazil in 1951-1953, followed by Argentina—were not anticipated by the creditors, although with hindsight their likelihood was clear. The creditors first negotiated bilaterally, but quickly organized themselves in the first of the creditor clubs—the Hague Club (1955) and the Paris Club (1956)—in which, having sustained very heavy losses, they put strict limits on the defaulters' future access to trade credit. (The British Export Credit Guarantee Department lost the whole of its accumulated surplus in Brazil and had to start 1953 in deficit.) And, in both cases, the resolution of the situation proved only temporary. By 1957 Argentina was in trouble again, and by 1961 so was Brazil, neither for the last time. The experience of loss, however, helped the creditor countries to reach an agreement to limit their enthusiasm for financing export trade with guaranteed credit. The "understanding" reached through the Berne Union of Credit Insurers in 1953 on the terms and conditions of trade credit, although constantly breached and renegotiated, was the first significant acknowledgment that it was the creditors, not the debtors, who needed to be restrained.

Perhaps it was significant that the creditors' dilemma first reappeared in Latin America and that the next serious threat of nonrepayment came from India. For, during most of the 1950s, the dismemberment of the French and British colonial empires in Africa had yet to come; there were still comparatively few developing countries outside Latin America that were politically free to borrow substantially abroad, just as the available channels of access to credit were still small and few. The Indian government embarked in 1956 on an ambitious Second Five-Year Plan of economic development. By 1958, India had used up most of the sterling credit balances accumulated during the war, and the 1957 check to world trade made it impossible to keep up repayments on past loans while paying for capital goods under the plan. The World Bank, which had lent comparatively heavily to India, then convened the first of the aid-consortia—meetings of ad hoc groups of countries providing aid to a developing country to review the country's economic progress (or lack of it) and to pledge, if possible, such disbursements of future loans as to avert the need for default.

At first a clear distinction was drawn between the "aid-consortia" set up for India and Pakistan and the "consultative groups" set up between donor countries with respect to Nigeria, Tunisia, Colombia, and the Sudan—the latter undertaking no pledges of credit to the developing country. But later, as the World Bank played a more active role of impressing on members of consultative groups the risks they ran by failing to keep the near-defaulters afloat, and as formal pledges to countries like India and Pakistan (actually at war with each other in 1965) became politically embarrassing, the distinction ceased to have much meaning.

Both arrangements, however, indicated the common concern of creditor countries: (1) to avert open default if at all possible and (2) to spread the costs and risks of doing so as widely as possible. The arrangements displayed an awareness by the rich countries of the credit trap they had created for themselves in lending in the first place—an awareness just as acute as the poor countries' perception of the debt trap: that dependence on continued financing made them susceptible to foreign, neo-colonialist intervention in their domestic economic management by the officials of the World Bank or the International Monetary Fund. But, as Christopher Prout has pointed out, the rich countries, as lenders, behave "like highly speculative fringe bankers devoted entirely to profit considerations and mindless of asset security," while later, as creditors, "they establish elaborate and lengthy procedures to salvage a financial disaster which need never have happened if even a fraction of the cooperation they displayed ex post the insolvency had been demonstrated ex ante the insolvency."[9]

In this respect, neither the imprudence of creditors nor the improvidence of debtors had changed significantly since the other longish period of widespread international credit creation from about 1870 to 1914. That period also laid the basis for the economic strength of both of today's superpowers. Both superpowers, in fact, had then managed to borrow on a quite unprecedented scale without ever paying it all back. In the United States, the foreign borrowing was mostly done early in the nineteenth century by a stage army of debtors beginning with the federal government, followed by state governments, followed by the railroads, the mineral industries, real-estate ventures, and a variety of commercial and financial enterprises. There were times, more than a few, when European creditors swore, in vain, never to be taken in again by American optimism and persuasion. The Russians borrowed later, mostly from France and only latterly from Britain. Herbert Feis remarked of the politically directed French involvement in Russia, "Towards the end the large volume of Russian securities already possessed by [the banks'] depositors would have compelled them to support Russian credit even though they might have wished to curtail new loans. The credit trap for France was a big one; between 11 and 12 billion francs of which 9 billion were directly or indirectly lent to the Russian government."[10]

The American and Russian examples underscore the fact that the use of punitive coercion on debtors was relatively rare even in the nineteenth century, if one considers the rapid expansion in international credit creation and the long string of defaulter debts. Many recall the Anglo-German-Italian naval blockade of Venezuela in 1902-1903. But the long history of Portuguese and Spanish default (in which nobody used force) is mostly forgotten. It is true the United States perfected the technique of the customhouse takeover to deal with Central American and Caribbean countries whose governments were not only overthrown quite frequently, but tended each time to gaily revoke their predecessors' external debt. It was debt, too, and the repetition of default that brought French administration into Morocco in 1911 and British administration into Egypt (and subsequently the Sudan) in 1883 after the failure of the Anglo-French Dual Control. But in both cases the intervention might never have happened if confidence on the creditors' side had not been checked by weak, ineffectual government on the debtors', so that instead of wanting their loans repaid the creditors would have been happy to lend more and more.

They did so easily enough with Japan, half of whose public

debt before 1914 was borrowed abroad, at a rate of interest that fell from 9 percent in 1870 to 4 percent by the end of the century. They even did so with the Ottoman Empire and with the Chinese, both before and after the revolution of 1911. In both these countries, the creditors elaborated new and sophisticated versions of the customhouse takeover, perhaps not so much to make sure the debt was repaid as to bolster the confidence of the bondholders. As Feis remarked in relation to the multilateral Debt Administration accepted by the Ottoman Empire as a supervisor of government revenues, "The existence of the Debt Administration secured it trust that otherwise would have been denied, trust on interest terms lower than 5% up to 1914."[11] In historical perspective, there seems little difference between that situation and contemporary ones in which the function of the World Bank, the International Finance Corporation, or the annual missions of the IMF is at least as much to stiffen the nerves of the foreign creditors as to enslave the debtor country's government in collective colonialism.

One may also search nineteenth-century history in vain for any consistent policy or any coherent and agreed doctrine regarding the rights and duties of international creditors and debtors. The famous Palmerston memorandum of 1848, which purported to lay down the principles of British foreign policy toward recalcitrant foreign debtors, evenhandedly proclaimed the right of British governments to intervene while denying the right of British creditors to rely on the government's backing if they had been foolish enough to risk their money in uncertain foreign ventures. As Feis says:

> Swayed between political and financial considerations, the government now resisted, now yielded to the pressure of the interested parties. The outlook of the Ministry in power, the course of domestic politics, the allies that injured bondholders could find—all these might and did enter to turn events. Small wonder that the record shows a fitfull, hesitant policy, a tendency now to drift with events, now to act with sternness, now to evade ... there is no simple formula by which the government's behavior can be summarized.[12]

(Substitute bankers for bondholders and *plus ça change . . . .*) Conversely, the 1902 attempt by an Argentinian foreign minister to assert the contrary Drago Doctrine, denying states the rights to use coercive force against recalcitrant debtors, was good public relations: it was followed up by the Hague Convention of 1907 which limited the employment of force for the recovery of contract debts. But that convention did not stop the British from using a warship to intimidate Guatemala in 1913 nor, later, the French from militarily occupying the Ruhr in 1923 to secure German reparations. In short, "ad hocery" ruled. Bankers like Bismarck's Bleichröder were often quite unable to keep up with masters whose policy changed more often in response to political than to financial variables.[13] Yet, astonishingly, despite a list of defaults far longer than the near-defaulters of the 1960s and 1970s, the system of international bond issue and public and private borrowing under no clear book of rules survived and grew. A variety of management measures were devised and practiced with more or less success.

Undoubtedly, far more crises would have rocked the creditors' boats but for two coincidental developments. One was the insatiable appetite of creditors—both individual investors and institutional intermediaries—for the profits to be made from credit creation. The other was the prudent elaboration, by Britain especially, of statutory fences insulating the domestic credit structure and its major institutions (the joint-stock banks especially) from too close an involvement with the uncertain international scene.

Reviewing the differences between the nineteenth and the mid-twentieth centuries twelve years ago, I now think that I misjudged the situation that was then emerging in two ways. Noting that major defaults historically had been associated with major upheavals in the international political system—with wars and their accompanying major revolutions—I suggested this might account for the complacent presumption in the mid-1960s that so long as World War III was averted, there was no need to worry about the debt situation. But in doing this, I unconsciously accepted another assumption: that the pre-1914 debt situation so vividly described by Feis could not have been resolved in any other way than by the wholesale default brought on by the system collapse of 1914-1918. The Russians, the Turks, and several others were so far in debt and had so little prospect of rapid economic growth that I assumed they could never repay it. But, on reflection, they might never have needed to. But for the war and its wasteful use of foreign credit and but for its destruction of financial confidence, the process of credit creation could have gone on and on—as it had more or less throughout the nineteenth century for the United States. In short, although identifying some of the behavioral patterns in relation to credit that the 1950s and 1960s shared with the pre-1914 period, I gravely underestimated the basic resilience of the international political economy so long as it is spared the trauma of general war.

That mistake led to a second misjudgment: to think that because the accumulated LDC debt situation had been so widely overlooked, it had been "suppressed," hidden out of sight, swept under the carpet, and that this suppression would make the ultimate problem more difficult and dangerous. That assumption was wrong. True, the proliferation in indebtedness, the creeping rise in the proportion of foreign exchange earnings taken by debt service, and the slowness of the rise in gross national product in some debtor countries were likely to create a dangerously unstable situation if other factors remained unchanged. But, although a ceiling in the expansion of buyers' and suppliers' credit perhaps had been reached by then and bilateral aid programs were already nudging their politically determined upper limits, it did not follow that credit creativeness had entirely run out of steam. The Eurocurrency market existed, although it was then still a mechanism for drawing deposits from the LDCs for use of multinationals and developed country governments. The banks had begun to organize themselves to operate transnationally though they were still busy lending in industry, property development, and commercial enterprises in the industrial world. Both were later to reverse their course and provide new inflatable cushions to keep at least most of the LDCs afloat and away from the rocks of default. The oil states were to appear as a new source of bilateral and multilateral lending.

Indeed, it is the continuing expansion of credit creation that has been the outstanding feature of the last decade. Once again, it is being assumed that the expansion cannot continue, that

Table 1
Gross Disbursements, Debt Service, and Net Transfers for 67 Non-Oil-
Exporting Developing Countries, 1965 and 1973 ($ millions)

	Disbursements		Debt Service		Net Transfers	
	1965	1973	1965	1973	1965	1973
Official Bilateral	3620	6786	719	2301	2901	4485
Multilateral	728	2057	331	1017	397	1080
Private	1372	7362	1177	4231	195	3051
Supplier Credit	571	1312	587	1417	-16	-105
Banks	546	4849	417	2001	129	2768
Other Private	255	1201	173	813	82	388
Total	5726	16281	2227	7661	3499	8530

Source: UNCTAD IV, International Financial Cooperation for Development, Nairobi, 1976.
TD/188/Supp. 1, Item 11, p. 9.
Note: Figures may not add to totals owing to rounding, unallocated flows, and adjust-
ments for liabilities due to nationalization.

other things will remain equal. Table 1 summarizes the extent of
the expansion before 1973 and before the addition of OPEC aid.
It shows a threefold expansion in credit and disbursement over
eight years and a particularly rapid increase in bank lending to
developing countries. The latter trend has continued since 1973,
the net figure for bank lending having increased fourfold over
the next three years, from an estimated $2.13 billion in 1973 to
an estimated $7.96 billion in 1976.[14] In the same years and par-
ticularly after the oil price rises in 1973-1974, a further major
source of credit opened up in the Eurocurrency markets. The
Organization for Economic Cooperation and Development
(OECD) estimates that between 1971 and 1975 Eurocurrency
credit expanded almost ten times from $1.47 billion to $12.70
billion, producing total credit of over $36 billion.[15] The
market, however, was far more discriminatory than official
lending, in that it practically ignored the higher-risk, lower-
income LDCs altogether. Their total borrowings in the period
from January 1971 to June 1975 amounted to only 2 percent
of the total, while 69 percent went to oil-producing LDCs and
the higher-income countries, especially those in Latin America
(69 percent).

Thus, by the end of 1976, the proportion of private credit
not publicly guaranteed in the total debt outstanding to LDCs
had risen perceptibly and was approaching a quarter of the
whole (22.6 percent).[16] Unpredictable as official aid flows had

proven in the past, they were not nearly so volatile as this private credit. As the figures show, new borrowing was capable of staying level one year and making a substantial jump the next. The creditors were not members of nor subject to any of the stabilizing pressures of aid-consortia or creditor clubs. So that when, as in the mid-1970s, the LDC trade balance was apt to be grossly upset by rising prices of major, necessary imports like oil or grain coinciding with flagging or restricted markets for some of their exports, the dangers of default were bound to loom closer.

Such trade pressures were also apt to fall unevenly, most affecting those least able to manage. For instance, the whole of the improvement in LDCs' total deficit in 1977 was achieved by five semideveloped countries: Mexico, Brazil, Argentina, South Korea, and Taiwan, which were then responsible for only a third instead of half of the overall total. "The most notable feature," reported the Bank for International Settlements of the developing countries' finances for 1977, "was the pronounced slow-down in new lending to non-oil exporting countries from nearly $18 billion in 1976 to $11.3 billion."[17] Yet new deposits from these countries which had accelerated sharply in 1976 continued to expand at a rapid pace, by $12.9 billion, so that they became net suppliers of credit to the tune of $1.6 billion in 1977.

3. Conclusions

The credit structure's response to the undeniable rise in liability to default caused by the increased number and volatility of political and economic variables may be criticized as inadequate. But it has not been negligible. The response has been under four heads: increased information; stricter control of creditors; improved welfare measures; and better provision of both public and private insurance. Still further steps in each of these four directions will certainly be required in the future. The key question, as always, will be whether the measures will go far enough and whether they will be taken in time.

Greater information could help defend against the domino danger of one default giving rise to others—defaults either of other debtors or of creditor institutions. This danger is increased by the cross-default clauses in credit contracts.[18] Only through improved information can time be gained to anticipate and thus prevent default. During the last five years, the data collection on debt profiles and on contingent risks has vastly improved.[19] The banks themselves, being well aware of the dependence of their balance sheets on profits from foreign operations, have also become more cautious in extending their liability in any one direction, and in extending the range of information required of borrowers. Although there may be resistance to making credit operations more transparent than they are at present, some information pooling will surely be found necessary in the general interests of the banks and their national monetary authorities. The Bank for International Settlements (BIS), noted for the discretion of its style as a Swiss-incorporated bank, might be a more acceptable coordinator than either the International Monetary Fund (IMF) or the World Bank. Some closer association by the BIS with a reformed Berne Union is also worth considering.

In the last few years, it has been evident that stricter control of creditors was necessary, and that this task should be left to national monetary authorities. They may consult and cooperate together, but it is they alone in the last resort who have the political and market-controlling power to compel credit institutions to bridle their profit-making instincts, to observe reserve/ asset ratios, to limit their exposure to any one debtor, and to guard against unforeseen combinations of risks. After the scare with REITs and New York City's finances in the United States, and of the Herstatt, the Slater-Walker, and the Reksten collapses in Europe, there is now a new awareness that preventive action by national monetary authorities must not be too little or too late. Recently, all the creditor countries have tended to increase the insulating fences that separate the institutions that lend domestically from those that lend abroad. It is increasingly being recognized that these tasks cannot realistically be expected of the IMF. As the Fund's secretariat identifies more and more with the interests of the developing countries, its tasks will be different: to act as a liaison body, a mediator and broker, between the debtor countries and the governments of the creditor countries.

By the mid-1970s, there were already clear indications of growing recognition (by the much-maligned Fund as well as by the World Bank) that the expansion of the credit structure required an acceleration in the provision of welfare, especially for the poorest countries. The IMF's oil facility, the World Bank's Third Window, the Fund's sales of gold, its increased provision for compensatory export financing, and the larger quotas and improved access to Fund drawings all added up to a steady expansion in the provision of multilateral credit on noncommercial terms. The accent of both the Fund and World Bank operations significantly shifted toward the most seriously affected (MSA) developing countries. This does not seem to be a merely temporary response to the oil price rise and the world recession, and can therefore be expected to continue in the future.

The complementary association of insurance with welfare and credit structures is something which is taken for granted in many developed countries, although the ways in which the three fit together vary quite considerably. To take one example, health and medicare insurance, which in some countries started as public welfare systems, have been increasingly supplemented, as in Britain, by private health insurance. In other countries, such as the United States, health services, at first predominantly provided by organized private insurance, have been very substantially extended in recent years with the aid of public welfare finance. So, in the international system, the provision of welfare and the better management of credit have already been accompanied by an elaboration of public and private international insurance practices. This trend can be expected to continue strongly in the future.

On the public international side, the first rather meager IMF scheme for compensatory export finance was put together in 1963. Sixteen years later, the argument still continues over the financial burden-sharing for commodity stabilization schemes. But the lead given in the Lomé Convention is significant of a dawning recognition that it may be in the interests of the creditor/consumer countries as well as the producer/debtor countries to take some of the uncertainty out of the developing countries' balance-of-payments accounts. Similarly, the greater

Fund and World Bank involvement with LDC debt is another kind of insurance, in which the increased liability of the international organizations adds to the confidence of private creditors. The holding of LDC government securities and even Treasury bills by these organizations would be a further step in the same direction.

The United States has also given a lead to other investing countries with the institution of OPIC (Overseas Private Investment Corporation), a federal agency that offers publicly financed insurance against the risks to U.S. corporations of expropriation by LDCs. Although OPIC's operations have been widely criticized, the principle is a valid one, and the integrity of the system and the national interests of the creditor countries are best served when risks are reduced, even if it is at some expense to the U.S. government.

Meanwhile in the private sector, the rapid, recent extension of reinsurance to the insurance enterprises of the LDCs also makes a significant contribution to the credit system. It may be argued that reinsurance costs the LDCs too much, or that London and New York insurance companies' profits are too large, and that these charges are yet another vehicle for channeling capital from the periphery to the center. Unquestionably, the fewer the risks borne solely and unaided by a developing country, the less likely it is to fall into an unforeseen and unavoidable default situation. And insurance, private and public, is one of the least costly and most politically acceptable ways in which the creditor countries maintain confidence in their expanding structure of international credit. Recognition is dawning that this is a national interest no less vital to the rich countries than the political advantages, the export opportunities, and the profits they have previously pursued.

A continuation of experiment and initiative in these four directions does not mean that the creditor countries are likely to alter their opinions on the question of a general debt moratorium. Nor does it imply that occasional defaults are inconceivable. Indeed, they are more likely to be easily tolerated in 1980 than in 1960. A moratorium, or at least the cancellation of the debts incurred by the poorest LDCs, was one demand of the Group of 19 LDC representatives at the 1976 Conference on International Economic Cooperation (CIEC) in Paris. It was resisted by the Group of 8 representatives of developed countries, as was the idea of systematic rescheduling of all North-South commercial debt. Bankers and creditors have always preferred to deal with debtors on a case-by-case basis, if possible, without being required even to explain or justify their decisions. Creditor governments are likely to behave no differently in the future. They will continue to resist all suggestions that general rules for the management of debt might be drawn up. Especially unacceptable was the idea promoted by the Group of 19 that renegotiation and rescheduling of debt should be managed so as to produce minimum growth rates in terms of per-capita income in debtor countries. Such rule-of-thumb arrangements proved equally unpopular with many of the countries (like Brazil and Mexico) with the largest accumulations of foreign debt. They correctly feared that such arrangements might detract from their creditworthiness with U.S. banks. But, while a blanket solution is unlikely to emerge, ad hoc arrangements such as the agreement reached in March 1978 will aim to avert avoidable defaults, to maintain confidence in the credit structure, and to agree upon mechanisms to renegotiate where debt problems arise.[20] In particular cases, it may be necessary to convert public debts into ex post grants to provide additional finance at preferential rates, even to transfer LDC debts to international organizations on a temporary or permanent basis. A continued softening of credit postures toward certain LDC debtors seems a hypothesis in accord with past experience.

The policy objectives, as in national credit structrues, are essentially quite simple: to keep expanding the edifice of credit, but to do so steadily and surely. It is not a balloon that is more apt to pop the more it is blown up. On the contrary, the bigger the credit structure, the stronger it is likely to be—always provided that the expansion is neither too irregular nor too rapid for confidence to be maintained. Looking back over the past thirty years, it is significant that Third World growth rates have been best in the Latin American countries, to whom most credit has been extended and who, therefore, are now the most deeply in debt. The historical perspective surely demonstrates the interests of those on the top of the heap in expanding the size of the heap. This applies to governments and banks alike.

Notes

1. Susan Strange, "Debts, Defaulters, and Development," *International Affairs*, July 1967.

2. It might be argued that the very largest of the multinationals do in fact exercise such directive powers over productive resources in the world economy. They can use land, buildings, plant and direct labor capital, and materials for research, exploration, and development, and now do so on a global scale. So long as home states permit their existence and countenance the operations of multinationals, and so long as host states do not exclude, nationalize, or severely constrict them, their power over the production structure is the source of their status in the international system; and no international authority exists to coordinate the operations of the many diverse multinational enterprises (MNEs) in such a way as to produce an overall global development plan.

3. "The Secondary Banking Crisis and the Bank of England's Support Operations," *Bank of England Quarterly Bulletin*, June 1978.

4. Dragoslav Avromovic, *Economic Growth and External Debt* (Baltimore: Johns Hopkins Press, 1966).

5. United Nations, *Export Credits and Development Financing*, E/4274 (ST/ECA/95) (New York, 1966); see especially Part 1: "Current Practices and Problems."

6. World Bank, "Suppliers' Credits from Internationalized to Developing Countries," (Washington, D.C., 1967).

7. Susan Strange, *Sterling in British Policy: A Political Study of an International Currency in Decline* (London: Oxford University Press, 1971), Chap. 4.

8. William B. Reddaway, S. J. Potter, and C. T. Taylor, *Effects of UK Direct Investment Overseas: Final Report* (London: Cambridge University Press, 1968).

9. Christopher Prout, "Finance for Developing Countries," in *International Monetary Relations*, Vol. 2 of *International Economic Relations of the Western World 1959-1971*, ed. Andrew Shonfield (London: Oxford University Press, 1976), p. 389.

10. Herbert Feis, *Europe, the World's Banker: 1870-1914* (New York: W. W. Norton, 1965), p. 218.

11. Ibid., p. 337.

12. Ibid., p. 105.

13. Fritz Stern, *Gold and Iron: Bismarck, Bleichröder, and the Building of the German Empire* (New York: Knopf, 1977).

14. Nicholas Sargen, "Commercial Bank Lending to Developing Countries," *Federal Reserve Bank of San Francisco Economic Review*, Spring 1976.

15. Philip A. Wellons, *Borrowing by Developing Countries on the Eurocurrency Market*, The Development Center (Paris: OECD, 1977).

16. The World bank's external debt division estimated that the total debt outstanding to eighty-five LDCs at $202 billion, of which $45 billion was private, nonguaranteed.

17. Bank for International Settlements, *Annual Report,* 1978. In 1978 the BIS produced for the first time a new data series giving information on the accumulated debts of LDCs to international banks, their deposits with the banks, and the extent of undrawn bank loans available to borrowers in each of the developing countries.

18. Cross-default clauses are dealt with in more detail in Jonathan David Aronson's contribution to this volume, Chap. 11.

19. Most notably by the World Bank's External Debt Department and by the Office of the United States Comptroller of the Currency.

20. For details on the March 1978 agreement, see Brian G. Crowe's article in this volume, Chap. 2.

2
International Public Lending and American Policy

Brian G. Crowe

Recent events in the world economy have focused increasing attention on the existing procedures and mechanisms for dealing with international debt problems. This chapter discusses U.S.-government debt policies and relates them to the realities of the current debt situation as it is perceived by creditor governments.

1. Borrowing for Adjustment

For the developing countries, partial reliance on external borrowing is both normal and responsible. In theory, efficiently utilized borrowed capital should contribute to overall national economic strength and permit the gradual liquidation of debt. However, the constantly rising economic expectations of the developing countries exert upward pressure on both consumption and investment requirements and have diminished the likelihood of debt liquidation for the vast majority of countries. As a result, even before the shocks of 1973-1974, projected development strategies anticipated large-scale, additional, foreign resource transfers. The oil price rise, coupled with world recession, added a striking new dimension to the debt situation. In the three-year period 1974-1976, the combined current-account surplus of the thirteen members of the Organization of Petroleum Exporting Countries (OPEC) averaged $49 billion.[1] Since

Views expressed are those of the author and do not necessarily represent the policy of the U.S. government.

Table 1
World Payments Patterns: Balance of Goods, Services, and Private
and Government Transfers ($ billions)

	Average 1971-73	Average 1974-76
Surplus Countries		
OPEC	2.8	49.0
OECD	12.3	15.3
Total Surpluses	15.1	64.3
Deficit Countries		
OPEC	-1.4	-2.0
OECD	-6.7	-37.3
Non-OPEC LDCs	-4.1	-23.0
Other[a]	-2.7	-12.3
Total Deficits	-14.9	-74.6
Residual[b]	-0.2	10.3

Source: "Special Report to the President and to the Congress on U.S.
participation in the Supplementary Financing Facility of the International Monetary Fund," The National Advisory Council on International
Monetary and Financial Policies, September 1977. Data are OECD and U.S.
Treasury Department staff estimates.

[a]Israel, South Africa, and the non-market economies of Eastern Europe,
the USSR, and the People's Republic of China

[b]Over the past several years the "residual" item has grown significantly.
Recorded exports exceed imports by a sizeable sum for any calendar year
due to goods in transit and inflation. The OECD staff has estimated
that $12-14 billion is involved in these factors. These factors by
themselves would make the residual negative rather than positive. Both
the IMF and the OECD attribute the positive residual to asymmetries in
the reporting of service transactions; that is, an over-reporting of
service imports or under-recording of service exports.

this surplus inevitably generated a corresponding deficit in non-
OPEC countries, balance-of-payments management for most oil-
importing countries became very difficult. Table 1 illustrates
the changing balance-of-payments situation.

   The magnitude of their collective deficit and its sudden appearance gave many of the oil-importing countries two broad
options. They could abruptly curb their development objectives
by deflating their economies and imposing tight import restrictions, a course of action that would have caused severe hard-
ships on their populations and might have jeopardized their
political stability. An abrupt curtailment of economic growth in
deficit countries also would have exacerbated greatly the world
economic recession by collapsing export markets through a
sharp reduction in demand. Alternatively, the oil-importing

countries could seek an increased level of external finance which would allow for a more orderly adjustment process stretched over a period of years. Most developing countries preferred the second option. Given the alternatives, borrowing to avert a disastrous economic contraction was prudent. This remains true even though much of the borrowing was, of necessity, utilized for consumption rather than investment.

2. The Nature of the Current Debt Situation

U.S. government estimates show that the external debt of the non-oil-exporting developing countries has more than doubled between 1973 and 1977, with debt service payments (interest plus amortization of outstanding debt) having increased to an annual level of more than $20 billion.[2] Significantly, as Table 2 shows, private lending has increased more rapidly than official lending. The rise in indebtedness does not in itself threaten to produce major debt-servicing problems. The nominal increases in debt in recent years appear far less dramatic in the context of continuing inflation and growth or real output and trade in the world economy. Between 1973 and 1977, for example, the exports of the non-oil-exporting developing countries rose from $67.4 billion to $135 billion.[3] Moreover, aggregate data obscure the widely diverse situations among developing countries, es-

Table 2
Non-Oil-Exporting Developing Country External Debt ($ billions)

	1973		1977	
Yearend Position	75.3		160.0	
Official	38.5	(51%)	69.0	(43%)
Private	36.8	(49%)	91.0	(57%)

Source: Data are estimates used within the U.S. Government and cover a seventy country sample which account for more than 95 percent of debt attributable to the non-oil-exporting developing countries. Data refer to disbursed credits, for which the debtor has incurred clear liability; they are distinguished from undisbursed credits, which have been committed but not yet drawn. Data include liabilities not guaranteed by the debtor country, amounting to $20 billion to $25 billion in 1976. Data do not include liabilities to the IMF, which amount to about $3 billion. The country samples do not include the member countries of OPEC or the more advanced Mediterranean countries (Greece, Spain, Turkey, etc.), two categories used in standard World Bank presentations.

pecially in their potential to earn foreign exchange and to manage their debt effectively. It is of particular importance that debt is distributed broadly in line with the servicing capacity of individual countries. Most of the new debt attributable to low-income countries has been on highly concessional terms. In addition, the bulk of private debt is, as Table 3 indicates, concentrated in economies with relatively high per-capita incomes and a fair-sized industrial base.

A clearer understanding of the current debt situation of developing countries is obtained by distinguishing three broad groups of developing country debtors. The first category includes a dozen relatively advanced countries which now depend largely on private markets for the external capital needed to support domestic development programs. Their productive, relatively diversified economic sectors have a history of sustained growth and appear to have the economies of scale and momentum necessary to continue generating adequate export earnings to service debt and maintain creditworthiness. They will face, however, a substantial bunching of debt service over the next several years, and their ability to attract adequate levels of new financing will be contingent on their continued economic efficiency and competitiveness. Their ability to avoid servicing difficulties will also depend on maintaining access to and demand from the markets of industrial countries for their exports. At the other extreme, a large number of low-income countries with a limited growth potential for exports and minimal access to capital markets have been hard hit by recent economic developments and confront a serious resource-transfer problem. Their inability to attract anything but concessional lending, however, means that very few have a debt problem as such. In the middle is a third category of developing countries with moderate per-capita incomes which now utilize both traditional aid-type financing and commercial borrowing. Their capacity to accumulate commercial debt is limited. Many still depend upon exports of a few commodities with highly cyclical prices and have, therefore, variable external-payments situations. Caught between official assistance efforts increasingly geared to low-income countries and commercial borrowings geared to more-dynamic economies, these middle-category

Table 3
Breakdown of 1977 Debt Attributable to Non-Oil-Exporting Developing Countries
($ billions)

	Official	Private	Total
High Income Countries	25.6	73.2	98.8
(1976 per capita greater than $600)			
Argentina	1.3	4.8	6.1
Brazil	5.0	26.5	31.5
Chile	2.2	2.5	4.7
China (Taiwan)	1.1	2.0	3.1
Colombia	1.9	1.0	2.9
Ivory Coast	0.5	1.0	1.5
Jamaica	0.5	0.7	1.2
Korea	3.3	5.5	8.8
Malaysia	0.9	1.4	2.3
Mexico	3.0	21.8	24.8
Panama	0.3	1.1	1.4
Tunisia	1.2	0.4	1.6
Other[a]	3.1	2.3	5.4
Middle-Income Countries	16.0	13.5	29.5
(1976 per capita between $200 and $600)			
Bolivia	0.7	0.5	1.2
Egypt	4.6	4.0	8.6
Morocco	1.5	1.1	2.6
Philippines	1.0	4.1	5.1
Sudan	0.7	0.7	1.4
Syria	1.0	0.3	1.3
Thailand	1.0	0.9	1.9
Zambia	0.9	0.6	1.5
Other[a]	4.6	1.3	5.9
Low-Income Countries	27.4	4.4	31.8
(1976 per capita less than $200)			
Afghanistan	1.7	---	1.7
Bangladesh	2.2	0.2	2.4
India	12.9	1.3	14.2
Pakistan	5.9	0.5	6.4
Tanzania	1.0	0.1	1.1
Zaire	0.6	1.9	2.5
Other[a]	3.1	0.4	3.5
Total	69.0	91.1	160.1

Source: U.S. Government estimates

[a]"Other" high-income countries are Costa Rica, Cyprus, Dominican Republic, Fiji, Guatemala, Guyana, Liberia, Nicaragua, Paraguay, Singapore, Trinidad and Tobago, and Uruguay. "Other" middle-income countries are Botswana, Cameroon, Congo, El Salvador, Ghana, Honduras, Jordan, Kenya, Madagascar, Mauritania, Mauritius, Senegal, Sierra Leone, Somalia, Swaziland, and Togo. "Other" low-income countries are Benin, Burma, Burundi, Central African Empire, Chad, Ethiopia, Gambia, Lesotho, Malawi, Mali, Niger, Rwanda, Sri Lanka, Uganda, Upper Volta, and the East African Community.

countries often face the most serious difficulties in securing finance for large-scale payments imbalances.

Individual country analysis shows clearly that there is no general debt crisis affecting the developing countries. It also shows that, while the financing needs of many deficit countries remain large, particularly for those with social and political constraints that curb the speed of balance-of-payments adjustment, acute debt-servicing problems are currently restricted to about a half-dozen countries. In assessing future debt-servicing prospects, there are certainly grounds for caution. Although the payments imbalance between OPEC nations and the rest of the world was reduced sharply in 1978, a sizable OPEC surplus remains. In addition, there is the imbalance resulting from Japan's burgeoning surplus. The need for economic adjustment and structural change will therefore be a continuing one, and the task of gearing payments deficits to individual countries' underlying productive potentials remains difficult.

During this adjustment period, the level of developing country indebtedness will continue increasing, albeit at a slower rate than during the last few years. Despite this increase, acute debt problems should remain concentrated on a small number of individual countries which require individual, specific solutions. This assessment is based on the maintenance of a reasonably favorable, international economic environment. Thus the foreign economic-policy implications of developing country indebtedness extend across the entire range of global economic management. In this context, a paper presented by industrial country "debt experts" at an UNCTAD meeting in December 1977 concluded, "Dealing with the international debt situation as we now find it entails five broad elements:

1. Maintenance of aggregate global demand;
2. Access of developing country exports to the major markets of the world;
3. Assurance of adequate financing to encourage internal adjustments in an orderly fashion;
4. Provision of development assistance flows, especially to the poorest countries, particularly those with limited export potential; and

5. Appropriate domestic policies and effective management of borrowed funds."[4]

3. U.S. Debt Policy

As of March 31, 1978, outstanding indebtedness of U.S. government credits (exclusive of indebtedness arising from World War I) totaled $43.4 billion, of which $42.8 billion related to long-term debt with a maturity of over one year. In the vast majority of cases, debts owed to the United States since World War II have been paid on time, with the United States receiving approximately $50 billion in principal and interest payments. The non-oil-exporting developing countries now owe the United States over $22 billion in long-term debt, with six countries (India, Pakistan, Brazil, South Korea, Egypt, and Chile) accounting for almost 60 percent of the total. The more-advanced developing countries have an increasing portion of their U.S.-government debt portfolio in commercial-type credit (i.e., loans extended by the Export-Import Bank and the Commodity Credit Corporation), while the debt of low-income countries remains concentrated heavily in concessional loans. For example, approximatley 95 percent of the debt owed to the United States by the least developed countries was extended under either the Foreign Assistance Act or Public Law 480.

U.S. policy on debt reorganization as approved by the interagency National Advisory Council on January 6, 1978, states:

1. Debt-service payments on international debt should be reorganized on a case-by-case basis only in extraordinary circumstances where reorganization is necessary to ensure repayment. Debt relief should not be given as a form of development assistance.
2. Debt-service payments on loans extended or guaranteed by the U.S. government will normally only be reorganized in the framework of a multilateral creditor-club agreement.
3. When a reorganization takes place that involves government credits or government-guaranteed credits, the U.S. will participate only if:
   a. the reorganization agreement incorporates the principle

of nondiscrimination among creditor countries, including those that are not party to the agreement;

b. the debtor country agrees to make all reasonable efforts to reorganize unguaranteed private credits falling due in the period of the reorganization on terms comparable to those covering government or government-guaranteed credits;

c. the debtor country agrees to implement an economic program designed to respond to the underlying conditios and to overcome the deficiencies which led to the need for reorganizing debt-service payments.

4. The amount of principal and interest to be reorganized should be agreed upon only after a thorough analysis of the economic situation and the balance-of-payments prospects of the debtor country.

5. The payments that are reorganized normally should be limited to payments in arrears and payments falling due not more than one year following the reorganized negotiations.[5]

This approach reflects congressional opposition to the use of debt relief as "backdoor aid," the economic soundness of case-by-case analysis, and the importance attached to maintaining contractual obligations.

Since July 1, 1975, dollar receipts from loans made under Part 1 of the Foreign Assistance Act are deposited in Treasury's miscellaneous receipts accounts. This reinforced concern in the executive branch that use of debt relief as a regular instrument of economic assistance would circumvent congressional responsibility and provoke legislative restrictions on executive-branch authority to use debt relief even in crisis situations. It also constrains U.S. policy from distinguishing between the treatment of debts owed on official commercial-type credit (e.g., Export-Import Bank loans) and those owed under concessional aid programs.

The U.S. position that official commercial debt should be renegotiated in creditor clubs only in imminent default situations is shared by all other industrialized creditor countries. There is no indication that any creditor country favors either a major restructuring of the creditor club as an institution or a significant weakening of current creditor-club operating criteria. However, other countries tend to be more flexible regarding the treatment of debt service on Official Development Assistance (ODA) and are not opposed, in principle, to considering the selective use of ODA debt relief as a form of development assistance. For most other creditors, such relief would constitute a portion of their aid budget and thus not necessarily represent a real increase in total resource transfers.

4. Creditor Policies and Debt Crises

While creditor-club efforts to maintain a healthy international economy constitute their most important contribution to global debt management, there is also a need for the international community to respond effectively when individual countries encounter debt servicing difficulties.

Factors Leading to Debt Problems

The debt servicing problems of the developing countries are not easily generalized. Even when deteriorating situations in individual countries require multilateral debt relief, it is difficult to attribute the origin of the crisis to a single cause. A 1971 IMF study of debt renegotiations noted "the gradual deterioration in the economic situations of debtor countries was the result of a complex series of economic and noneconomic events." The same study identified the basic problem as "a prolonged domestic imbalance between resource demand and availability" which led debtor countries to "rapidly increase foreign borrowing largely on commercial terms in order to raise more resources particularly for investment."[6] Still, common elements frequently reappear among the underlying causes of servicing difficulties. These include:

1. *Excessive government spending* and the financing of the resulting government deficits by either large-scale domestic borrowing (aggravating inflation) or short-term external debt;
2. *Overambitious investment programs* that, with little in the

way of project evaluation, have high import content, are
long range in nature, and are not directly productive;
3. *Lagging exports* due to both external factors, such as
   deteriorating terms of trade and world recession, and
   internal policy decisions, such as stressing heavy industrial
   development rather than export promotion;
4. *Adverse capital flows* resulting from a political/economic
   environment that encourages private capital flight and discourages new flows;
5. *Excessive use of short-term credits*, often acquired without
   central control, on a scale incompatible with the debtor's
   capacity to generate an adequate foreign-exchange return;
   and
6. *Creditor country policies* on export and suppliers' credits,
   sometimes influenced by competitive pressures rather than
   either the loan's economic viability or the borrower's
   debt absorptive capacity. The trade and aid policies of
   creditors also fall short of developing country expectations.

Debt servicing crises in recent years also, of course, reflect the
massive 1973-1974 upswing in petroleum prices which increased
significantly the demands on available foreign exchange, disrupted development in a number of countries, and prompted unprecedented external borrowing, much of it on commercial
terms.

Multilateral Debt Renegotiations

There have been thirty-eight multilateral negotiations involving twelve developing countries since 1956. The incidence of
renegotiations, viewed on an annual basis, has been relatively
infrequent, since creditors generally have seen renegotiation as
a last resort to be used only when a debtor's balance of payments deteriorated to the point where renegotiation was unavoidable. Up to 1965, multilateral debt renegotiations focused
almost exclusively on commercial debt since it was a major
factor in the debt servicing difficulties being encountered. This
commercial debt either was offered by official export agencies
in the creditor countries or was guaranteed or insured by credi-

tor country governments. The 1965 Chilean renegotiation marked the first time any intergovernmental loans were included in multilateral rescheduling. Usually short-term credits, unguaranteed bank credits, and loans from the multilateral lending institutions such as the World Bank had been excluded from negotiations. In a few cases, payments arrears were included; in others, the agreement included a provision concerning the elimination of arrears. In several cases involving repeated renegotiations, previously renegotiated maturities were left outside the new agreement; in other cases, they were included. Although renegotiations differentiated among the types of debt obligations, often outstanding debt considered eligible for renegotiation constituted one-half or more of the total debt outstanding. The portion of eligible debt consolidated has ranged between 60 and 100 percent in the majority of cases and, as Table 4 shows, the total value of maturities covered frequently has been substantial.

The consolidation periods of past reschedulings have been rather short (one year is now the norm), but most grace and repayment periods have been at least six years and were extended to ten years or more in most cases.[7] Interest rates on the renegotiated debt have usually been determined bilaterally, although some multilateral agreements provided for an interest ceiling. The highly concessionary 1970 Indonesian rescheduling agreement provided for no additional interest payments on the rescheduled debt. Most other multilateral agreements—India, Ghana (1970/71 and 1974), and Pakistan (1974) being exceptions[8]—resulted in interest rates comparable with prevailing commercial interest rates in the creditor countries. This reflected the creditors' view that debt relief should be considered as a conventional refinancing operation. Factors upon which interest rates were based included the original contractual interest rate of the renegotiated debts, the existing borrowing rate for new loans of the same type as the debt being rescheduled, and the cost of the borrowing by the creditor governments. Reflecting the upward global trend in interest rates, the interest charged on renegotiated debt has usually been somewhat higher than in the original contract.

In most multilateral debt-relief agreements, all creditors pro-

Table 4
International Debt Rescheduling Exercises: 1956-1978

Year	Country	Total Amount Rescheduled ($ million)	Amount of U.S. Debt Rescheduled ($ million)	Consolidated Period
1956	Argentina	500	0	Arrears to 6/30/56
1959	Turkey	400	0	5 yrs., 5 months
1961	Brazil	300	0	4 yrs., 7 months
1962	Argentina	240	0	2 years
1964	Brazil	200	44.5	2 years
1965	Chile	96	43	2 years
1965	Turkey	220	15	3 years
1965	Argentina	76	18	1 year
1966	Ghana	170	.511	2 yrs., 7 months
1966	Indonesia	247	51	1½ years
1967	Indonesia	95	23	1 year
1968	India	300	27	3 years
1968	Peru	58	0	1½ years
1968	Indonesia	85	22	1 year
1968	Ghana	100	.141	3½ years
1969	Peru	70	0	2 years
1970	Indonesia	2100	215	All Maturities
1970	Ghana	25	0	2 years
1971	India	92	9	1 year
1971	Yugoslavia[a]	59	59	2 years
1971	Egypt[a]	145	145	4½ years
1972	Cambodia	2	0	1 year
1972	Chile	258	110	1 yr., 2 months
1972	Pakistan	234	51	2 yrs., 2 months
1972	India	153	29	1 year
1972	Cambodia	2.5	0	1 year
1972	Turkey[a]	114	0	All Maturities
1973	Poland[a]	32	32	2 years
1973	Pakistan	103	23	1 year
1973	India	187	29	1 year
1974	Ghana	290	0	Pre-1966 Commercial
1974	Chile	460	232	2 years
1974	Pakistan	650	196	4 years
1974	India	194	45	1 year
1975	Chile	230	95	1 year
1975	India	167	0	1 year
1976	India	160	0	1 year
1976	Zaire	170 (est.)	46	1 year
1977	India	n.a.	0	1 year
1977	Zaire	200 (est.)	68 (est.)	1 year
1977	Sierra Leone	n.a.	0	2 years
1978	Turkey	1100 (est.)	225 (est.)	13 months

Source: Office of Monetary Affairs, Department of State

[a]Bilateral. Note: The concept of grant element is a measure of concessionality of lending terms. It compares a loan on given terms with a hypothetical loan at 10 percent with no grace period; the lower the grant element (expressed as

Terms	Comments
No grace, 9 yrs. - 3½%	---
No grace, 12 yrs. - 3%	Only U.S. Commercial Debt Rescheduled
6 mos. grace, 5 yrs. - various %	Eximbank rescheduled $305 million separately
No grace, 6 yrs. - various %	Eximbank refinanced a $72 million loan in 1963
2 yrs. grace, 5 yrs. - various %	Eximbank only
2 yrs. grace, 5 yrs. - various %	---
5 yrs. grace, variable	---
2 yrs. grace, 5 yrs. - various %	Eximbank only
2½ yrs. grace, 7½ yrs. - various %	Eximbank only
3 yrs. grace, 8 yrs. - 3-4%	Interim Rescheduling
3 yrs. grace, 8 yrs. - 3-4%	Interim Rescheduling
62% grant element	---
1-1½ yrs. grace, 4 yrs. - various %	Only U.S. Commercial Debt Rescheduled
3 yrs. grace, 8 yrs. - 3-4%	Interim Rescheduling
2 yrs grace, 7¼ yrs. - 6%	Eximbank Only
1 yr. grace, 4 yrs. - 8-9%	---
30 yrs. - 0%	Incorporates 1966-67 and 1968 Rescheduling
Variable	---
62% grant element	---
2 yrs. grace, 10 yrs. - 5%	---
27 mos. grace, 5 yrs. - 6.6%	No Grace on CCC Credits
2 yrs. grace, 8 yrs. - 3%	---
2 yrs. grace, 6 yrs. - 5-6%	---
2 yrs. grace, 3 yrs. - 5% (maximum)	---
59% grant element	Continuation of 1971 Agreement
2 yrs. grace, 8 yrs. - 3%	---
5 yrs. grace, 25 yrs. - 3%	Proceeds assigned to Reimburse U.S.
4 yrs. grace, 8 yrs. - 6%	---
2 yrs, grace, 3 yrs. - 5% (maximum)	Temporary, Partial Extension of 1971 Agreement
55% grant element	Continuation of 1970 and 1971 Agreement
10 yrs. grace, 18 yrs.- 2½%	Incorporates 1966-68 and 1970 Rescheduling
80% @3 yrs. grace, 7 yrs. - various %	---
62% grant element	Resolves Debt Issues From 1971 War
52% grant element target	---
80% @3yrs. grace, 6½ yrs. - various %	---
62% grant element target	US, Canada, Italy Did Not Participate
62% grant element target	US, Canada, Italy Did Not Participate
85% @3yrs. grace, 6½ yrs. - various %	---
n.a.	---.
85% @3yrs. grace, 6½ yrs. - various %	Bilateral US-GOZ Agreement Not
80% @2½yrs grace, 7½ yrs. - various %	---
80% @3 yrs. grace, 5 yrs. - various %	Includes $500 million arrears on short-term debt , to be repaid @2yrs grace, 4 yrs, various %

a percentage), the closer the rescheduling terms are to this hypothetical loan. The 1974 agreement with Pakistan was linked directly with an agreement under which Bangladesh assumed responsibility for debts on projects visibly located in its territory. As part of the multilateral accord, the U.S. rescheduled $85 million in debt services on obligations assumed by Bangladesh.

portionally share the burden of rescheduling. It is standard practice to use a most-favored-nations (MFN) clause to extend this
principle of nondiscrimination to nonparticipating creditors.
Under such an MFN provision, debtor countries receiving relief
agree not to accord any creditor better treatment than that
being provided to participating creditors. The 1968 Indian debt
renegotiation introduced the additional concept that creditors
who had lent on relatively hard terms should reschedule relatively larger amounts than those who had lent on softer terms.
Strong opposition to this principle by some creditor countries,
however, precluded its application beyond the 1973 Indian
agreement.

The Creditor-Club Mechanism

Debt renegotiations usually take place in a multilateral framework to ensure that creditors share the risks of lending identi-
cally. The creditor club has been the most frequently used institutional forum. Most creditor-club negotiations have been in the
Paris Club although there have also been London Clubs (for
Peru and Ghana) and a Hague Club (for Brazil). The World Bank
has also sponsored debt relief exercises through its aid-consortia
for Pakistan and India. As a result of unique political/economic
factors, renegotiations of Turkey's debt have been conducted
in the framework of the OECD consortium for Turkey.

The creditor-club mechanism has been used only in actual
debt-problem situations where there is a strong possibility of
imminent default. Developing countries approaching or experiencing acute debt-servicing problems seek relief through the
creditor-club mechanism after establishing an understanding
with the International Monetary Fund. Then they apply to a
major creditor for a convening of negotiations. The club, which
in the case of the Paris Club is usually chaired by the French
Ministry of Finance, is convened by the chair after appropriate
consultation with major creditors. Participants generally include
representatives from major creditor nations, the debtor country,
the IMF, observers from the World Bank, and, on occasion,
observers from the regional development banks. Negotiations are
normally carried out in two stages in each of which the credi-

tors first meet alone and then meet with the debtor nation. The first stage is characterized by an assessment of the facts and a request for further information from the debtor country. In the second stage, an umbrella agreement between creditor countries and the debtor nation is negotiated. This nonbinding agreement extends equal treatment to all creditors and serves as a basis for subsequent, individual bilateral agreements to implement the terms of rescheduling.

The viability of the creditor-club mechanism for dealing with debt servicing crises rests on three basic elements: the case-by-case approach, conditionality, and the confluence of interests between debtors and creditors.

1. *Case-by-Case Approach.* The creditor countries entertain requests for creditor-club rescheduling on a case-by-case basis. This approach allows creditors the necessary flexibility to consider and negotiate rescheduling on the merits of each individual case. Suggestions made by developing countries for more-generalized approaches to rescheduling, which generally entail the use of trigger mechanisms to determine eligibility for relief, have been rejected consistently by creditor countries.

2. *Conditionality.* Renegotiations are conditioned on the debtor country undertaking a comprehensive economic program designed to strengthen its underlying balance-of-payments situation. This linkage of debt relief with performance standards has proved a key element in restoring debtor countries' normal commercial/financing relationships both with creditor governments and—usually after a delay of several months following the renegotiation—with private lenders. The conditional nature of relief also has limited the incidence of rescheduling applications by confining them to serious debt situations and discouraging requests for the use of debt relief as a means of resource transfer.

3. *Confluence of Interests of Debtors and Creditors.* In a debt rescheduling situation, there is a fundamental confluence of interests between debtors and creditors. If the terms of rescheduling payments are met, debtors reestablish their

creditworthiness and creditors ultimately receive payments, albeit at a later date than was planned. The mutual interest of debtors and creditors in securing such a result is in large part responsible for the effectiveness of the creditor-club mechanism.

The International Monetary Fund also plays an important role in creditor-club negotiations by providing an assessment of the debtor's balance-of-payments situation and, in the great majority of cases, supporting a financial program adopted by the debtor country. More than two-thirds of the debt renegotiations that involve a creditor club were related to IMF standby arrangements, usually involving second or high-credit tranches.[9] In all but one case not involving a standby, the IMF was requested to survey the implementation of the debtor's financial program and/or transmit performance data to the creditors. Twice the Fund also helped the debtor country prepare for a debt renegotiation with private banks and then attended the meetings.

Rescheduling in Aid-Consortia

While there is a solid creditor-country consensus regarding the nature and the criteria of creditor-club operations, there is no such consensus on the role of World Bank aid-consortia in debt reorganizations. Some creditors view aid-consortia as the most appropriate forums for dealing with servicing problems related to low-income developing countries with debt portfolios based primarily in concessional debt.

The United States has participated in ten debt renegotiations within the aid-consortia framework: seven for India (1968-1974) and three for Pakistan (1972-1974). Policy preference, however, clearly favors the use of the creditor club. The United States sees rescheduling in aid-consortia as posing three serious difficulties. First, aid-consortia are, by definition, concerned primarily with the provision of economic assistance, and dealing with debt in them suggests that debt relief is being used in an aid context. On this basis, some policymakers believe that regular U.S. participation in aid-consortia exercises could generate congressional criticism. Second, unlike most industrial creditors, the United States does not include debt relief as budgeted assistance. For other countries, where debt relief on ODA debt is a budget item, it may not represent a real increase in resource transfers. Thus on burden-sharing grounds, the United States may be placed at a disadvantage in aid-consortia renegotiations. Third, the conditionality of past creditor-club exercises has been significantly stricter than experienced in aid-consortia.

The Effectiveness of Past Debt Renegotiations

Multilateral debt renegotiations are directed to the financial aspects of debtor country situations. They seek to alleviate an unsustainable pattern of debt servicing obligations and thereby regularize commercial relationships. While this objective, in the long run, should facilitate a sustainable pattern of economic growth, development criteria per se are not an integral part of the renegotiation process.

The key to the effectiveness of a renegotiation generally has been the debtor country's implementation of its economic policy commitments. As a result, the impact of debt relief cannot be analyzed independently from these policies. Often the pursuit of more conservative monetary and financial programs by the debtor country was followed by a significant improvement in the balance of payments which allowed a buildup in international reserves and provided a firm basis for avoiding new debt problems. A 1976 IMF staff study concluded that "in about four-fifths of the cases in which stand-by arrangements were associated with debt renegotiations, there was an improvement in the overall balance of payments performance, while in about two-thirds of the cases the current account performance improved."[10] Although private lenders have tended to be considerably more cautious about resuming normal lending activity than official lenders, in several situations the past rescheduling flow of public and private capital substantially exceeded the amount of direct debt relief. One result of the emphasis renegotiations have placed on debt control has been a marked improvement in the debt management policies of the debtor countries. Debt surveillance procedures for monitoring new foreign indebtedness were usually strengthened significantly and, where necessary, debt management was centralized. More-

over, the IMF programs, which usually precede debt renegotiations, increasingly place limitations on the level and structure of
new indebtedness.

Renegotiations sometimes have been followed by disappoint-
ing economic performances. In some cases, balance-of-payments
pressures continued because domestic financial policies, often
constrained by strong political pressures, did not improve sufficiently. Several times, economic problems facing debtors were
so great that substantial improvements in overall economic
performance could not realistically be expected quickly. This
reflects the fact that most applicants delay debt renegotiation
until it is the unavoidable consequence of a severe economic
crisis. In such situations, the complicated task of recovery is far
more difficult than had they acted earlier.

Although most renegotiations are repeated, this does not
itself indicate a failure of the initial renegotiation to improve
the debtor country's overall position. Repeated debt renegotiations have tended to occur within one to three years after the
initial renegotiation and often reflect a continuance of the
economic problems that initially forced the debt relief. Moreover, even when the severity of the country's problems clearly
required longer-term measures, creditors usually preferred to
reschedule debt only one or two years at a time—the "short-
leash" approach—in order to be able to apply maximum leverage in support of the debtor country's adherence to its ecnomic
policy commitments.

The Need for New Institutional Arrangements

Developing and creditor countries differ sharply regarding the
effectiveness of the creditor club. Many developing countries
resent the club mechanism, viewing it as a means for the creditors to "gang up on" individual debtor countries. They specifically criticize the "last resort" nature of club operations,
advocating that international action should be taken well in
advance of crisis situations. Developing countries also feel
strongly that creditor-club deliberations fail to give adequate
consideration to developmental issues and claim that only the
highly concessionary Indonesian debt renegotiation provided a
long-term framework for the pursuit of development objec-

tives.[11] They cite the need for repeat reschedulings as proof that the initial terms of rescheduling were too hard and therefore failed to remedy the underlying problem conditions. The views of debt experts from developing countries as expressed at a 1977 UNCTAD meeting were summarized as "the existence of ad hoc consortia for only a few individual countries,[12] the absence of any permanent international institution competent to receive requests for debt relief and the absence of any internationally agreed guidelines for debt reorganization were all factors leaving developing countries dissatisfied with existing machinery."[13] As a remedy, the developing countries have proposed new institutional arrangements that would, in effect, treat debt renegotiations in a development and resource-transfer oriented framework.[14]

Creditor countries, however, believe that the creditor-club mechanism has worked reasonably well and maintain that development considerations are one of the many factors taken into account. They do not feel that the emphasis accorded development criteria in the case of Indonesia is universally appropriate, and they argue that using concessionary funds to provide relief to middle- and higher-income countries, whose debt problems are largely attributable to excessive commercial borrowings, could divert scarce aid resources away from poorer, less-indebted countries.

Most creditor countries would agree that the creditor club could be more responsive to the feelings and perceptions of debtor countries. Specifically, they are willing to establish guidelines to assure the debtor countries of equitable and efficient creditor-club treatment. Creditor countries, however, remain firmly opposed to any new arrangements that could increase the incidence of rescheduling requests or reduce the conditionality now associated with debt relief.

5. Topical Aspects of Debt Policy

Recent developments in indebtedness have highlighted the relationship of creditor policies to private lenders, the role of the IMF, and the emergence of debt as a major issue in the North-South dialogue. While creditor policies have been refined to some extent, the substantive aspects of traditional policy remain little changed.

The Relationship between Official and Private Lending

Rough data indicate that global, cumulative current-account deficits totaled about $225 billion in the period of 1974 through 1976, of which some $179 billion—plus about $40 billion of debt repayments—were financed by market-oriented borrowing.[15] This expansion of private lending has generated concern that easy access to private credits would prompt developing countries to postpone indefinitely the adjustment policies necessary to gradually bring their balance of payments into a sustainable pattern.

The availability of bank lending clearly induced a number of developing countries to delay recourse to the conditional lending of the IMF. The private banks also made some serious errors of judgment in their assessments of country risk in Peru and Zaire, and continued lending to Turkey well beyond reasonable limits in order to accommodate the trade-related activities of their domestic clients. Despite these problems, the lending standards of private lenders in developing countries have generally been high. Private lending is concentrated in countries with the most promising growth prospects, and losses on bank loans to developing countries have remained below loss-ratios on domestic credits. Given the favorable economic potential of a number of countries, it is reasonable to expect that private markets will continue to have a significant role in assuring finance for the development of those countries.

As expected, developing countries now have a significant portion of debt—and, as shown in Table 5, an even larger share of debt service—attributable to private sources. Should debt renegotiation prove necessary, private debt often will constitute the primary source of servicing difficulty. Recognizing this fact, creditor governments have increasingly emphasized their support for the principle of roughly comparable treatment of both public and private lenders. They believe risks of lending should be shared by public and private creditors and that governments should not "bail out" their private creditors since bailouts would eventually lower lending standards by projecting the false impression that private lenders do not bear full responsibility

Table 5
Proportion of Non-Oil-Exporting Developing Country Debt Attributable
to Private Sources

	% of Yearend 1977 Debt Attributable to Private Sources	% of 1977 Debt Service Related to Private Sources
All Non-Oil-Exporting LDCs	57%	73%
High-Income Countries	74%	82%
Middle-Income Countries	46%	62%
Low-Income Countries	14%	39%

Source: U.S. Government estimates

for their contractual lending. Therefore, U.S. policy explicitly conditions government participation in debt reorganization on agreement by the debtor country to make all reasonable efforts to reorganize private credits falling due in the period of reorganization on terms comparable to those covering government-guaranteed credits.

Private lenders do not participate in creditor-club negotiations. Moreover, most creditor governments have no legal authority to bind private creditors. A number of debt renegotiation agreements have, however, contained the provision that the debtor country seek to renegotiate private debt on terms similar to those accorded participating governments. Such a provision was first utilized in the 1964 negotiations with Brazil, and more recently has been employed in negotiations with Chile, Zaire, and Turkey. The responsibility for ensuring comparable treatment falls on the debtor country, whose leverage with the private lenders will vary according to circumstances. In the 1972 Chile renegotiation, large amounts of bank credits were negotiated outside the framework of the Paris Club on terms broadly comparable to those assigned official creditors. In the case of Zaire, however, the international banks have resisted a conventional refinancing arrangement even though Zaire's economic position is more precarious than other recent instances—which entailed no renegotiation of official debt—where the private banks rolled over or refinanced debt service obligations.

The Role of IMF Conditionality

As noted earlier, creditor governments have usually made their participation in creditor-club operations contingent on the debtor country adopting a stabilization program which, as a general rule, would be worked out with and monitored by the IMF. Given the emphasis these governments now attach to gradual but effective global economic adjustment, it is difficult to see creditors taking action on any request for renegotiation that was not preceded or accompanied by debtor action on a comprehensive economic program to strengthen its underlying balance-of-payments position. Moreover, private lenders have now begun to insist on the IMF playing the leading policy role in debt crisis situations. IMF stabilization programs are intended to assist countries in restoring equilibrium in their payments position. In short, the benefits of a Fund program are three-fold: (1) Fund resources become available to the borrower, (2) the stabilization plan benefits the borrower's economic performance, and (3) the Fund-endorsed program strengthens the borrower's domestic and international credit standing.

The degree and type of conditionality entailed in a program depend largely on the overall financial circumstances faced by the country. In general, the more serious and protracted a country's problems, the greater the degree of financial discipline required to effect the necessary adjustments. Some critics are concerned that Fund stabilization programs force the adoption of austerity measures which impact adversely on the poor. This concern has been prompted largely by the fact that efforts to establish a viable payments position have, in a number of recent instances, required difficult structural adjustments. It is the country's economic situation, however, rather than the IMF, that necessitates adjustment. In this context, former IMF Managing Director Witteveen points out that "all too many countries approach the Fund for financial assistance only when, as a result of protracted delay in taking corrective action, the economic situation has already become critical . . . much of the difficulty associated with Fund conditionality arises from the severity of the adjustment measures needed at that late stage."[16] Moreover, implementation of Fund programs is intended to spread the impact of needed reforms over time, and thus minimize the disruption and hardship that would otherwise have taken place. Where the adjustment process is difficult, it remains appropriate for official and multilateral agencies to supplement Fund resources by providing the type of development-oriented assistance that is beyond the scope of the Fund.

The United States does not become directly involved in IMF/borrowing-country stabilization negotiations, and its role is confined to encouraging both sides to continue their efforts to reach a mutually acceptable solution. Other Fund members adopt a similar stance, realizing that efforts to compromise traditional Fund standards could undermine the very market confidence a Fund-endorsed program was intended to instill.

Debt in the North-South Dialogue

The issue of developing country debt has attracted considerable attention within the United Nations system, and become a major issue in the dialogue between the industrial countries and the Third World. As a result of the serious economic difficulties they confront, some low-income developing countries now view debt relief as a vehicle for providing balance-of-payments relief and/or a means of supplementing what they consider to be inadequate flows for development assistance. The Group of 77, the caucus of developing countries in the United Nations, argues that the case-by-case approach is no longer valid and that generalized, across-the-board debt relief is necessary for all poor countries. The emphasis is not on whether individual countries have the capacity to service debt, but on the inconsistency between development objectives and the continued absorption of limited financial resources by debt payments. They believe that debt policies should be considered in the context of resource transfer goals, and that debt relief should be recognized as an appropriate means of reaching internationally agreed-upon development targets. From the point of view of the Group of 77, generalized debt relief would be an ideal form of assistance since it is unconditional, untied, and quickly disbursed.

The Manila Declaration issued in February 1976 formed the basis of the developing country position for UNCTAD IV, and called for action on both official debts and commercial debts.[17] For official debt, it requested (1) cancellation of debt owed by the least developed, "land-locked," and "island" developing countries, (2) cancellation or "at a minimum" a highly concessionary rescheduling of debt owed by other poor countries, and

(3) the provision of debt relief to other countries seeking such relief. The Manila Declaration also called for a consolidation of commercial debt owed by *interested* developing countries,[18] possibly via a multilateral financial institution, and the rescheduling of payments over a period of at least twenty-five years.

The developing countries in general have attempted to focus North-South debt discussions on relief for the official concessionary debt held by low-income countries. Most of the pressure for generalized relief came from the few countries, such as India and Pakistan, that would receive most of the benefits from the Group of 77 proposals.[19] For many other low-income countries, however, the issue assumed a political importance far beyond its economic significance. Higher-income countries, such as Brazil and Mexico, disassociated themselves from demands for debt relief, realizing their creditworthiness in international capital markets would otherwise be harmed.

Demands of developing countries for generalized debt relief were resisted strongly by most creditor countries who feel that the wide diversity of debtor country situations fully justifies the traditional case-by-case approach. The creditor countries also stressed their doubt that generalized debt relief is an efficient mode of resource transfer since benefits would be distributed on the basis of the historical profile of borrowers rather than on a country's current performance or need. They point out that most of the poorest countries, particularly the smallest, do not have a large accumulation of debt and would gain little in absolute terms by the Group of 77 proposals.

Substantive North-South agreement on debt has been slow to emerge. The United States and the European Community, with the support of most developed countries, have proposed procedures to guide creditor-club operations. These procedures, in effect, codify current practice and represent no substantive change in the policies of creditor countries. A new policy element was provided, however, by including a set of procedures to provide additional external support for low-income countries experiencing structural balance-of-payments problems, of which debt is an element, that impinge unduly on development prospects. Under these procedures, donor countries would "enhance assistance efforts" to eligible countries judged to be taking corrective measures in their own behalf. Some developing countries have shown interest in the United States/European Community proposal, although the Group of 77 as a whole has not accepted it.

In March 1978, a ministerial-level meeting of the UNCTAD Trade and Development Board adopted a resolution that appears to have defused debt as a confrontational issue in the North-South dialogue. The resolution had two basic elements. The first was a commitment by donor countries to seek to adopt measures that would allow the terms of past aid loans to be adjusted to the easier terms of today. The commitment, sometimes referred to as a commitment to retroactive terms adjustment (RTA), is framed as an aid enhancement device rather than debt relief, and other equivalent measures are also allowed. Each donor country is left free to determine the distribution of the measures, with most donors expected to restrict RTA to those countries on the United Nations list of thirty countries that are relatively least developed. The second element of the March resolution was an agreement on four basic concepts to guide international action on future debt problems, with a commitment to continue efforts to expand those concepts. The agreed concepts are as follows:

1. International consideration of the debt problem of a developing country would be initiated only at the specific request of the debtor country concerned.
2. Such consideration would take place in an appropriate multilateral framework consisting of the interested parties with the help, as appropriate, of relevant international institutions to ensure timely action, taking into account the nature of the problem which may vary from acute balance-of-payments difficulties requiring immediate action to longer-term situations relating to structural, financial, and transfer-of-resources problems requiring appropriate longer-term measures.
3. International action, once agreed upon by the interested parties, would take due account of the country's economic and financial situation and performance, of its develop-

ment prospects and capabilities, and of external factors, bearing in mind internationally agreed-upon objectives for the development of developing countries.
4. Debt reorganization would protect the interests of both debtors and creditors equitably in the context of international economic cooperation.

While the concepts appear modest, and in some cases self-evident, their implicit endorsement of the case-by-case approach is significant in the context of the Group of 77's previous position of focusing almost exclusively on demands for generalized measures. The favorable position adopted by donor countries on retroactive terms adjustment was undoubtedly an important factor in securing Group of 77 acceptance of the concepts.

The Foreign Assistance Act for fiscal year 1979 which passed Congress in October 1978 has two provisions authorizing the United States to ease the terms of past American loans. Both provisions, the Javits amendment which relates to Foreign Assistance Act loans and the Solarz amendment which relates to Public Law 480 loans, call for case-by-case application and restrict eligibility to the least developed countries. Total receipts on past AID and PL-480 loans to the least developed countries have approximated $20-$25 million in recent years.

6. Conclusion

The international monetary system has coped reasonably well with the strains imposed upon it by the current account surpluses of the OPEC countries and the most severe recession of the postwar era. Disruptive pressures were contained in part because deficit countries were able to obtain the borrowing necessary to cushion economic adjustments, enabling their impact to be spread over a number of years.

The level and structure of the resulting indebtedness underscore the importance of efficient debt management by debtor countries. The situation also places a responsibility on industrial countries to maintain a global economic environment that facilitates debt repayment. Adequate aggregate demand, trading opportunities, adjustment finance, and—for the poorest countries—concessionary assistance flows are key factors in sustaining current and projected levels of developing country debt. If a reasonably healthy international economy can be maintained, serious debt-servicing problems should continue to be confined to a relatively few countries where they can be handled effectively in a manner similar to the approach used in the past.

Lending policies could, however, be improved by greater coordination among official and private creditors and the IMF to ensure that country performance criteria become a more critical element in the early stages of the lending process. It is, for example, clearly unsatisfactory for private lenders to delay seeking IMF-type conditionality until an actual crisis arises. Moreover, creditor countries should be willing to consider applications for debt relief before the default or imminent-default stage as long as the debtor demonstrates a willingness to undertake appropriate stabilization measures. If necessary adjustments are adopted at an early point in an emerging problem, their disruptive impact on the debtor's economy would be far less traumatic than if reform is delayed until it becomes unavoidable.

This chapter has addressed the financial aspects of the debt situation. Another important aspect is the unique problem of poorer developing countries whose lack of resources makes it difficult to undertake effective development programs. Official lending to many such countries has not kept pace with the level of official and private flows to middle- and higher-income countries. The problem is not essentially that of debt but of development. In this context, there is ample room for improved performance by the industrial countries, including the United States, in the provision of increased concessionary lending.

Notes

1. OPEC members are Algeria, Ecuador, Gabon, Indonesia, Iran, Iraq, Kuwait, Libya, Nigeria, Qatar, Saudi Arabia, United Arab Emirates, and Venezuela.

2. UNCTAD Trade and Development Board, "Report of the Intergovernmental Group of Experts on the External Indebtedness of Devel-

oping Countries on Its Second Session," Annex 1 D. (The Non-OPEC Less Developed Countries: External Debt Positions and Prospects, Paper Submitted by the United States of America), TD/B/685/Add. 1 (Geneva, December 29, 1977).

3. IMF, *International Financial Statistics*, May 1978, June 1978.

4. UNCTAD Trade and Development Board, "Report of the Intergovernmental Group of Experts on the External Indebtedness of Developing Countries on its Second Session," Annex 1 B. (The Debt Situation of Developing Countries, Paper Submitted by France on Behalf of Countries Members of Group B), TD/B/685/Add. 1 (Geneva, December 29, 1977).

5. National Advisory Council on International Monetary and Financial Policies, "Action 78-5" (Washington, D.C., January 6, 1978).

6. IMF, "Multilateral Debt Renegotiations—Experience of Fund Members" (Washington, D.C., August 6, 1971), p. 3.

7. The consolidation period is the period of time during which the original maturities of debt fall due for payment and are made subject to the renegotiation.

8. The renegotiation of India's debt and the establishment of repayment terms with a high grant element reflected the concessional nature of India's outstanding debt, and the country's poor development prospects which included an inability to generate high rates of return on invested capital. The 1974 Ghana rescheduling, although covering pre-1966 commercial debt, was also highly concessional but reflected unique political/economic factors. The 1974 Pakistan renegotiation also reflected unique circumstances, i.e., the need to maintain full servicing of all prewar Pakistan debt following the independence of Bangladesh.

9. Renegotiations involving India, Indonesia, Pakistan, and Turkey are excluded from the data here.

10. IMF, "Avoidance and Resolution of Debt Servicing Difficulties" (Washington, D.C., September 23, 1976), p. 20.

11. The terms of the 1970 Indonesia agreement provided for an unusually long repayment period of thirty years, and a complete waiver of additional interest charges during the repayment period. The $2.1 billion renegotiated also included debt that had previously been rescheduled.

12. This refers to developing country preference for use of the aid-consortia framework rather than the creditor club for treatment of debt problems.

13. UNCTAD Trade and Development Board, "Report of the Intergovernmental Group of Experts on the External Indebtedness of Developing Countries" (Geneva, July 18-22, 1977), p. 3 (TD/B/670-TD/AC.2/7, July 28, 1977).

14. UNCTAD Trade and Development Board, "Report of the Inter-

governmental Group of Experts on the External Indebtedness of Developing Countries," Annex II. (Proposal of Developing Countries on Future Debt Renegotiation for Interested Developing Countries) (Geneva, July 18-22, 1977).

15. National Advisory Council on International Monetary and Financial Policies, "Special Report to the President and the Congress on U.S. Participation in the Supplementary Financing Facility of the International Monetary Fund" (Washington, D.C., September 1977), p. 9.

16. *IMF Survey*, May 22, 1978.

17. The Manila Declaration and Program of Action was adopted by the Group of 77 at its February 1976 ministerial meeting in Manila and is contained in UNCTAD document TD/195.

18. The word "interested" was inserted by developing countries currently active in private capital markets, and was intended to dissociate themselves from this portion of the proposal.

19. India and Pakistan together account for roughly two-thirds of the official development-assistance debt owed by low-income countries.

3
Private Overseas Lending: Too Far, Too Fast?

Jane D'Arista

Since 1974, international bank debt of non-oil-exporting developing countries has grown rapidly. Although debt expanded more slowly in real than in nominal terms, debt accumulation accelerated in real terms in 1974 and 1975[1] and probably in 1976 and 1977 as well. Significantly, private Eurocurrency banks provided a large portion of the new funds. Since private banks did not become important in public sector and development finance until the 1970s, the scale of their 1974-1976 lending, when they supplied 60 percent of new credit to non-oil developing countries, appears remarkable. Thus, disagreement concerning the appropriate speed of private debt creation emerged. Analysts who focus on the debt itself, rather than on the shifting sources of funds, usually see no danger. Those focusing on the source, structure, and terms of LDC debt are more concerned. In order to clarify these issues, this chapter examines the speed of and reasons for the rapid rise in commercial bank credit to LDCs from the perspective of both the borrowers and the lenders.

1. Demand: The Borrowers

LDC borrowing has spurted three times in the past two decades. In the 1960s, industrial countries' prosperity and the Third World's emerging political and economic significance underscored the need for greater LDC development and led to the creation of new lending institutions to channel more funds to developing countries. The sources and structure of LDC borrowing in the 1960s reflected the fact that stimulating development was seen largely as a governmental responsibility. About 60 percent of the funds loaned to LDCs were bilateral credits on easy terms; 6 percent were multilateral; and the remaining one-third were supplied by the private sector, mostly in the form of direct investments and suppliers credits.[2]

Industrial countries' efforts to hasten the development process by government-to-government grants and credits succeeded. Between 1960 and 1973, the real domestic product of developing countries as a group grew at a 6 percent annual rate—significantly higher than the growth rates of both the industrial countries and centrally planned economies. Since their average annual increase in real output throughout the first half of the century was only 2 percent, the strides of the 1960s appeared even more remarkable.[3]

By the early 1970s, the political survival of certain LDC governments appeared to depend on rapid development. By 1970, however, about half of the official foreign-exchange receipts of developing countries went to repay debts to official lenders. LDC governments feared that debt servicing requirements undermined further progress. Developed country aid and investments declined as a percentage of OECD countries' gross national product (GNP) from 0.52 percent in 1960 to 0.33 percent in 1974.[4]

Industrial countries also began concentrating their assistance in lower-income countries. Although the World Bank continued to lend to middle-income countries, it did raise its rates to cover the cost of its own borrowing in private financial markets,[5] making it a less-attractive source of funds for higher-income LDCs. Impatience with the limitations and conditions of official aid also helped convince the faster-growing LDCs to turn to the Eurocurrency banks for development funds. The banks were willing lenders.

In the second borrowing rush, LDC growth was made possible by the private funds. Non-oil-exporting developing countries borrowed $300 million from Eurocurrency banks in 1970, $900 million in 1971, $1.5 billion in 1972, and a staggering $4.5 billion in 1973.[6] The non-oil-exporting LDCs' share of new Eurocurrency credits grew from 6.3 percent in 1970 to

20.7 percent in 1973. The World Bank estimates that the total external debt of non-oil developing countries was $78.5 billion at the end of 1973. Thus their 1973 Eurocurrency borrowings were 5.7 percent of total external debt, almost the same proportion as in 1976. Clearly, debt escalation preceded the increase in oil prices.

In accepting expensive Eurocurrency credits, LDCs gambled that economic progress would outstrip debt service repayments. Rising 1972 commodity prices made the gamble seem worthwhile, but by 1974 the situation was bleak. Lower prices following the collapse of the commodity boom resulted in declining export earnings. Import prices for oil, fertilizer, and food increased sharply. Exports to OECD countries slowed in 1974 and declined in 1975. Imports from OECD countries did not begin to slow until late in 1974.[7] Combined LDC current-account deficits reached $38.2 billion for 1975, an $8.7 billion increase over the 1974 deficit and an almost fourfold increase over that for 1973.[8]

LDC borrowing spurted a third time between 1974 and 1977 in the wake of massive balance-of-payments shifts between countries caused by the oil price increases. The cumulative balance-of-payments deficits for all countries between 1974 and 1976 are estimated at $180 billion.[9] The combined, cumulative non-oil developing countries' deficit was $78 billion. The remaining $100 billion cumulative deficit was incurred by OECD countries, about half by France, Britain, Italy, and Canada.

As LDC cumulative deficits mounted, so did their borrowings. It is generally agreed that LDC debt rose from about $80 billion in 1973 to $180 billion in 1976 and that LDCs financed about 60 percent of their current account deficits during this period by bank loans.[10] *World Financial Markets* estimated that by the end of 1976 the LDCs owed $76.8 billion to the private banks, of which $52 billion was owed to U.S. banks, but the Bank for International Settlements and the IMF estimate that bank claims on LDCs had risen to $89.1 billion.[11]

In 1976, LDCs' balance-of-payments position improved significantly; their combined deficit was only $25.8 billion. But their 1976 private borrowing increased to $20.1 billion, and their total bank debt rose by 29 percent.[12] Thus, some said that the LDCs "overborrowed" in 1976, adding $11.6 billion to their reserves. LDC reserve accounts rose to $42.7 billion in 1976, or 23.7 percent of their total external debt.[13]

Optimists contended that the LDCs' current account improvements and increase in reserves indicated that LDC debt was manageable. They also argued that escalating worldwide inflation had undercut the burden of previous debt, making recent debt accumulations more supportable.[14] Optimists also saw the slowing rate of increase in LDC borrowing from Eurocurrency banks as further evidence of an improved position, arguing that the LDCs adjusted better to the oil price increase than most industrial countries. Pessimists feared that the decline was evidence of banks' overextension and subsequent readjustment. They viewed the cutback as undesirable, inviting a decline in aggregate world demand.

Evidently neither view was wholly correct. The LDCs continued borrowing, and the banks extended them an additional $13.4 billion in 1977.[15] Although the LDCs' share of Eurocurrency credits was only 32.2 percent, down from 38.2 percent in 1976, credits to industrial countries, OPEC, and communist countries were all up sharply. In macroeconomic terms, the shift was desirable since LDC current account deficits had improved while other countries' deficits had worsened. In any event, LDCs increased their Eurocurrency bank borrowing in 1977 and nearly doubled the amount of funds they raised by international bond issues.[16] The demands of the major LDC borrowers were met by the financial markets.

2. Supply: The Lenders

The discussion so far may suggest that the debt increase was demand driven.[17] Some analysts question that assumption. Robert Solomon argues that "it is easy to demonstrate that as long as OPEC members in the aggregate remain in surplus, funds will be available from the proceeds of that surplus to finance the deficits of oil-importing countries in the aggregate. The OPEC surplus provides the means for its own financing."[18] Robert Weinert suggests "that LDC indebtedness results as much from the need of lenders to lend as from the need of borrowers to borrow."[19]

As evidence, Weinert cites the remarkable variation in the margin-of-lending rates over the cost of funds during the period 1970-1978, from 2.75 percent to 0.625 percent for the same country. Maturities also varied between five and twelve years over this period. He notes that terms "became more favorable to the LDCs from 1970 to 1973, stiffened from 1974 to 1976, and have been slowly easing since."[20] He posits that banks were anxious to increase their international lending to enhance growth and that the process of petrodollar recycling made them "necessitous lenders."[21]

Federal Reserve Board Governor Henry C. Wallich has also voiced concern, noting that, for fifteen borrowing countries, the spreads between lending rates and the cost of money reached a low of approximately 1.11 percent in the fourth quarter of 1973, a period he characterizes as "a time of dangerous euphoria" propelled by "the expansive forces of the international economy."[22] Comparing the stiffening of Eurocurrency bank rates from 1974 to 1976 and the U.S.-bond market rates during the same period, Wallich indicated that in the American market, lower-quality risks paid more relative to the higher-grade issuers. By contrast, the Eurocurrency markets "appeared to wipe out differences among borrowers and to assign to all of them a similar higher risk rating."[23]

Wallich attributes the recent sharp decline in spreads to diminishing risks as conditions improve and to increased pressure to lend. He notes that liquidity is high in Eurocurrency markets. The absence of international monetary controls means that funds will remain plentiful even as demand diminishes, since "rising assets and liabilities . . . do not absorb limited supplies of reserves, as they would in national money markets."[24] Wallich sees an impetus to relax credit standards as inevitable, although highly undesirable.[25]

The present situation resembles the prevailing pattern in the early 1970s. The Eurocurrency markets received substantial inflows of funds from the United States as domestic offices of American banks repaid their foreign branches the $14 billion borrowed during the 1969 credit crunch. As funds flowed back into overseas branches, Japan and several European countries imposed capital controls to prevent increased Eurocurrency lending to their domestic borrowers. This effectively severed relations between the U.S. banks' foreign branches and their major customers—the European subsidiaries of U.S. multinational corporations. The banks seeking new markets found the LDCs waiting in the wings with long-standing, previously ignored demands. Then, as now, banks and LDCs found a marriage between a need to lend and a need to borrow.

Another factor encouraged bank lending to developing countries after 1974. The recession weakened domestic loan demand in the United States and then in other OECD countries, where low demand for domestic credit remains. In the United States, the banks faced a $13 billion drop in domestic commercial and industrial loans between the end of 1974 and the end of 1976. Slack demand, coupled with losses on REIT loans and other recession-related problems, flattened income from domestic sources.

Liability management, the legacy of banking's "go-go" years and its principal mechanism for growth, above all requires profits. During the growth-oriented late 1960s and early 1970s, bank managers looked to their stocks' price-earnings ratios as the significant performance measure. Larger banks relied on the domestic money market for liquidity, funding loans by selling certificates of deposit (CDs) and issuing commercial paper to finance their expanding holding-companies' operations. Abroad, they relied on the interbank market as a source of and use for funds.

The 1974 international banking crisis demonstrated the unreliability of money markets as a source for liquidity.[26] Between May and September 1974, interbank liabilities of U.S. banks' foreign branches dropped by $8.3 billion, a decline of 11.2 percent. This decline partially reflected the withdrawal of dollar funds to pay for higher-priced oil, but also signaled the lack of confidence in Eurocurrency banks in the wake of the Franklin and Herstatt failures. OPEC deposits replaced about $4 billion of the lost liabilities. The remainder was supplied by the parent banks' headquarters.[27] What appeared as an interim shift in overseas branches' sources and uses of funds has persisted. U.S. banks continue to fund about half of new foreign lending by their branches from U.S. sources.[28]

Until recently, banks and bank regulators generally ignored the implications of an increased portion of foreign lending based on U.S. deposits. They erroneously viewed the net out-flows of funds to foreign branches as an interim phenomenon which would abate when domestic business lending picked up. Meanwhile, there is pressure to maintain earnings growth, although the penalty for failure is being downgraded by security analysts. If a bank's stock falls, its ability to raise new capital diminishes. And banks must raise new capital if they are to ex-pand their lending.[29] To attract funds to lend, banks must also maintain market confidence. The balance sheets of some larger money center banks reveal that as much as two-thirds of their liabilities is borrowed or purchased in interbank and money markets at home and abroad. Multinational banks have become captives of the markets they sought to manipulate.

There is a significant relationship between earnings pressure and escalating international lending. The fact that the thirteen largest banks earned half of their profits from international operations in 1975 is widely quoted.[30] But it is the terms of as well as the increase in foreign lending that make their international business more profitable than domestic operations. For a managing bank, a large, syndicated international loan provides substantial fees which are "earned" merely by transferring deposits (or borrowing) into profits. The banks are assured of immediate current earnings. But they must continue to generate new loans on similar terms, since the typical large, syndicated credit provides for long grace periods during which no interest or principal payments flow back to the bank.

There are no domestic loan syndications of comparable size or structure. Thus, there are real advantages in lending to foreign public-sector borrowers. The ability to realize immediate and sizable profits may have been the key not only to growth, but to survival for some banks pressed for profits in 1975. If so, then the margin on loan spreads to foreign countries and the differentiation between more or less creditworthy borrowers might, indeed, appear less important. The front-end fee would be the dominant concern.

3. Too Far? A Summary of Views

Have LDCs borrowed too much? The U.S. Treasury and State Department say no.[31] The administration has, however, strongly

supported an IMF special lending facility, the so-called Witteveen Facility, on the grounds that, if Fund lending becomes
more important, it can influence borrowers to accept needed
balance-of-payments adjustments. If countries are pressed to
adjust, less borrowing will be needed. But successful adjustment
is also seen as helping to maintain the flow of bank lending in the
long run. As Undersecretary of the Treasury Anthony Solomon
explained, "Private lenders would actually . . . be more willing
to lend to a country that has a 'good housekeeping seal.' "[32]

Current Fund resources are insufficient for this role. The
quota system, linking the amount of funds each country lends
to the amount it can borrow, makes most countries' available
IMF credit seem miniscule next to their bank borrowings. Even
IMF credits to Italy and the United Kingdom were buttressed
by bilateral assistance and private bank credits, and Mexico's
1976 devaluation was smoothed by an $800 million U.S. swap
agreement.

In contrast, the Congress generally has been more pessimistic.
Some foresee possible defaults, financial crises, and even a
worldwide depression.[33] Members of Congress questioned
whether the Witteveen Facility's size was sufficient to allow
anything but symbolic deficit financing. Some members suggested that encouraging further bank lending to countries by
"certifying" their creditworthiness and pressuring them to
reduce imports and public assistance to their neediest citizens
to insure repayment of private bank debts would convey a
somewhat cynical attitude.[34]

Bank regulatory authorities are in the middle. In March 1977,
Arthur Burns electrified the financial world by suggesting that a
problem might exist and by admitting that the monitoring of
external debt was clearly inadequate to its size.[35] Shortly thereafter, Governor Wallich acknowledged that risks were greater in
foreign lending than in domestic lending.[36] However, the Federal Reserve Board ultimately accepted the status quo, while
urging greater self-regulation of banks' international activities.

4. Measuring How Far

Like the Federal Reserve Board, the Office of the Comptroller of the Currency (OCC) believes that current international bank loans are manageable, but fears that overextension is possible and could jeopardize individual banks. Recently the OCC released a 1974 letter that expressed reservations about the amount of one bank's lending to a certain country. It has been surmised that the bank was Chase Manhattan and the country, Italy.[37] The bank had lent almost $550 million to various public-sector borrowers in that country, none of which could repay the loans independent of the central government. Moreover, the OCC identified one credit where funds were not used by the stated borrower but were turned over to the central bank. The aggregate loans to the country involved were about 25 percent of the bank's capital, far in excess of the 10-percent legal limit on loans to one borrower.

The OCC is actively seeking a reasonable way to apply the statutory limit on loans to one borrower to international lending. The problem is complicated by the fact that the 10 percent lending limit applies only to national banks. Thus, state member banks in New York, including Morgan Guaranty, Manufacturers Hanover Trust, Bankers Trust, and Chemical Bank, are permitted to loan up to 25 percent of their capital funds to individual borrowers.

A glance at Tables 1 and 2 indicates that the OCC's view is not unreasonable. The commitment of the nine largest banks to almost all groups of countries is very high. But the ratio of capital to loans for individual LDCs is worrisome only with respect to Brazil and Mexico, where all U.S. lenders' aggregate loans to public borrowers exceeded 10 percent of their combined capital in June 1977. Loans to the Brazilian government dropped from 10.4 percent of bank capital to 8.3 percent between June and December 1977. The Mexican government's borrowings declined from 16.3 percent to 13.3 percent over the same period. In both cases, the decline was offset by significant increases in bank placements—from 0.9 to 9.3 percent for Brazil and from 1.2 to 5.5 percent for Mexico. This shift in funds at the end of the year may reflect roll-overs of maturing credits channeled through banks. They help improve the appearance of year-end statements for both borrowers and lenders. The year-end reductions in public borrowers' shares of bank credit, as

Table 1
Ratios of Foreign Loans of U.S. Banks to Bank Capital[a]
(By Groups of Countries, Groups of Banks, and Types of Loans) (December 31, 1977)

Groups of Countries	9 Largest U.S. Banks				15 Other Money Center Banks				95 Other U.S. Banks				All U.S. Banks			
	Total Claims	Claims on: Banks Placements	Public Borrowers	Other Private	Total Claims	Claims on: Banks Placements	Public Borrowers	Other Private	Total Claims	Claims on: Banks Placements	Public Borrowers	Other Private	Total Claims	Claims on: Banks Placements	Public Borrowers	Other Private
G-10 Countries + Switzerland	371.9	211.7	34.0	126.2	184.6	145.4	13.0	26.2	78.5	60.2	7.3	11.0	231.1	145.3	20.4	65.5
Non-G-10 Developed Countries	81.3	20.1	21.0	40.3	44.1	18.4	12.9	12.8	17.8	6.5	6.7	4.6	51.5	15.0	14.3	22.2
Eastern Europe	28.5	14.3	11.4	2.8	17.3	9.5	6.6	1.3	7.5	3.7	3.0	.8	18.9	9.6	7.5	1.8
Oil Exporting Countries	67.7	13.9	28.5	25.3	30.3	9.9	12.9	7.4	12.0	3.5	3.7	4.8	40.6	9.5	16.7	14.4
Non-Oil-Exporting Developing Countries	186.3	40.5	64.9	81.0	118.7	44.0	41.0	33.7	63.9	25.0	22.8	16.2	129.7	35.8	45.3	48.6
Latin American + Caribbean	(128.2)	(24.1)	(44.1)	(60.0)	(87.7)	(30.4)	(31.0)	(26.3)	(50.2)	(17.5)	(19.4)	(13.4)	(92.7)	(23.1)	(32.8)	(36.8)
Asian	(46.3)	(14.7)	(12.3)	(19.3)	(26.5)	(12.7)	(7.1)	(6.7)	(12.1)	(7.2)	(2.5)	(2.5)	(30.3)	(11.7)	(7.8)	(10.9)
African	(11.7)	(1.7)	(8.4)	(1.6)	(4.5)	(1.0)	(2.9)	(.6)	(1.6)	(.4)	(1.0)	(.3)	(6.7)	(1.1)	(4.7)	(1.0)
Offshore Banking Centers	86.3	64.0	1.6	20.8	59.3	49.4	.9	9.1	41.9	34.4	.6	6.8	65.3	50.7	1.1	13.5
Miscellaneous	.7	---	.7	---	---	---	---	---	1.1	---	1.1	---	6.9	---	6.7	---
Total Foreign Loans	822.7	364.4	162.0	296.2	454.3	276.6	87.2	90.5	222.7	133.4	45.3	44.2	544.0	265.8	112.0	166.1

Source: Federal Reserve Board

[a] Equity capital and loan loss reserves reported in 1977: $16,130 million for the 9 largest U.S. banks; $7,438 million for 15 other money center banks; $12,607 million for 95 other U.S. banks; and $36,175 million for all three groups of banks.

Note: Due to rounding, figures in this and all following tables may not add to totals.

Table 2
Ratios of Loans of U.S. Banks to Bank Capital for Selected Less Developed Countries[a]
(By Groups of Banks and Types of Loans) (December 31, 1977)

Country	9 Largest U.S. Banks				15 Other Money Center Banks				95 Other U.S. Banks				All U.S. Banks			
	Total Claims	Claims on: Banks Placements	Public Borrowers	Other Private	Total Claims	Claims on: Banks Placements	Public Borrowers	Other Private	Total Claims	Claims on: Banks Placements	Public Borrowers	Other Private	Total Claims	Claims on: Banks Placements	Public Borrowers	Other Private
Argentina	10.9	1.8	5.8	3.2	6.1	1.9	2.2	2.0	3.4	1.3	1.1	1.0	7.3	1.7	3.4	2.2
Brazil	47.9	9.1	10.9	27.8	31.2	14.3	8.1	8.8	15.5	6.6	5.0	3.8	33.2	9.3	8.3	15.6
Chile	3.3	.8	1.7	.8	2.0	1.0	.6	.4	1.1	.5	.3	.3	2.3	.7	1.0	.6
Korea	13.4	5.5	2.2	5.8	6.0	3.6	1.2	1.2	3.7	2.5	.5	.8	8.5	4.0	1.4	3.1
Malaysia	2.5	.4	1.2	.8	1.1	.3	.7	.1	.24	.1	.1	.04	1.4	.3	.7	.4
Mexico	37.6	5.0	15.1	17.5	33.3	7.2	14.3	11.7	21.2	5.0	10.3	5.9	31.0	5.5	13.3	12.3
Peru	6.6	.9	4.2	1.5	5.9	2.0	2.6	1.3	2.6	1.2	1.0	.4	5.1	1.2	2.8	1.1
Philippines	7.8	1.8	2.1	3.8	6.4	2.3	1.3	2.8	2.5	1.1	.5	.9	5.7	1.7	1.4	2.6
Taiwan	11.6	3.0	4.0	4.6	7.3	3.1	2.7	1.5	3.1	1.9	.8	.3	7.8	2.6	2.6	2.5
Thailand	3.9	1.4	.6	2.0	1.6	.5	.1	1.0	.8	.5	.1	.2	2.4	1.1	.3	1.0
Subtotal	144.2	28.6	47.8	67.8	100.9	36.2	33.8	30.8	54.1	20.7	19.7	13.6	104.7	28.1	35.2	41.4
Other NO-LDCs	42.0	11.8	17.0	13.1	17.8	7.8	7.2	2.9	9.8	4.3	3.1	2.6	25.0	7.7	10.1	7.2
Grand Total	186.2	40.5	64.8	80.9	118.7	44.0	41.0	33.7	63.9	25.0	22.8	16.2	129.7	35.8	45.3	48.6

Source: Federal Reserve Board

a Equity capital and loan loss reserves reported in 1977: $16,130 million for the 9 largest U.S. banks; $7,438 million for 15 other money center banks; $12,607 million for 95 other U.S. banks; and $36,175 million for all 3 groups of banks.

Table 3
U.S. Bank Loans to Selected Foreign Governments: June 1977 and December 1977 [a]
($ millions)

Country	9 Largest Banks June 1977 Amount	% of Capital	December 1977 Amount	% of Capital	15 Other Money Center Banks June 1977 Amount	% of Capital	December Amount	1977 % of Capital	95 Other U.S. Banks June 1977 Amount	% of Capital	December 1977 Amount	% of Capital	All U.S. Banks June 1977 Amount	% of Capital	December 1977 Amount	% of Capital
Mexico	3,287	20.4	2,436	15.1	1,141	15.3	1,067	14.3	1,478	11.7	1,299	10.3	5,910	16.3	4,802	13.3
United Kingdom	1,775	11.0	2,260	14.0	427	5.7	473	6.4	272	2.2	347	2.8	2,475	6.8	3,079	8.5
Brazil	2,549	15.8	1,757	10.9	602	8.1	601	8.1	594	4.7	635	5.0	3,748	10.4	2,992	8.3
Venezuela	1,959	12.2	1,652	10.2	313	4.2	227	3.1	178	1.4	197	1.6	2,450	6.8	2,076	5.7
Italy	1,192	7.4	785	4.9	269	3.6	257	3.4	255	2.0	201	1.6	1,717	4.7	1,243	3.4
Indonesia	1,019	6.3	875	5.4	231	3.1	201	2.7	98	.8	91	.7	1,350	3.7	1,166	3.2
Spain	939	5.8	734	4.6	208	2.8	229	3.1	114	.9	130	1.0	1,264	3.5	1,093	3.0
Peru	902	5.6	670	4.2	235	3.2	196	2.6	187	1.5	129	1.0	1,328	3.7	995	2.8
Taiwan	743	4.6	650	4.0	308	4.1	204	2.7	144	1.1	104	.8	1,198	3.3	958	2.6
Algeria	871	5.4	722	4.5	207	2.8	143	1.9	50	.4	63	.5	1,129	3.1	928	2.6
South Africa	729	4.5	490	3.0	208	2.8	175	2.4	247	2.0	259	2.1	1,186	3.3	924	2.6
U.S.S.R.	839	5.2	478	3.0	175	2.4	138	1.9	96	.8	93	.7	1,112	3.1	709	2.0
Poland	736	4.6	390	2.4	168	2.3	51	.7	111	.9	59	.5	1,016	2.8	501	1.4
Total	17,540	108.8	13,899	86.2	4,492	60.4	3,963	55.3	3,824	30.4	3,608	28.6	25,883	71.5	21,468	59.4

Source: Federal Reserve Board

a   Equity capital and loan loss reserves reported in 1977 were $16,130 million for the 9 largest banks; $7,438 million for 15 other money center banks; $12,607 million for 95 other U.S. banks; and $36,175 million for all three groups of banks.

shown in Table 3, indicate that the phenomenon is fairly wide-spread.

Nevertheless, as Turkey's recent experience suggests, distinguishing between public and private borrowers may become irrelevant if falling reserves provoke restrictive measures, preventing private borrowers from using foreign exchange for debt repayment. Thus, external currency loans to both public and private borrowers in individual countries which aggregate 35 or 40 percent of capital can be worrisome.

One additional measure is indicative of the overall commitment of U.S. banks to balance-of-payments lending. Table 3 lists thirteen countries to each of which U.S. banks had made loans of more than $1 billion as of June 1977. These loans totaled $25.9 billion—71.5 percent of the capital funds of the 119 lending banks, 6.1 percent of total U.S. bank lending to foreign governments, and 15.8 percent of total foreign loans in external currencies. At the end of 1977, the banks had reduced their exposure to most of these countries. However, they reported a 65-percent increase in the ratio of total bank placements to capital. For example, loans to banks in Eastern Europe rose from 4.3 percent of capital to 14.3 percent between June and December as the ratio of public sector loans to capital declined from 17.9 to 11.4 percent over the same period. To the extent that these shifts reflect roll-overs of credits to public sector borrowers, the year-end figures would appear to understate their share of bank lending. Data in Table 3 reveal that, as of June 1977, the commitment of U.S. banks to the governments of these few countries was sizable.

Despite fiascoes in Indonesia and elsewhere, some analysts argue that banks have not been reckless in their LDC lending. They cite as evidence a Federal Reserve Board study showing that loan loss experience on foreign loans has been significantly lower than on domestic loans.[38] An obvious question arises: Is it possible that the same banks that lent $22 billion to REITs were miraculously more prudent when lending to foreigners?[39] Albert Fishlow suggests that this could be so if banks are more willing to *accept* losses on domestic portfolios than on foreign. Domestic bankruptcy laws offer some protection unavailable abroad, especially where governments are involved.[40] It may be rational for banks to accept refinancing or rescheduling of foreign loans rather than default.

Thus, evidence of problems in international lending may lie elsewhere. The Securities and Exchange Commission has, in fact, turned over a stone ignored by other bank regulatory authorities. It requires bank holding companies to report aggregate nonperforming loans and sometimes has pressed banks to break out these loans by source and state their earnings' impact. At the end of 1976, a few U.S. multinational banks reported nonperforming foreign loans at levels almost as high as those for domestic borrowers. While much more information is needed to assess the source of international lending problems, it is clear that loan loss experience is an inadequate measure of foreign lending prudence.

5. The Terms of Lending

Those most concerned with the structure of LDC debt argue that combining short-term stabilization borrowings and medium-term commercial credits for development purposes results in a "potentially dangerous" bunching of maturities.[41] Some see bunching as dangerous because it leads to high debt-service ratios, reduces net fund transfers, and thus constrains LDC growth prospects.[42] Others fear that, by reducing LDCs' capacity to import from developed countries, the prospects for world recovery diminish.[43] Although some argue that the bunching of maturities represents only a short-run liquidity problem,[44] all agree that a substantial portion of major LDC borrowers' debt matures before 1982 and must be refinanced.

Governor Wallich's data on the average maturity of LDCs' Eurocurrency credits confirm that a bunching of maturing debt will occur in the early 1980s (see Table 4) and that the medium-term characteristics of LDC bank borrowing will probably cause a repetition of the bunching of payments between 1984 and 1986. Thus, the system apparently faces not a rescheduling of debt, but refinancing.

Profit considerations make banks reluctant to reschedule debt. They are more willing to refinance since this incorporates the old debt into the new and permits profit-taking in the form

Table 4
Maturity Structure of LDC Debt

Borrowed by Year and Quarter	Avergae Maturity of Loans (Years)	Year Debt Matures
1973 Q4	10.9	1984 Q2
1975 Q4	5.4	1981 Q1
1976 Q4	5.1	1982 Q1
1977 Q3	4.6	1982 Q2
1977 Q4	7.3	1985 Q1
1978 Q1	8.3	1986 Q3

Source: Federal Reserve Board (from IBRD, Borrowing in International Capital Markets, various issues).

of management fees. Rescheduling offers borrowers breathing space without additional costs and the opportunity to negotiate new credits on independent terms. The refinancing option assures a continued flow of income for the bank lender but condemns the borrowers to more debt, higher costs, and too short a time limit for repayment. But, setting aside the borrowers' concerns, can huge debt refinancings be easily accomplished? The current condition of the world economy, the possibility of distributional shifts of surpluses and deficits affecting the availability of lendable funds, and the future prospects of the LDCs themselves are all critical factors. The only solution may be to allow the LDCs to "export their way out of debt."[45]

Lending to Less Favored LDCs

Discussion of the structural problem of the short-term nature of commercial bank lending usually focuses on the ten countries accounting for the bulk of LDC commercial bank claims. Given this focus, the view that LDC bank debt is manageable is plausible.[46] But what of the other LDCs? Most observers assume that their $83 billion of external debt at the end of 1976 was owed "mainly" to foreign governments and international organizations. It appears, however, that the other LDCs increased their private borrowing significantly in 1976.[47] Since 1975, for example, Morocco has become an important borrower ($641 million in 1975 and $777 million in 1976). In 1977,

Morocco was the fifth largest LDC borrower—after Brazil, Mexico, South Korea, and Argentina. *World Financial Markets* reports that the cumulative Eurocurrency borrowings of "other" LDCs were $6.9 billion for the years 1973-1977. U.S. banks reported outstanding claims of $9.1 billion on nonmajor LDC borrowers as of December 31, 1977 (see Table 6)—$5.0 billion on Latin American and Caribbean borrowers; $1.7 billion on Middle Eastern, Asian, and Pacific countries; and $2.4 billion on African non-oil LDCs. Over half of these credits have maturities of less than one year; a substantial portion is to public borrowers. The short-term nature of these bank credits reflects their lower "perceived" creditworthiness. Given the obvious lending risks of these countries,[48] their substantial, newfound access to Eurocurrency markets is remarkable.

Their access, however, may be due largely to the need for the banks to lend. As the tables on bank loans to capital ratios indicate, the banks are at, or near, prudent loan limits to the more favored borrowers. Lending to those countries probably cannot continue to increase at past rates. Thus, they need new borrowers. Since increased 1977 borrowings by industrial countries, OPEC, and the Soviet bloc apparently did not absorb available funds, the lower-income LDCs were given a larger slice of the pie.

Will the extension of short-term Eurocurrency credits to the poorer LDCs promote growth, helping countries without previous access to private credits reach the high-growth rates already achieved by those with earlier access? Or will it cause financial problems for poorer countries and impede future growth? Precise answers to these questions are not yet possible, but the case of Pakistan indicates the kinds of problems some of the poorer countries may face in borrowing from Eurocurrency markets.

The Case of Pakistan

Pakistan has not been an important Eurocurrency borrower. Only five of the eighty-four countries listed in the Country Exposure Lending Survey have a smaller amount in outstanding loans to U.S. banks than does Pakistan. As of December 1977, Pakistan had borrowed $400 million from all Eurocurrency banks[49] and only $60 million from U.S. banks, of which $8 million was in loans to local banks, $31.1 million to public borrowers, and $20.2 million to other private borrowers.[50] In addition, Pakistan has obtained commitments to borrow an additional $318 million from U.S. banks. It is possible that Pakistani borrowers intend to utilize these commitments to increase their Eurocurrency credits. But the commitments may reflect U.S. bank guarantees (for a fee) that most of Pakistan's $400 million Eurocurrency debt will be rolled over.

The key factor in Pakistan's debt to U.S. banks is its maturity. Of the $60 million owed, only $10 million has a maturity of over one year. Thus, $50 million was to mature in 1978. That factor appears to have triggered Pakistan's decision to request a rescheduling of $71.1 million of official 1978 debt.[51] It is also noteworthy that all but $6 million of Pakistan's U.S. debt is owed to the nine largest U.S. banks. It is probably owed to far fewer than these nine, since earlier Federal Reserve Board surveys of twenty-one U.S. banks[52] indicated that only the six largest had outstanding Pakistani loans.[53] It is also probable that not all six reporting banks were lenders. According to the surveys, the outstanding loans of those banks dropped from $54 million in December 1975 to $6 million in September 1976. It is likely that they were short-term loans which were repaid in 1976 and then reextended, since there was no significant increase in Pakistan's U.S. bank debt in the twenty-four months from December 1975 to December 1977.[54] For the most part, the U.S. portion of Pakistan's debt has been merely rolled over, perhaps with additional finance charges which raise the total amount outstanding.

The stagnant level of U.S. bank funds lent to Pakistan may be unusual. Non-U.S. banks may have increased their lending since 1975; BIS data indicate that Japanese banks loaned Pakistan an additional $200 million between June and December 1977. At current world price levels, however, Pakistan's $400 million of private debt is significant only if most of it must be repaid within a single year to assure a continued flow of funds. In such a situation, Pakistan's ability to obtain Eurocurrency financing is not a blessing. High-cost, short-term funds contribute little to either development or stabilization policies. The possibility that they may create an insupportable near-term debt burden is, in fact, highly destabilizing.

6. Concentration: The Lenders

The concentration of both OPEC deposits and LDC loans in a few U.S. banks recently became apparent.[55] As of December 31, 1975, approximately two-thirds of the total non-oil LDC credits of twenty-one major U.S. banks was loaned by the six largest U.S. banks. These six banks also held 76 percent of all OPEC funds deposited in U.S. banking offices.[56] The claims reported for fifteen LDCs totaled $12 billion, or 5 percent of the total assets of this group of banks, with claims on Mexico and Brazil each about 1½ percent of total assets. By comparison, their domestic real-estate loans were also 5 percent of their total assets and domestic consumer loans only 3 percent, an amount equal to their combined claims on Mexico and Brazil.[57]

More recent, not totally comparable, data collected by the House Banking Committee revealed that through September 1976 the six largest U.S. banks held over 79 percent of OPEC deposits reported by twenty-one U.S. banks, up from 76 percent nine months earlier, and that OPEC deposits accounted for almost 7 percent of their total domestic and foreign liabilities. Of the $26.3 billion of claims on fifteen LDCs reported in September 1976, $17.7 billion, or 67.3 percent, were held by those six banks. While their share of LDC lending and foreign lending in general was very high compared with other U.S. banks, the total assets of the six largest were only 22.7 percent of all U.S. bank assets at that time.

More recent data aggregate the banks differently and do not provide deposit data. Table 5 shows that the nine largest U.S. banks held over two-thirds of the total external-currency loans to foreigners by 119 American banks on December 31, 1977. Bolstered by their global networks, they probably also held the bulk of the $44 billion of local currency loans to foreigners (not reported here)[58] and, thus, an even larger share of total foreign lending. Their extensive branch networks also help explain their higher proportionate lending to non–G-10 developed countries and to Africa. The lower proportion of their claims on offshore

Table 5
U.S. Bank Loans to Foreign Countries by Groups of Countries, Groups of Banks, and Types and
Maturities of Loans (December 31, 1977)   ($ Millions)

Groups of Countries	Total Claims of 9 Largest Banks	% of Total Claims of All US Banks on this Country	Total Claims of 15 Other Money Center Banks	% of Total Claims of All US Banks on this Country	Total Claims of 95 Other Banks	% of Total Claims of All US Banks on this Country	Total Claims	% of Total Claims of All Non-Oil-Exporting LDCs	Claims on: Banks Amount	As % of Total Claims on these Countries	Public Borrowers Amount	As % of Total Claims on these Countries	Private Borrowers Amount	As % of Total Claims on these Countries	Maturity Distribution: 1 Year & Under Amount	As % of Total Claims on these Countries	Over 1 Year Amount	As % of Total Claims on these Countries
G-10 Countries & Switzerland	59,986.8	71.7	13,729.4	16.4	9,893.9	11.8	83,610.1	43.0	52,551.4	62.8	7,375.5	8.8	23,688.6	28.3	65,242.7	78.0	18,356.4	22.0
Non-G-10 Developed Countries	13,114.4	70.3	3,278.2	17.6	2,247.4	12.1	18,640.0	9.6	5,423.1	29.1	5,184.9	27.8	8,028.7	43.1	9,094.8	48.8	9,545.3	51.2
Eastern Europe	4,597.1	67.2	1,290.4	18.8	950.3	13.9	6,837.8	3.5	3,447.6	50.8	2,705.5	39.6	660.6	9.7	3,094.9	45.1	3,758.4	54.9
Oil-Exporting Countries	10,922.3	74.3	2,251.4	15.3	1,512.5	10.2	14,686.2	7.5	3,425.6	23.3	6,037.0	41.1	5,227.2	35.6	8,209.5	55.9	6,479.4	44.1
Non-Oil-Exporting Developing Countries	30,046.0	64.0	8,829.8	18.8	8,058.4	17.1	46,934.2	24.1	12,955.2	27.6	16,387.4	35.9	17,592.8	37.5	24,073.6	51.3	22,861.5	48.7
Latin America & Caribbean	(20,685.5)	(61.7)	(6,525.1)	(19.4)	(6,324.5)	(18.9)	(33,535.1)	(17.2)	(8,349.8)	(24.9)	(11,863.3)	(35.4)	(13,322.0)	(39.7)	(15,985.5)	(47.7)	(17,545.6)	(52.3)
Asia	(7,465.2)	(68.0)	(1,968.5)	(18.0)	(1,531.5)	(14.0)	(10,965.2)	(5.6)	(4,214.4)	(38.4)	(2,827.5)	(25.8)	(3,926.8)	(35.8)	(6,988.6)	(63.7)	(3,979.9)	(36.3)
Africa	(1,895.3)	(77.9)	(336.2)	(13.8)	(202.4)	(8.3)	(2,433.9)	(1.3)	(391.0)	(16.1)	(1,696.9)	(69.7)	(344.0)	(14.1)	(1,099.5)	(45.2)	(1,336.0)	(54.9)
Offshore Banking Centers	13,926.0	59.0	4,412.5	18.7	5,279.6	22.3	23,618.1	12.1	18,334.4	77.6	399.7	1.7	4,883.1	20.7	20,213.6	85.6	3,369.6	14.3
Miscellaneous	111.5	45.0	---	0.0	136.4	55.0	247.9	.01	1.1	11.6	245.0	98.8	---	0.0	38.1	15.4	206.9	84.5
Total	132,704.1	68.2	33,791.7	17.3	28,078.5	14.4	194,574.3	100.0	96,167.4	49.4	38,335.0	19.7	60,081.0	30.9	129,967.2	66.8	64,577.5	33.2

Source: Federal Reserve Board

banking centers reflects the activity of smaller banks, which do most of their interbank lending through shell branches in Nassau or the Cayman Islands.

Table 6 indicates that the nine largest banks were somewhat less dominant in their loans to major LDC borrowers. The highest proportion of loans of the smaller banks are to the ten most-favored borrowers and to Latin American countries. Among other things, this reflects long-standing trade and financial relationships between the United States and Latin America. The fairly equal distribution of Latin American lending is even more apparent for individual countries. Mexico and Peru are favored borrowers of both the second and third groups of banks. The second group's share of loans to Taiwan and the Philippines is also higher, reflecting large numbers of California-based banks.

7. Concentration: The Borrowers

It is estimated that at the end of 1976, Mexico and Brazil had borrowed about half of total Eurocurrency credits and eight other countries—Argentina, Chile, Colombia, Peru, South Korea, the Philippines, Taiwan, and Thailand—had borrowed most of the other half. The Country Exposure Lending Survey reveals that U.S. bank claims on these ten LDC borrowers account for over 80 percent of their claims on all LDC countries, with loans to Mexico and Brazil taking about half of the total. The nine largest banks provided 72 percent of the remaining 20 percent lent to other LDCs. The poorer LDCs had a higher proportion borrowed by their governments and banks than is the average for the more-favored borrowers and also a higher proportion of loans maturing in less than one year.

Overall, there is a surprisingly high level of LDC private non-bank borrowing.[59] Even Africa seems less dependent on public sector borrowing for capital flows than the summary table indicates. A substantial amount ($1.8 billion) in private credits is borrowed in Liberia, an offshore banking center. Since 62 percent of these credits are externally guaranteed, they apparently reflect borrowings by multinational corporations for use by subsidiaries throughout Africa. Private sector borrowing in Thailand is also especially notable, since it amounted to 73.5

Table 6.
U.S. Bank Loans to Selected LDCs by Groups of Banks and Types and Maturities of Loans
(December 31, 1977) ($ millions)

Country	Total Claims of 9 Largest Banks	% of Total Claims of All US Banks on this Country	Total Claims of 15 Other Money Center Banks	% of Total Claims of All US Banks on this Country	Total Claims of 95 Other Banks	% of Total Claims of All US Banks on this Country	Total Claims	% of Total Claims of All Non-Oil-Exporting LDCs	Claims on: Banks Amount	As % of Total Claims on these Countries	Public Borrowers Amount	As % of Total Claims on these Countries	Private Borrowers Amount	As % of Total Claims on these Countries	Maturity Distribution: 1 Year & Under Amount	As % of Total Claims on these Countries	Over 1 Year Amount	As % of Total Claims on these Countries
Argentina	1,753.4	66.4	457.1	17.3	429.1	16.3	2,639.6	5.6	598.0	22.7	1,238.4	46.9	803.1	30.4	1,669.4	63.2	970.3	36.8
Brazil	7,721.7	64.4	2,320.2	19.3	1,950.5	16.3	11,992.4	25.6	3,364.2	28.1	2,992.5	25.0	5,631.9	47.0	4,062.7	33.9	7,927.6	66.1
Chile	535.7	65.2	149.1	18.2	136.3	16.6	821.1	1.7	256.6	31.3	359.3	43.8	204.5	24.9	520.5	63.4	300.1	36.6
Korea	2,160.5	70.3	444.7	14.5	466.7	15.2	3,071.9	6.5	1,458.7	47.5	503.9	16.4	1,111.1	36.2	1,823.1	59.3	1,250.8	40.7
Malaysia	399.7	78.2	82.8	16.2	28.6	5.6	511.1	1.2	106.4	20.8	259.4	50.8	145.1	28.4	216.8	42.4	294.3	57.6
Mexico	6,063.3	54.1	2,478.4	22.1	2,671.4	23.8	11,213.1	23.9	1,982.6	17.8	4,801.8	42.8	4,434.1	39.5	5,418.6	48.3	5,794.9	51.7
Peru	1,059.4	57.8	442.1	24.1	329.8	18.0	1,831.3	3.9	450.8	24.6	995.4	54.4	383.8	21.0	1,021.7	55.8	809.4	44.2
Philippines	1,258.5	61.4	475.7	23.2	315.7	15.4	2,049.9	4.5	611.1	29.8	505.6	24.7	933.4	45.5	1,250.1	61.0	800.0	39.0
Taiwan	1,870.8	66.7	546.6	19.5	388.3	13.8	2,805.7	5.8	954.9	34.0	958.3	34.2	893.5	31.8	1,895.7	67.6	910.9	32.4
Thailand	633.3	73.9	122.2	14.3	101.3	11.8	856.8	1.8	390.7	45.6	108.9	12.7	357.3	41.7	715.0	83.5	141.7	16.5
Subtotal	23,456.3	62.1	7,518.9	19.9	6,817.7	18.0	37,792.9	80.5	10,174.0	26.9	12,723.5	33.7	14,897.8	39.4	18,593.6	49.2	19,200.0	50.8
Other NOLDCs	6,589.7	72.1	1,309.8	14.3	1,239.7	13.6	9,139.2	19.5	2,779.6	30.4	3,662.7	40.1	2,693.7	29.5	5,477.9	59.9	3,658.6	40.1
Total	30,046.0	64.0	8,828.7	18.8	8,057.4	17.2	46,932.1	100.0	12,953.6	27.6	16,386.2	34.9	17,591.5	37.5	24,071.5	51.3	22,858.6	48.7

Source: Federal Reserve Board

percent of the country's external debt in June 1977 and 41.7 percent in December. Only 4.7 percent was externally guaranteed by residents outside the country in June and 10.2 percent in December. For all LDCs, externally guaranteed credits averaged 6 percent of total loans in June and 9.5 percent in December 1977.

In the past, debt service ratio estimates for many LDCs excluded private borrowing because data were not available. Discussions of private borrowing usually assumed that as much as half was externally guaranteed, that most of it reflected loans to multinational corporations, and that another sizable portion was guaranteed by governmental entities such as the U.S. Export-Import Bank in industrial countries. The Country Exposure Lending Survey contains a few surprises. Table 5 points out the surprising fact that almost a quarter of U.S. banks' loans in external currencies are to LDCs.[60] If interbank placements are excluded, U.S. banks have lent $31.1 billion to public and private sector borrowers in the G-10 countries and Switzerland, $13.2 billion to non–G-10 developed countries, $3.4 billion to Eastern Europe, $11.2 billion to OPEC, and $34 billion to LDCs. A residual of $5.5 billion of loans to public and private nonbank borrowers booked in offshore banking centers remains. Thus, the LDCs are the largest public and private nonbank borrowers, with 34.5 percent of total loans going to these two sectors.[61]

8. Effects of Concentration: The Borrowers

The concentration of Eurocurrency lending in a few wealthier LDCs has reoriented official lending toward the poorer countries. As a result, the middle-income countries suffer most from inadequate financing.[62] Those countries are especially sensitive to reductions in credit flows and are particularly vulnerable to short-term stabilization programs.[63] Some analysts advocate the extension of more official resources to broaden credit availability, and slower adjustment to avoid social and political upheaval.[64]

In the late 1960s, official lending shifted to poorer countries because disparities in growth rates and in the distribution effects within those countries were thought to be partially linked to the magnitude and focus of official aid. The growth rate of higher-income LDCs accelerated from 6 percent in the early 1960s to 7 percent a decade later, while that of the poorer countries fell from 4 to 2 percent over the same period. The sudden increase in Eurocredit flows to the higher income countries in the early 1970s widened the growth disparities among LDCs. The more-favored borrowers increased industrial production and real imports by 9 percent annually between 1965 and 1973, while production and imports grew by less than 4 percent in the poorer countries. As a result, the ten largest Eurocurrency borrowers now have over one-half of the combined gross national product of all LDCs but only a quarter of the population of the developing world.[65]

The allocation of so large a share of international financial resources to so few countries, both before and after 1973, solidified and increased their growth rates above those for any other group of countries. Recently, their growth in new industrial capacity and in exports has surpassed the industrial countries' performance.[66] The effects of this growth level may have a greater direct impact on industrial countries than on other LDCs.

The improved 1976 LDC balance-of-payments results were due partly to the improvement in their terms of trade with the United States.[67] For the first time, these nations experienced a balance-of-trade surplus with the United States.[68] LDCs' export performance to other industrial countries has been less significant than their decline in imports, spurred partly by the 1976 "adjustment" and partly by import substitution.[69]

A shift in world trade patterns might be expected given these variations in economic performance, but so far there has been little discussion outside the U.S. Congress of the implications of those shifts. Most discussion of LDC debt has focused on the impact of developed countries' policies on LDCs—on the industrial countries' role in promoting world economic recovery, in assuring continued credit flows to LDCs, and in preventing a cutback in LDC exports necessary to service debts by eschewing protectionist policies. Few analysts consider the importance of the higher-income LDCs in the world economy and that their economic policies will significantly contribute to or impede recovery.

9. Effects of Concentration: The Lenders

In June 1977, an *IMF Survey* supplement on international lending claimed:

> Although the international credit and interbank markets remain highly concentrated, the picture is now changing somewhat. The principal oil-exporting countries have increased from a handful to about 20 the number of banks with which they deposit their surplus funds. The interbank market continues to be dominated by about 40-50 large banks. This concentration, coupled with limits on these banks' credit lines to other banks, constrains the access of smaller banks to interbank funds and thus their ability to expand their lending activities. However, when only the larger and more experienced banks are operating in the market, there is more stability.[70]

The assertion that international market concentration contributes to stability is debatable. If market confidence rests on too few banks, the pressure to retain that confidence can lead to lax lending[71] and can result in pressures to restore order "at any political and social price."[72] Several recent, private debt negotiations have demonstrated that, where so few lenders are involved, discussions take on characteristics more appropriate to a poker game than to the operations of supposedly impersonal credit markets.[73]

As the IMF and others have noted, the concentration of OPEC deposits is a major factor reducing the number of banks heavily involved in international lending. The growth in OPEC claims on the largest banks is also significant. The nine largest U.S. banks have made almost 75 percent of loans to OPEC countries; the top twenty-four banks have made 90 percent (see Table 5).

Over 40 percent of total U.S. bank claims on OPEC countries are to public sector borrowers which, in turn, provide more funds to the banks than any other single source. This indicates how few and how powerful are the major actors in international financial markets.[74] The relationship between the banks and the oil cartel has cartelized the banks. This concentration of control over a critically important financial market cannot be taken lightly. It is clearly no longer a free market—nor even a private market. And the absence of a strong countervailing force working in the interst of the majority in both developed and developing countries enhances the potential for conflicts. When so few control the allocation of such vast resources, defensive policies may develop in national economies. If such defensive policies proliferate, "the world could encounter a monetary and economic crisis."[75]

10. Some Proposed Solutions

Private banks probably will continue to be the principal source of funds for the higher-income LDCs. For some, this is a matter of concern. Not only balance-of-payments financing but also development financing worries them, particularly since, for most developing countries, the two are inextricably intertwined. Some analysts believe bank credit is a poor substitute for direct equity investment in promoting development.[76] The relatively short terms and high rates of private loans make debt less supportable than when equity investment provided most private funds. The profit orientation of banks necessarily results in financial flows that ignore global requirements. Moreover, recent heavy reliance on bank credit has tended to favor capital-intensive, export-oriented development programs which has helped create diverging LDC growth rates and has worsened national income distribution within some of the faster-growing LDCs.[77]

If LDCs continue to rely heavily on private bank credit, these problems may persist. The number of alternative financing proposals under discussion are evidence of substantial agreement on this point. Expanding the resources of multilateral lending institutions, expanding the resources of the International Monetary Fund (both through increased quotas and the Witteveen or special lending facility), and encouraging cofinancing arrangements between public and private lenders are among the more modest solutions which have been offered. All three are likely to be implemented.

Another proposal put forward during congressional hearings on the debt problem advocates that the IMF assume a larger role in deficit financing,[78] the Witteveen Facility being a first step. The second step, requiring many more funds, would be financed, like the so-called safety-net proposal, by IMF borrowing in the market, backed by guarantees from member countries. IMF borrowing would shift the lending burden away from the banks while absorbing a substantial amount of the funds they now control. As purchasers of IMF securities, banks would remain major lenders to deficit countries but would no longer decide who would receive funds and on what terms. In return for taking a back seat, the banks would receive the benefits of official guarantees and improved liquidity,[79] reducing their vulnerability to market confidence.

Meanwhile, there is increased awareness of the structural problems in the world economy that, given the greater integration of national economies, can be dealt with effectively only on an international scale. Surplus capacity is no longer a national problem for the textile, steel, and shipbuilding industries. Institutions to deal with the problem of global surplus capacity do not yet exist, while regional solutions advance the interests of only one country or a group of countries and may intensify the international problem.[80]

And yet, all countries have a responsibility to protect their own interests. The U.S. Congress has grappled with this dilemma in setting policies for foreign aid. Foreign aid programs are concerned with the larger good and seek to benefit other countries. But the conflict between these benefits and U.S. interests has become apparent. In response, the House of Representatives has directed the Export-Import Bank to "take into account any serious adverse effect on the competitive position of U.S. industry and the effect on U.S. employment" in approving loans and guarantees. Specifically, the report of the House Committee on Appropriations states:

> The Committee is very concerned with Export-Import Bank financing of overseas production of certain overcapacity industries or commodities that cause injury to United States producers. The specific concern has been centered on the overseas production of iron and steel products. Although the Committee is certainly not advocating a protectionist stance regarding United States trade or assistance to foreign countries, it does have difficulty understanding why we have to provide help in financing foreign producers of com-

petitive commodities in order to qualify as supporters of free enterprise. Because of Congressional concern in this area, the Committee
has included a general provision that would prohibit direct foreign
assistance, the Export-Import Bank, and the Overseas Private Investment Corporation from financing the production of any commodity
for export, if it is in surplus on world markets and if the assistance
will cause substantial injury to United States producers of the same,
similar, or competing commodity.[81]

The committee report also emphasizes the need to rely less
on external capital for development by creating internal
savings.[82] Implicit in the committee's policy prescriptions is
the view that developing countries should rely more on internal
growth than on exports to promote capital formation. Such an
approach might help integrate development goals into a policy
framework for world recovery. If a greater reliance on domestic
growth and consumption in industrial countries will contribute
to recovery, perhaps a similar policy orientation within the
higher-income developing countries would also contribute to
that end. But will it help those countries in servicing existing
debt? Maybe not, and perhaps that is why the banks have
emerged as "the new champions of freer trade and greater
market access."[83]

There are others who also argue for freer trade, stressing the
dangers of disengagement for both developing and developed
countries. Reliance on internal growth might have the desired
effect of reducing LDC exports, but it would also reduce their
need to import. If the industrial countries lose those markets,
they risk endangering their own prospects for recovery. For this
reason, Ronald Müller has proposed a "Marshall Plan" for
developing countries, arguing that an effort comparable to U.S.
assistance in rebuilding Europe and Japan after World War II is
needed to end "stagflation" by stimulating the growth of new
markets.[84]

As this brief summary indicates, there are significant differences among the solutions offered. Nevertheless, most analysts
acknowledge that the manageability of LDC debt depends on
worldwide economic recovery. Increased protectionism and the
failure of industrial countries to achieve adequate growth rates
are closely linked to the question of debt manageability. Ex-

change rate instability has also been seen as a threat to the
expansion of world trade and as an impediment to maintaining
growth. The stability of the international monetary system is
another underpinning critical for recovery. Recent developments in international financial markets indicate that a new
constellation of destabilizing factors has emerged. These developments are discussed in the following section.

11. Mirror Images:
The Eurocurrency Market and Recycling

Most analyses of Eurocurrency lending focus on the identity
of borrowers and on the use of funds. It is feared that defaults
by heavily indebted countries without adequate foreign exchange earnings to service debts could threaten the system's
stability. Some pessimists, focusing on the sources of funds as
a problem, also fear that the Eurocurrency market's role in
recycling OPEC surplus funds to deficit countries could create
structural problems. But these analyses are weakened by a
failure to examine the system as a whole.

The counterargument dismissing the OPEC "threat" is plausible. Funds withdrawn from one bank or any given nation's
banks can be readily recaptured through the interbank market.[85] Although banks losing funds may have to buy them
back at a higher price, perhaps adversely affecting their profits
and market confidence, central bank guarantees can effectively
stabilize such disruption and restore confidence.

Petrodollar holders' options are also somewhat limited in
switching to assets denominated in other currencies. The availability of stronger currencies is finite because of the size of the
various economies relative to the United States and because of
governments' actions to restrict foreign investment in domestic
holdings. The scarcity of nondollar assets may even have contributed to destabilizing exchange markets.[86] There are wide
gaps between the demand for currencies and their availability.
But the implications of such problems extend to all holders of
dollar assets, not just to OPEC investors.

Pessimists also erroneously assumed that OPEC surpluses
would remain at 1974-1976 levels.[87] In fact, some OPEC coun-

tries have fallen into deficit and have become net borrowers from Eurobanks. As Table 7 shows, even the Middle Eastern OPEC countries had $37 billion net deposits in Eurobanks at the end of 1977, only slightly more than U.S. residents. Moreover, their deposits in U.S. banks declined in the fourth quarter of 1977, while their borrowings increased throughout the year. The growth of the newly formed Arab banks, which are probably borrowing from U.S. and other Eurobanks for relending, could explain some of these shifts. Apparently, OPEC countries have begun to enter the Eurocurrency markets and have taken on some of the burden of recycling their own surplus funds.[88]

But there are systemic weaknesses in the Eurocurrency market. Sizable outflows of private capital from the United States, coupled with the inadequacy of private capital flows from Germany and Japan, help create instability. As the memoranda to Table 7 indicate, the United States was a net supplier of funds to the Eurocurrency market in 1977 while Germany and Japan were net borrowers. Such an inverse relationship between surplus and deficit countries and private capital flows requires a compensating mechanism. The U.S. current account must be financed, and the German and Japanese surpluses must be used to finance deficits if the international monetary system is to continue to function. If the financing is not undertaken by the private sector, the public sector must do the job.

Table 8, the U.S. Capital Account Summary, lists the level of net capital outflows from 1975 through the first quarter of 1978. In 1975, the U.S. current account surplus of $18.4 billion accommodated a net capital outflow of the same magnitude. The $26.7 billion outflow of private capital was partially offset by the investment of $7 billion of OPEC funds in the United States. In 1976, the current account surplus shrank to $4.3 billion as the trade balance shifted from a $9 billion surplus in 1975 to a $9.3 billion deficit.[89] But the sizable trade deficit did not inhibit private capital outflows, which declined by only $1.7 billion. These outflows were again partially offset by inflows of foreign official funds—$9.6 billion from OPEC countries and $8.5 billion from other nations.

The U.S. current account shifted into deficit in 1977 and was financed by an investment of $37 billion in the United States

Table 7
Eurocurrency Market: Sources and Uses of Funds by Groups of Countries, December 1977
($ billions)

	All Eurobanks (Including U.S. banks) December 1977			Change Q4		Change A2		Change for Year		U.S. Banks Foreign Branches December 1977			Change Q4		Change A2		Change for Year	
	Claims	Liabilities	Net Claims-Liabilities	Claims	Liabilities	Claims	Liabilities	Claims	Liabilities	Claims	Liabilities	Net Change Liabilities	Claims	Liabilities	Claims	Liabilities	Claims	Liabilities
G-10 Countries & Switzerland	319.7	384.0	(64.3)	37.5	44.0	46.8	52.0	50.2	64.4	110.5	131.3	(20.8)	5.7	10.2	13.1	16.9	16.2	23.4
Non-G-10 Developed Countries	70.2	41.1	29.1	5.7	4.5	9.9	8.2	15.7	6.1	16.9	11.0	5.9	1.6	1.3	2.4	2.0	3.2	2.2
Eastern Europe & U.S.S.R.	32.9	7.8	25.1	2.8	1.8	3.3	2.3	4.1	.2	4.9	.4	4.5	1.4	0	1.4	-.1	1.6	-.5
Offshore Banking Centers	97.8	71.1	26.7	8.4	5.3	8.9	9.4	14.3	15.1	23.9	20.6	3.3	.4	-1.4	-1.2	-.9	.3	-.3
OPEC Countries	35.4	77.6	(42.2)	3.5	4.5	5.7	4.9	11.3	13.4	13.3	19.1	(5.8)	.8	-.3	1.8	-.9	4.6	1.4
Non-OPEC LDCs: Middle East	4.6	10.1	(5.5)	.4	.7	.5	1.9	.2	2.8	.7	.8	(.1)	.1	0	.1	-.1	.1	.1
Non-OPEC LDCs: Other Africa	5.5	6.7	(1.2)	.6	.4	.6	.8	1.1	1.4	1.7	.6	1.1	.2	.1	.5	.1	.7	.2
Non-OPEC LDCs: Other Asia	18.1	20.0	(1.9)	1.0	1.4	2.0	2.2	3.4	5.1	7.2	8.8	(1.6)	.8	.1	1.1	.9	1.9	1.9
Non-OPEC LDCs: Latin America & Caribbean	64.0	25.9	38.1	3.7	2.2	5.7	3.2	6.6	3.6	24.4	6.1	18.3	.8	.5	1.1	1.4	2.8	1.3
Unallocated	9.1	14.1	(4.9)	1.3	.5	1.7	1.7	2.4	2.3	2.9	4.7	(1.8)	.3	.4	.5	.7	.5	1.0
Total	657.3	658.3	(1.0)	64.9	65.3	85.1	86.6	109.3	114.3	206.4	203.4	3.0	12.1	10.9	20.8	20.0	31.9	30.7
Memo Items:																		
U.S.	39.1	73.9	(34.8)	-1.1	5.8	5.1	8.1	5.8	17.6	11.7	44.3	(32.6)	-.4	3.7	4.2	6.3	3.6	11.1
Japan	29.4	7.3	22.1	.4	.5	-.8	.2	-4.7	-2.9	12.9	5.8	7.1	.7	.4	1.3	1.2	1.6	1.1
West Germany	36.2	24.0	12.2	6.6	2.7	N.A.	N.A.	N.A.	N.A.	9.1	6.1	3.0	.8	.4	1.1	1.6	1.8	-.2
Mid-East OPEC	14.2	51.3	(37.1)	1.7	3.5	N.A.	N.A.	N.A.	N.A.	5.4	14.3	(8.9)	.4	-.3	1.0	-.3	2.5	.6
Total, LDCs	92.2	62.7	29.5	5.7	4.7	8.8	8.1	11.3	12.9	34.0	16.3	17.7	1.9	.7	2.8	2.3	5.5	3.5

Sources: Bank for International Settlements, Forty-Eighth Annual Report, Basle (June 1978),
p. 92; Federal Reserve Board, Statistical Releases, (June 13, 1978).

Table 8
U.S. Capital Account Summary ($ millions)

Item	1975	1976	Change 1975-6	1977	Change 1976-7	Q4 1977	Q1 1978	Quarterly Change
Private and Official Capital Flows (Net)	-18,446	-4,338	-13,108	15,222	19,560	6,934	6,953	19
Foreign Official Assets (Increase +)	6,907	18,073	11,166	37,124	19,051	15,543	15,691	148
U.S. Reserve Assets (Increase -)	-607	-2,530	1,923	-231	-2,299	---	246	246
Other U.S. Government Assets (Increase -)	-3,470	-4,213	743	-3,679	-534	-838	-900	62
Private Capital Flows (Net) (Outflow -)	-26,725	-24,968	-1,757	-16,994	-7,974	-9,340	-11,507	2,167
Statistical Discrepancy (Unrecorded Transactions)	5,449	9,300	3,851	-998	-10,298	1,569	3,423	1,854
Memo Items								
Foreign Official Transactions (Increase +)								
OPEC	7,092	9,581	2,489	6,733	-2,848	1,024	1,810	786
Other Foreign Official Institutions	-185	8,492	8,677	30,391	21,899	14,519	13,881	-638
Foreign Official Purchases of U.S. Treasury Securities	4,408	9,333	4,925	30,294	20,961	12,900	12,965	65
Bank Reported Private Capital Flows (Net)	-12,904	-10,378	-2,526	-4,708	5,670	-5,607	-6,584	977
Claims (U.S. Assets Abroad) (Increase -)	-13,532	-21,368	7,836	-11,427	9,941	-8,750	-6,270	2,480
Liabilities (Foreign Assets in U.S.) (Increase +)	628	10,990	10,362	6,719	-4,271	3,143	-314	-3,457

Source: Bureau of Economic Analysis, U.S. Department of Commerce (as reported in Federal Reserve Bulletin, July 1978, A54)

by foreign official institutions. Private capital outflows diminished, but the net outflow of nearly $17 billion was larger than the current account deficit ($15 billion). Moreover, in the last quarter of 1977 and the first quarter of 1978, the cumulative private capital outflow rose to almost $21 billion, only $6 billion less than the outflow in 1975. During those same two quarters, foreign official institutions bought about $32 billion of U.S. assets, $26 billion of which were U.S. Treasury securities. Total foreign official holdings of U.S. government debt rose above $100 billion, approximately 15 percent of the national debt.

OPEC investments declined in 1977 both absolutely and as a share of total, foreign official investment in the United States. One explanation for the sizable investments of other countries is that some intervened in foreign exchange markets to support the value of their currencies against the dollar and invested the dollars acquired in U.S. government obligations. Others—LDCs in particular—may have borrowed more dollars than needed to finance their current account deficits and so increased reserves, a portion of which were invested in U.S. Treasury securities. In any event: Did the inflow of foreign official funds stimulate an outflow of private capital or vice versa? Did intervention (and the inflow of publicly held dollars) permit a greater degree of monetary ease in the United States, which encouraged the outflows? Given present data, there is no conclusive answer. But the increase in capital outflows did occur before the inflow of foreign official funds. In 1975, non-OPEC central banks actually reduced their holdings in the United States.

If foreign central banks did not intervene, would the dollar exchange rate fall enough to reverse the trade deficit? Conventional wisdom suggests that free floating would improve the dollar's position, but it might not have ended capital outflows. Moreover, the absence of intervention creates instability in international financial markets. A measure of that instability is the fall of the overnight rate on Euro–Swiss francs to 0.0 percent on August 16, 1978, as the Swiss National Bank resumed intervention.[90] In addition, a fall in the value of the dollar affects deficit as well as surplus countries, and developing as well as industrial nations. Taiwan, for example, revalued its currency 5.6 percent in relation to the dollar in July 1978 rather than continue to accept a 30 percent increase in its money supply and an annual inflation rate of 7 percent.[91]

U.S. interest rates rose significantly in 1978, and the discount rate surpassed the peak level of 1974.[92] Interest rates in countries with strong currencies also fell significantly. Yet interest rate differentials have not helped modify shifts in exchange rates because the cost of hedging is prohibitive.[93] The premium for forward cover reflects present expectations about trends in future exchange rates. It also helps fulfill those expectations.

Rising interest rates could also induce a recession in the United States. A recession might—as in 1975—result in a trade surplus (which would mitigate the effects of continued private capital outflows) and reduce the level of foreign official investment in the United States (since a U.S. current account surplus would result in matching deficits elsewhere). The effects of a sell-off of foreign official holdings of U.S. government securities in a recession is difficult to predict; it could help intensify the recession.

Whatever the cause, it seems that the key problem facing the United States is the continuation of private capital outflows. As Table 9 and the memoranda for Table 8 indicate, the bulk of these outflows occurs through the banking system, with most of the funds deposited in the overseas branches of U.S. banks. Outstanding net liabilities of U.S. banks' foreign branches to U.S. residents rose to approximately $40 billion in March 1978. Net U.S. liabilities were almost 20 percent of total branch liabilities, a reversal of the pattern in 1969-1970, when the foreign branches lent over 17 percent of their funds to their parent banks and other U.S. borrowers. Table 9 also shows that, in the first quarter of 1978, U.S. banks' foreign branches increased their total lending by only $1.6 billion while increasing their net U.S. liabilities by $7 billion. Apparently, it was cheaper to obtain funds at home than abroad. Thus, U.S. banks contributed to the dollar glut by reducing their Eurodollar deposits while bringing in more dollars to add to an existing oversupply.

Moreover, the banks have used some of these funds to lend or buy assets denominated in other currencies. The Bank for International Settlements reported that Eurodollar deposits at

Table 9
Claims (Liabilities) of U.S. Banks' Overseas Branches ($ millions)

Year	Total Claims/Liabil. of Overseas Branches^a		Net Claims (Liabilities) to U.S. Residents				Ratio of Net Claims (Liabilities) U.S. to Total Claims/Liabilities		
	Outstand-ing at Year-End	Change From Previous Year	Total Due to or from U.S. (Net)	Change From Previous Year	Due to or from Par-ent Bank (Net)	Due to or from other U.S. (Net)	Total Due to or from U.S. (%)	Due to or from Par-ent Bank (%)	Due to or from Other U.S. (%)
1970	40,476	- - -	7,165	- - -	6,532	632	17.7	16.1	1.6
1971	48,597	8,121	1,692	-5,473	1,642	50	3.5	3.4	0.1
1972	66,698	18,101	1,177	-515	1,116	61	1.7	1.6	0.1
1973	103,635	36,937	(189)^b	-1,366	724	(912)	(0.2)	0.7	(0.9)
1974	124,964	21,329	(5,082)	4,893	(1,345)	(3,738)	(4.1)	(1.1)	(3.0)
1975	142,382	17,418	(13,478)	8,396	(8,500)	(4,979)	(9.5)	(6.0)	(3.5)
1976	175,050	32,668	(24,832)	11,354	(15,452)	(9,380)	(14.2)	(8.8)	(5.4)
1977	206,335	31,285	(32,800)	7,968	(17,192)	(15,607)	(15.9)	(8.3)	(7.6)
1978 Q1	207,914	1,579	(39,847)	7,047	(20,952)	(18,894)	(19.2)	(10.1)	(9.1)

Source: Federal Reserve Bulletin, various issues

^a Data are net of claims (liabilities) to other foreign branches of parent banks.

^b Figures in parentheses indicate a net liability position to U.S. residents.

banks in eight European countries exceeded their Eurodollar assets by $8.3 billion at the end of September 1977.[94] For U.S. banks, the gap between their dollar assets and liabilities on that date was $4.8 billion.[95] The excess of Eurodollar liabilities over assets has grown steadily since June 1976 when it amounted to only $100 million.

The growing tendency of banks to convert dollar deposits into other currencies is also reflected in the data on Euromark and Euro-Swiss franc assets/liabilities. In September 1977, Euromark assets exceeded Euromark liabilities by $1.3 billion; Eurofranc assets exceeded Eurofranc liabilities by $1.1 billion.[96] These gaps appear to have widened further. In March 1978, the foreign branches of U.S. banks reported that the difference between their dollar liabilities and assets had risen to $5.1 billion.[97] Shifts of this size, especially if fed by new dollar funds, would necessarily have important effects on the dollar's value.

The outflows from the United States undermine current assumptions about the sources of funds for Eurocurrency lending and the market's function. Even the staff of the International Monetary Fund assumes that the largest proportion of funds drawn into the market is derived from surplus industrial countries.[98] As Table 7 shows, that is true in the aggregate: G-10 countries and Switzerland are net suppliers of Eurocurrency funds. But the fact is overlooked that, as noted, Germany and Japan are net borrowers,[99] and thus some deficit countries must be suppliers.

Can it be assumed that the Eurocurrency market recycles the funds of surplus countries to countries with current account deficits? That is an oversimplification at best. Some deficit countries are net borrowers, but many of the deficit countries do not have access to the market. The non-oil-exporting developing countries of Asia and Africa were net suppliers of funds in 1977. The United States has the largest current account deficit and is the largest single supplier of funds. Obviously, surplus funds are recycled. But the more significant exchanges of funds appear to take place at U.S. Treasury–bill auctions—not in the private international capital markets. After surplus funds are received by the U.S. Treasury, they are absorbed by U.S. financial markets and passed on through U.S. banks for relending outside the United States.

Has the Eurocurrency market become superfluous as a recycling mechanism? Probably not, if private banks are to continue to make the majority of loans to governments. The Eurocurrency market is needed to distribute the funds among banks for relending. But, with the exception of OPEC and other developing countries, governments do not contribute funds back to the market. Thus, its role as a financial intermediary will continue to be undermined by imbalances in the supply and demand for funds.

Perhaps private markets actually have failed to recycle payments imbalances. The U.S. government has borrowed over $100 billion from other governments so that its private sector could continue to invest abroad and to import more than it exports. The decision to let the private sector handle the balance-of-payments problems of the world has not excluded governments from direct involvement. Conceivably, the United States should have met the need for deficit financing at the official level; such a role was implicit in the Kissinger safety-net proposal. Other, more recent proposals for IMF borrowing in capital markets suggest an alternative. The U.S. government could have supplied dollars to the Fund for relending to deficit countries. Had the dollars been exchanged for special drawing rights (SDRs), the United States would by now have built up an impressive level of reserves. Since reserve levels are viewed by speculators as an important measure of a currency's strength, the exchange of dollars for SDRs might have supported the dollar more effectively than intervention on the massive scale that has occurred.

Moreover, the United States could have used its reserves to finance its own current account deficit, exchanging SDRs for dollars accumulated by foreign central banks as a result of imbalances in trade or private capital investment. Instead, U.S. reserves are valued at less than 20 percent of its liabilities to foreign official institutions, and its best policy prescription appears to be the hope, contingent on substantial policy shifts by other governments, of reversing its trade deficit.

The Federal Reserve Board has recognized the need for

monetary action other than interest rate increases to modify the net capital outflow. It is attempting to induce a return flow by removing reserve requirements on loans made by the branches to their U.S. parents and other U.S. borrowers. The reserve requirements were placed on Eurodollar inflows as a result of the $14 billion lent by the branches to U.S. residents during the 1969 credit crunch. In 1975, the Federal Reserve Board lowered the reserve requirement from 8 percent to 4 percent—to the level of domestic CDs—to encourage a reflow of funds, and lowered them further (to 1 percent) in December 1977. As the tables indicate, this strategy has had no significant effect in reducing net bank-related capital outflows. Nevertheless, in August 1978, the Federal Reserve Board decided to try again and struck the reserve requirements on Eurodollar inflows altogether.[100] Whether or not this latest action will attract an inflow of dollars remains to be seen. The increase in the federal funds rate in August 1978 may prove more effective in curbing outflows than the effort to induce inflows. Because there is no reserve requirement on federal funds, the relatively low federal fund rate over the previous winter, and again in the summer of 1978, encouraged borrowing by money center banks for relending abroad. The higher cost of funds in the United States and the shrinking margins on Eurocurrency loans could encourage banks to keep funds at home if the domestic demand for credit remains strong.

Alternatively, the Federal Reserve might impose reserve requirements on U.S. banks' foreign branch liabilities.[101] If the cost of funds is a significant factor in bank-related capital flows—and the Federal Reserve's actions indicate that it thinks so—it would seem more useful to tax dollar outflows through reserve requirements rather than attempt to reduce net outflows through interest rate increases. Higher U.S. interest rates will not necessarily attract foreign investors. They will continue to prefer assets denominated in other currencies at less than 3 percent rates of interest if the cost of forward cover remains at present levels. But higher interest rates will, in time, have important effects on the U.S. economy. Some of those effects, such as lowering the rate of inflation, may be desirable. But the trade-offs in terms of positive and negative effects should continue to be weighed in relation to their impact on the domestic economy rather than on capital flows.

Opting for policies aimed at maintaining the strength of the U.S. economy in no way diminishes the importance of strengthening the international monetary system, since the two are very much interrelated. But policies that attempt to strengthen one at the expense of the other are likely to fail. Making it attractive for foreigners to hold excess dollars issued both by the U.S. banking system and through trade deficits seems somewhat expensive in terms of domestic economic growth. Curbing bank-related capital outflows would help restore the balance between the supply and demand for funds in Eurocurrency markets. If the flow of excess dollars from this source were reduced, the international monetary system could more readily support the U.S. trade deficit.

Notes

1. Nicholas Sargen, "Commercial Bank Lending to Developing Countries," *Federal Reserve Bank of San Francisco Economic Review*, Spring 1976, p. 25.

2. Ibid., p. 20.

3. David C. Beek, "Commercial Bank Lending to Developing Countries," *Federal Reserve Bank of New York Quarterly Review*, Summer 1977, p. 1.

4. Pierre Latour, "Euromarkets Wait for LDCs' Credits to be Repaid," *Euromoney*, October 1975, p. 33. The OECD's Development Assistance Committee (DAC) estimates that official assistance as a percentage of the donor countries' GNP was 0.35 in 1975, 0.33 in 1976, and 0.31 in 1977 (*IMF Survey*, July 3, 1978, p. 200).

5. Beek, "Commercial Bank Lending," p. 3.

6. Morgan Guaranty Trust Company, *World Financial Markets*, March 1978, p. 4. Note, *WFM* estimates tend to be understated. Nevertheless, the data accurately reflect the rapid rise in Eurocurrency lending in this period. Total Eurocurrency credits for all countries in 1970 were $4,730 million, roughly the amount loaned to the LDCs in 1973. There was an almost fivefold increase—to $21,851—between 1970 and 1973.

7. Sargen, "Commercial Bank Lending," p. 24.

8. Robert Solomon, "A Perspective on the Debt of Developing Countries," *Brookings Papers on Economic Activity*, 2 (Washington, D.C.:

Brookings Institution, 1977), p. 489.

9. The OPEC nations, West Germany, Japan, the Benelux countries, Switzerland, and, in 1975, the United States experienced most of the matching $180 billion surplus.

10. Solomon, "A Perspective on the Debt," p. 481. The U.S. Treasury estimates that 75 percent of all payments deficits were financed by private international loans (Eurocurrency credits and Eurobond issues), 7 percent were financed by the IMF, and 18 percent by other sources.

11. Morgan Guaranty Trust Company, *World Financial Markets*, June 1977, p. 7; Bank for International Settlements, *Forty-Seventh Annual Report*, Basle, June 1977; *IMF Survey, Supplement in International Lending*, June 1977. The *WFM* data cover all banks in the United States, including U.S. agencies, branches, and subsidiaries of foreign banks, and foreign branches of U.S. banks. The Country Exposure Lending Survey published by U.S. bank regulatory authorities in January 1978 states that as of June 30, 1977, U.S. banks and their foreign branches had loaned $40.1 billion of external credits to non-oil-exporting developing countries. The survey excludes U.S. offices of foreign banks. The World Bank Debt Tables list LDC external debt to private creditors for 1976 at $71.9 billion; this includes creditors other than banks but excludes debt with a maturity of less than one year. Debts with shorter maturities are included in the Morgan estimates and the Country Exposure Lending Survey.

12. *IMF Survey*, June 1977, p. 182.

13. Solomon, "A Perspective on the Debt," pp. 481, 483.

14. Paul M. Watson, *Debt and the Developing Countries: New Problems and New Actors*, Development Paper No. 26 (Washington, D.C.: Overseas Development Council, April 1978), pp. 17-20.

15. Morgan Guaranty Trust Company, *World Financial Markets*, March 1978, p. 4.

16. Ibid., p. 3.

17. Irving S. Friedman, *The Emerging Role of Private Banks in the Developing World* (New York: Citibank, 1977), subscribes to this view.

18. Solomon, "A Perspective on the Debt," p. 481.

19. Robert S. Weinert, "Why the Banks Did It," *Foreign Policy* No. 30, Spring 1978, p. 143.

20. Ibid., p. 144.

21. Ibid., pp. 143, 146.

22. Henry C. Wallich, "International Lending and the Euromarkets," remarks at the 1978 Euromarkets Conference sponsored by the *Financial Times*, May 9, 1978, p. 2.

23. Ibid., p. 7.

24. Ibid., p. 8.

25. Ibid., p. 10.

26. The 1975 New York crisis demonstrated that domestic money markets also can be unreliable. New York banks were forced to pay higher rates for CDs than banks in other regions. Whether or not they paid higher rates for deposits overseas during this period is unknown, but there is some surmise that California banks were getting better rates in London at that time.

27. Andrew F. Brimmer and Frederick R. Dahl, "Growth of International Banking: Implications for Public Policy," Address before the Joint Session of the American Economic Association and the American Finance Association, December 28, 1974.

28. Jane D'Arista, "U.S. Banks Abroad," *Financial Institutions and the Nation's Economy*, Compendium of Papers Prepared for the FINE Study, Book II, Committee on Banking, Finance, and Urban Affairs, U.S. House of Representatives, June 1976, pp. 821-23; Federal Reserve Bank of Chicago, *International Letter* No. 367, April 14, 1978, p. 1.

29. Wallich, "International Lending," p. 90.

30. Thomas H. Hanley, *United States Multinational Banking: Current and Prospective Strategies* (New York: Salomon Brothers, June 1976); Karin Lissakers, *International Debt, the Banks, and U.S. Foreign Policy*, Staff report prepared for U.S. Congress, Senate, Committee on Foreign Relations, Subcommittee on Foreign Economic Policy, August 1977 (Washington, D.C.: U.S. Government Printing Office, 1977), pp. 10-11; *IMF Survey*, June 1977, p. 180.

31. U.S., Congress, House, Committee on Banking, Finance, and Urban Affairs, Subcommittee on Financial Institutions Supervision, Regulation, and Insurance, *Hearings on International Banking Operations*, April 5, 1977 (Washington, D.C.: U.S. Government Printing Office, 1977), pp. 545-669.

32. U.S., Congress, Senate, Committee on Banking, Housing, and Urban Affairs, Subcommittee on International Finance, *International Debt*, Hearings, August 29, 1977 (Washington, D.C.: U.S. Government Printing Office, 1977), p. 44.

33. Lissakers, *International Debt, the Banks, and U.S. Foreign Policy*, pp. 5-8. See testimony of Senator Jacob Javits, U.S., Congress, Senate, *International Debt*, pp. 3-26.

34. See remarks of Representative Parren J. Mitchell and Representative John J. Cavanaugh, Transcript, Markup of H.R. 9214, "IMF Special Lending Facility, U.S. Congress, House, Committee on Banking, Finance, and Urban Affairs, February 23, 1978, pp. 14-17, 26-29, 31, 34, 42-45, 82, 83.

35. Arthur F. Burns, Chairman, Board of Governors of the Federal

Reserve System, Testimony before the Committee on Banking, Housing, and Urban Affairs, U.S. Senate, March 10, 1977; and Burns, "The Need for Order in International Finance," Address, Columbia University Graduate School of Business, April 12, 1977.

36. U.S. Congress, House, *Hearings on International Banking Operations*, p. 5.

37. Robert A. Bennett, ed., *Econocast World Banker*, May 3, 1978.

38. Marina v. N. Whitman, "Bridging the Gap," *Foreign Policy* No. 30, Spring 1978, p. 151; *IMF Survey*, June 1977, p. 180; Bank for International Settlements, *Forty-Seventh Annual Report*, p. 102.

39. See John H. Karaken's discussion of Robert Solomon's paper (Solomon, "A Perspective on the Debt," p. 505).

40. Albert Fishlow, "Debt Remains a Problem," *Foreign Policy* No. 30, Spring 1978, p. 142.

41. El Colegio de México, *Interim Report of the Meeting on Alternative Solutions of the External Public Debt Problem of the Developing Countries*, October 27-30 (Mexico City, 1977), p. 11.

42. Fishlow, "Debt Remains a Problem," p. 134.

43. El Colegio de México, *Interim Report*, p. 13; Kenneth Lipper, "Cartels Are No Solution," *Foreign Policy* No. 30, Spring 1978, p. 157. Robert Z. Aliber presents an alternative view with respect to LDCs' role in maintaining economic recovery by borrowing to sustain imports. He argues that adjustments to higher oil prices by industrial countries have been delayed by the process of debt creation. LDCs have borne the brunt of the deficits which are the counterpart of OPEC surpluses even though they consume only one-tenth of the amount of oil consumed in developing countries. He argues that it is "cynical" to rely on the developing countries to incur the deficits as a way to avoid pressures on the industrial countries to curtail oil consumption and increase production; testimony, "U.S. Participation in the Supplementary Financing Facility of the International Monetary Fund," U.S. Congress, House, Committee on Banking, Finance, and Urban Affairs, Subcommittee on International Trade, Hearings on H.R. 9214, September 29 (Washington, D.C.: U.S. Government Printing Office, 1977), pp. 172, 174-84.

44. Solomon, "A Perspective on the Debt," p. 490.

45. Beek, "Commercial Bank Lending," p. 5; El Colegio de México, *Interim Report*, pp. 8, 26; Solomon, "A Perspective on the Debt," p. 499.

46. Beek, "Commercial Bank Lending," p. 5; El Colegio de México, *Interim Report*, pp. 8, 26; Solomon, "A Perspective on the Debt," p. 499.

47. Beek, "Commercial Bank Lending," p. 3.

48. The June 1977 Country Exposure Lending Survey reveals that only 6 percent of U.S.-bank external currency claims on all LDCs were guaran-

teed by residents of other countries. For all countries, guarantees were 20 percent, but only 8 percent if bank placements were excluded from both total loans and guaranteed loans.

49. Bank for International Settlements, *Report*, November 1977.

50. Country Exposure Lending Survey.

51. Pakistan has received substantial amounts of assistance from the United States and other Development Assistance Committee countries, the international financial institutions, and from both the USSR and the People's Republic of China.

52. U.S., Congress, Senate, Committee on Foreign Relations, Subcommittee on Multinational Corporations, *Multinational Corporations and United States Foreign Policy*, Part 15, Hearings, 94th Cong., 1st sess. (Washington, D.C.: U.S. Government Printing Office, 1975), pp. 128-33; material supplied by the Federal Reserve Board to the House Committee on Banking, Finance, and Urban Affairs, February 1977.

53. These six banks are: Bank of America, Citibank, Chase Manhattan, Manufacturers Hanover Trust, Morgan Guaranty, and Chemical Bank.

54. Some of the fifteen money center banks outside the largest groups lent the government of Pakistan $5 million in 1977.

55. U.S., Congress, Senate, *Multinational Corporations and United States Foreign Policy*, pp. 128-33.

56. The aggregation of the data for these banks masks the fact that there are probably significant disparities in the proportionate levels of LDC loans and OPEC deposits between them.

57. Call report data, 1975.

58. Most of the $44 billion of local currency loans are claims on the G-10 countries and Switzerland and are partially offset by $37 billion of local currency liabilities.

59. It is probable that a substantial portion of LDC private nonbank borrowing is guaranteed by the public sector (Philip A. Wellons, *Borrowing by Developing Countries on the Eurocurrency Market*, The Development Center [Paris: OECD, 1977], p. 85).

60. As footnote 11 indicates, a substantial amount in loans to LDCs is also made by U.S. offices of foreign banks.

61. The June 1977 data reveal that the amount in bank placements in LDCs is usually less than for any other group of countries. Some interbank placements are used to finance public and private nonbank borrowers in the home country of the borrowing bank. Some reflect the use of U.S. bank funds by non-U.S. Eurocurrency banks to finance loans to nonbank borrowers in other countries. Nevertheless, a substantial portion reflects interbank redepositing. Thus, measuring LDC borrowing on the basis of known public and private nonbank borrowing is not unreasonable. On that

basis, this group of countries emerges as the primary borrowers of U.S. bank Eurocurrency resources.

62. Whitman, "Bridging the Gap," pp. 149-50.

63. Fishlow, "Debt Remains a Problem," p. 139.

64. Whitman, "Bridging the Gap," p. 152.

65. Beek, "Commercial Bank Lending," pp. 5-6.

66. Solomon notes that, between 1973 and 1976, the five LDCs for which data are available—Brazil, the Philippines, South Korea, Thailand, and Taiwan—outperformed industrial countries in terms of the rise in export volume (Solomon, "A Perspective on the Debt," p. 493).

67. Fishlow, "Debt Remains a Problem," p. 139.

68. Morgan Guaranty Trust Company, *World Financial Markets*, February 1978, p. 6; *Federal Reserve Bulletin*, April 1978, pp. 259-60.

69. Fishlow, "Debt Remains a Problem," p. 140.

70. *IMF Survey, Supplement on International Lending,* June 6, 1977, p. 179.

71. Wellons, *Borrowing by Developing Countries*, pp. 24, 65. Wellons also notes that the entry of Japanese banks into the Eurocurrency markets with some of the foreign exchange reserves of the Japanese government for use in lending had considerable effect in lowering interest rates. The price of stability may be oligopolistic pricing practices (p. 61).

72. El Colegio de México, *Interim Report*, p. 18.

73. "The Sick Men of the Euromarkets," *Euromoney*, March 1978, pp. 10-41.

74. While the bulk of loans to OPEC borrowers go to only five countries—Venezuela, Indonesia, Iran, Algeria, and Ecuador—and they do not account for the bulk of OPEC deposits, these countries nevertheless have a significant role in decisions affecting the investment and pricing policies of the group as a whole.

75. Lipper, "Cartels Are No Solution," p. 158.

76. Sir Arthur Lewis, "The Less Developed Countries and Stable Exchange Rates," 1977 Per Jacobsson Lecture, in International Monetary Fund, *The International Monetary System in Operation* (Washington, D.C., September 25, 1977), pp. 42-43.

77. A Congressional Budget Office report points out that this is not true for Korea and Taiwan, where the emphasis has been on employment creation, involving policies to promote labor-intensive manufactured exports (U.S., Congress, Congressional Budget Office, *Bilateral Development Assistance: Background and Options*, [Washington, D.C., February 1977], p. 27).

78. The following have testified in favor of IMF borrowing in the market before congressional committees: Peter B. Kenen, Princeton (Joint

Economic Committee, Subcommittee on International Economic Policy,
April 21, 1977); Irving S. Friedman, Citibank (Senate Banking Committee,
Subcommittee on International Finance, August 30, 1977); Frederick
Heldring, Philadelphia National Bank (Senate Banking Committee, Sub-
committee on International Finance, August 30, 1977; and House Banking
Committee, Subcommittee on International Trade, September 29, 1977);
Marina v. N. Whitman, University of Pittsburgh (House Banking Commit-
tee, Subcommittee on International Trade, September 30, 1977); Robert
Solomon, the Brookings Institution (Senate Banking Committee, October
13, 1977).

79. The liquidity issue is of considerable importance. Currently so-
called country loans are not disposable. A bank in need of liquidity has no
assets to sell; its only recourse is to permit maturing interbank placements
to run off. But this affects other banks' liquidity and may set off a domino
reaction such as occurred in 1974. In 1974, however, the smaller and
regional U.S. banks were more liquid than they are today and were all too
eager to upstream funds (at a federal funds rate of 13 percent) to the
money center banks for use in bailing out foreign branches. Now, the
smaller banks in agricultural areas have high loan-to-deposit ratios and
regional banks made the bulk of the domestic loans during the 1977 credit
expansion. Thus international markets are more vulnerable to a credit
crunch now than in 1974.

The substitution of IMF securities for country loans would better protect the system from such a crisis. An individual bank needing liquidity
could sell its securities in the Eurobond or national bond markets that
have developed secondary markets; this would lessen the possibility of a
chain reaction.

80. W. Michael Blumenthal, "Steering in Crowded Waters," *Foreign
Affairs*, July 1978, pp. 734-36, 738, 739.

81. U.S., Congress, House, Committee on Appropriations, *Foreign Assis-
tance and Related Programs Appropriation Bill*, H.R. No. 95-1250, 95th
Cong., 2nd sess., June 1, 1978 (Washington, D.C.: U.S. Government
Printing Office, 1978), pp. 56-57.

82. Ibid., p. 8.

83. Fishlow, "Debt Remains a Problem," p. 141.

84. Ronald E. Müller, "LDC Debt and U.S. and World Economic
Stagnation: Overcoming Contradictions in Global Interdependence," pre-
sented to the Experts Meeting on Alternative Solutions to the External
Public Debt Problems of the LDCs, El Colegio de México, Mexico City,
October 27-29, 1977; see also Dr. Müller's testimony, U.S. Congress,
House, *International Banking Operations*, pp. 833-35.

85. U.S., Congress, Senate, *Multinational Corporations and United*

States Foreign Policy, p. 128.

86. "Who's to Blame for the Dollar?" *The Economist*, August 19, 1978, pp. 53-54.

87. "Report on International Lending," *IMF Survey*, July 31, 1978, p. 230.

88. Henry S. Reuss, press release, March 18, 1977.

89. The largest offsetting increase was a $3.2 billion rise in net investment income (Bureau of Economic Analysis, U.S. Department of Commerce, as reprinted in *Federal Reserve Bulletin*, July 1978, A54).

90. Federal Reserve Board, Division of International Finance, Financial Markets Section, *Selected Interest and Exchange Rates*, (Washington, D.C., August 28, 1978); "Calm Before What?" *The Economist*, August 26, 1978, p. 73.

91. *Far Eastern Economic Review*, July 28, 1978, p. 90.

92. *Wall Street Journal*, November 2, 1978, p. 1.

93. *The Economist*, August 26, 1978, p. 70; Federal Reserve Board, *Selected Interest and Exchange Rates*, various issues.

94. Federal Reserve Bank of Chicago, *International Letter* No. 363, February 17, 1978, p. 1.

95. *Federal Reserve Bulletin*, June 1978, A62.

96. Federal Reserve Bank of Chicago, *International Letter* No. 363, February 17, 1978, p. 1.

97. *Federal Reserve Bulletin*, June 1978, A62.

98. *IMF Survey*, July 31, 1978, p. 230.

99. This can be explained in part by the fact that the dollar is the world's principal transactions currency. Some 80 percent of Eurocurrency lending is in dollars; dollars are used to pay for oil and to finance trade between countries whose currencies are not traded in major financial markets. Thus, even surplus countries need to borrow dollars to engage in international transactions. The issue here relates to the fact that some surplus countries do not return more funds to the Eurocurrency market than they borrow, while some deficit countries deposit more funds than they borrow.

100. Federal Reserve Board, press release, August 28, 1978.

101. Letter from Henry S. Reuss to Federal Reserve Board Chairman Arthur F. Burns, December 9, 1977; Robert Z. Aliber, *The Stability of the International Banking System*, Contract No. 1722-520100 (Washington, D.C.: U.S. Department of State, June 1977), pp. 18-34; "International Banking," *FINE Study* Compendium, Part 4, pp. 768-70, 816.

4
Financial Interrelations, the Balance of Payments, and the Dollar Crisis

Hyman P. Minsky

It is the duty of every bank and most of all of a central bank to be rich.

—R. S. Sayers[1]

Professor Sayers's proposition that it is the duty of a bank and especially a central bank to be rich helps us understand the disarray of the world monetary system since, first, the demonitization of gold in 1968 and, then, the final abandonment of the Bretton Woods system of fixed exchange rates in 1973. What does it mean for a bank, a central bank, or a country whose money serves as the international currency "to be rich"? What happens when a bank, a central bank, or a key-currency country is no longer rich? These are the questions that need to be addressed in the light of the insight by Sayers. We want to look beyond the obvious implication of being rich, which is having power, and examine the mechanisms by which the richness and, therefore, power of a bank are exercised. To do this, we will look at the financial relations that make banks powerful and then extend the argument to cover the effect of the balance-of-payments structure upon the richness or power of a country whose currency serves as an international money.

In essence, the current crisis exists because the structure of the balance of payments of the banking center of the Bretton Woods system, the United States, became that of an impoverished economy in the late 1960s; with this impoverishment, demand liabilities denominated in dollars lost some of their attractiveness. The impoverishment is not due to any fundamental decline of the United States as a producing entity. It is largely due to inept policies that reflect the dominant economic theory, which misspecifies the nature of the economy. The United States and other capitalist economies are now intensely financial, and standard economic theory (which is used by the advisers to U.S. policymakers) ignores the financial aspects of their economies. Only after we fully integrate financial inter-relations into our analysis of the international economy will we have the understanding that will enable us to develop policies that can reverse the impoverization of the United States and establish an international monetary system conducive to sus-tained economic progress. The United States in the late 1970s must be seen as an "ailing bank" whose management either does not understand its problems or is not able to take the steps necessary to resolve the difficulties. The U.S. policy establish-ment and political leadership dither, while, like Macawber, they hope "something will turn up."[2]

In the autumn and winter of 1977-1978, the world witnessed the queer spectacle of the chief U.S. financial officer, Secretary of the Treasury Blumenthal, cheering on the decline of the dol-lar on the international exchanges. Aside from welcoming developments that were planting the seeds for a subsequent accelerating inflation—which duly occurred in the spring and summer of 1978—it is evident that Secretary Blumenthal and his house economists deemed the existence of a vast number of dollar-denominated, offshore financial instruments unimpor-tant. Official reasoning seemed to disregard the need to keep the owners of offshore and domestic dollars happy with holding dollar assets; they seemingly did not understand that if dissatis-faction with holding dollars became widespread, the terms of trade would so turn against the dollar that rapid impoverish-ment and "banana republic" rates of inflation would surely occur. Secretary Blumenthal and his advisers were applying the price-specie-flow analysis, which sees no flaws in currency devaluation. This theory is fully relevant only for economies without financial interrelations; it is of limited relevance for economies in which debts denominated in dollars are abun-dant.[3] The normal functioning of a world economy character-ized by a maze of financial instruments denominated in dollars depends upon the willingness of governments, businesses, banks, and individuals to hold monetary instruments denominated in dollars. This is so because such dollars largely arise in the process of financing activity and any attempt to change the currency of denomination will reduce the amount of activity that can be financed.

A fundamental proposition of the following argument is that, although currencies that are not used to denominate transactions and debts may depreciate without destabilizing the world economy, when the key world money depreciates, a "flight" of liabilities from the banks and money markets that denominate in that currency is likely to occur. At worst, this leads to financial crisis and crash, as the flight makes the refinancing of positions by banks and other financial units impossible; at best, it leads to a world recession as the volume of financed economic activity contracts.[4]

1. Defining "Being Rich"

The liabilities of a rich person or institution are scarce and valuable, not because they are few in number but because the assets controlled generate a large cash flow to the rich. AT&T bonds are valuable because the U.S. telephone network generates a cash flow to the company that is much larger than the cash payments required for current telephone network operations. New York City bonds are not marketable now because the assets New York City controls, the New York tax base, do not set up reliable cash flows that exceed by a substantial margin the current operating costs of New York City. The key determinant of the value of liabilities of any organization is the cash flow its assets are expected to generate.

The world in which we live acts out its events and determines its asset values in calendar time. This means that there is an inherent uncertainty to events. The time dimension, and thus uncertainty, is an essential factor in the valuation of assets. This is especially true in international financial relations, where political uncertainty must be added to the uncertainty inherent in capitalist economies with capital assets that are technically and institutionally dynamic.[5] The time dimensions of an economy are of special significance for banks—be they commercial banks, central banks, or a country whose currency serves as the international money—for banks are organizations whose liabilities are of a shorter term to expected cash payments than their assets are to expected cash receipts. This means that banking institutions must always be refinancing their position; they must be issuing new liabilities in order to fulfill obligations as outstanding liabilities fall due.

Banks issue their liabilities in exchange for assets. The assets acquired may be gold, government debt, private debt, or liabilities of other banks. Gold and the liabilities of other banks are valuable because they enable the acquiring bank to fulfill financial obligations, and, if put at the service of bank customers, they enable customers to fulfill financial commitments and to acquire goods, services, or assets. A bank acquires government and private debt in the expectation that the borrowing unit will supply it with cash or with the bank's own liabilities on an agreed-upon schedule. These debtors to banks generate the basic demand for money—and, in particular, bank money—so as to be able to fulfill financial commitments. This demand for bank deposits due to the existence of debts payable in bank deposits makes bank deposits valuable.

In any money-using economy, every unit can be characterized by its cash receipts and cash payments. In a capitalist economy, debts are used to finance control over capital-assets as well as to finance the production of investment output. Part of the debt used by business to finance investment and control over capital-assets is owed to banks and other financial institutions. Banks and other financial institutions use their own debt to finance their financing of business. In our type of economy, demand deposits, which are part of the money supply, emerge from the financing process at commercial banks. Financing activity also leads to the central bank acquiring assets and issuing liabilities. In the same way, bank debts denominated in the key international currency emerge as international trade and investment are financed. A special characteristic of an organization that acquires debts to finance its activities by issuing its own debts that others use as money, or as near-money, is that the amount of activity it can finance and the amount of its own debts that can be outstanding are flexible. The amount of financing a bank can engage in is limited only by the amount of its own liabilities it is willing and able to sell or emit.

When banking and the process by which money is created are

analyzed, it is usually assumed that the amount of their own liabilities banking institutions sell or emit is determined by the value of high-powered (or reserve) money outstanding and by the legal reserve requirements against these liabilities. Given the complex and convoluted banking system of today, this view is patently false. In today's world banking system, dollar-denominated demand deposits and certificates of deposit are created and exist as debts of institutions that are not chartered by U.S. authorities. Furthermore, demand and passbook savings deposits are of decreasing importance in the liability structure of all banks, both in the United States and in other countries. As a result, Federal Reserve control of bank reserves does not, except under very short-run and exceptional conditions, determine the acquisition of assets by banks and the volume of bank liabilities outstanding.

2. Financing Relations and Central Bank Power

The liabilities that banks are willing and able to emit and the assets they acquire are determined by market usages and prevailing views as to admissable financing relations rather than by any mechanical linkages between reserves and deposits.[6] Among the determinants of admissable financing relations are the conditions under which maturing debt structures can be refinanced. In particular, commercial banks depend upon the refinancing available through direct borrowing from the facilities of their national central bank. This refinancing takes the form of direct borrowing from their national bank or borrowing from or selling to a market that is rigged by the central bank. The power that a central bank has over commercial banks largely stems from this dependency. In a smoothly functioning banking system, assets owned by the central bank yield a cash flow to the central bank from the economy. The cash flow reduces the commercial banks' cash or reserve position and their direct or indirect debt to the central bank.

Either directly or indirectly, commercial banks finance part of their asset holdings by debts owned by the central bank. By acquiring new assets even as its other assets are maturing, the central bank makes it possible for commercial banks to sustain their total asset holdings. Whereas payments to the central bank being considered here are due to terms on contracts owned by the central bank, asset acquisition by the commercial bank is at the initiative of the central bank or at terms set by the central bank.

The normal functioning of our economy depends upon the continued viability of the banking system, which, in turn, depends upon the central bank's discounting and open-market operations. However, the dependency we have described is not that which is emphasized in the standard reserves and reserve requirement analysis of the money-creating process. The serious dependency, which makes central banks potent, is that central banks finance a significant portion of the positions of commercial banks.

This relationship between the central bank and commercial banks is very clear when the central bank acquires assets by a discounting process. Discounting is equivalent to a collateralized loan to the "borrowing" bank. Some of the activity financed by commercial banks and a part of the position of commercial banks are financed by "loans" from the central bank. When the central bank acquires assets by open-market operations in government debt, the ability of commercial banks to acquire private debt depends upon their being able to sell some of their government paper. The ability to acquire cash by selling assets is a vital influence upon commercial bank behavior, and is equivalent to financing part of a total position by selling participations to the central bank.

Commercial banks can finance activity by acquiring debts in exchange for demand deposits if a demand for commercial bank liabilities exists. This demand exists when there is a wide array of liabilities that can be satisfied by the payment of demand deposits. specifically, this demand depends upon the existence of numerous debtors to banks who have to pay sizable sums to banks over a relatively short period. If the business of banking is visualized as a two-phase process, in which banks first acquire debts (contracts) in exchange for their own liabilities and then collect a "premium" on their own liabilities as the debts (contracts) become due, it becomes clear that the assets of banks determine the value of bank money. It is the cash flow to banks from the rest of the world—because of the contracts owned by banks—that makes bankers rich and powerful. If the assets of banks are well structured, which means that banks, if they need to, can force a cash flow in their favor, then bank money is valuable. The units with debts due to banks exchange their labor and their produce for bank deposits so they can meet their commitments. It is this offer of goods and services in exchange for bank money by debtors to banks that makes bank money valuable.

In his great rebuttal to Jacob Viner's review of the *General Theory*, John Maynard Keynes asked, "Why should anyone outside a lunatic asylum wish to use money as a store of wealth?"[7] Keynes's answer to his own question was that "the possession of actual money dulls our disquietude."[8] We can ask a second question: Why should anyone outside a lunatic asylum accept demand deposits in exchange for useful goods and services? Our answer is that there are debts that can be satisfied by the payment of demand deposits to banks and the debtors are willing—nay, eager—to exchange goods and services for bank money.

3. Exchange Rates

Foreign currencies are valuable to economic units in various countries because the units have financial obligations denominated in the foreign currency, the foreign currency yields command over desired goods and services, or the foreign currency dulls the disquietude of which Keynes wrote. A distinction has to be made among financial, production and trade, and precautionary or speculative demands for money. Whereas the demand for a noncentral currency in the international monetary system is determined almost entirely by the place of the country's output in international markets, a large portion of the demand for the international monetary system's key currency is determined by financial flows due to outstanding financial instruments, the buying and selling of financial instruments, and precautionary and speculative considerations.

If a bank's or a central bank's liabilities are to be valuable, then its assets must generate a large, favorable cash flow. Such cash flows can result from contractual commitments to pay principal and interest (as stated in debts), from the sale of assets, or from issuing debts that do not function as money. Note that if a liability is used as money, then selling assets or issuing nonmonetary debts decreases the amount of "money" liability outstanding. If this occurs without a concomitant decrease in the incoming cash flow because of the "bank" assets, the money liabilities will become scarcer and, therefore, more valuable. This explains why, when the Bank of England was the linchpin of the successful international monetary system based upon the relatively fixed exchange rates of a gold standard, a loss of gold by the Bank of England had a powerful effect upon the course of exchange rates. By decreasing the liabilities of the Bank of England without changing the sterling-denominated cash payments commitments or the values of transactions denominated in sterling, an outflow of gold made the pound more valuable. The increasing value of the pound made holders of financial assets eager to hold assets denominated in pounds. Pounds, also, were valuable as precautionary and speculative balances because any turn against sterling was sure to be transitory.

In April 1978, Henry Kaufman remarked that "in order [for the dollar] to be a valid international currency, there must be a strategy which resists efforts of others to switch from dollar to other currency-denominated obligations if we are to prevent a depreciation in value of the massive assets denominated in dollars. This obviously would create a serious financial danger."[9] Before there can be a strategy which resists switching from the dollar to other currencies, there has to be a structure of financial relations or a financial environment in which the strategic operations can be effective. The financial environment hospitable to operations designed to resist efforts to switch is one that makes the reserve currency scarcer, and thus more valuable, whenever switches are attempted. The "rules" of the sensitive international gold standard when Britain "ruled the roost" were well designed to make pounds more valuable whenever substantial switches out of pounds were attempted. Any fall in Bank of England holdings of gold led to a rise in British interest rates and, thus, to a decline in the pace of foreign borrowing in London in the form of long-term loans to developing nations. This London lending was critical in supplying the funds needed to fulfill debt commitments denominated in sterling and for precautionary and speculative sterling balances: the Bank of England could make the rest of the world scamper for pounds by turning off the international lending spigot that supplied pounds.

4. Balance of Payments

Inasmuch as dollars are made available to the rest of the world by a variety of means and are used by the rest of the world for a variety of purposes, a way of looking at the balance of payments that focuses on those means and purposes needs to be developed. A country's balance of payments can be broken down into four tiers: (1) current imports and exports of goods and services, including remittances and other invisibles; (2) receipts and expenditures due to income from capital assets owned abroad; (3) long-term private investments; and (4) short-term debts or the movements of international reserves (gold) among countries. The last item is strictly a balancing item. In addition to the four tiers, in the contemporary balance of payments there is a "policy intrusion" in the form of military expenditures and government investment abroad. This policy intrusion is now of rather minor importance. In Table 1, the U.S. balance of payments in 1960, 1964, 1971, and 1977 are shown in this four-tier plus policy-intrusion format. Results for 1960 and 1964 are consistent with the dollar serving as an international currency. Those for 1971 and, more dramatically, 1977 are inconsistent with the survival of the dollar as an international currency.

In each of the four years the United States had a balance-of-payments deficit as measured by the net acquisition of U.S. short-term balances and gold by the rest of the world. However, in 1960 the foreigners' acquisition, net of banking relations, of $3.3 billion of dollar assets was offset by a $3.9 billion private investment abroad; in 1964 the foreign acquisition of dollars was $2.6 billion and U.S. private investment abroad was $6.6 billion. In the absence of the private long-term investment

Table 1
United States Balance of Payments

	1960	1964	1971	1977
TIER I				
Merchandise				
Receipts	19.7	25.5	43.3	120.5
Expenditures	14.8	18.7	45.6	151.7
Balance	+4.9	+6.8	-2.3	-31.2
Net Travel, Transportation, and Services	-0.4	-0.1	+0.2	+2.5
Remittance, Pension, and Other Unilateral Transactions	-2.3	-2.8	-3.7	-2.0
Current Balance	+2.2	+3.9	-5.8	-30.7
TIER II				
Investment Income				
Receipts	3.4	5.4	9.5	n.a.
Expenditure	-1.1	-1.5	4.9	n.a.
Balance	+2.3	+3.9	+4.6	+11.9
Basic Balance: Trade and Investment Income	+4.5	+7.8	-1.2	-18.8
Policy Intrusion				
U.S. Military Transactions	-2.8	-2.1	-2.9	+1.4
U.S. Government Investment	-1.1	-1.7	-1.9	-2.7
Basic Balance plus "Policy"	+0.6	+4.0	-6.0	-20.1
TIER III				
Private Investment Abroad Net	-3.9	-6.6	-9.8	-10.3
TIER IV				
Foreign Acquisition of Short-Term Dollar Balance and Gold from United States	+3.3	+2.6	+15.8	+30.4

Source: Economic Report of the President and Later Release

abroad, the U.S. basic balance of payments, even after allowing for policy intrusions, would have been in surplus: $0.6 billion in 1960 and $4.0 billion in 1964. Furthermore, if policy intrusions were excluded, the balance of payments due to the current transaction balance and investment income was a hefty (for those days) surplus of $4.5 billion and $7.8 billion; if the United States had not had military and civilian spending and gifts abroad, the net acquisition of dollars and gold from the United States would have been negative. In the 1960s, it was said that if the United States caught a cold, Europe caught pneumonia; the ability of the rest of the world to fulfill its commitments on outstanding financial instruments and to purchase inputs from abroad at the level it did depended upon the flow of dollars from U.S. investments abroad and U.S. foreign military and civilian aid.

The 1971 data reflect a transition year from a strong dollar position to the current weak position. The balance of trade was in deficit, as was the current trade balance, but the deficit in the current trade balance was almost offset by investment income: the Basic Balance was a mere $1.2 billion in deficit. However, a $4.8 billion policy intrusion item and a $9.8 billion private investment bill made the total foreign acquisition of short-term assets and gold $15.8 billion.

The 1977 balance of payments is strongly and fundamentally inconsistent with the U.S. dollar retaining its status as the international currency. The high, current account deficit shows that there is no way, except by measures that would seriously deflate the economy in order to reduce imports, the Federal Reserve can make dollars scarce. And, without the Federal Reserve being able to make dollars scarce relative to foreigners' payment commitments by "controlling" offshore investments, the continued use of the dollar as an international currency is in jeopardy.

The big difference in the U.S. balance of payments between 1977 and the earlier years is the size of the current deficit (Tier I) and, in particular, the merchandise deficit. The only balance-of-payments item that the Federal Reserve can affect is merchandise expenditures, and it can only affect this item by lowering U.S. domestic income (by inducing a recession/depression in the United States). Secretary Blumenthal's "cheering on" of the dollar's deterioration was grounded in the belief that by changing the exchange rate the balance on the merchandise account could be reversed. The evidence to date is that the relative price effect that Blumenthal and his colleagues rely upon is ineffective except when it is pushed so far that it also leads to financial market disruption. Blumenthal's strategy will work only as it leads to recession, if not deep depression.

Secretary Blumenthal's position rests upon the price-specie-flow theory of the balance of payments which assumes that merchandise transactions take place in markets and that, within quite narrow limits, buyers and sellers take prices as parameters. In truth, we live in a world of cartels, monopoly power, and transnational enterprises. Not only is the assumption that "prices are parameters" violated, but, as Victoria Chick has pointed out,[10] the very concept of price becomes amorphous when dealing with transnational transactions among units of transnational enterprises. For a transnational enterprise, price is a device for determining in which country it shows profit and in which currency it holds cash assets. A transnational enterprise's effect upon a country's balance of payments depends upon which currency it chooses to denominate debts and in which to hold financial assets.

Whereas the Federal Reserve cannot bring the merchandise balance into a posture that is consistent with the continued functioning of the dollar as an international currency without forcing a serious recession, the government could. The government may use tariffs, excise taxes, and direct controls to raise the price or restrict the availability of particular merchandise imports. In particular, the government could act to cut back the huge U.S. use of foreign oil and gas, although, in truth, the reduction of any dimension of the import bill of goods through taxes or controls would suffice. The only reasons for emphasizing the dependency on the foreign oil are the size of the bill for imported oil and gas, the recent explosive growth of this bill, and the fact that oil and gas prices are set by a cartel (i.e., are the result of an exercise of power).

In the world economy, international dollars are created by the banking process and by the U.S. balance-of-payments deficit. If dollars created in the banking process are the result of well-structured bank loans and investments, then a "reflux" of dollars from the markets of the world to the creating banks will occur. For example, if all international dollars are the result of 90-day discounts and if the annual interest rate is 8 percent, then over a 90-day period borrowers are committed to pay the banks 102 percent of the amount of dollars outstanding. If the supply of international dollars is depleted by banks, allowing their positions to decrease, then the amount of activity that is financed decreases and debtors will be hard pressed to meet their commitments. The result of banks not lending as much as they receive in repayment on outstanding loans is financial stringency followed by a decline in economic activity. Bank loans are well structured if they generate cash flows as stated in the loan agreement. This, in turn, means that there are economic transactions, financed by the loans, that will generate the needed funds. The "commercial loan doctrine" of banking is not so much a theory of the determination of the "apt" amount of money as it is a rule of prudent banking.

Whenever bankers deviate from the financing of well-structured business transactions, they must continue to focus on the capacity of borrowers to generate the cash to fulfill commitments. If they are financing government deficits, bankers need be concerned about the ability of the borrowing government to execute tax and spending policies. If bankers are financing balance-of-payments deficits, they must be concerned about the ability of the borrowing countries to generate a sufficiently favorable merchandise balance to at least service the outstanding debts. When bank money is created to finance a New York City or a Zaire, then the reflux to banks of funds, which originate in cash flows from operations earned by New York City through taxes or by Zaire through its trade balance, may not be forthcoming. If New York City or Zaire is engaged in "Ponzi" finance, borrowing in order to pay interest on debts, then the liabilities of the banks that are financing these operations will depreciate in value when the increase in bank liabilities without an offsetting increase in bank receipts is felt in commodity and financial markets. Until the comeuppance of a financial crisis, financing by bank loans that do not yield a reflux leads to inflation, if domestic money creation is involved, and to a depreciation on the exchanges, if international money is involved.

Restricting ourselves to current international monetary connections, any large excess creation of dollar liabilities by banks over the dollar reflux to banks to repay outstanding loans will lead to (1) a decline of the exchange value of the dollar under flexible exchange rates or (2) an outflow of gold from the United States under fixed exchange rates. Inasmuch as an extrapolation of a depreciation of the dollar would lead to a run on the dollar, the depreciation must set in motion processes

that lead to a quick appreciation in order for the dollar to continue as the international money. The reaction may be the
result of normal functioning market processes or central bank
(or government) actions to "correct" the depreciation or the
gold outflow under fixed exchange rates.

Assume that the balance of payments consists only of Tier I
items, or only of the items in the merchandise balance, and that
these items are normally close to being balanced. Then if a
country ran a deficit, the depreciation of its currency would
lead to a rise in the price of its imports and a fall in import prices in the surplus country. Assuming that demands
are sufficiently elastic, small exchange rate variations would
eliminate the imbalance. Under fixed exchange rates, the end
result is the same, except that the mechanism involves movements in the price levels of the trading partners. The addition of
investment income adds a fixed amount of payments in the
currency of denomination. Since World War II, the currency of
denomination usually has been dollars, and the "rest of the
world" has had a fixed "nut" of dollars that it has had to earn.
In this case, a depreciation of the debtor's currency increases
the domestic currency sales that must be made if the financial
commitments on debts are to be met.

However, currently—and in the classical nineteenth and early
twentieth centuries—there are a full four tiers to the balance of
payments. Furthermore, in both epochs the currency of denomination of both financial instruments and many international
transactions was and is a particular currency (pounds when the
Bank of England ran an international gold standard and dollars
since World War II). The story that Professor Sayers tells in
Bank of England Operations, 1890-1914 shows that the primary
equilibrating variable between the "center" and the rest of the
world in the years he studied was in the net private investment
abroad by the "center." Whenever the Bank of England felt it
was losing specie on the exchanges, it would raise the bank rate
—the discount it took in acquiring money market paper. Because the Bank of England had demonstrated that it was willing
and able to make the bank rate effective, the various bank
interest, money market, and capital market rates moved with
the bank rate. The higher, long-term (capital market) rates sig-

nalled a transitory, unfavorable time for London capital market placements. Potential borrowers in the London capital market cut down on their borrowings. That was sufficient to turn the exchanges around.

For this technique to work, the sum of Tier I and Tier II had to be positive—as it was for the United States in 1960 and 1964 and as it almost was in 1971. The technique of managing the net foreign acquisition of international money by influencing private investment abroad requires that the basic balance—the sum of Tier I and Tier II—be in surplus. Note that managing the exchanges is feasible even if the trade balance is in deficit: the effective constraint is that the current trade deficit must be substantially smaller than net investment income. In 1977, a foreign trade deficit of some $5 billion to $8 billion would have been compatible with the maintenamce of a strong international posture by the United States.

5. A "Run" in International Banking

A basic concern of any bank is that a run can occur if one of its basic liabilities becomes unacceptable. Historically, a run meant that customers tried to exchange bank deposits for specie or notes of the central bank. In the 1974 Franklin National Bank failure, the run took the form of an inability of Franklin National to purchase Eurodollar "deposits" by selling its dollar-denominated certificates of deposit. For the central bank of a country that supplies the key currency for the world's monetary system, a run occurs when holders of monetary assets denominated in the key currency try to decrease their holdings of this asset. Within a country, a flight from money leads to a sharp rise in the price of other assets and in the nominal demand for output. One aspect of the inflationary process is a rise in velocity as units decrease their holdings of cash relative to transactions. Between countries, an attempt to decrease holding of the key currency leads either to a drain of gold from the key central bank, under a regime of fixed exchange rates, or to a sharp drop in the exchange rate of the key currency in a world of flexible exchange rates.

For the international banks that acquired dollar-denominated assets as they emitted dollar-denominated liabilities, a run on the dollar means that they cannot sell new dollar liabilities as such liabilities mature. Thus, they have to cut their asset acquisition. Even if their national central bank refinances their position, so that they fulfill their obligations to deliver dollars to depositors, the run will lead to pressure to cut commitments. Either a panic and a deep and long recession or financing constraints and a recession will take place. In either case, the exchange rate of the key currency that is being challenged will fall far below what any purchasing power parity or relative inflation rates indicate. As in Britain, the route from being a key currency to being just another national currency is by way of a rapid decline in the exchange rate and a burst of inflation.

6. Conclusion: Requisites of a Viable International System

The continued viability of any particular international monetary system and the longer-term prosperity of the various countries require that the key or international money not decline relative to the community of other currencies. A particularly strong currency can and should appreciate relative to the key currency, but, even as this happens, other currencies must depreciate. Furthermore, the expected trend of the intertemporal purchasing power of the key currency must be such that sizable groups will willingly hold the currency. A long-run trend of slightly falling prices in the key currency makes for financing terms that require only minimal cash flow commitments and a strong willingness to hold the currency. Thus one essential element of a successful key currency is a strong commitment to stable or slowly falling prices in the "home" country.

Another necessary element is a positive Basic Balance, so that the growth in offshore holdings of short-term debts in the key currency that are liabilities of the banks domiciled in the key-currency country is less than the key-currency country's investment abroad. The key-currency country, envisaged as a bank, must borrow short to finance the acquisition of long-term assets. The short borrowing by the banks of the country becomes the net increase in offshore monetary liabilities. This is analogous to the growth in commercial bank reserves through central bank open-market operations in the standard story of bank behavior.

It follows that the country whose currency is functioning as a key or reserve currency in international monetary relations, and therefore as the currency of denomination in international transactions, must act as if it is on a gold standard. However, in today's non–gold-standard world, there is no obvious substitute for a "protection-of-gold" policy for the central bank. There is an obvious trading position relation that must be maintained: the Basic Balance must be solidly positive. Thus, in today's world the central bank and the government of the key-currency country must work together.

The key element threatening the current international monetary structure is the huge current trade deficit of the United States. An improvement of at least $20 billion and perhaps $25 billion is necessary. This could be accomplished in a variety of ways: one way is to force the appreciation of the currency of the country with a huge non-oil, export-based surplus in current account. However, the Japanese economy is inherently fragile, so that this dimension cannot be squeezed too far; furthermore, every appreciation of the Japanese yen lowers the yen price of oil imports and debt servicing. The key item is, of course, oil imports. The basic change that is necessary if a dollar-based international system is to survive is to cut the U.S. oil-import bill by a major portion of the $30.7 billion current trade-balance deficit.

The dollar's decline in the international markets has been cushioned by the demand for dollar assets and assets in the territorial United States as protection against political instability. The "very rich," regardless of nationality, want to hold assets in the United States—be they real estate, agricultural land, companies, or common shares. The political situation in much of the world is a "prop" behind the dollar. Furthermore, a vast amount of politically insecure money that would seek, but is not now seeking, haven in the United States is being held back by the downward pressure on the dollar (not by the U.S. inflation rate). Once the conviction grows that the dollar has hit bottom, there will be a flood of funds to the United States.

Undoubtedly, a stabilized dollar would soon be transformed into an appreciating dollar; this would spark a stock-market boom.

There are two areas needing policy intervention. One is to reduce the balance-of-payments deficit in the United States so that the Basic Balance is positive, the other is to fund a major portion of the excess supply of short-term dollars. The details of getting the U.S. balance of payments into line is beyond the scope of this chapter. The problem of how to fund the excess supply of dollars is within its scope; funding short-term dollars into long-term foreign currency debt reduces the supply of, but not the demand for, short-term dollars.

As mentioned before, there is a strong demand by the world's rich for the political security and commitment to capitalism that characterize the United States, even as there is a reluctance to purchase dollar-denominated financial instruments. The U.S. government should offer to any and all holders long-term Treasury securities denominated in the principal foreign currencies. Simultaneously, the United States should make a commitment to the establishment of a dollar that either appreciates or does not depreciate relative to the currencies of trading partners.[11]

By transforming some of the short-run dollar holdings into long-run holdings of U.S. obligations denominated in other currencies, the funding operation decreases the threat of a run on the dollar. A desire to get out of those other-currency securities and into other assets would not lead to a decline in the exchange value of the dollar, but to a decline in the market price of those long assets relative to other assets denominated in the same currencies. Instead of a deficit pushing a dollar-denominated, short-term asset into the hands of reluctant holders, the substantial (but not overwhelming) volume of offshore-currency–denominated U.S. Treasury securities needed to fund a substantial portion of the current deficit would find eager buyers. In fact, such an instrument, issued in sufficient quantity to fund a major portion (but not necessarily all) of the trade deficit would become a superior object of portfolio diversification for the world's rich, for it would provide them with a substitute, in a currency whose short-run strength they trust, for holding physical assets in the United States.

Over the longer run, the U.S. Basic Balance must be in surplus if the dollar is to be the world's key currency. In the shorter run—as the dollar moves to a current account posture that makes dollar holdings if not scarce then verging on scarce—a major portion of the accruing short-term assets generated by the deficit need be funded into long-term debt denominated in currencies other than dollars. Such an offshore-currency debt would not only generate a U.S. national interest in an appreciating currency, but it would also create a financial instrument well suited to soothing the fears and apprehensions of many of the world's rich.

However, even funding the merchandise deficit in offshore currencies is but a transitory step unless the Basic Balance can be brought into surplus. The "center" must not only be a currency of denomination, but it must also be increasing its net assets position abroad. The world's net holdings of short-term dollars must increase because the United States is generating a dollar surplus that finances a part of the U.S. investment abroad; i.e., the United States must act as a banker. International progress requires a rich, effective banker. The United States, in spite of its current difficulties, remains the strongest candidate for that assignment.

Notes

1. R. S. Sayers, *Bank of England Operations, 1890-1914* (London: P. S. King and Sons, 1936), p. 27.

2. Hyman P. Minsky, "The Dollar: U.S. Economy Must Be Seen as an Ailing Bank," *Money Manager*, April 24, 1978.

3. The fact of dollar denominating is not of critical importance; what is critical is the existence of a dominant center for international financial transactions and a dominant currency for denominating debts and transactions.

4. Henry Kaufman estimates that "the U.S. dollar external liabilities of U.S. banks and foreign banks to non-bank creditors" were $130 billion and the U.S. dollar external interbank liabilities were $345 billion in 1977. This is just a fraction of the assets whose holders have to be willing to keep in dollars because dollar holdings are good assets for their portfolios (Henry Kaufman, "The Future of the Dollar," a talk delivered in New York, April

10, 1978, Salomon Brothers, mimeographed).

5. See Hyman P. Minsky, *John Maynard Keynes* (New York: Columbia University Press, 1975) for a discussion of uncertainty and asset values.

6. The classic exposition of the mechanical linkage between deposits and reserves is Chester Arthur Phillips, *Bank Credit* (New York: Macmillan Co., 1931).

7. John Maynard Keynes, "The General Theory of Employment," *Quarterly Journal of Economics* 51, February 1937, p. 216.

8. Ibid.

9. Kaufman, "Future of the Dollar."

10. See Victoria Chick, "Transnational Enterprises and the Evolution of the International Monetary System," Faculty of Economics, University of Sydney, Information and Research Project on Transnational Corporations Research No. 5, 1976, mimeographed.

11. Since November 1, 1978, the U.S. has gold treasury bills denominated in strong currencies. Although it has not succeeded in convincing the exchange markets of its determination to support the dollar, the dollar strengthened against all major currencies except sterling in the first half of 1979. (*J.D.A.*)

Part Two

Debt and Development

Banks are theoretically quite simple machines, either private or public. The pendulum swings steadily between the two, sometimes favoring risk and sometimes caution. The bankers' principle almost without exception consisted in collecting other people's money.

—Fernand Braudel

Introduction

The surging demand of newly independent, impoverished nations for the benefits of modern industrial development has reoriented international relations in the past two decades. The focus of Western scholars and diplomats on East-West security affairs has been supplemented if not totally subsumed by the impatient quest of less developed countries for "more" and for "better." Although beset by uncertain goals and ambiguous perceptions concerning appropriate development, OPEC's success in raising petroleum prices has galvanized a chorus of ultimatums among developing nations seeking a "new international economic order." Just as Japan's victory over Russia in 1905 echoed throughout the non-Caucasian world undermining the myth of occidental invulnerability, OPEC's triumph and its members' enrichment added insights and determination to the dreams of the world's poor nations.

The Manila Declaration of the Group of 77 and the Conference on International Economic Cooperation allowed the Third World to take the initiative away from the industrial world as the United Nations Conference on Trade and Development had tried, but failed, to do. The developing world demanded and received greater representation within the International Monetary Fund and the World Bank (even if such representation diluted these institutions' ability to act as independent agents). Questions involving technology transfer, the law of the sea, and the power of transnational enterprises all came under close scrutiny by nations no longer willing to move slowly into the twentieth century.

Naturally, the efficient contribution of external debt to the process of self-determined development became a priority item in many nations. The increasing tendency of developed nations to offer loans (official or private) instead of aid created concern in LDC capitals. Recipient nations also began questioning the contribution of external funds to their development plans and wondering aloud whether their creditors had not unfairly tempted them into unwise borrowing.

It is therefore important to carefully examine the role of debt, both domestic and external, in the process of development. How can debt be efficiently utilized within developing nations? In addition, has external official and private debt contributed to well-rounded development or created distorted growth and untenable, dependent links between key sectors in the developing countries and their metropolitan creditors? The four essays in this section explore these questions, with special reference to Latin America.

Clark W. Reynolds suggests some ways in which financial policy may be explicitly linked to planning in developing countries to foster structural change and development. He shows that financial intermediaries in developing states frequently are not neutral and that national planners frequently have misunderstood the nature of various types of rent and their variable contribution to growth and development policies. Professor Reynolds also suggests the appropriate use of financial intermediaries in the channeling of economic rents. By employing a social accounting framework for the reconciliation of real and financial flows of funds, Reynolds seeks to explain how policy-makers might match production planning of the private and public sectors for maximum consistency with the availability of domestic and foreign savings. In addition, Reynolds argues for the "separation of the income and flow-of-funds accounting framework into enough sectors to permit a functional analysis of net lending and borrowing over time."

Arthur B. Laffer looks at another possible approach developing countries might choose to adopt to stimulate savings that could contribute to future development. He extends his work on taxation to the problems of debt and the LDCs and suggests that fewer controls and lighter taxation in these nations would stimulate greater savings and growth. He points to Puerto Rico and Chile as examples of economies that have shown marked improvement in overall growth since such open policies were promulgated. He argues that growth and development are identical and not two separate processes.

W. Ladd Hollist's assessment of Brazilian external debt is more gloomy. He asks whether that country's "economic miracle" has in fact produced worsening economic and social conditions for the majority of Brazilians. He questions whether Brazil's industrialization-based development policies enacted by the economic and military elites and financed through extensive external borrowing have not actually increased Brazil's dependence on the developed world. Finally, Professor Hollist examines whether Brazil's development policies have concentrated aggregate national product in areas that will make eventual repayment extremely difficult except by further subjecting the majority of the population to continued and even worsening poverty.

This section concludes with R. Peter DeWitt and James F. Petras's more general attack on the "dynamics of finance capital." Their radical analysis of the "dynamics of international debt peonage" argues that private capital was drawn inevitably to developing countries and helped industrial nations reinforce their dominance over developing nations. The results of the expansion of global debt harms the true development prospects of developing nations and also increases the instability of the global economic system. Eventually, the developed as well as the developing nations may regret this extension of modern capitalism.

In sum, these four essays paint quite different pictures of the impact of debt on development. Clark Reynolds and Arthur Laffer each suggest (although for very different reasons) that, although the current system has major flaws, there exist at the same time major avenues of reform that could lead to significantly improved utilization of external debt by LDCs. The other authors in this section believe that systemic and structural problems associated with debt are more likely to lead to impoverization of borrowing countries (or at least most of their populations) and perhaps to marked instability in the functioning of the world monetary and economic systems as well.

—*J.D.A.*

Bankers as Revolutionaries
in the Process of Development

Clark W. Reynolds

What role, if any, might financial intermediaries play to facilitate the goals of radical structural change in the developing economies? This chapter offers some reflections on the subject based on several years of research on Latin American finance and development. Despite Charles Anderson's suggestive work on the Mexican banking system after the revolution,[1] there is little evidence yet that rapid growth of banking and financial intermediation in most of Latin America has done much to broaden social participation in the distribution of income and wealth.[2] Attempts have been made to use financial institutions to favor housing construction, employment, and savings of workers, as in Brazil and Colombia. But for the most part, net distributive effects have been ambiguous.[3] And, in the case of Allende's Chile, financial policy was relegated to last place in the order of priorities. It was as though the monetary authorities adopted the simplistic view of their "Chicago school" adversaries, that finance is a mere veil over real transactions, having no direct impact on the process of production or distribution. Under the Unidad Popular, the monetary base was expanded at will to cover any and all deficits brought to the government's attention by sympathetic pressure groups. The shambles in which this left the Chilean economy prompted an observer, who had watched with dismay the decline of the

The author gratefully acknowledges the opportunity to prepare the present draft while a visiting research scholar at the International Institute for Applied Systems Analysis, Laxenburg, Austria. An earlier version of this paper was presented at the Latin American Studies Association, Houston, Texas, November 1977.

Allende regime, to comment recently, "The lesson of Chile is that whoever wishes to be a political revolutionary had better be a monetary conservative." Yet, since financial orthodoxy is the hallmark of some of Latin America's most reactionary regimes, the appropriate role of finance in revolution needs careful assessment.

This chapter suggests some ways in which financial policy may be linked to planning for structural change, through the dynamic use of flow-of-funds analysis. Actual and potential sources and uses of funds are related to the behavior of the real structure of the economy, with particular attention to the generation and channeling of "economic rents." The concept of economic rent is extended to include all returns to scarce factors over and above their opportunity cost. As such, rent, broadly defined, is seen to be a true economic surplus. It is shown why banking and financial policy may serve to generate and mobilize such rents for growth and distribution, so that an apparently orthodox financial system can serve revolutionary goals.

1. Is the Financial System Neutral?

Financial institutions, including banks and other nonbank intermediaries, serve as links between surplus and deficit sectors in the economy. They also facilitate transactions through the provision of liquidity, the diversification of risk, term transformation, and other financial services. The charge for such intermediation services is reflected in the spread between net borrowing and net lending rates of interest per unit of financial flow per period.

- *Loan rate:* the average charge per unit of loan per period (including loan fees, opportunity cost of maintaining minimum balances, and related charges)

  (MINUS)

- *Deposit rate:* the average payment per unit of deposit per period (including the unit cost of related services, overdraft privileges, gifts for account holders, and other nonprice benefits to depositors)

(EQUALS)
- *Spread:* expressed as an average cost per unit of loan per period and includes:
  1. charge for loan risk
  2. charge for loan liquidity
  3. cost of entrepreneurship in the intermediation process (valued at opportunity cost)
  4. cost of labor (valued at opportunity cost)
  5. cost of land, buildings, or other fixed assets and working capital (valued at opportunity cost)
  6. cost of other inputs in the intermediation process (valued at opportunity cost)
  7. economic rent on intermediation services (in pure competition this item would be zero, since all inputs have already been paid their opportunity cost); since rent includes returns to any factor, including labor, over and above its opportunity cost in a competitive market, it might well be disguised in the accounting definition of "costs."

Where financial markets are atomistic and competition is keen, one may expect the spread to fall to the level of the marginal cost of intermediation services. Under these circumstances, the spread would include no more than a normal return to items (1) through (6) above and would not contain any excess profit (7). Competition would prevent intermediation rents from being earned either in lending or in borrowing, since, wherever excess profits existed, new institutions would enter the market, raising borrowing rates or lowering lending rates and thereby reducing the spread. Hence, in a hypothetical, purely competitive market, the neutrality of banks and other financial institutions would be assured.

However, the existence of barriers to entry could permit the spread between borrowing and lending rates to grow beyond the marginal cost of intermediation services. In such conditions, discriminatory pricing of financial services could be used against lenders and borrowers, so that monopsony and monopoly profits could accrue to financial institutions operating in imperfect markets. In such cases, economic rent would be earned on intermediation, shifting income distribution toward the owners of financial institutions. Banks would also be in a position to ration credit, thus limiting investment and distorting resource allocation. Under such circumstances, finance would cease to be neutral, and decision makers in banks and other financial institutions could assume an active voice in the economy, influencing the level and direction of credit flows.

Customarily, state permission to engage in banking and other forms of financial intermediation has been more restricted than that applying to other corporations. This arises from the desire to protect the public from excessive competition among financial institutions to ensure that the privilege of entry into a protected market is matched by the need for responsible conduct of banking affairs. In the case of banks of issue, a pure legal monopoly is common, so that the income from seigniorage (the issuing of money) tends to be concentrated in one institution. In many Latin American countries, such banks were historically, as some still are, private or semiprivate enterprises combining commercial banking activity with that of "central bank." Their profits accrued to private shareholders as well as to the government.

In developed countries, all but the largest banks (and the smallest, with virtual monopolies, in small towns and rural areas) face a high degree of competition. Hence, they are relatively neutral in the sense that no single financial institution can block a potentially profitable credit transaction and none can engage for long in the subsidization of credit, transfer pricing, or other measures, as these would lead to losses and eventual bankruptcy. However, the largest banks of developed countries have rather more degrees of freedom, since their decisions as market leaders can affect both lending and borrowing rates. In view of the interdependence among the largest banks, business, and government, their major financial decisions tend not to be neutral in political/economic terms.

For developing countries, financial markets are more subject to imperfections. However, while relatively wide spreads between borrowing and lending rates are common in developing countries, evidence of excess profits in banking is ambiguous. There seems to be a form of transfer pricing operating in many countries, whereby banks are linked to business and commercial groups that borrow at competitive rates from captive financial institutions, even when conditions in credit markets might have compelled them to be charged monopoly rates. The surplus from such transactions is internalized in the profits of the borrowing firm. Hence the "intermediation rent" from financial institutions in such credit markets is passed on to the ultimate borrower. Since nonfinancial enterprises are usually freer from government audits and regulation, they earn higher profits while their banks appear to break even. Another phenomenon in developing countries is that financial intermediaries use their monopoly spread to cover cost increases, swell payrolls, raise executive salaries and fringe benefits, and construct luxurious office buildings and employee villas, rather than to maximize profits. This is as likely to hold for government banks as for those in the private sector, since both operate behind legal barriers to entry.

Whether excess profits or excess costs predominate, the power to ration credit services exists, permitting nonneutral finance. Credit flows are likely to be restricted and resource allocation distorted for the benefit of those in the financial sector, their associates, and those with the power to raise or lower barriers to entry. The loser is society at large. In designing a financial system for operation during periods of radical structural change, one must avoid the replacement of old monopolies by new ones. And one should not fail to take advantage of the neutrality of potentially competitive financial markets. It is quite possible, for example, that in a country subject to the domination of one or a few traditional financial institutions, the chartering of new private or government banks could do more to improve the competitiveness of financial intermediation and its responsiveness to government policy than any change in ownership or management of existing institutions. Indeed, it would make sense to force traditional banks to face much-increased competition. If they fail, their charters could then be auctioned to the highest bidder while relying on new public or private participants in the market to increase the competition and neutrality of the banking system.

2. Nonneutral Banks and Development—A Conservative Bias?

Since banks are frequently nonneutral, especially in developing countries, what role might they be expected to play in the process of radical transformation? The answer will depend, to some extent, on the nature of their respective activities. Those involved in the provision of short-term credit for working capital, commerce, or consumption loans are likely to be most interested in the security of their asset and liability portfolios and in the opportunity to cover costs with a reasonable spread. Such institutions are not likely to be closely involved in aspects of structural change and will tend to go with the tide provided that they can cover costs plus their customary "intermediation rent." However, since radical change in the economy tends to alter the banks' base of action, those most able to respond to the shifting locus of borrowing and lending will be more likely to benefit from change and, therefore, to support the government. Those least flexible will use their leverage to slow the process of reform. In Latin America, many governments have used selective deposit creation and borrowing practices to secure support for their policies from nonneutral banks. Those supporting change have tended to prosper.

Banks involved in growth-related activities, such as mortage and investment lending, venture capital provision, and other forms of medium- and long-term finance, present more serious problems. Their degree of conservatism or resistance to experiments with new approaches to development finance will depend on their history and their ability to profitably alter asset and liability structures. For example, mortage lending institutions tend to have heavily locked-in asset portfolios, with loans subject to longer maturities at fixed rates of interest, so that they are particularly susceptible to pressure for change in portfolio structure, interest rates, reserve requirements, and inflation. The spread that they earn on "term transformation" between short-term deposits and long-term liabilities is very sensitive to changes in real rates of interest on lending or borrowing. This is especially true if they must compete for deposits with other institutions offering flexible borrowing rates. As deposit rates rise while loan rates remain contractually fixed at historic levels, the spread is squeezed and, with it, their profits. Not surprisingly, mortage banks tend to be among the most-conservative financial institutions, and even new government housing banks will tend to be pushed in that direction by the constraints of term transformation if they are not to require continual subsidization.

The need for banks to maintain portfolio balance, both within asset and liability structures and between total assets and liabilities, leads them to reflect a kind of conservatism which should not be confused with a congenital bias against reform. Rather, it indicates the need for reform to be made consistent with sound banking principles. To illustrate this point, it is useful to list eight major problems relevant to banking in a developing economy, each of which is likely to be affected by revolutionary policy:

1. price stability
2. savings mobilization
3. investment stimulation
4. financing the government deficit
5. financing real resource transfers among domestic institutions, sectors, and regions
6. financing international resource transfers
7. provision for intermediation services to previously marginal groups
8. improvement of economic and technological efficiency in production, including that of intermediation services.

The finance and development literature has tended to focus on problems of policy-induced inflation (1) and imperfections in financial markets (8) with particular attention to the costs of disequilibrating financial policies on real savings, investment, and allocative efficiency (2), (3), and (8). The restoration of "full financial intermediation" in such economies has been persuasively advocated so as to achieve these three goals. However, the effects of financial policy on the structure or production or distribution of income and wealth, problems of central importance to revolutionary policymakers, are given less attention.

In the previous sections, it was argued that financial systems in developing countries are customarily nonneutral with a potentially large influence on resource allocation. The following sections deal with items (4) through (7) above, in the framework of flow-of-funds analysis, to show how a nonneutral financial system may be utilized to mobilize and allocate economic rents for purposes of growth and distribution.

3. The Nature and Significance of Economic Rents for Growth[4]

Much contemporary Third World growth, as that of presently developed countries, has depended on the mobilization of natural resource rents from agriculture, mining, and petroleum. Scarcity rents, which accrue to inframarginal suppliers, have provided a surplus for reinvestment in new sectors of production which offer further potential for yields over and above a normal return on capital. The pattern of rent-generation takes three major forms:

1. *Natural resource rent:* the returns to natural resource endowments over and above the normal costs of capital, labor, and premiums for risk and liquidity essential to permit the activity to occur (Ricardian rent)
2. *Innovation rent:* the returns to entrepreneurial combinations of innovations with financial capital, subject to patents and other barriers to entry essential to permit the rents to occur (Schumpeterian rent)
3. *Protection rent:* the returns to barriers to entry (legal, social, institutional, illegal) permitting monopoly and monopsony profits (Bain rent).

Natural resource rents are common in developing countries. To the extent that they accrue to factors of production in inelastic supply, they tend to exceed the opportunities for reinvestment in the same sector. This is especially true if the sector faces a downward sloping demand curve so that supply restraints are necessary for profit maximization. In the case of mineral exports, such as copper, those firms that traditionally dominated the world market for the red metal tended to save and reinvest their rents in other rent-generating sectors of the world economy and not in copper which would have expanded supply unduly and brought down the price. Thus Chilean copper rents were transformed into investment in overseas processing plants, timber, lead, zinc, and other activities in order to diversify the investment portfolio of the rent-generating firms and to prevent excess supply of copper.

The pattern has been for copper to finance, through its rents, a broader pattern of growth. However, there has been little tendency for copper to foster growth in the same sector or region of the economy where the rents were initiated. Instead, the rents have provided what one might call "footloose capital" which has gone abroad seeking other rent-generating opportunities. Such rents, plus innovation and protection rents, provide a major potential source of financial capital for new development. But there is no assurance that they will find their way into productive investment, especially in the locale where they originated. The Swedish economic historian Eli Heckscher showed that copper rents from the great Falun mine helped to finance commercial and military expansion of seventeenth-century Sweden, leading eventually to the growth of other industries in the country by providing a surplus to new investors.[5] Montana copper was first a borrower and then a supplier of "Boston dollars," helping to finance industrial growth in the eastern United States.[6] Rents from sugar and cotton in the Brazilian Northeast supplied the financial capital for the growth in the São Paulo area according to Werner Baer.[7] In each case, resource rents provided the funds to permit real transfers into other domestic activities. There are countless instances in which the vicissitudes of history and geography caused rent-generating sectors to be on one side of a natural boundary line and net borrowing sectors on the other. And where the owner of resources resided abroad, rents often left their region of origin, never to return. While some might argue that this was optimal from the point of view of world welfare, given the distribution of international wealth and political power, it was nevertheless detrimental to the growth of output and employment in the rent-generating region.

History is filled with examples of ghost towns and abandoned areas of national economies where extractive industries had once given rise to thriving commercial centers, where agriculture had provided a surplus for the building of great plantation houses, railroads, port facilities, and theaters. Jerome, Arizona; Manaus, Brazil; Falun, Sweden; and Iquique, Chile are all cases in point, struggling to survive now that the rental income bonanza from copper, rubber, and nitrate is over. National economic policymakers in today's developing countries are well advised to examine the history of rent-generating industries to facilitate their approach to (a) the maximization of resource rents and (b) the channeling of these rents into new investments, preferably in activities generating innovation rents.

The first step in the generation of economic rents from natural resources is one of exploration, development, and investment in plant, equipment, and other physical infrastructure. This step usually requires a net flow of resources including capital goods, skilled labor, intermediate goods, and technology into the sector. In the first phase, the sector will be a net borrower from the "rest of the world." If the domestic economy does not have sufficient net savings to finance this initial borrowing by the new rent-generating sector, resource transfers will have to come from abroad. In either case, the transfers may take the form of direct or indirect finance or fiscal subsidies (concessional aid represents foreign fiscal subsidies). Such flows occurred in the past under the aegis of private enterprise. The finance of new rent-generating activities was often done directly in the form of equity investment by firms that had accumulated rents else-where, or by financial intermediaries which provided indirect finance so as to permit a leverage of equity, thereby increasing entrepreneurial rents. Stephen Hymer's now-classic doctoral dissertation analyzes the process of leverage in which rental incomes from multinational enterprises are concentrated in the hands of equity investors who maximize borrowing, often in the host country, while retaining a maximum command over profits.[8] In this way, the "normal returns to capital" flow to indirect investors, while rents accrue to equity investors at rates of return on sunk capital well above international borrowing rates. Wherever resource, innovation, or protection rents are possible, such practices would be rational for profit maximization. This would also hold for government-owned equity in productive enterprises, and, indeed, the state should maximize the use of leverage to cover capital costs while retaining the rental income shares for itself. For this reason, a fully functioning financial system will permit the government to maximize its share of economic rents.

The second stage of rent-generating activities is the phase of production, during which rents accrue in excess of normal costs of labor and capital *if* (and only if) the enterprise has been successful. What is often forgotten by developing countries, which assume the role of owners and managers of such industries, is that they are generally very risky. Mining and petroleum exploration are a case in point. For every mine or well that proves to be a bonanza, dozens are unable to cover the sunk costs of exploration and development. John D. Rockefeller recognized this problem and determined to concentrate control of the U.S. petroleum production at the processing rather than the drilling stage, since Pennsylvania petroleum deposits were difficult to locate and risky to drill. Hence, "normal costs of capital" must include an element to cover such risks as well as those reflecting the volatility of world prices. Since rent-intensive activities reflect relatively inelastic supply conditions, they are especially vulnerable to price fluctuations (as we have seen for copper in recent years, not to mention coffee or sugar). Having accounted for these costs, the second stage should permit the repayment of earlier borrowings and the gradual accumulation of positive net worth in the form of new physical and financial assets (assuming that the rent is not fully consumed in the current period).

This leads to the third stage of rent-generating activities, one of diversification through savings and investment in new activities on the part of those with access to rental income. It should be noted that future rental streams may be capitalized at their present value and sold by the original investors so as to earn capital gains. These gains, in turn, may be saved and reinvested, though it should be stressed that since they arise from a financial transfer rather than a real transaction, their net effects on real savings and investment is ambiguous. After such a transaction, the subsequent rental streams flow to net investors as normal returns on their financial capital. It is this circumstance that makes it difficult in practice to characterize rental income streams as a surplus. They are indeed surplus in the sense that they provide an excess return on sunk physical capital, labor, and other operating costs. But from the viewpoint of the new owners who have paid full value for the future rental stream, a considerable capital loss would be experienced if such rents were to be subsequently taxed or otherwise diverted. This problem is less serious in cases where the state initially owns the rent-generating resources.

But it should be recognized that the opportunity cost to the state of maintaining such assets ownership is the return on the income which might be obtained from divestiture of the assets at their capitalized value. The Guggenheims, Rockefellers, and other groups who engaged in entrepreneurial ventures of this type frequently "went public" and capitalized the rents at rates that permitted substantial capital gains, especially if financial market conditions were unduly favorable to the enterprises relative to reasonable long-term expectations.[9] On the other hand, many governments in the past have sold the rights to domestic resource rents at prices far below any reasonable present value of the concessions, though this practice is less widespread today with the growing emphasis on social accountability of public officials. (The more democratic the system, the more likely that government officials will be held accountable for such transactions. It is, therefore, understandable that few rent-rich export economies are governed democratically. The potential for personal enrichment in such cases more than compensates for the risks inherent in totalitarian rule.)

4. The Role of Finance in the Channeling of Economic Rents

The rents for growth initiating sectors permit potential resource transfers to other regions and sectors. These transfers may be regarded as an "export surplus" provided by the initiating sector to deficit sectors in the same manner that a country exporting more than it imports enjoys a surplus in its balance of payments on current account. The transfers may be voluntary or involuntary, the latter being associated with taxation of the initiating sector for the benefit of deficit sectors. Here we are concerned with voluntary transfers through the banking system. To what extent can such transfers, which arise from rents in surplus sectors, serve to finance investment in deficit sectors, so as to keep the stream of rents steadily growing? Such intersectoral flows tend to cancel each other out in conventional social accounting frameworks, owing to the high degree of aggregation of the sectors involved, though some flows among major institutional groups such as households, business, and government may be captured in the statistics. Regional flows are rarely estimated, nor are flows among production sectors even as important as agriculture, manufacturing, and extractive industries. If finance were fully neutral, if entrepreneurship were fully effective, and if politics dictated that the structure of production and distribution be relegated to the operation of market forces, it might be reasonable to ignore intersectoral financial flows. Indeed, no budgeting of capital flows or related financial flows would be necessary for policy purposes.

However, we have argued that in developing countries finance is rarely neutral, public policy is normally committed to some degree of reform, and neither the public nor the private sector has evidenced expertise in the sustained generation of economic rents from sector to sector. Hence, there is a case for financial planning at the sectoral level which becomes more important as such economies receive a greater share of their income from scarcity rents and as they are increasingly committed to an equitable distribution of income among all sectors of society. The opportunity to generate and channel rental income into further growth-inducing investments provides a windfall to those economies fortunate enough to possess abundant resources. But they also require the technological potential capable of producing such a surplus over labor and capital input costs, together with entrepreneurship and financial capital which will make the enterprises possible. In this sense the Schumpeterian role of the entrepreneur, who links innovation and financial capital, is seen to be central to the success of both state and private ventures in presently developing countries. But no less important is financial capital.

Financial planning in economies that depend upon the rents from wasting resources involves the determination of optimal patterns of resource use. While this can be left solely to market forces, such was not the case in most of the now-developed countries. Most governments were actively involved in the provision of infrastructure, securing of legal and other claims to rents, obtaining financial capital at favorable rates, patenting of technological processes (permitting innovation rents), marketing, and distribution. Internationally, the state often intervened to secure permission for enterprises under its flag to develop rent-generating activities abroad, to extract the rents, and to reinvest them in third countries, using diplomatic, military, and security forces as well as economic pressures. In short, real and financial planning did not take place in a political-economic vacuum historically, and it should not be expected to do so today. All aspects of capital budgeting of new ventures, and especially those regarded as sources of future finance, are likely to be the concern of policymakers, however much market forces are utilized to expedite decision making and to promote efficiency.

To accomplish the multiple and potentially conflicting goals of growth, efficiency, and equity, policymakers require:

1. measures to match production planning of the private and public sectors for maximum consistency with the availability of domestic and foreign savings
2. instruments and guidelines for the mobilization of savings from actual or potential surplus sectors, through both finance and taxation (with careful consideration of the trade-offs between the two approaches)
3. instruments and guidelines for the allocation of savings to investment in potential rent-generating activities
4. a basis for the estimation and simulation of sectoral savings and investment behavior under conditions of alternative real and financial policies and alternative projections of external borrowing
5. a set of criteria for the determination of optimal degrees of external borrowing (and lending) for consistency between internal and external financial management and the capital requirements of macroeconomic planning.

While most developing countries pursue all of these objectives to some degree, the current external debt problems of many suggest that insufficient attention has been given to links between real and financial planning and the banking system. There is rarely a consistency framework for the estimation of internal sectoral surpluses and deficits and their matching domestic and foreign financial flows. To illustrate the consequences of this failure, one may take the recent cases of two countries. One borrowed abroad while maintaining an internal surplus, thus causing an increase in the monetary base (and inflation)—Chile. The other country borrowed abroad to cover an internal deficit, again with inflationary consequences for the monetary base—Peru. Mexico recently followed the Peruvian example of funding internal deficit with external savings, leading to inflation and devaluation of its currency.

If the mechanism suggested in the fifth requirement were adopted, and if social accounting techniques were used to project real and financial flows by major sectors of economic activity, it would begin to be possible to determine whether planned investment could be financed out of internal savings. Where sectoral surpluses or deficits were projected, it would become clear to what extent financial flows (and in extreme cases fiscal transfers) would be required to bring about internal balance. Given domestic investment requirements and domestic savings capability, net foreign borrowing (or lending) needs would become clear under alternative expansion paths. Research by the Organization of American States (OAS) on flow-of-funds analysis for Latin American countries indicates that the financial savings potential of a given country is flexible and sensitive to a variety of financial policies. A number of cases exist in which the financial savings of some sectors are used to finance dissavings of others. In these cases net financial savings would rise as a share of gross domestic product (GDP) if the use of funds were shifted from current to capital expenditures.[10]

From the viewpoint of foreign indebtedness, such an approach would make it possible to predict a variety of alternative foreign resource gaps under different fiscal, financial, and investment incentive programs. This would facilitate the matching of net foreign borrowing to net import requirements and help avoid the use of foreign savings to fund domestic resource gaps with inflationary consequences. This would improve the creditworthiness of borrowers and lessen their vulnerability to external pressures.

Failure to relate current foreign borrowing to medium-term planning goals tends to produce a succession of stop-and-go measures, as balance-of-payments support loans become due without the requisite foreign exchange to repay them. The stop-and-go measures have adverse effects on both profits (credit squeeze) and labor income (wage freeze) and exacerbate investment uncertainty, social unrest, and political pressures to increase the domestic deficit. The cases of Argentina in the 1960s and Peru in the 1970s illustrate the consequences of failure to coordinate internal and external balance. The resulting inflation makes such coordination even more difficult, as rising prices and costs make it almost impossible to budget in real terms. In addition to normal surpluses and deficits on capital account, financial flows in an inflationary economy reflect distorting capital gains and losses resulting from changes in the real value of financial assets and liabilities from period to period.

It is the purpose of this chapter to deal with the first and fourth of the list of policymakers' requirements by suggesting a framework for the reconciliation of real and financial flows permitting alternative projections of external borrowing. In terms of the first item, the rent-generating sectors are likely to pass through a "rent cycle" in which they are, first, net borrowers and, then, net lenders. Hence, economies characterized by a significant share of resource rents are particularly vulnerable to a loss of potential investment in future rent-producing activities. Much of the following analysis is devoted to such cases. Indeed, where the rents reflect foreign exchange earnings, foreign deficits in the initial period to finance imports of goods and services for exploration and development may be justified independently of other components in the domestic accounts. And in later periods, export surpluses may be justified for the accumulation of foreign financial assets. This would hold not only for stabilization funds, but also for those economies in which future production growth potential is limited, at least in terms of the capacity to absorb imports. In short, this is an argument for a separation of the income and flow-of-funds accounting framework into enough sectors to permit a functional analysis of net lending and borrowing over time, including the role of financial intermediation between surplus and deficit sectors.

5. A Social Accounting Framework for the Reconciliation of Real and Financial Flows: Sectoring the Accounts[11]

Sectoring of the flow-of-funds accounts should take into consideration the functional behavior of specific sectors as key actors in the national economy and should be consistent with those in the national income accounts. For a rent-generating export economy, the following sectoring is suggested:[12]

Basic Flow of Funds Sectors to be Linked with
Capital Accounts of the National Income Accounts
(If possible divide each sector into deficit and surplus
  components)
Nonfarm households and nonprofit institutions
Agriculture (including farm households)
Principal export industries
Other manufacturing
Other private nonfinancial corporations
Unincorporated enterprise
Central bank
Insurance and pension funds
Commercial banks
Nonbank financial intermediaries
Public enterprise
Government
Rest of world

The objective is to provide sufficient detail on real production sectors to estimate net savings and investment flows (net financial flows), and to provide sufficient detail of the financial institutional sectors to determine their role in the channeling of funds from net lenders to borrowers.

6. A Complete Sectoral Source and Use of Funds Statement

A complete statement of the source and use of funds of a given sector integrates information from both national income accounts and flow-of-funds accounts. The latter are customarily prepared from annual statements of financial assets and liabilities, using the first difference of year-to-year changes in stocks to generate corresponding "financial flows." Such statements tend to be available in consolidated form for financial intermediaries and other corporate enterprises. Sample surveys facilitate the preparation of flow-of-funds statements for households, unincorporated enterprises, and agricultural enterprises. Cross-referencing may permit the disaggregation of financial institutions' assets and liabilities with respect to nonfinancial institutional sectors (e.g., business and households; government; rest of world). Since each financial asset has a corresponding liability entry with respect to a given sector, this permits gaps in the flow-of-funds accounts on the asset side to be filled from information on the liability side and vice versa.

If balance-sheet data are used for the estimation of net flows of financial assets and liabilities from year to year, income statements are helpful in preparing annual national income and product accounts. These, in turn, permit the estimation of sectoral savings (real savings) and investment. The difference between the two is the net financial surplus (or deficit) of the sector. By definition, the net financial surplus (or deficit) from the income and product accounts must equal the net financial surplus (or deficit) from the flow-of-funds accounts for the same sector. However, in practice they rarely match because of different estimation procedures. The problem of reconciliation of a sector's real and financial flows is analogous to that of the current and capital account in the balance of payments. An item for "errors and omissions" should be included to reconcile the independently derived estimates.

Figure 1 shows a complete "sources and uses of funds statement" for a single sector. Above the solid line are real income and expenditure flows taken from the sector's current account in the national income accounts. Below the solid line and above the dotted line are the real flows of investment and savings from

Figure 1
A Complete Sector Sources and Uses of Funds Statement (given time period)

	Uses	Sources
Income Statement	Current Expenditures (C) Saving (S)	Current Receipts (Y) Net Fiscal Transfers (F)
	Saving $\longrightarrow$	(ΔNW)
	Real Investment (ΔRA)=(I) Net Financial Surplus (or Deficit –) (NFS)	=
Change in Balance Sheet — Flow of Funds	Lending (ΔFA) Accumulation of Cash Balances (ΔM)	Net Financial Surplus (or Deficit –) (NFS) Borrowing (ΔL)
	Σ =	Σ

the sector's capital account in the national income accounts. Below the dotted line are the financial flows that correspond to those in the flow-of-funds account. "Net financial surplus (or deficit)" is a balancing item $(S - I)$ in the capital account of the national income accounts. In Figure 1, it cancels out when both accounts are consolidated. The "net fiscal transfers" item in the income statement refers to net subsidies (minus taxes) of the government with respect to the given sector. For most sectors, this item will be negative. An offsetting item of opposite sign will be entered in the government sector.

7. A Flow of Funds Matrix for the Whole Economy

Having shown the complete source and use of funds statement for a given sector in Figure 1, a general source and use of funds statement such as would apply to the whole economy appears in Figure 2. The small letters represent data on sector saving (s), investment (i), borrowing (b), lending (l), and accumulation of cash balances (m). The large letters represent the total of each category for the economy as a whole. Thus,

$$s_a + s_b + s_c = S \text{ and } i_a + i_b + i_c = I \text{ et cetera.}$$

As we have seen, for each sector,

$$s + b = i + l + m$$

but b need not equal $l + m$, and s need not equal i. However, for the economy as a whole,

$$S + B = I + L + M$$

and

$$B = L + M$$

$$S = I$$

where no net foreign borrowing or lending occurs.

Figure 2
Flow of Funds Matrix for the Whole Economy

149

		Sector A		Sector B		Sector C		All Sectors	
		U	S	U	S	U	S	U	S
Saving	(ΔNW)		s_a		s_b		s_c		S
Investment	(ΔRA)	i_a		i_b		i_c		I	
Borrowing	(ΔL)		b_a		b_b		b_c		B
Lending	(ΔFA)	l_a		l_b		l_c		L	
Accumulation of Cash Balances	(ΔM)	m_a		m_b		m_c		M	
		Σ = Σ		Σ = Σ		Σ = Σ		Σ = Σ	

(In the All Sectors column: S = I; L + M braced = B)

Sources: Lawrence S. Ritter, "The Flow of Funds Accounts: A Framework for Financial Analysis," The Bulletin, Graduate School of Business Administration, New York University, 1968; Clark Reynolds and Lewis Spellman, Financial Intermediation and Economic Development as Seen Through the Flow of Funds Accounts, draft, 1975.

8. Open Economies with Net Foreign Borrowing or Lending

If the economy is open to the rest of the world, it is reasonable to suppose that lending and borrowing will take place beyond its borders. This case could lead to a situation in which domestic savings (S_d) might not be equal to domestic investment (I_d) by the amount of the balance-of-payments surplus (or deficit) on current account. In this case, if we let X represent exports and M imports for the economy as a whole,

$$S_d = I_d + X - M$$

or

$$S_d + M = I_d + X.$$

Since net foreign lending $(X - M)$ represents the net domestic accumulation of foreign monetary and nonmonetary financial assets, less liabilities to foreigners, the general flow of funds matrix for the whole economy, presented in Figure 2, could be adapted to an open economy by allowing one of the sectors (such as Sector C) to represent the rest of the world.

9. Intersectoral Financial Flows

Note that the balance-of-payments concept that relates the economy to the rest of the world in terms of real flows (current account of the balance of payments) and financial flows (capital account of the balance of payments) is analogous to intersectoral transactions within a given economy. Just as some countries are in surplus and others in deficit in their balance of payments on current account $(X \neq M)$, with associated offsetting financial flows, so individual sectors, regions, or income groups within an economy may be in surplus or deficit with the rest of the economy. The flow-of-funds accounts can be designed to reveal such intersectoral real and financial flows. These flows may be as important in permitting accumulation and growth of the domestic economy as are real and financial flows between countries. Yet they are rarely considered by social accounting analysis, partly because of the difficulty of obtaining reliable flow data at the sectoral level. The application of such an approach to transfers between the agricultural and nonagricultural sectors in Taiwan is presented in T. H. Lee's pioneering work.[13]

Earlier in the chapter, it was noted that sectors that have a large share of resource rent in their income stream eventually may be capable of providing net financial savings for investment in other sectors. Of course, in their early stage they may be net borrowers from other domestic sectors and/or the rest of the world. This would hold for "vent for surplus" resource-intensive activities such as those described by Richard Caves.[14] In Figures 3a and 3b, an example of a rent-generating activity is presented in terms of hypothetical real and financial flows in early and late stages of development.

In the first phase, the mining sector is engaged in exploration and development. Since this requires imported inputs, it borrows abroad 100 units, increasing the external debt by that amount. If any of the 100 units were not spent on imports (net savings of rest-of-world = $M - X$), then the economy would accumulate foreign exchange or other rest-of-world liabilities in the amount of the difference, reducing rest-of-world savings accordingly and increasing domestic savings for that sector holding the claims. During the process of development, the mining sector will experience income growth. If it is successful, income will exceed expenditures permitting positive real savings (Figure 3b). The savings of 60 units are used, in part, for additional physical investment in the mining sector (10 units). Part are used to retire debt contracted earlier (30 units). (Note: Debt service payments appear as current costs which are deducted from sectoral income flows before arriving at sectoral savings. Business savings may be gross or net of depreciation but should include retained earnings—undistributed profits—of enterprise.) The remaining "net financial savings" are lent to the financial sector (government development bank) in the amount of 20 units under the assumptions of Figure 3b. These funds may be re-lent to the manufacturing sector if investment opportunities exist in excess of internal savings capacity.

In developing countries, flows from resource rents to invest-

Figure 3
A Resource Intensive Activity's Real and Financial Flows During the
Raw Material Product Cycle

A) Stage of Exploration and Development

	Sector A Mining		Sector B Manufacturing		Sector C Government Development Bank		Sector D Rest of World		All Sectors	
	U	S	U	S	U	S	U	S	ΣU	ΣS
Saving (ΔNW)								100		100
Investment (ΔRA)	100								100	
Borrowing (ΔL)		100								100
Lending (ΔFA)							100		100	

B) Stage of Maturity (before significant depletion)

	Sector A Mining		Sector B Manufacturing		Sector C Government Development Bank		Sector D Rest of World		All Sectors	
	U	S	U	S	U	S	U	S	ΣU	ΣS
Saving (ΔNW)		60						-30		30
Investment (ΔRA)	10		20						30	
Borrowing (ΔL)		-30		20		20				10
Lending (ΔFA)	20				20		-30		10	

ments, which give rise to innovation or protection rents in manufacturing and commerce, are often supported by policies that favor financial intermediation. In many cases, if intermediation were not provided by the banking systems, investment would decline.[15] But financial intermediation also may transfer the rents from surplus sectors to consumption loans or to the finance of current expenditure of the government. In such cases, the opportunity for accumulation and growth is lost to the economy, as net savers finance dissavers through the passive role of banks. In such circumstances, policies should be pursued by the financial authorities to promote investment banking activities by providing security for financial institutions engaged in longer-term lending. It may also be possible for the country to hold short-term foreign financial assets against longer-term foreign liabilities, thus shifting the risk of term transformation to the rest of the world.

An alternative, less-desirable means of mobilizing and channeling resource rents would be through fiscal transfers, in which the mining sector would be taxed to provide funds for investment subsidies elsewhere (such as loans at low or negative real rates of interest). This procedure is common in the Latin American experience. It tends to distort resource allocation to the extent that further investment in the rent-generating sector is discouraged and new investments occur at yields below levels that would be obtained if the capital markets were competitive. Also, favored sectors often enjoy rents that derive from high rates of effective protection. Such protection permits monopoly pricing and excess profit-taking, especially where the size of the domestic market is small. Transferring rents derived from efficient export production to protected domestic manufacturing works against efficient resource allocation and sustained growth.

10. Bankers as Revolutionaries:
The Need for Financial Planning

Developing countries have greatly increased their international borrowing and lending in recent years. The result has been a radical shift in world financial flows and real resource transfers. Those developing countries in surplus tend to be earners of resource rents (OPEC is a current example) that have reached the stage of maturity, have paid off their initial exploration and development expenses, and are unable to absorb increased imports in proportion to their export growth. In fact, many of those countries should be showing even larger surpluses than they do and are overimporting from the viewpoint of efficient resource management. They have many characteristics of the false-front mining towns of the North American West which, while they boomed, imported every luxury from the East and squandered their wealth on unproductive adornments, only to eventually decline.

This chapter suggests that, given the political will, a small

investment in statistics, and the formation of rudimentary national income and flow-of-funds accounts, it would be possible
to prepare a financial plan at the sectoral level. This would permit a more effective channeling of resource rent income toward
new rent-generating investments at home, plus the accumulation
of financial assets abroad which could eventually be drawn upon
to finance future growth-related imports once domestic absorptive capacity had expanded. A competitive banking system
could facilitate such a function, provided that the returns to
intermediation were sufficient to cover costs.

Recent work on the functional distribution of income in the
Central American Common Market indicates that 30 to 40 percent of value added in those economies represent economic rent
(returns in excess of normal costs of labor and capital).[16] Yet
their domestic rates of savings and investment are only 10 to
15 percent, and their rates of direct taxation are only a few
percentage points of GDP. Rental incomes in such countries
accrue only to a small number of property owners and tend to
be used to finance luxury consumption or overseas deposits. By
bypassing domestic financial institutions, the rental incomes are
lost for purposes of investment, distribution, and growth. In
addition, the protection rents in new import-substituting industries have not been saved and reinvested at significant rates. This
is attributable, in part, to the monopolistic character of such
rents, which discourages further investment in the same sector
and, in part, to the limited size of national markets. Another
reason is the fact that the market offers little promise of innovation rents given a business climate in which protection is seen to
be more profitable than innovation.

But a final explanation is the relatively backward state of financial intermediation in Central America, in which banks tend
to concentrate on commercial credit and other short-term lending rather than on the finance of venture capital. Here, there is
ample scope for the stimulation of more rigorous financial
activity. There is no reason why major structural changes in
regions such as Central America, where revolution is long
overdue, could not be made consistent with conditions of
portfolio balance, insurance against risk, price stability, and
other sound banking requirements. With financial planning

linked to the real economic needs of reform, banks could serve revolutionary goals by capturing rents and reallocating them under conditions of maximum neutrality.

Notes

1. Charles Anderson, "Bankers as Revolutionaries: Politics and Development," in *The Political Economy of Mexico*, two studies by Glade and Anderson (Madison: University of Wisconsin Press, 1968).

2. Clark Reynolds and Jaime Corredor, "The Effects of the Financial System on the Distribution of Income and Wealth in Mexico," *Food Research Institute Studies* 15:1, 1976.

3. Clark Reynolds and Robert Carpenter, "Housing Finance in Brazil: Towards a New Distribution of Wealth," in *Latin American Urban Research*, Vol. 5 of *Urbanization and Inequality: The Political Economy of Urban and Rural Development in Latin America*, ed. W. A. Cornelius and F. Trueblood (Beverly Hills, Calif.: Sage Publications, 1975), pp. 147-74.

4. Aspects of this and the following sections were presented at the meeting on Alternative Solutions of the External Debt Problem of the Developing Countries, Mexico City, October 27-30, 1977.

5. Eli F. Heckscher, *An Economic History of Sweden* (Cambridge: Harvard University Press, 1963).

6. C. B. Glassock, *The War of the Copper Kings: Builders of Butte and Wolves of Wall Street* (New York, 1935).

7. Werner Baer, *Industrialization and Economic Development in Brazil* (Homewook, Ill.: Richard D. Irwin, 1965).

8. Stephen H. Hymer, *The International Operations of National Firms: A Study of Direct Foreign Investment* (Cambridge: M.I.T. Press, 1976).

9. Harvey O'Conner, *The Guggenheims: The Making of an American Dynasty* (New York: Covici Friede, 1937).

10. Clark Reynolds and Lewis Spellman, "Financial Intermediation and Economic Development as Seen through the Flow of Funds Accounts," draft, 1975.

11. An earlier discussion of flow-of-funds accounting for development analysis is contained in Reynolds and Spellman, "Financial Intermediation and Economic Development."

12. Note that this sectoring is essentially that of Frank B. Rampersand, "An Integrated System of Real and Financial Accounts," *Social and Economic Studies*, Institute of Social and Economic Research, June 1962, pp. 128-56. The OAS flow-of-funds project disaggregated households,

business, government nonfinancial sector, central bank, other financial institutions, and the rest of the world.

13. Teng-Hui Lee, *Intersectoral Capital Flows in the Economic Development of Taiwan, 1895-1960* (Ithaca, N.Y.: Cornell University Press, 1971).

14. Richard E. Caves, "Export-Led Growth and the New Economic History," in *Trade, Balance of Payments, and Growth*, ed. Jagdish Bhagwati, R. Jones, R. Mundell, and J. Vanek (Amsterdam: North Holland Publishing Co., 1971).

15. Ronald I. McKinnon, *Money, Capital, and Economic Development* (Washington, D.C.: Brookings Institution, 1973).

16. Clark Reynolds and Gustavo Leiva, *Employment Problems of Export Economies in a Common Market: The Case of Central America*, Brookings/SIECA Study, June 30, 1977 (Washington, D.C.: Brookings Institution, forthcoming).

6

Debt, Indenture, and Development

Arthur B. Laffer

In the last half decade several economies have made major strides toward economic development. In the case of OPEC countries the source of the catalyst appears obvious. Yet, in a few non-OPEC economies, the development process has also begun in spite of a substantial deterioration in the specific economy's terms of trade. Historically, as today, development has arisen from widely divergent sources. Maintenance of the development process, however, requires adherence to basic economic principles. This remains true whether the economy has high or low real income per capita.

In the words of Will and Ariel Durant, "the experience of the past leaves little doubt that every economic system must sooner or later rely upon some form of the profit motive to stir individuals and groups to productivity. Substitutes like slavery, police supervision, ideological enthusiasm, prove too unproductive, too expensive or too transient. Normally and generally men are judged by their ability to produce—except in war, when they are ranked according to their ability to destroy."[1] Restated in the vernacular of modern economics, individuals and groups of individuals allocate resources according to after-tax yields. If market activities are profitable to perform, the society will shun leisure and nonmarket ventures while concentrating on ever-increasing market successes. If, however, successful market performance encounters waxing discrimination in the forms of high and progressive taxes, regulations, and other forms of societal disapprobation, the development process will be retarded. Ultimately, poverty results.

1. Traditional Analysis

The more traditional approach to development economics has focused on the economy's need to acquire capital. Less developed economies have been viewed as areas of labor surplus with high levels of both unemployment and underemployment. As such, the marginal product of labor is taken as being close to, if not literally, zero. In other words, any increase in the labor force will have little, if any, effect on total production unless, of course, that increase in the labor force is accompanied by an increase in the total quantity of capital.[2] More specifically, the most pressing need for capital in a preponderance of the less developed economies is so-called infrastructure, such as highways, schools, health facilities, power generating plants, or sewer systems.

Within a traditional framework, the problems of capital paucity are heightened further by the low savings ratio found to exist in a majority of the less developed economies. Speculation has isolated cultural factors as perhaps the principal source of the low savings rates. Whatever the source, low, private savings rates combined with low levels of per-capita income inextricably lead to low rates of capital formation.[3] Low rates of capital formation, high rates of growth of the population, and the incumbent political instability connote a poverty trap. Natural forces, so the traditional approach contends, condemn less developed countries to remain less developed. Malthusian considerations define the floor. A vicious cycle locks poverty into poverty unless somewhere along the line the causal sequence can be broken.

2. Traditional Policy Recommendations

Moving from this framework of analysis to the realm of policy formulation, traditional development economists have stressed the need for massive, once-and-for-all development programs—the "big push." A large infusion of capital would have the effect of breaking the vicious poverty cycle and elevate per-capita real incomes. Higher real incomes would lead to greater savings rates and lower birth rates. This would, in turn, carry the process forward under its own natural forces.

The specifics of a "big push" strategy for development usually include: protection for domestic manufacturing; high excises on luxuries so as not to waste precious domestic resources on nonessential products; high and progressive taxes to transfer resources to a central organization for coordinated development planning; large public or government development projects to provide the requisite infrastructure; and lastly, tight and pervasive exchange and investment controls such as licensing to assure productive and nonexploitive foreign investment. To the extent possible, these coordinated development programs also envision concerted efforts to extract foreign aid concessions from developed economies. These foreign aid concessions can take the form of outright grants, low interest loans, special concessions on sales in developed markets, and specific cartel efforts to improve the less developed country's terms of trade.

One recent example of a traditional development program is the Tobin report to the governor of Puerto Rico.[4] The recommendations of the Tobin report consisted of:

1. An increase in taxes including maintenance of a 5% income tax surcharge, increased excises and luxury taxes, increased property taxes, and increases in the prices charged to consumers of products produced by publicly owned companies. The logic here was simply that Puerto Rican private savings rates were so low that increased taxes would transfer the income to the public sector where a larger share would be saved.
2. Development of an intellectual group within government whereby public and, to some extent, private resource allocation could be coordinated to attain social objectives.
3. A reduction in the wages and an increase in the work input levels of government and publicly run enterprises. Again by reducing the real costs of public services (and, as mentioned above, an increase in the prices charged for public services) so that publicly owned enterprises could use surpluses and thereby increase Puerto Rican state savings.
4. An elimination of the minimum wage.
5. Solicitation of additional net transfers from the mainland

United States. Here again Puerto Rican real resources available for capital accumulation would be expanded.

The problem with these stylized development programs is not so much that capital accumulation per se is not important. It is. The problem is simply with the analytic framework illustrating how an economy can truly effectuate rapid capital growth. If relevant variables are treated as constants via deletion from the analysis, no matter how carefully the model is developed and implemented the results are inevitably going to be misguided.

In the case of traditional theorizing about economic development, incentives are virtually completely ignored. As such the schemes and plans profered to less developed economies will, to a large extent, overlook the very incentives required to obtain development.

3. Critique of the Traditional Framework

With few exceptions, incentive-oriented analysis indicates that less developed economies should proceed along lines precisely the reverse of those recommended by the aforementioned Tobin report.

Traditional approaches operate almost exclusively within a Keynesian framework. In that framework, personal savings depend upon personal income and the "culturally determined" savings propensities. Public savings, on the other hand, are the difference between governmental tax revenues and governmental consumption expenditures. Business savings correspond to earnings retained by enterprises located within the economy less those earnings repatriated abroad.

Capital formation requires increased total savings. A one-dollar increase in personal taxes, therefore, will reduce personal savings by much less than one dollar. If government consumption doesn't increase, the dollar tax increase will raise public savings by the full dollar. As a result, most traditional analyses recommend an increase in public savings and public investment. Failure to consider the effects of economic incentives leads to the conclusion that tax rates should be increased and public investment expanded.

Savings and employment depend primarily on the after-tax yields savers and workers can expect. Progressive and high tax structures, in conjunction with capital mobility, lead to the plight found in many less developed economies today. To make matters even worse, less developed economies generally have inefficient publicly operated enterprises. A major outlet for public investment has included the acquisition of productive enterprises. In addition, some of these public industries are granted monopoly status while others are subsidized. Private competition is virtually, if not literally, precluded. Along with explicit taxes on work, minimum wage laws and "means" and "needs" tests for the state welfare provide additional disincentives to work.

Adding it all together, for the law-abiding individual it pays little to work. High unemployment, low productivity, widespread tax evasion, and official corruption are prevalent. The Tobin report's recommendations, if implemented, would make matters substantially worse. Savings, employment, and wages would fall because of the onerous additional taxes proposed. In addition, government revenues often decline while mandated spending rises. Pursuit of traditional policy prescriptions, as often as not, raises the specter of bankruptcy.

To encourage economic expansion the first objective should be a reintroduction of basic incentives. Tax rates of all sorts, especially those of a progressive nature, should be reduced sharply. "Means" and "needs" tests as well as minimum wages should be reduced. To the extent possible, publicly operated enterprises should be returned to the private sector.

The Tobin report suggestions are by no means an isolated case in point. Official U.S. policies as well as policies of other developed countries toward the less developed world include a consistent package of policies the effects of which are to destroy what precious few incentives for development exist. Developed nations' policies include a distinct tendency for less developed countries to incur vast amounts of foreign debt obligations by the governments of less developed lands. The purpose of the debts is ostensibly to acquire social capital. These obligations, in due course, require massive debt servicing that forces the less developed countries to impose ever-burdensome taxes on the productive sectors of their economies. Thus, these counterproductive debt-oriented policies lead progressively to indenture, stagnation, and unnatural dependence.

Policies of the developed economies toward the less developed countries also encourage heavy tariffs on imported consumer goods and exorbitant excise taxes on luxuries. Here again, such actions reduce the ability of the productive factors in the less developed economies to acquire the products they desire in exchange for their effort expended. A precise equivalence between product taxes, such as tariffs and excise taxes, and factor taxes, such as the income and payroll taxes, exists. Therefore, tariffs, excise, and sales taxes have the same effect on incentives as do factor taxes. Incentives being retarded, the retraction of effort expended soon follows.

Developed nations also exert pressure on the less developed nations to diversify and increase exports while providing substitutes for and reducing imports. These trade objectives are often stated in terms of improving the less developed country's trade balance or balance of payments. Export diversification and import substitution attempts encouraged by developed economies lead inevitably to production inefficiencies and, as a consequence, retard the efficient use of already scarce resources. Balance of trade and balance of payments policies include capital controls, tariffs, and export subsidies. Specific restrictions on foreign investors are frequently part of an overall development strategy. The licensing of foreign exchange purchases in conjunction with unrealistic exchange rates is also quite prevalent. Each of these policies, in turn, reduces incentives and leads to slower development.

Incentives—Internal

Domestic fiscal and regulatory policies are unquestionably the most cruicial policies impacting on the development process. Governments, however ordained, that provide a framework conducive to personal enrichment commensurate with personal endeavor will eventually experience economic growth. A government framework that constrains or, in the extreme, eliminates the personal gain associated with personal effort will fail to achieve economic progress.

Government spending, be it on income transfers, public works, defense, or state-run enterprises, must meticulously avoid the preemption of equivalent or more efficient private efforts. State monopolies rarely are able to achieve the production efficiencies of private competition. State transfer payments to subsidize inefficient industries, such as export- or import-substitute industries, rarely provide the incentives for these industries to become efficient. Defense, in many cases, is a pure waste of scarce development resources.

Regulations, too, can substantially distort relative prices much as taxes do. Minimum wages, artificial price controls, and elaborate requirements for obtaining permission to carry out some activity are but a few examples. These regulations raise the real costs of doing business and provide a fertile environment for graft, bribery, and other forms of corruption. Merely maintaining an elaborate structure of licensing requirements and other forms of state-controlled privilege-granting does nothing short of placing economic decisions in the hands of people motivated by considerations other than economics. The power to alter what otherwise would be purely economic decisions corrupts the very criteria needed for economic development. To the extent regulations are needed, they should exist at the lowest level feasible and should be made so as to allow as little discretion as possible by representatives of the state.

Taxes, perhaps, are the key to internal incentives. In *Progress and Poverty*, published first in 1879, Henry George summarized the relevant canons of taxation for economic development. These canons of taxation are as appropriate today as they were in times past.[5]

The best tax by which public revenues can be raised is evidently that which will closest conform to the following conditions:
1. That it bear as lightly as possible upon production—so as least to check the increase of the general fund from which taxes must be paid and the community maintained.
2. That it be easily and cheaply collected, and fall as directly as may be upon the ultimate payers—so as to take from the people as little as possible in addition to what it yields the government.
3. That it be certain—so as to give the least opportunity for tyranny or corruption on the part of officials, and the least temptation to

law-breaking and evasion on the part of the taxpayers.

4. That it bear equally—so as to give no citizen an advantage or put any at a disadvantage, as compared with others.

Let us consider what form of taxation best accords with these conditions. Whatever it be, that evidently will be the best mode in which the public revenues can be raised.

Two western hemisphere economies provide vivid illustration of the benefits obtainable by adroit fiscal and regulatory reform. One, Puerto Rico, has produced astounding results within a fully democratic framework while the other, Chile, has proceeded under military rule.

Up until 1976, government intervention in the Puerto Rican economy had been advancing at a rapid pace. From 1947 until 1976 Puerto Rico experienced a massive increase in government intervention in its domestic economy. By way of example, total government expenditures as a share of the island's gross product rose from slightly less than 20 percent in 1947 to something over 45 percent in 1976. Tax rates on taxable personal income also rose quite substantially peaking in 1976 with the highest marginal rate at 87.1 percent. In 1976 taxable income recipients reached the 50 percent tax bracket at $22,000. As a share of total Puerto Rican tax receipts other taxes were substantially larger than personal income taxes.

Private savings as a share of gross product fell throughout the entire period and turned negative in the middle to late 1960s. By 1976 the private savings rate was an incredible –7.5 percent. Even public savings fell in the mid-1970s. In fact, in 1975 Puerto Rico had its first current budget deficit. Unemployment rates, which had been inching up through the mid-1960s on into the early 1970s, rose to over 20 percent by 1976. Even labor force participation rates experienced a dramatic decline. Private investment followed a similar pattern. As a ratio to domestic product, private investment peaked in 1972 at a little over 20 percent and then fell to slightly over 10 percent in 1976.

Perhaps the single most comprehensive measure of the performance of the Puerto Rican economy is the growth rate of real gross domestic product itself. With few exceptions real growth rates ranged between 5 and 10 percent over the period 1947 through 1972. 1973, 1974, 1975, and 1976, however, were far below the historical pattern. In fact, real gross product actually declined in 1975, the sole decline since the 1930s.

In January of 1977 Puerto Rico embarked on an entirely new policy direction. The elections in 1976 were focused on tax rates.[6] Carlos Romero-Barcelo, running on tax rate reductions, unseated the incumbent governor, Hernandez Colon. In 1977 income tax rates were cut 5 percent across the board. In 1978 they were cut another 5 percent and rates for 1979 were reduced an additional 10 percent. Excise taxes and import duties have also been lowered.

Since 1976, the Puerto Rican current deficit has moved strongly into surplus. Unemployment rates have fallen and real output growth has returned back to its historically higher range. Other indicators have not had enough time to show the recovery pattern incumbent in a reinstatement of incentives. Prospects appear good.

For a number of decades up until the mid-1970s, the path of incentive reduction in Chile had been proceeding virtually without respite. In the late 1960s and early 1970s the Fabian pace accelerated, leaving the economy in the midst of economic chaos. In 1973 an entirely new economic order was abruptly instituted.

The economic reforms in Chile included:

1. A substantial liquidation of nationalized companies via auction to private interests.
2. Drastic reductions in tariffs and elimination of foreign exchange controls.
3. A substantial reduction in income tax rates via widening of the income tax brackets.
4. An elimination of investment discrimination along the lines of investor nationality.
5. A complete elimination of all wage and price controls.
6. A substantial reduction in the real value of the liabilities of the central government to foreigners.

The record of performance is clear. Chilean inflation has dropped markedly. Real growth in the past year is the highest it has been in some forty years. Foreign investment is returning and real after tax rates of return are at unprecedentedly high levels.

Equivalent counter-examples are also available for Western Hemisphere economies. Brazil after removing a substantial amount of disincentives in and around 1964 began reimposing them in the early 1970s. The process has continued to the present. Brazil's growth rates have fallen. Peru, Ecuador, and other nations acquired large amounts of foreign indebtedness, necessitating austerity measures leading those nations to their present state of economic deprivation.

Without substantial internal incentives, growth to the extent it occurs will not persist.

Investment and Savings Incentives

From the standpoint of the individual saver or investor, investment is not an end in and of itself. Individuals save and invest in order to consume in the future. Investment is merely the means of transferring current goods earned in the present into future goods. However, impediments occur; anything that reduces the amount of future goods an individual receives for abstaining from consuming current goods will lead to less investment and savings. The primary sources of these impediments are taxes, regulations, and restrictions on the use of resources.

From the standpoint of economic theory there is a precise equivalence between consumption taxes and investment taxes. There exists on the international front another precise equivalence between repatriation taxes or capital repatriation prohibitions and taxes or prohibitions on foreign investment itself. If an investor feels that repatriation of profit or even the return of the capital itself may be impaired in the future, he will reconsider the investment act itself.

In a number of less developed economies, as well as some developed ones, capital repatriation prohibitions have been instituted. The results of these actions have been to drag up the original source of capital. Even in the case of domestic savers and investors, international diversification is a powerful motivating force behind the savings and investing desire. With such options either legally prohibited or expensive due to regulations savings and investment within the economy decline. As a consequence, economic growth declines.

The recent experience of Brazil illustrates this phenomenon. In recent years the tightening of exchange controls and repatriation restrictions have led to slow growth and chronic balance of payments problems. Chile, on the other hand, has experienced a resurgence of investment along with higher growth.

Rapid economic development requires incentives. The incentive for a foreigner to invest in a less developed land is ultimate retrieval of an after-tax income stream. Fears as to the ability to repatriate funds reduces the anticipated ultimate retrieval. Capital controls of all sorts drive a wedge between the investment and the return on that investment. Capital controls reduce growth and economic development. The freer the country is from regulations of this sort the more it can rely on foreign capital in the development process.

Incentives—External

A number of less developed economies can be characterized as having an abundance of labor and a shortage of capital. In some instances land is plentiful yet in others available land is at a premium. Whatever the specifics of the country in question the relative factor endowments tend to differ greatly from those of the rest of the world. International trade tends to provide markets for products intensive in the services of the abundant factors and simultaneously provides relatively less expensive products that require large amounts of the services of factors that are scarce in the less developed economy. As such, trade raises wages and increases both the quantity and the spectrum of goods available to the less developed economy.

Trade barriers erected in an effort to balance a country's trade balance or to protect a country's "infant" industry have a number of interesting effects. The first and most important implication is that tariffs imposed on imports have a precise equivalence with taxes on exports. This theorem is referred to as the Lerner symmetry theorem. The meaning of the theorem in this context is quite clear. There is no reason to believe a priori that tariffs will improve a country's trade balance.

People export products for reasons other than altruism and making foreigners happy. Exports represent the acquisition of the wherewithal to acquire imports. The sole purpose of exports is to import. Any act that reduces the amount of imports obtainable from a given amount of exports will in and of itself reduce exports. A tariff policy, therefore, will reduce the volume of both exports and imports and will have little, if any, effect on the overall trade balance. Tariffs will, however, have a marked effect on the efficiency of trade and economic growth. Tariffs will reduce the exchange value of domestically produced products. As such, incentives will be lowered, work effort will be retarded, and resources will be less efficiently allocated. Domestic industries, protected by tariff walls, will experience less competition and will become less efficient.

An overall development program should include large reductions in tariff and nontariff barriers. Only by reducing international distortions can an economy truly benefit from the rest of the world. Without freer trade the development process becomes more burdensome.

Income Distribution versus Growth

A widely misunderstood theme inherent in basic economics is that economic policies oriented toward income growth tend also to be those policies that relieve poverty in subsectors of the economy. Income growth and social and economic equity are highly compatible. They are by no means inimical.

A fundamental tenet of basic economics is that the burden of a tax is not the same as the incidence of a tax. Stated alternatively, the incomes or products upon which taxes are placed are by no means necessarily the same ones which bear the burden of that tax.

In general, the burden of a tax depends upon the elasticity of supply of the factor of production and the elasticity of demand for that factor. The less elastic the supply and the more elastic the demand the greater will be the burden borne by that factor irrespective of the precise incidence. Thus, taxes on luxuries and progressive income taxes may well reduce the after-tax wages of low income earners and the consumers of necessities.

In general, tax and incentive structures that lead to rapid economic growth are those same tax and incentive structures that benefit the poor and the unemployed the most. Income growth and economic development go hand in hand. Policies designed to redistribute existing income generally have little effect on the distribution of income and, in turn, reduce the total amount of income.

Notes

1. Will and Ariel Durant, *The Lessons of History* (New York: Simon and Schuster, 1968), p. 54.

2. Richard R. Nelson, T. Paul Schultz, and Robert L. Slighton, *Structural Change in a Developing Economy—Colombia's Problems and Prospects* (Princeton, New Jersey: Princeton University Press, 1971).

3. Harvey Leibestein, *Economic Backwardness and Economic Growth* (New York: John Wiley & Sons, 1957).

4. Report to the governor by the Committee to Study Puerto Rico's Finances, chaired by Professor James Tobin, December 11, 1975.

5. Henry George, *Progress and Poverty* (first published 1879; New York: Robert Schalkenbach Foundation, 1939).

6. More specifically, the issue at hand was the 5 percent tax surcharge instituted in 1974. In the local Spanish vernacular, this surcharge was referred to as *la vampirita* ("the little vampire"); see Jude Wanniski, *The Way the World Works* (New York: Basic Books, 1978).

7
Brazil's Debt-Burdened Recession: Consequences of Short-Term Difficulties or of Structures of Production and Consumption?

W. Ladd Hollist

Brazil's impressive rate of growth in real gross national product has attracted a widening circle of admirers. Although not entirely unprecedented in Brazil's history, such a growth record following a period of slow growth, between 1 and 4 percent from 1959 to 1965, is striking. Many praise the policies of post-1964 military regimes as the primary determinants of Brazil's "success." However, the "economic miracle" of average annual growth rates around 10 percent from 1968 to 1973 declined to 4 percent or less in 1975 and 1976. Brazilian financiers and government officials, hardly distinguishable in many contexts, blame external, short-term difficulties, particularly the oil-crisis induced increase in oil, lubricant, and fertilizer import bills. Financing current account deficits, associated with both goods and service accounts, has resulted in the depletion of international reserves and the rapid buildup of international debt.

Since 1974, the slowing growth rates, the more than doubling of international debt, the worsening inequities in income distribution, renewed increases in inflation, and increased social repression have brought the "Brazilian development model" into question. Some see these reversals as short-term consequences of the 1974 global recession, others see them as inevitable results of inappropriate production and exchange structures worsened by the deepening of deficit-financed industrialization which emphasized the production of consumer durables (automobiles, refrigerators, televisions, etc.).

This analysis explores the following:

1. Although Brazilian policymakers have blamed the vagaries of the external market for recent difficulties, can these factors be considered independently of domestic economic and social structures?[1]
2. Industrialization-based development, emphasizing heavy machinery and equipment and the consumer durable sector, has superseded the development of consumer non-durables (food, clothes, etc.), which are more significant in the consumer basket of at least 70 percent of the Brazilian population. Has the "economic miracle" created worsening social conditions for the majority of Brazilians?
3. Are claims that Brazil's emergence as a "world power" has lessened its dependence and external vulnerability over-touted?[2] Have certain types of dependence merely given way to increased international market, monetary, and domestic production dependence?
4. Finally, has Brazil's deficit-financed development, with its purposeful creation of a resource gap where imports consistently exceed exports, been wise? Will the deepening of this debt cycle, by extending further public and private loans which are increasingly used to service already outstanding debts, bring undesirable long-term effects associated with short-term problem solving? Does current internationalization of capital and development financing policies produce aggregate growth of an increasingly concentrated national product, but fail to eradicate poverty and improve the quality of life?

1. Brazil's Production Profile

Since 1964, Brazilian economic policy has been oriented toward aggregate growth of production. To achieve this objective, Brazil has argued that in the short run it would be necessary to allow imports to exceed exports. This resource gap would be offset by attracting external investment and incurring international public and private debt. As Table 1 suggests, to a marked extent this objective has been realized for the years 1968 through 1974. If the increasing rates of growth of the late 1960s and early 1970s were primarily a function of govern-

Table 1
Brazil's Real Output Growth Rates by Major Sector

Year	Gross Domestic Product Percentage	Agriculture Percentage	Industry Percentage
1965	2.7	13.8	-4.7
1966	5.1	-3.1	11.7
1967	4.8	5.7	3.0
1968	9.3	1.4	15.5
1969	9.0	6.0	10.8
1970	9.5	5.6	11.1
1971	11.3	11.4	11.2
1972	10.4	4.5	13.8
1973	11.4	3.5	15.0
1974	9.6	8.5	8.2
1975	4.0	3.4	4.2
1976	3.8[a]	n.a.	n.a.

Source: Pedro S. Malan and Regis Bonelli, "The Brazilian Economy in the Seventies: Old and New Developments," World Development, 5:1&2, January/February 1977, p. 36.

[a]Estimate based on Malan and Bonelli's observations.

mental management of the economy—including astute responses to international conditions—then why does the trend reverse itself in 1974? Explanations can be grouped into two categories: domestic production structure and international context factors.

A Period of Expansion: 1968-1973

During the 1950s, Brazilian utilization of manufacturing capacity hovered around 80 percent. Although Kubitschek's push for industrialization for export and import substitution during the late 1950s and early 1960s produced even greater utilization, by 1965, capacity utilization was down to 76 percent. As a result, the growth in production output from 1968 to 1973 was a comparatively "easy" growth, as underutilized capacities were pressed into use. However, Malan and Bonelli estimate that, by 1973 and through 1974, production capacity was completely utilized.[3] The fortuitous existence of unused capacity permitted a major increase in growth.

Malan and Bonelli also identify a second internal factor affecting increases in output.

The policy of expanding credit for the acquisition of durable consumer goods, and the simultaneous enlargement of private [family]
indebtedness due to the purchase of such goods . . . [increased demand for economic output] . . . . As a result between between 1966
and 1974 the output of durable consumer goods expanded at an
average growth rate of nearly 21% per year, while the total manufacturing figure reached 12.1% yearly.[4]

This expansion of the consumer durables sector, a sector largely
aimed at consumer demand of upper classes, sparked overall
production-output expansion at previously unattained rates.
Similar emphasis on luxury consumption, production, and imports abounded prior to the more socially oriented production
policies of the Quadros and Goulart regimes (1960-1964).

These domestic factors stimulated aggregate growth in conjunction with policies of import substitution and expansion of
manufactures via external inputs. After the military seized
power in 1964, the Brazilian economy was reopened to widespread, foreign direct investment. Foreign investment increased
from 18.9 percent of total investment in the manufacturing
sector in 1965 to 28.6 percent in 1975.[5] Attracting external
capital required the import of production processes oriented
toward high-technology, capital-intensive outputs and also
forced the adoption of production systems capable of generating surplus rents. These processes and systems were oriented
toward production for a global market which had only a relatively small complementary market within Brazil. Consequently, there emerged a tendency toward production oriented for
consumption by less than a quarter of the Brazilian population.

External factors also played a role in this growth spurt, but
not necessarily the principal role. Fortuitous, temporary international conditions existed from 1966 through 1973. The postwar expansion of the main industrial societies generated surplus
rents as well as, by the mid-1960s, abundant dollar-denominated liquidity outside of the United States. Particularly after
1969, private banks became eager to extend medium-term loans
to richer developing nations such as Brazil. Brazil's explicit
intention of engaging in deficit-financed development was
fueled by the availability of relatively easy global credit. In
addition, the resurgence of Western economies stimulated inter-

national trade, and Brazil's new role as an exporter of manufactured goods fortunately occurred during this period of expanding world markets. Such favorable international conditions led Brazil's ministers to proclaim trade as "the engine of growth."

A Period of Economic Recession: 1974-

Surprisingly, until the coming of the oil crisis and global recession in 1974, policymakers forgot that these favorable global conditions, when viewed in the light of long-term economic cycles, were likely to be temporary. Although the 1974 recession hurt virtually every industrialized economy, the downturn was particularly devastating for Brazil, *given its unbalanced domestic production system.*

True, increased energy-import bills hurt Brazil's balance of payments on current account, but this was not Brazil's primary difficulty. Brazil also was forced to pay greater prices for imported, industrial heavy equipment.[6] The major industrial countries quickly passed some of their increased oil cost on to foreign consumers of their industrial equipment by raising the prices of their manufactured products. Prices of consumer durables imported from abroad also were increased. Since Brazil's new industrial exports were concentrated in only a few sectors, its economy proved particularly susceptible to imported oil and manufactures price increases and was far less able to transfer higher prices on to consumers of Brazilian exports, exports already faltering in world demand.

Interestingly, during this recession some tremendous drops in domestic demand for consumer durables occurred. From 1967 through 1973, production of these goods grew at an average rate of almost 24 percent annually; their production grew at an estimated rate of only 3 percent in 1975.[7] The domestic production system simply could not bear the strain of world recession, primarily because its growth sectors had been so narrowly focused for the market basket of about 20 percent of the population.

Yet, despite these major strains on Brazil's economy, the root difficulty perhaps may be found in the failure of earlier growth efforts to stimulate expanded production capacity in excess of consumption. "From 1967 through 1973 the rate of capital accumulation was high, domestic production of capital goods rose by an impressive 20.5% a year on the average between 1967 and 1973, but simultaneously high rates of growth in consumption mainly by the upper classes, largely offset these gains."[8] By 1973, there was no more slack in Brazil's production capacity and the possibility for easy growth via improved production utilization was gone. Yet consumer consumption practices remained skewed, placing greater and greater strains on Brazil's ability to generate more and more domestically produced capital goods.

Malan and Bonelli summarize a major difficulty of this kind of "internationalized capital" domestic production structure. "This conjunction of high investment effort with high propensity to consume was only made viable through a policy of rapidly expanding international indebtedness. . . . Brazilian total foreign debt, therefore, increased almost four-fold" from $3.3 billion in 1967 to $12.6 billion in 1973.[9] By the end of 1977, Brazil's foreign debt reached $31.5 billion, $26.5 billion of which came from private sources.[10] Moreover, Brazil had the highest debt to U.S. banks of any developing country, almost $12 billion at the end of 1977.[11] Compounding this expanded debt burden was the fact that a greater and greater share of the debt was held as private credits, rising from 20 percent in 1967, to 62 percent in 1973, to about 85 percent at the end of 1977.[12]

Financing these increased current account and service deficits via further borrowing, forced upon Brazil by a worsening production output picture no longer capable of offsetting much of the trade deficit, also put pressure on the domestic monetary system. Money supply necessarily expanded more rapidly than rates of production output, resulting in a worsening inflation rate. Whereas rates of inflation averaged some 20 percent during the late 1960s and early 1970s, by 1974-1976, inflation was increasing by 30 to 35 percent annually.[13]

Apparently, the major reason the 1974 global recession struck Brazil so severely was its asymmetrical production structure oriented toward a narrow domestic consumption market, and the stagnation of its previously flourishing trade market which was unable to shift its emphases from weak sectors to relatively strong sectors. Moreover, attempts at improving Brazil's export sector to offset the increased post-oil-price-rise deficit have been impeded by the large and rapidly expanding foreign debt. To increase the attractiveness of Brazilian exports by lessening their prices via a policy of currency devaluation has been severely constrained by the increased debt burden that such a policy necessarily entails. Already debt servicing annually requires more than 40 percent of foreign exchange earnings on current account.[14] Indeed, Brazil's economic miracle may be faltering precisely because its domestic production structure can ill adapt to a worsening international context.

2. Deficit-Financed Industrialization: Development for Whom?

Having considerd the significance of the domestic production structure in determining the ups and downs of Brazilian aggregate growth, we turn now to the broader question of development. The Brazilian government has conceded that Brazilian economic growth would incur "social costs" but also has declared that, if endured for a time, the "trickle down" of growth successes would greatly improve the living standard of the entire population. Yet as late as 1974, Brazilian President Geisel admitted that, although the Brazilian economy was flourishing, the people were not.

To some, the social failures of Brazilian economic policies are really little more than the result of impatience, and they contend that the economic strategy eventually will bear fruits for all people. This contention had some support until the 1974 reversals of economic growth rates. However, this author believes that the social failings are not temporary, even if Brazil continues to grow, but will remain unless the production structure is drastically modified. Moreover, the chances of modifying this production structure are lessened as Brazil pursues a production system based more and more on international capital and continued deficit financing. The resulting increased debt reinforces the linkage of the production system to international capital as the capability to service the debt increasingly requires continued inflows of international capital via export earnings, foreign investment, or continued foreign loans. As Brazil's production and financial systems become more and more dependent upon international capital and financial flows, the chances for altering the production system in favor of the majority of the people are necessarily worsened.

These claims can be substantiated by reviewing the production system as it evolved during the period of rapid economic growth. Clearly, the first indication that Brazil's post-1964 production system was oriented toward the few rather than the many was the rapid expansion of the production of consumer durables. As noted earlier, average annual growth rates in this sector approached 24 percent, while growth in agriculture averaged 5.5 percent.[15] This figure takes on added meaning since per-capita food production actually may have declined during the decade of rapid economic growth in Brazil ending in 1974.[16] One basis for making this comparison is represented in Table 2. The data indicate that the food index increased by 13.3 percent from 1966 to 1974, whereas the manufactures index increased by 124.3 percent from 1966 to 1973. The extreme difference suggests that the Brazilian food sector has

Table 2
Indexes of Brazil's Per Capita Production in Food and Manufactures: 1962-1974

Year[a]	Index of Per Capita Food Production	Index of Per Capita Industrial Manufactures Production
1962	98	51
1963	--	61
1964	95	--
1965	109	--
1966	98	--
1967	102	70
1968	101	81
1969	104	90
1970	105	111
1971	106	127
1972	109	147
1973	104	157
1974	111	---

Source: James W. Wilkie and Peter Reich (eds.), Statistical Abstract of Latin America, UCLA Latin American Center Publications, Vol. 18 (1977). Table 206, p. 41 and Table 207, p. 42.

[a]Missing data are missing in original source.

been the stepchild of Brazil's industrial development efforts.

The worsening food supply is further highlighted by production records of beans and rice, the stable foodstuffs of most Brazilians. From 1970 through 1974, a scant five years, per-capita production of beans declined 12.2 percent while per-capita production of rice declined by 19.2 percent.[17] Contrast this with a 360 percent increase in the production of passenger cars during the 1960s, a trend that has probably accelerated through 1974.[18]

Finally, as an indication of the indirect taxation of food and other consumer nondurables to support the industrial capital and consumer durable product expansion, consider the changes in constant value added for these sectors. The value added for the consumer nondurable sector has declined from 51 percent of the total in 1959 to 17 percent in 1975, while the percentages of value added for consumer durables and for capital goods have doubled or nearly doubled. The percentage of value added for consumer durables increased from 5.1 percent in 1959 to 10.5 percent in 1975. The comparable values for capital goods are 10.6 percent and 18.4 percent.[19] Indeed, growth has been imbalanced in favor of concentrated aggregate growth and to the disadvantage of the majority of the people.

Census data from 1970, represented in Table 3, indicate that as a function of this asymmetrical economic system, income distribution has worsened for the lower classes, with a clear improvement for the top 5 percent of the population. This mal-distributed income, coupled with inflation which caused the

Table 3
Changes in Brazil's Income Distribution

	Percentage of Total Income		Per Capita Income in U.S. Dollars	
	1960	1970	1960	1970
Lowest 40 Percent	11.2	9.0	84	90
Next 40 Percent	34.3	27.8	257	278
Next 15 Percent	27.0	27.0	540	720
Top 5 Percent	27.4	36.3	1645	2940

Source: Werner Baer, "The Brazilian Growth and Development Experience: 1964-1975," in Brazil in the Seventies, ed.Riordan Roett (Washington: American Enterprise Institute for Public Policy Research, 1976), p. 52.

consumer price index to explode from 55.0 in 1967 to 260.0 in 1975, has worsened the standard of living for all but the upper 20 percent of the Brazilian population.[20] Summarizing the condition of the lower classes, Brady Tyson writes:

> In 1971 it took a worker on minimum salary 113 hours and 26 minutes to earn sufficient buying power to buy his own minimum diet for a month, as determined by the official (WHO) [World Health Organization] standards of minimum nutrition, whereas in 1965 it took a worker on minimum salary only 87 hours and 20 minutes to do the same. . . . Brazil is creating a Scandinavian-size consumer economy superimposed on an Indonesian-size pauperized mass.[21]

This type of concentrated production system creates further ill effects on long-term economic growth. A production system oriented primarily to a narrow domestic market, with a widening dependence on purchases of its products on the international market, is particularly subject to global economic reversals. Unless greater external economies of production can be realized within Brazil, involving a greater proportion of the total population, overall aggregate growth rates will decline further. This is the case since Brazil's production capacity is now near 100 percent utilization and Brazil's international economic position will likely weaken as debt servicing becomes a greater burden. Brazil's capability to attract foreign resources via direct investment and deficit financing may well decline.

Hope for such an enlightened policy in Brazil came with Geisel's declaration in early 1974 of forthcoming "decompression," defined as "a promise that tension would be relaxed in all areas of Brazilian society as the military led revolution matured."[22] At the same time, Minister of Trade and Industry Serevo Gomes urged the government to turn attention to the domestic market, limiting the role of foreign corporations. In what appeared to be a recognition of the plight of the Brazilian masses, but what was probably motivated by the realization that economic growth could not continue as before unless the domestic market were expanded, Gomes further declared, "Social equality is more important than growth."[23] A prominent industrialist concurred that there could be "no security in the country while there exists hunger, despair, and anguish. . . . [I] sn't it possible to give the worker simple justice, restoring his real wage?"[24]

However, the tenuous commitment to these types of policy became clear as the oil crisis and worsening economic conditions threatened the gains of Brazil's new industrial upper class. These deteriorating economic conditions were coupled with some long-repressed expressions of social violence. In July 1975, low-income train passengers smashed nine train stations and stoned riot police.[25] Given the increasing frequency of these types of domestic political events, and the evident popularity of the opposition Movimento Democrático Brasileiro (MDB) party, Geisel entered upon retrenchment. In quick succession, Geisel told congress that much of the "decompression" talk was rumor. MDB leaders began to be arrested in increasing numbers so that full political repression was in evidence by September 1975. Finally, the "bombshell burst when the President addressed a national television audience on October 9, revealing a totally new policy toward foreign oil firms":

1. 25 percent increase in domestic petroleum prices
2. 15 percent cut in imports for the public sector
3. new fiscal incentives for exporters
4. permission for Petrobras . . . to contract non-Brazilian oil companies to search for oil and to develop existing offshore fields
5. media were forbidden to discuss oil contracts.[26]

The return to emphasis on international capital, even in such a vital sector as energy exploration and development, doomed Gomes's hopes of limiting transnational enterprise activities in Brazil and of concentrating on producing goods for a wider domestic consumer market. The return to emphasis on production for export was also clearly foretold. Indeed, it appears that the current political, economic, and social structure, a structure based on long-term trends reinforced by the post-1964 crusade for rapid economic growth, virtually precludes the possibility of shifting the production gains from a near-total emphasis on serving the demands of the few to an extended concern for the many. Although this structure is indigenous to Brazil, it is reinforced and supported by a widening dependence of the Brazilian economy on the international market.

3. Brazil's Shifting, Deepening External Vulnerability

Although lessening the impact of his declaration by multiple caveats, Robert Packenham has recently concluded that national dependence in post-1964 Brazil has actually declined.[27] Of five indicators selected to measure dependence, Packenham concludes that four have evidenced declines.[28] Although Packenham may be correct in suggesting that certain features of national dependence may be waning, others seem to be heightening. A shift in international dependence, as well as a deepening of certain key components of external vulnerability, seem to be taking place. Packenham does conclude that external penetration of Brazilian resources and production capacities has increased. Agreed, but this type of dependency has become so critically important and so efficiently employed that Brazil's overall external vulnerability has increased, even if Packenham is correct in arguing that other facets of national dependence have declined.

For purposes of elaboration, consider three interrelated types of external penetration: production dependence, market dependence, and finance dependence. Production dependence is here defined as the degree to which production decisions are conditioned by reliance on external sources of capital. The expanding role of foreign capital is shown by the increase of foreign investment from 18.9 percent of total investment in Brazilian manufacturing activities in 1965 to 28.6 percent in 1976.[29] Moreover, foreign capital investments have reinforced the trend toward import substitution industrialization which has produced significant increases in aggregate growth. Further investments by foreigners are likely to continue in this sector; breaking away from this emphasis will likely prove difficult.

Market dependence is probably an even more intense factor of external vulnerability. Given Brazil's production system emphasis, reinforced by foreign investors' involvements, declines in global demand schedules have had a devastating impact on the attractiveness of Brazilian exports. The oil crisis, for example, was highly debilitating to Brazil since major industrial nations passed on some of their increased costs in higher prices for their export products. Since Brazil's production system requires imports of the major industrial country products for continued expansion of its industrial efforts, and since Brazil's exports have become less attractive as major nations seek to reduce imports to offset the rising cost of oil imports, Brazil has been severely hampered by worsening export and import market conditions. Many of these difficulties are rooted in the dilemma that Brazil's production output is aimed at a narrow domestic market and at an expanding external market. External market demand constrictions, which might in some countries be offset by greater domestic sales, are not readily absorbed via increased domestic consumption in Brazil. Recently, Brazil's gross national product depended on trade for 24 percent of its total.[30] Although this figure has declined appreciably since World War II, the growth sectors of Brazil's economy are still overly reliant on external markets.

It is important to note, however, that Brazil has achieved some success since 1964 in creating a more-diversified product mix. Volatile prices in a particular product market are less devastating than they once were, since other products may well be experiencing more-favorable market conditions. Nevertheless, since so much of Brazil's "new" industrialization has been associated with oil-related products such as automobiles, fertilizer, and heavy equipment, the energy crisis has had a marked impact. And, since these industries have been in "growth" sectors, the impact on Brazil's production output has been severe.

Finance dependence, potentially the most-limiting type of external vulnerability, has gone relatively unrecognized until recently. Dependency authors have historically emphasized trade (market) dependence or investment dependence. However, Brazil's purposeful incurrence of debt to fund its "resource gap" has made it vulnerable to decisions outside its control. About 85 percent of Brazil's $31.5 billion external debt at the end of 1977 was privately held. As early as October 1973, one financial analyst warned that "Brazil's ability to match [its] growing debt burden by export earnings is expected to decline."[31] Brazil's enormous and expanding foreign debt is likely to increase its future vulnerability to financial decisions by bankers outside Brazilian political control. To merely service existing debt now requires 41 percent of Brazil's annual export earnings, forcing Brazil to incur even greater debt obligations. To continue past growth patterns, Brazil must rely on foreign credits. This is particularly true in the light of recent slowing in capital transfers to Brazil in the form of foreign direct and portfolio investments. Compounding this difficulty, public lending has also been increasingly limited, again causing Brazil to turn to the more stringent private market.

If, as some believe, Brazil's foreign debt is dangerously high,[32] are debt renegotiations in the offing? If debt renegotiations were necessary, they would undoubtedly be more difficult and complex than Brazil's official debt rescheduling exercises of 1961 and 1964.[33] Given the inreased proportion of debt held by private entities, which prefer to avoid formal reschedulings and refinancings, the probability of resorting to debt renegotiations seems small. Moreover, since Brazil must continue to attract foreign loans and since private banks have funds they wish to lend, Brazil is unlikely to even contemplate debt renegotiations, a posture it has assumed repeatedly of late.

Finance dependence is also closely linked to production and market dependence. If Brazil cannot attract credits, then its present production structure cannot expand as rapidly as national goals would suggest as desirable. Moreover, if Brazil wants to devalue its currency to increase export earnings, then it must carefully consider the impact this will have on its foreign debt, which is increasingly denominated in other currencies.

In summary, although Brazil may have more production capacity now than in 1964, and may have greater entrepreneurial experience than it previously enjoyed,[34] important impediments remain that curtail Brazil's options for controlling its own economy.

4. Summary and Conclusion:
Questioning Brazil's "Deficit-Financed Development"

Suppose the Brazilian economic "miracle" were evaluated in terms of criteria promoted by the International Labor Organization—namely the provision of basic human needs for all.[35] Virtually no analyst would claim that Brazil has done as well in terms of these criteria as might reasonably have been expected given its high growth rate. Undoubtedly, the official response would be that short-term savings, necessarily entailing sacrifice, must precede improvements of goods and services. Eventually, growth will benefit all Brazilians. If fault is to be laid anywhere for the reversal of Brazil's growth rates, the argument continues, then the vagaries of the international arena in which Brazil must compete with overwhelmingly stronger economies must be blamed. The situation will improve when global equity emerges in world exchanges. Brazil then will return to concerns of equity, and social policies will increase.

Yet, Brazil's social performance, even in times of high production output, was weak at best and perhaps little more than a political ploy to diffuse regime opposition. Of programs aimed at improving wage earners' living standards, Skidmore writes:

> Relatively minor gestures toward social welfare (which is how I would define the net redistribution effects of such programs as the Programma de Integracão Social [PIS] and the small increase in real wages resulting from the minimum wage decision of 1975) can be made with little impact on overall development strategy. In practice, the much publicized PIS-type programs will probably turn out to be little more than new means of generating forced savings to finance public sector investment. In sum, over the next five years it seems unlikely that the Brazilian government will choose to sacrifice, or feel itself forced to sacrifice, growth for social welfare.[36]

Although Skidmore is undoubtedly correct, there remains the lingering implication that, if the Brazilian government chose to improve the lot of the masses, policies of reform would be available to it that would leave the present production structure largely unmodified. Our analysis leads to quite a contrary conclusion.

Impediments to socially oriented policies and production practices are endemic. The growth sectors of the Brazilian production system have long been those oriented toward production for a narrow domestic consumer market and a widening international market. Over time, Brazil's capacity to supply goods for these markets has declined. Previously unutilized production capacities have now been pressed into action, while extremely large increases in consumption by this narrow market have consumed much of the surpluses which could have been reinvested in production. Consequently, further advances in production will require acquisition of surplus rents through infusions of foreign capital and loans. In addition, Brazilian society will be forced to provide even greater savings than previously exacted. *It is very unlikely that in periods when production capacity is limited that resources will be diverted into the provision of production capacity for sectors more oriented toward domestic consumption by the majority of Brazilians.* The transfer of gains in present growth to sectors oriented toward domestic consumption is further impeded by increased debt-service burdens which require foreign exchange earnings, earnings that come via exports of current growth-sector products, and a diminishing demand for Brazilian exports as previously high-consuming importers limit their imports to offset worsening balance-of-payments problems.

Consequently, transfers of production outputs to sectors more significant to mass consumption is increasingly doubtful. The structure of domestic production and the existing structural linkages with markets for international goods and services and with foreign capital and loan finance markets needed for further expansion of existing growth sectors impede such transfers. Short of altering the entire production system, the majority of Brazilians can expect little improvement in their standard of living. Particularly hard hit are persons newly attracted to the monetary economy who, once they immigrate to urban areas, find that this economy ill provides for their wants.

In sum, if any major industrial nation is indeed concerned with the provision of basic human needs for all, not the furtherance of luxury consumption for the few, then policies of extending surplus rents via foreign loans and capital exports perhaps should be challenged. However, the national pursuit of self-interest, which lies at the root of such "internationalization of capital" policies, must be vanquished before progress will become likely.

Notes

1. Structures are simply defined as relationships having persisted over relatively long periods of time, generally being less susceptible to change than day-to-day alterations via social policies.

2. External vulnerability or vulnerability has multifaceted connotations that are more fully discussed later in this chapter. However, it is important to note here that claims of lessening dependence may actually be correct in terms of reductions of certain kinds of dependence, but are likely better understood if they are considered shifts in the elements of enduring relationships. See Robert A. Packenham, "Trends in Brazilian National Dependency since 1968," in *Brazil in the Seventies*, ed. Riordan Roett (Washington, D.C.: American Enterprise Institute for Public Policy Research, 1976), pp. 89-116.

3. Pedro S. Malan and Regis Bonelli, "The Brazilian Economy in the Seventies: Old and New Developments," *World Development* 5:1/2, January/February 1977, p. 29.

4. Ibid., p. 22.

5. Ibid., p. 34.

6. Ibid., p. 26.

7. Ibid., p. 27.

8. Ibid., p. 26.

9. Ibid., p. 24.

10. Figures cited in Brian G. Crowe, "International Public Lending and American Policy," chap. 2 in this volume.

11. Federal Reserve Board, Comptroller of the Currency, and the Federal Deposit Insurance Corporation, "Country Exposure Lending Survey," (Washington, D.C., June 8, 1978).

12. Malan and Bonelli, "The Brazilian Economy," p. 24; Brian G. Crowe, "International Public Lending."

13. Robert M. Levine, "Brazil: The Aftermath of 'Decompression,'" *Current History* 70:413, February 1976, p. 54.

14. A brief consideration of difficulties surrounding Brazil's servicing its foreign debt is found in William R. Cline, "Brazil's Emerging International Economic Role," in Roett, *Brazil in the Seventies*, pp. 70-75.

15. Average annual agricultural growth rate calculated from data in Table 1.

16. Fernando Henrique Cardosa, "Associated-Dependent Development: Theoretical and Practical Implications," in *Authoritarian Brazil*, ed. Alfred Stepan (New Haven: Yale University Press, 1973), pp. 149-50.

17. These figures were calculated on the basis of data in James W.

188   W. Ladd Hollist

Wilkie and Peter Reich, eds., *Statistical Abstract of Latin America*, UCLA
Latin American Center Publications, Vol. 18 (Los Angeles: UCLA, 1977),
Table 1507, p. 238.

18. Ibid., Table 210, p. 44.

19. Malan and Bonelli, "The Brazilian Economy," p. 39.

20. In considering the standard of living of the majority of Brazilians,
we would do well to consider the governmental provision of certain valued
services. However, the record of the Brazilian post-1964 government has
been less than laudatory. Public health expenditure per inhabitant in 1972
was $1.33 (Wilkie and Reich, *Statistical Abstract*, Table 2303, p. 319).
This figure, with the exception of expenditures in Ecuador and Peru, is
the lowest in Latin America. Venezuela spends $42.92 per inhabitant,
Chile spends $22.12. Moreover, Brazil's record in providing educational
opportunities, though often lauded, is also mixed. Although enrollments
have increased, the increases are disproportionately distributed in favor of
the few, upper-class clients. For example, while the percentage change in
enrollment at the primary level was 71.3 percent, the increase at the university level was 486.6 percent (Wilkie and Reich, *Statistical Abstract*,
Table 1003, p. 132). Education seems increasingly geared to the provision
of technical skills needed by a small proportion of the working class to
produce industrial products. This explicit policy is elaborated in the
annual report of Secretaria-Geral do Conselho de Desenvolvimento Social,
Julho a dezembro, de 1975, pp. 57-69.

21. Brady Tyson, "Brazil: Nine Years of Military Tutelage," *World
View*, July 1973, pp. 33-34.

22. Levine, "Brazil: The Aftermath of 'Decompression,' " p. 53.

23. Ibid.

24. Ibid.

25. *Latin America*, July 25, 1975, p. 230.

26. Levine, "Brazil: The Aftermath of 'Decompression,' " p. 55.

27. Packenham, "Trends in Brazilian National Dependency," pp.
110-15.

28. Ibid., p. 110.

29. Malan and Bonelli, "The Brazilian Economy," p. 34.

30. This estimate is based on data from the Ministry of External Relations, *Brazil: Resources and Possibilities*, 1976, pp. 241-43.

31. O'Shaughnesy, "Brazil's Foreign Debt . . . in 1980 Could Increase
by 800 Percent," *Financial Times*, October 10, 1973, as cited in Philip
A. Wellons, *Borrowing by Developing Countries on the Eurocurrency Market* (Paris: OECD, 1977), p. 102.

32. Roett, *Brazil in the Seventies*.

33. United Nations Conference on Trade and Development, Secretariat,

Debt Problems of Developing Countries (New York: UNCTAD, 1972), pp. 19-26.

34. Packenham, "Trends in Brazilian National Dependency," pp. 93-94, 102-3.

35. International Labor Office, *Employment Growth and Basic Needs: A One-World Problem* (New York: Praeger Publishers, 1977).

36. Thomas E. Skidmore, "Brazil's Changing Role in the International System: Implications for U.S. Policy," in Roett, *Brazil in the Seventies*, p. 14.

8
Political Economy
of International Debt:
The Dynamics of Financial Capital

R. Peter DeWitt
James F. Petras

As Marx brilliantly observed, one of the central features in the development of the capitalist system has been the growing tendency toward greater concentration and centralization of capital. Today, that phenomenon has been extended on a world scale, increasingly involving all nations, regions, and productive systems. The clearest recent evidence of this process of Western-centered accumulation has been the growth of multinational corporations and commercial enterprises and, since the 1960s, multinational banking. In the earlier phases of overseas expansion, the growth of industrial and commercial capital was facilitated by public loans which were, in large part, export subsidies for Western manufacturers and instruments for financing international corporate investments. The cumulative consequences of externally oriented development were to heighten dependence. Unequal terms of exchange, fluctuating prices, and massive transfers of earnings created severe balance-of-payments problems in the periphery, most of which preceded the so-called oil crisis, which merely exacerbated the problem. The growth of long-term, large-scale movements of finance capital thus must be seen as part of a larger picture of externally controlled industrial and commercial investments linked to public finance; the debt crisis is only one aspect of a larger crisis of world capitalist development.

During the last decade and a half, major banks have become increasingly multinational. The U.S. banks, which followed the American corporations abroad, accounted for the lion's share of this expansion, establishing a complex global network of

191

branches, subsidiaries, and other offshore affiliates. In 1960, eight U.S. banks had branches abroad with assets of $3.5 billion; by mid-1976, over one hundred twenty U.S. banks maintained foreign branches with assets of $181 billion.[1] A recent study by Andrew Beveridge and Philip Wellons underscores the extent of U.S. commercial bank activity abroad, noting that in 1975 the Eurocurrency market for developing countries was dominated by two North American nations, the United States (44 percent) and Canada (18 percent). Indeed, they found that the Bank of America alone was involved in 42 percent of all loans in 1975.[2] Similarly, a 1977 study by the Subcommittee on Foreign Economic Policy of the Senate Committee on Foreign Relations noted that financing in private capital markets is not only concentrated in a few countries but also in a few, large multinational banks. For instance, 66 percent of all non-OPEC private bank debt is owed to U.S. banks. Furthermore, a survey by the Subcommittee on Multinational Corporations indicates that two-thirds of all U.S. private bank lending to twenty-five selected countries was done by six banks.[3]

The growth of private bank lending by U.S. banks has been particularly precipitous since the credit crunch, caused by the now sixfold increase in the price of petroleum, created a dramatic demand for loans, especially to non-oil-exporting less developed countries. The amount of international debt extended by U.S. multinational banks to non–oil-exporting LDCs by the end of 1977 equaled some $91 billion, over half of the outstanding external debt of these countries.[4] This very substantial debt was supplemented by large amounts of long-term public debt. Indeed, it is estimated that international debt has been expanding at a rate of 20 to 25 percent a year since the oil crisis in 1973.[5]

International lending has proved a bonanza for the largest U.S. banks. Foreign earnings of thirteen of the largest of these banks rose from $177 million in 1970 to $885 million in 1976. Domestic earnings of these same banks only increased from $884 million in 1970 to $908 million in 1976. Thus, for these large banks, international operations produced over 95 percent of the increase in total earnings during the six-year period.[6] Figure 1 compares international earnings to domestic earnings for each of the thirteen banks for 1972 and 1976. As a group,

Figure 1
Total, International and Domestic Earnings
of 13 Large U.S. Banks for 1972 and 1976

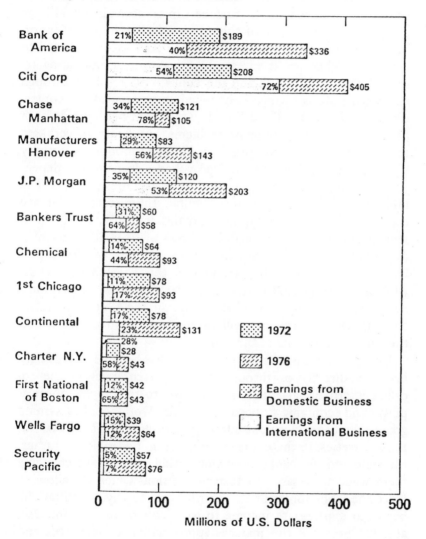

Source: Karin Lissakers, *International Debt, the Banks, and U.S. Foreign Policy*, Staff Report Prepared for U.S. Congress, Senate, Committee on Foreign Relations, Subcommittee on Foreign Economic Policy (Washington, D.C.: U.S. Government Printing Office, 1977), p. 10.

these banks derived about 50 percent of their earnings internationally in 1976.

If the oil crisis had not existed, it would have had to be invented. The movement of finance capital abroad was, in large part, a necessary result of the relative decline in profit opportunities in the metropolitan centers as well as of the need to maintain higher profit rates in the wake of accumulating reserves. The problems facing the banks were resolved through movements abroad which heightened and extended the contradictions within the Third World. Bank loans neither aided nor ameliorated the development problems, but rather exacerbated the balance-of-payments problem, hindered productive activity by capturing local savings, and provoked a deepening of dependency by appropriating local productive facilities as assets. The internationalization of finance capital, the merger of finance capital with industrial capital, and the appropriation of local savings and industry through purchases of financially troubled local firms has inalterably linked the survival of the largest Western banks to profits accrued in the Third World. Thus, while in the early 1970s internationalization of capital became a necessary outlet for surplus loan capital, in the 1980s the profits from these commitments will become an essential element in the overall operations of the banks.

Recognizing this, the capitalist state has become increasingly involved—directly or through their representatives in the so-called international banks—in attempts to restructure political power and economic systems in the Third World, while assuming greater direct involvement in the operations of the banks within those societies. In this context, default is not a real issue: rather, the state and the banks are manipulating regimes (and changing them when necessary) to foster conditions which (1) allow or force the labor forces of the Third World to pay, (2) allow the banks to appropriate income to pay debts before anyone else, and (3) promote the massive appropriation of resources and strategic goods. The "debt threat" to the bank thus has been transformed into an instrument for threatening the livelihood of Third World labor and, indeed, the sovereignty of nations, as recent developments in Zaire, Peru, and elsewhere graphically illustrate.[7]

Citibank's senior vice-president Irving Friedman, in commenting on the criteria of creditworthiness by private banks, illustrated the leverage these institutions have for restructuring the economies and the social and political structures in the debtor LDCs:

> General economic management and external debt management are of critical importance. General economic management consists, however, of the totality of government policies and their effects on the economy. Fiscal, monetary, savings, investment and exchange-rate policies, exchange controls, foreign trade policy, public versus private ownership, the treatment of foreign investment, the role of the central bank—all exemplify, but not exhaustively, major areas of public policy that determine country risk.[8]

Clearly, Friedman suggests that continued lending to LDCs will be conditional on meeting the above criteria to be imposed by the private banks, the IMF, or other bilateral or multilateral lending agencies as a condition for future assistance. The scope and importance of these policy target areas in determining "risks" indicate the growing role of private banks and their governments in restructuring the LDCs.

The capitalist world economic system is not threatened by debt as long as the multinational banks and their countries can receive payments through neo-colonial regimes which can intensify exploitation of labor (austerity) and resources. The debt problem will become a threat to world stability when mass-movement–based regimes refuse to follow the dictates of the banks, nationalize their holdings, and prevent them from collecting their debts. Western intervention in Zaire had more to do with bank and corporate interests than with saving white expatriate lives.

For the banks, intervention in Zaire was crucial to maintain the production of state-owned mines that must produce ore to pay international debts. Military intervention has been followed by far-reaching economic and political intervention. In exchange for standby credit to Zaire in the form of $200 to $250 million in special drawing rights, IMF designees will wield effective power over Zaire's central bank and its Finance Ministry and regulate taxes, customs, the budget, and exchange controls. In addition, in 1978, Zaire agreed to return to the former owners 50 percent and control of the more choice plantations seized in a 1973-1974 confiscation drive. These Western interventions in Zaire illustrate the banks' and the developed nations' ability to restructure the LDC debtors.[9]

1. Dynamics of International Debt Peonage

For years, bank officials and academics partial to banking interests argued that creditworthiness was the key criteria for loans. The term itself, however, was so nebulous in practical terms that it was rather useless as a guide to bank loan behavior. For example, Chile after 1973, Argentina after the spring of 1976, and Brazil after 1964 experienced severe recessions and monstrous inflation and yet received massive financial support.[10] Clearly something else was involved beyond the rather vacuous notion of creditworthiness.

A cluster of factors seem to characterize regimes that get loans: (1) the regimes are deeply committed to an open-door policy to foreign flows of capital of all sorts; (2) the countries have strategic resources and regimes whose policies promote easy access to raw materials; (3) the countries have large internal markets and regimes that do not hinder foreign penetration; and (4) the countries have substantial surplus labor pools and regimes willing to promote platforms for foreign capital. Indeed, most of the easy terms of loans are intimately tied with Third World regimes that facilitate the internationalization of capital. The "model" most likely to be financed is one based on "growth from above and outside." Finance capital both promotes and deepens this approach. In some cases (South Korea, Hong Kong, Taiwan), external finance led to extended growth based on export industries exploiting cheap labor. In other cases, loans have led either local investors to transfer capital to nonproductive sectors (construction, speculation, etc.) or states to increase military spending; or the loans to productive sectors have failed to generate the surplus to repay the loans, especially loans to finance the exploitation of resources that have declined in price on world markets (copper) or failed to materialize (oil).[11] In still other cases, Third World export-oriented industrialization has suffered from the recession in the metropoles and from the protectionist measures adopted. Finally, in some cases, externally funded industrialization may raise wage levels causing capitalists to move their assembly plants to new, lower-wage areas within the Third World, leaving the country with the debt and declining revenues; Puerto Rico is illustrative.[12] Externally financed economic expansion is a precarious undertaking which contains within it numerous possibilities of falling into the "debt trap."[13] Regimes that loyally pursue the "growth from above and the outside" model periodically enter into crisis for one or more of the cited political or economic reasons.

Several structural features of dependency contribute to the growth of indebtedness and the growing centrality of finance capital. Third World growth based on the expansion of multinational capital carries with it the massive remittance of profits and payments for licenses, patents, etc. In addition, as Brazilian authorities have recently noted, most multinational corporations produce an unfavorable balance of payments, importing far more goods than they sell abroad.[14] Also, the terms of exchange, overall, have been unfavorable for Third World countries specializing in a limited number of raw materials, resulting in declining income and severe balance-of-payments problems. Investment and trade policies based on growth through dependency produce payments imbalances which are covered by external loans. As the imbalance deepens during cyclical downturns, debts increase, and the regime turns toward intensifying its debt position.

The dynamics of international debt peonage are intimately tied to the dependent structures of Third World productive systems. As the crisis deepens, the terms of loans become more onerous. Local entrepreneurs become bankrupt, state firms are sold, and foreign capital gains greater concessions—in some cases, the banks themselves take over enterprises. Hence, the rise of regimes oriented toward dependent growth leads to greater concentration of ownership by foreign capital (not homogenization or leveling between countries), greater internal inequalities, intensification of exploitation of labor to pay for the "recovery," and, hence, greater regime repression to sustain the overall effort.[15]

When the oil crisis hit and world recession began to take hold, non-oil-exporting less developed countries were caught in a credit squeeze. Private banks, however, not public international lending agencies like the World Bank or the IMF, have underwritten most of the massive debt buildup that resulted. LDC demand for credit to meet the increased cost of petroleum provided one incentive for commercial bank lending abroad. This was heightened by stagnation in domestic bank earnings, a result of the impact of near-global recession. If one analyzes this debt over time, the net foreign indebtedness of the sixteen non-oil-exporting LDCs that have done most of the borrowing has increased at an annual rate of 15 percent in real terms, allowing for inflation.[16] In the same period, the countries' combined real, gross national product grew about 4.5 percent per annum. Thus, clearly, external indebtedness has been growing faster than the capacity of those economies to carry it.

Although current fears of widespread default appear exaggerated, legitimate reasons for concern do exist. Commercial bank lending to developing countries has grown at a very rapid rate, and loans are concentrated on both the borrowing and the lending side. Mexico and Brazil, for example, account for one-half of the U.S. private bank claims on the non-oil LDCs, and most of the lending to the developing countries is done by a few large banks. This pattern of lending by the private banks poses problems in terms of portfolio diversification and risk dispersion. Of the one hundred or more LDCs in the world, ten countries accounted for the bulk of commercial bank claims on developing countries. In addition to Mexico and Brazil, eight other high-income nations in Latin America and East Asia (Argentina, Chile, Colombia, Peru, Korea, the Philippines, Taiwan, and Thailand) accounted for half of the outstanding commercial bank debt.

While all of the higher-income LDCs have avoided default, all have had difficulties in managing their international debt and have become increasingly dependent on the IMF and other international lending agencies to bail them out of their debt crises. For instance, the Philippines, after the fall of sugar prices in 1975, tried to maintain its high rate of imports by borrowing from foreign commercial banks, but by 1976 it was forced to institute a stabilization program in agreement with the IMF. Likewise, in Latin America, Argentina, Chile, and Peru have all experienced difficulty in rolling over maturing bank credit. To a lesser degree, Mexico and Brazil, the two largest borrowers, have experienced the same difficulties. Mexico has been forced to institute a comprehensive stabilization program in agreement with the IMF as a condition for receiving financial support from the Fund, while Brazil has been forced to institute austerity measures to curb inflation and offset her growing trade deficit.[17]

Another indication of the high cost of debt to the less developed countries is a study by American Express that estimates that one out of every four dollars borrowed abroad by the LDCs in 1977 would go for debt servicing. By 1980, it is estimated that one out of every two dollars will be used to repay old debts.[18] Clearly, these figures seem to indicate that LDCs generally are becoming more debt dependent and it is perhaps only a matter of time until many of them find the cost of default and rescheduling less than continuing payment. What impact such an eventuality would have on the entire international economic system and on host and sponsoring nations alike is an issue of widespread concern in banking circles.

The debt burden has a cumulative impact on the overall structure of dependency between the LDCs and their creditors. One issue is, of course, the growth of the debt, up nearly seven times in the decade since 1967. For debtor countries, the servicing of this debt is weakening their economic development capacity and lowering their national standards of living as the interest on the debt consumes between 20 and 50 percent of foreign exchange export earnings. Another important factor is that an increasing proportion of LDC debt comes from private sources and, typically, carries a higher rate of interest and a shorter repayment period. The stiffer terms of the commercial banks have placed new economic burdens on the LDCs. Increasingly, the commercial banks are using the offices of the IMF to impose conditions on poorer countries. Governments are forced to impose austerity programs to ensure repayment which increases economic hardship and places increasing demands on the stability of the political system.

Table 1
Average Interest Rates on Loan Commitments, Selected Countries (in percentages)

	1967-1970	1971-1972	1974	1975
Afghanistan	2.1	2.2	1.7	1.3
Argentina	6.0	7.8	7.0	6.6
Bangladesh	n.a.	1.9[a]	2.6	1.7
Costa Rica	5.7	6.9	8.0	7.8
Ecuador	5.7	6.0	5.5	6.4
Ethiopia	3.7	2.2	0.7	1.4
Indonesia	2.6	3.4	4.9	7.6
Ivory Coast	5.4	6.5	7.1	7.9
Jamaica	6.2	6.4	10.5	8.8
Korea	4.6	4.6	7.7	6.6
Malaysia	5.0	5.8	5.8	8.5
Paraguay	4.2	5.4	5.9	3.9
Philippines	5.9	5.2	6.1	6.4
Singapore	3.8	5.8	6.3	7.8
Sri Lanka	3.2	2.4	5.0	2.9
Sudan	4.1	2.6	6.4	4.2
Taiwan	5.4	6.3	7.2	8.3
Thailand	5.7	6.2	5.7	7.6
Turkey	3.2	4.4	5.6	7.4
Uruguay	6.0	7.5	9.0	8.8
Zaire	4.5	6.4	7.2	6.6
Zambia	4.3	4.7	4.6	5.8
Average 22 Countries	4.63	5.03	5.93	6.10

Source: Gordon W. Smith, The External Debt Prospects of the Non-Oil-Exporting Countries (Washington: Overseas Development Council, October 1977), p. 10.
[a]1972 only

Note: All countries for which 1975 numbers were available that had at least $400 million in debt outstanding and disbursed by December 31, 1975 were included.

Significantly, the World Bank has estimated that only 31 percent of the debt owed by less developed countries to international organizations is due in less than five years while 79 percent of the debt owed to private sources matures in five years or less. In 1971, the average maturity for all loans, both public and private, was thirty-two years for low-income countries. By 1974, the average maturity for loans to those same countries had dropped eight years.[19] Table 1 illustrates that, as the maturity structure has shortened, the interest rates have increased, thus intensifying the LDC debt burden.

According to conventional economic theory at least, the relationship between banks and the LDCs is one of mutual benefit. In fact, however, the beneficiaries usually have been the multinational banks who have profited from the postembargo credit squeeze placed on the LDCs by their historically dependent position. Most less developed countries are not borrowing for development reasons, but rather to resolve balance-of-payments problems or to maintain a national standard of living. The latter has certainly been the case of the largest borrowers of the LDCs, namely Brazil and Mexico.[20]

The structural basis of growth through debt, however, poses some serious problems for both the developed and the developing nations. Domestic lending in the developed world normally carries a government-imposed reserve requirement of about 10 percent. However, unregulated Eurocurrency lending allows multinational banks to be more flexible in the reserve requirements for LDC lending and has the effect of artificially creating money. The aggregate amounts of offshore deposits has been estimated at over $300 billion, and it appears that the amount created by offshore banks runs into the many billions of dollars.[21] The consequences and implications of this unprecedented explosion in multinational banking in the last ten years are far reaching. Commercial banks have experienced enormous increases in profits from their overseas operations which have important effects in both the developing and the developed world. Thus, the artificial creation of money by the offshore banks is a factor in generating inflation on a global scale which can increase the debt crisis for developed and developing nations.

Offshore banking has had a serious impact on international liquidity and inflation. Federal Reserve Chairman G. William Miller recently voiced concern for this potential crisis. "The Eurodollar market is a deep concern to us because of the very large amounts of dollar denominated money is out there over which the central bank has very little control. A lot of money is created in the international market outside of the control of any central bank, and this is one of the greatest worries in this period of time."[22] The concern is that stateless money, because of its unregulated nature, has no reserve requirements on the international bank operations. Since there are no reserve requirements on the banks, for instance, operating in the Euromarket, there is no real limit to the amount of credit they can create off their deposit base. A single dollar on deposit can serve as the base for $10 or $100 in loans. Moreover, there is a multiplier effect among the international banks that makes the pyramiding even worse. Constant Frannsen, managing director of Credit Banque de Luxembourgeois, has reported, "If I have $1 and put it in Barclays in London, and Barclays in turn lends it to a Swiss Bank, we can keep on building up liquidity and that is a potential inflation creator."[23]

Another problem with this huge pool of stateless money outside the control of national authority is that it has been used to circumvent government anti-inflation policies. To fight inflation, developed nations' governments have instituted tight credit policies that send up interest rates on loans. Multinational banks (MNBs) can now circumvent such anti-inflation policies merely by going to the Eurodollar pool. Thus, the international banks have been generating inflation on a global scale, which is impacting on developed and developing societies alike. Global inflation generated by the banks could provoke crises where (1) borrowing countries are forced to reschedule or default on loans and, thus, are faced with national crises as a result of their inability to continue to import supplies on which they have become heavily dependent; (2) political instability in LDCs results from austere conditions imposed on the debtors by public and private international lenders and domestic inflation; and (3) multinational banks are threatened by defaults in a period of decline in world economic growth or by "stagflation" which holds the potential of undermining the international monetary system.

Thus, as the new international banking order generates worldwide inflation, it weakens both creditor and debtor nations alike in their ability to deal with the debt crisis. Continuing global inflation will weaken LDC governments' ability to extract the money to service their debt from their populations through economic austerity. In addition, foreign assistance loans to bolster LDC debt servicing capacity may become increasingly unpopular in developed countries (DCs) as their inflation-driven recession increases. Such conditions could certainly result in massive defaults in LDCs followed by bank failures in the DCs that could rock the entire international monetary system.

2. Bank Capital's Impact on Development, Social Structure, and Political Structure

A regime's policies, class character, and willingness to use force to sustain its international obligations importantly influence bank capital's impact on diverse, polarized Third World societies with conflicting interests. Therefore, it is important to stress the differential interests of conflicting classes and their relations to multinational banks, corporations, and metropolitan states.

Bank capital has been channeled predominantly toward regimes favorably oriented toward international capital. Most recipient regimes have been authoritarian and/or highly repressive. Bank loans, open-door regimes, and repressive policies have frequently coincided. Bankers are less concerned with human rights than with the "bottom line." More important, repression selectively applied to class-conscious social forces and economic nationalist political groups has been supported by bank officials. Citibank's president recently reassured the Brazilian authorities of the bank's concern: "The problem of human rights has nothing to do with the loan policies adopted by the large international banking organizations. Brazil's debt to Citibank is about 2,000 million United States dollars and we still are not imposing any restrictions."[24]

The pursuit of policies encouraging foreign capital inflows prevents regimes from securing the support of popular majorities through welfare ideological appeals. At best, paternalistic measures (job security) and horizontal mobility (rural to urban movements) complement the use of force. The bulk of the loans are extended to multinational corporations, local big capital (rural or urban based), and the state. Most state investments help promote low-cost infrastructure development and facilitate the spread of private activity. Hence, the prime beneficiaries of private bank loans are the economically powerful. The loans strengthen their social, economic, and political power and contribute to widening the inequalities within society. Studies of major loan recipients such as Brazil, Chile, Argentina, Peru, and Zaire indicate that, although bank capital does not necessarily contribute to the growth of productive resources, it has contributed to exacerbating the inequalities.[25]

While the loans are channeled to particular classes and groups, debt repayment is the responsibility of the population at large. Whether the loans went into urban real-estate speculation, someone's Swiss bank account, or factory construction, the debt payments are assumed by the entire society. When creditors or the IMF demand "austerity" (cutbacks in public spending, wage freezes, credit squeezes) and freedom for private capital as a condition for loans to deal with past debts, the burden is borne by the classes that least benefit from the initial loans.[26] External credit thus reinforces political systems in which loan beneficiaries and debt payers are distinct and opposing classes. Thus, in the economic sphere, bank capital contributes to economic dependency; in the social structure, it leads to further concentration of income at the top; while in the political sphere, its policies contribute to increasingly authoritarian practices. One crucial necessity in interpreting and understanding the dynamics of indebtedness and repayment is the demystification of the interactions by going beyond "national" units and identifying the class actors who play the game.[27]

Most discussions of bank pressure on Third World Countries focus on economic policies that facilitate loans, rescheduling of payments, or debt financing. But the recommendations of private banks and the Fund also have major consequences for the structure of society and economy, as well as on the state's political-economic orientation. Bank demands for cutbacks in public spending and salaries adversely affect wage earners as well as those sectors, such as construction, where national capital is tied to public contracts. The constraints on wages lead regimes to impose constraints on unions, thus strengthening the power of employers; increases in prices raise profits for property owners at the expense of nonproperty owners. The net effect of bank policy is to alter the distribution of income and power in society toward propertied groups and classes.[28]

In the economic sphere, the emphasis on "market" criteria, the "lowering of productive costs" through the elimination of tariff barriers, adversely affects both private and state national industries and aids the multinationals. State enterprises are transferred toward the private sector and previously subsidized national capital goes bankrupt, increasing the economic importance of private foreign capital. In essence, the measures lead to a restructuring of the economy, a shift in the basis of production.

Finally, bank policies are not only "recommended" but in a period of crisis are imposed: regimes in severe financial difficulties that refuse to abide by the measures are denied loans and pressured to meet their obligations.[29] Government officials who lack the banks' confidence because of their previous association with nationalist/populist policies or their unwillingness to follow the demands of the banks are pushed aside. New officials emerge who, by background or ties, are willing to collaborate with the banks in the execution of their class-biased stabilization programs. Thus, bank policies are linked to societal, structural, and governmental changes that transcend simple financial transactions and encompass the political economy as a whole. The technocratic posturing and apolitical rhetoric of bank officials is merely a mask for far-reaching political actions.

Underlying this international debt management crisis lies the Third World's deteriorating international economic position, traceable in part to both rising import prices and related falling export earnings. Developed and less developed nations each have proposed solutions to this problem. The LDCs advocate alleviating the debt directly (through reschedulings or debt moratoriums) or redistributing wealth by establishing commodity price agreements on their exports. The developed countries, on the other hand, blame the Third World debt crisis on the oil crisis and on LDC economic mismanagement.

The developed, capitalist countries, therefore, call for debt management through a belt-tightening process, the imposition of which influences Third World development policy and political stability. Economic austerity is imposed from within by some LDC governments and externally by international agencies to smooth the repayment of debt. These austerity measures aim to reduce the consumption standards of LDC populations by deflating national economies with restrictive monetary and fiscal policies; by holding down wage increases with restrictions on labor's right to strike; and by reducing real wages with income policies, import controls, and import tariffs.

Economic austerity sometimes has resulted in riots, strikes, and changes in governments. Often LDC governments have increased repression in order to impose austerity measures on a recalcitrant population. Riots in Egypt, civil war in Zaire, and strikes and the fall of several finance ministers in Peru are recent examples. Austerity programs and repressive regimes have negatively affected individuals living in LDCs who have been forced to lower their already minimal consumption standards. External public and private creditors of Third World debtors are the real beneficiaries of this development through austerity. This strategy is now being assisted and institutionalized by industrial governments to the benefit of the private multinational banks.

The debt crisis is allowing the private banks, via the International Monetary Fund and other international lending agencies, to impose harsh economic restrictions on the already weak LDC economies. The impact of these internal constraints is to create greater inequalities within the host nations which may destabilize their societies and undermine the LDCs' ability to service their private debt. Such political and social unrest could force LDCs to default on their loans, causing failures of numerous private banks that are interlinked on a global scale, and thus undermine the stability of the international monetary system.

3. U.S. Policy toward Third World Debts and Finance Capital: Role of the State in Corporate Capital

Multinational banks are concerned about Third World repayment and are continuing to encourage internal policy changes. Since their Peruvian experience, private banks no longer see themselves as direct policymakers.[30] They support expanded IMF lending capacity and stricter enforcement of austerity programs. In May 1977, U.S. Treasury Secretary W. Michael Blumenthal suggested: "It seems to me important, therefore, to give careful study to the possibilities of developing closer interaction, a smoother transition, between financing through the private market and official financing through the International Monetary Fund."[31]

Increasingly, American multinational banks look to the government to bail them out by providing foreign assistance to debtor nations who can, in turn, use their public moneys to repay their private bank debt.[32] In this regard, the Carter administration recently urged that the IMF's lending capacity be doubled to $90 billion.[33] President Carter, in his March 25, 1977, press conference, reiterated the government's strong support for U.S. banks' Third World lending, avowing, "I'm not in favor of a debt moratorium."[34] The U.S. government would rather take a case-by-case approach to debt relief, which enables it to influence, directly or indirectly through the IMF, the internal policies and development strategies of particular LDCs. This approach, of course, helps ensure continuous repayment of LDCs' private external debt.

The United States is also concerned with the role of the commercial banks in the Third World because of the fear for international monetary stability. There is a growing concern that if enough Third World countries default on their loans, the whole international monetary system may collapse. Concern for the stability of the international banking system and its linkage to the whole international monetary structure has intensified since several recent U.S. and European bank failures and since recent defaults and near-defaults by debtor nations. These international debt difficulties created a growing awareness of the seriousness of the debt situation.[35] Individual bank failures are not isolated from other components of the international banking system. These individual bank crises spill over to other banks because much of the current international banking activity is composed of interbank transactions.[36] When a bank fails, it affects other banks doing business with that institution. Indeed, banks' loss experiences illustrate the interdependence of the world's major banks and how bank failures (because of interbank linkages) can create instability in the international banking system and, therefore, affect the international monetary system.

The failure of major international banks would mean a crisis of the dollar and other major currencies and the probable collapse of international financial markets. The unregulated nature of the international bank system today is similar to the unregulated condition of the U.S. banking industry before the depression. This current lack of regulation makes it difficult, if not impossible, to maintain the current system and, therefore, makes it difficult to predict just how far-reaching the failure of major international banks would be on the international monetary system.

The Basle Agreement of July 1974, in which the Board of Governors of the Bank for International Settlements agreed that each nation's central bank should make good the losses of its branches, illustrates the growing concern over bank failures. Indeed, the Basle Agreement suggests that the central bankers give credence to the domino theory of international banking, that several failures could set off a chain reaction throughout the interbank network and perhaps bring down the whole international economic system. Concern about bank failures has recently been heightened still further by reschedulings and potential defaults of LDC debtors whose outstanding liabilities to U.S. commercial banks are over $100 billion and could destabilize the entire banking system.

This Cassandra-like prediction is being taken seriously enough that the U.S. government is encouraging the creation of the IMF's Witteveen Facility to provide $25 billion of financing to help offset the burden of the less developed countries' debt.[37] Although this facility has not been established to safeguard private banks that have lent unwisely or excessively, the banks will certainly benefit from its establishment. This public, international bail-out of the commercial banks is not new. One recent study "charges that a substantial amount of money the International Monetary Fund funnels to developing countries now goes to repaying old, high interest loans made by private multinational banks, rather than to development projects."[38]

Both U.S. and foreign banks actually make loans on the assumption that the Federal Reserve or the IMF would intervene in an emergency. Robert Triffin has commented, "Lending abroad by foreign branches of U.S. banks has increased enormously, and foreign profits greatly exceed domestic profits. These banks believe that the Fed will never let one of their foreign branches fail, which leads them to take ever greater risks. There are some very powerful interests that do not want more central bank intervention."[39] This belief on the part of the banks that the U.S. government will bail them out allows them to assume greater risks which contributes to the potential international debt crisis.

There is an intimate relationship between the state, international lending institutions, and big business.[40] According to one calculation:

> For every dollar that went out in debt to the developing countries, about one and one-half dollars has been estimated to have come back in increased demand for exports from the industrialized countries. So one does have a very tightly connected system here between the nature of the debt and the industrialized countries in the real sense and not merely the financial.[41]

This relationship between the banks and the state in the industrialized world is seen as one of mutual benefit and provides support for the IMF's Witteveen Facility. As the risk of massive default and global financial collapse increases with the extension of large amounts of LDC debt, the role of the state widens. Recent testimony before the Senate Foreign Relations Committee has suggested that international agencies such as the World Bank, the Export-Import Bank, the Inter-American Development Bank, the Asian Development Bank, and the African Development Bank should also come to the assistance of the commercial banks. A rather significant swap between the private commercial banks and the official banks has been suggested. Under this scheme, the World Bank would issue its bonds to private commercial banks and would, in turn, accept some of the portfolio loans to developing countries that the commercial banks currently have outstanding.[42]

The commercial banks and the state, therefore, have been employing the leverage of the looming, international financial crisis as a bargaining tool to shift the burden of debt to public institutions. Whether or not crisis and potential default are likely is difficult to predict. Regardless, fear of trouble has led to austerity programs in many LDCs, which are difficult for the lower classes to absorb. Since default could mean economic and political chaos for the ruling classes, including a precipitous drop in essential imports and a stifling of multinational enterprises' business and profit, it will probably be avoided at all costs. Developing country governments are likely to work with developed countries and their commercial banks and continue the process of international indebtedness as long as the commercial banks can continue to make profits and the labor force of both developed and developing countries can be made to absorb the cost.

The international bankers are acting on the assumption that the governments of the creditor nations and the World Bank and IMF cannot afford to allow their client governments or their own major international banks to fall into bankruptcy. This attitude is clearly expressed in the pages of *Euromoney*:

> Though it was never articulated in so many words, most bankers must also have assumed that loans lent to LDC governments would be underwritten by the official aid programs of the developed world. No Western government had any wish to see a debtor country default, or to inflict a major loss on its own banking system.[43]

> On the other hand, a purely technical analysis of the NODC's current financial position would suggest that defaults are inevitable; yet on the other hand, many experts feel that this is not likely to happen. The World Bank, IMF, and the governments of major industrialized nations, they argue, would step in rather than watch any default seriously disrupt the entire Euromarket apparatus with possible secondary damage to their own domestic banking systems, which in many cases are already straining under their own credit problems.[44]

> In the case of such countries as South Korea, the Philippines, Taiwan or Israel, it is reasonable to expect that the day of default would be forestalled indefinitely as long as the stake of the U.S. government in their economic and political stability remains high.[45]

It is clear that the bankers are proposing that the governments of creditor nations come to the aid of their Third World clients by increasing the public bilateral and multilateral aid programs by massive amounts in order to ensure that debtor nations can contrive to service their debt to the international banks.

The crisis for international monetary stability will come when the impact of LDC defaults accelerates as a result of the unwillingness or inability of client regimes to meet the externally imposed demands for economic austerity by the IMF and when this is coupled with a declining ability in the creditor nations to provide sources of official aid to bail out the banks. Foreign aid programs are becoming unpopular in the United States as a result of domestic problems such as double-digit inflation, massive trade deficit, possible recession, and a population that is recalcitrant with regard to increasing government expenditures that do not benefit them. A scenario that would bring together these factors would cause default in the most debt-ridden LDCs and bankruptcy for the international commercial banks. The collapse of several major international financial institutions could set off an economic crisis in the entire international banking network, because of existing interbank linkages, that would bring the entire international financial system down. While we do not predict such a scenario for the immediate future, the potential now exists for a financial crisis of major proportions that could plunge the world into depression.

4. Conclusions

The debt crisis in the Third World has served as a major lever through which international capital is restructuring societies, economies, and states. Throughout the Third World in the post-World War II period, state-promoted and -protected productive enterprises have increasingly come under the influence or control of multinational capital. The whole ensemble of national development policies has come under attack and is being undermined. Protective tariffs, state subsidies, foreign exchange controls, restrictions on profit remittances, limitations on foreign investment, etc., all have been eroded by the IMF banks as part of their debt financing. This massive transformation over the past several years involves the privatization of state enterprise, the denationalization of national firms, and the respecialization of Third World countries into a new international division of labor. Thus, while most commentators have focused on the issues of debt payments, default, and the monetary crisis, the real issue that seems to be unfolding is the role of the banks in the restructuring of Third World economies and societies to facilitate the free flow of international capital. Through the levers of debt payments, the banks are, in effect, reversing the nationalist-statist development trends of the last several decades and creating a new neo-mercantilist world order. This process has advanced unevenly, but appears to be the historic direction in which the global push of bank policies is directed. The bankers' vision of a world free-enterprise system is setting in motion opposition at all levels of national societies: disruption and disorder lurk behind each freeing of prices; bankruptcy and industrial stagnation behind each lowering of tariffs; hunger and unemployment behind each austerity measure. The radical transformations wrought by the bankers in pursuit of their global neo-mercantile vision are engendering an equally radical adversary within the Third World.

Notes

1. Karin Lissakers, *International Debt, the Banks, and U.S. Foreign Policy*, staff report prepared for U.S. Congress, Senate, Committee on Foreign Relations, Subcommittee on Foreign Economic Policy, 95th Cong., 1st sess. (Washington, D.C.: U.S. Government Printing Office, 1977), p. 1.

2. Andrew A. Beveridge and Philip Wellons, "Societal Effects of International Bank Lending" (unpublished, 1977), pp. 29-32.

3. Ibid., p. 56.

4. Figures from Table 2 of Brian G. Crowe's article (chap. 2) in this volume.

5. David O. Beim, "Rescuing the LDCs," *Foreign Affairs*, July 1977, p. 1.

6. Lissakers, *International Debt, the Banks, and U.S. Foreign Policy*, pp. 9-10.

7. See the articles by Barbara Stallings (chap. 9) and Jonathan David Aronson (chap. 11) in this volume; also "Two LDC Borrowers Justify the Worries," *Business Week*, June 5, 1978, p. 58; *Latin American Economic Report*, April 21, 1978, p. 113, May 19, 1978, p. 146, and May 26, 1978, p. 154; *New York Times*, April 27, 1977, p. A5, and April 5, 1976, pp. 51-53.

8. Irving S. Friedman, *The Emerging Role of Private Banks in the Developing World* (New York: Citicorp, 1977), p. 48.

9. "Zaire: Economic Therapy for a Basket Case," *Business Week*, July 3, 1978, p. 34.

10. See the articles by John S. Odell (chap. 10) and W. Ladd Hollist (chap. 7) in this volume; also "Bankers Put Welcome Mat Out for Argentina," *Latin American Economic Report*, April 17, 1978, p. 97; "Chile Returns to Favour with Foreign Bankers," *Latin American Economic Report*, July 1, 1977, p. 98; James F. Petras and Morris Morley, *The United States and Chile* (New York: Monthly Review Press, 1975), pp. 43-78; "The Brazilian Gamble," *Business Week*, December 5, 1977, pp. 72-81; and "Latin America Opens Door to Foreign Investment Again," *Business Week*, August 9, 1977, pp. 34-38.

11. See "Even before Zaire the Outlook was Bleak," *Business Week*, June 5, 1978, p. 69.

12. See James Petras and Juan Manuel Carrion, "Contradictions of Colonial Industrialization and the Crises in 'Commonwealth' Status" (unpublished, 1977).

13. See Cheryl Payer, *The Debt Trap* (New York: Monthly Review Press, 1975).

14. See "Brazil Takes Harder Line on Transnationals," *Latin American Economic Report*, April 21, 1978, p. 114; and Richard J. Barnet and Ronald E. Müller, *Global Reach* (New York: Simon and Schuster, 1974), pp. 152-53.

15. Barnet and Müller, *Global Reach*, pp. 153-55.

16. Computed from data in the *IMF Survey*, June 5, 1978, p. 176.

17. Federal Reserve Bank of New York, *Quarterly Review*, Summer 1977, pp. 6-8.

18. Lissakers, *International Debt, the Banks, and U.S. Foreign Policy*, p. 51.

19. Howard M. Wachtel, *The New Gnomes: Multinational Banks in the Third World* (Washington, D.C.: Transnational Institute, 1977), pp. 20-21.

20. U.S., Senate, Report to the Subcommittee on Foreign Economic Policy of the Committee on Foreign Relations, *Market Power and Profitability of Multinational Corporations in Brazil and Mexico*, 95th Cong., 1st sess. (Washington, D.C.: U.S. Government Printing Office, 1977).

21. Paul M. Sweezy, "Multinational Corporations and Banks," *Monthly Review*, January 1978, pp. 8-9.

22. *Business Week*, August 21, 1978, p. 76.

23. Ibid., p. 75.

24. *Latin American Economic Report*, April 1, 1977, p. 51.

25. See Barabara Stallings's article on Peru (chap. 9) and W. Ladd

Hollist's article on Brazil (chap. 7) in this volume; also see Payer, *The Debt Trap*; "The Brazilian 'Economic Miracle,' " in *Latin America from Dependence to Revolution*, ed. James Petras (New York: John Wiley and Sons, 1973); and Irma Adelman and Cynthia Taft Morris, *Economic Growth and Social Equity in Developing Countries* (Stanford, Calif.: Stanford University Press, 1973).

26. See Wachtel, *The New Gnomes*, pp. 23-37.

27. The case for Peru is most stark and striking. See Barbara Stalling's article, chap. 9 in this volume.

28. See *Latin American Economic Report*, July 1, 1977, p. 99; and *New Times*, March 21, 1976, p. 3.

29. Wachtel, *The New Gnomes*, pp. 28-29.

30. U.S., Congress, House, Committee on International Relations, *Dollars, Diplomacy, and Development*, 95th Cong., 1st sess., July 26-27, 1977 (Washington, D.C.: U.S. Government Printing Office, 1977), p. 85.

31. Remarks by W. Michael Blumenthal, International Monetary Fund Conference, Tokyo, May 24, 1977.

32. Cheryl Payer, "Will the Government Have to Bail Out the Banks?" *Banker's Magazine*, Spring 1977, pp. 86-87.

33. Bernard D. Nossiter, "U.S. Urging Allies to Join $16 Billion Expansion of the IMF," *Washington Post*, April 1, 1977, p. D11.

34. Wachtel, *The New Gnomes*, p. 38.

35. See Emma Rothschild, "Banks: The Coming Crisis," *New York Review of Books*, May 27, 1976, pp. 11-12; Philip A. Wellons, *Borrowing by Developing Countries on the Eurocurrency Market* (Paris: OECD, 1977); and Gordon W. Smith, *The External Debt Prospects of Non-Oil Exporting Developing Countries* (Washington, D.C.: Overseas Development Council, 1977).

36. See Jonathan David Aronson, *Money and Power: Banks and the World Monetary System* (Beverly Hills, Calif.: Sage Publications, 1978), pp. 115-23.

37. U.S., Congress, Senate, Committee on Foreign Relations, Subcommittee on Foreign Economic Policy, *The Witteveen Facility and the OPEC Surplus*, 95th Cong., 2nd sess. (Washington, D.C.: U.S. Government Printing Office, 1978), pp. 25-26.

38. Dan Morgan, "Much IMF Help Goes to Repay Commercial Loans, Study Finds," *Washington Post*, June 25, 1977, p. 1.

39. *Business Week*, August 21, 1978, p. 78.

40. See, for example, R. Peter DeWitt, *The Inter-American Development Bank and Political Influence* (New York: Praeger, 1977), and Petras and Morley, *The United States and Chile*, for a more detailed analysis of the U.S. probusiness influence in international lending institutions.

41. U.S., Congress, Senate, *The Witteveen Facility and the OPEC Surpluses*, p. 57.

42. Ibid., pp. 61-63.

43. Pierre Latour, "Euromarkets Wait for LDCs' Credits to be Repaid," *Euromoney*, October 1975, p. 4.

44. David I. Levine, "Developing Countries and the $150 Billion Euromarket Financing Problem," *Euromoney*, December 1975, p. 14.

45. Charles G. Gravel, "US Banks' International Loans Under Security," *Euromoney*, March 1976, p. 13.

Part Three

The Politics of
International Debt Renegotiations

A customer who insists on repaying is just a nuisance who is putting the banker to the trouble of finding another customer.

—W. Arthur Lewis

Part Three

The Politics of
International Debt Renegotiations

Introduction

The players change; the game remains the same. International loans, enthusiastically signed and extended, sour. Creditors and debtors meet, usually in Paris, to reschedule or refinance loans that have fallen into payments arrears. Compromise is reached allowing the borrower to retain some creditworthiness and assuring the creditor repayment over a longer period of time. The process begins again.

But there are two important differences today. On the borrowers' side, there is a new sense of confidence and bargaining skill born in OPEC's success in dealing with the industrialized nations and fortified by the jihad for a New International Economic Order. The key lenders have also changed. Private banks have replaced governments and international organizations as the primary lenders to the wealthier developing nations.

This final section explores the changing interactions between debtors and creditors when things fall apart and projects possible changes in the interactions among developed and developing countries, private bank lenders, and the International Monetary Fund in the handling of international debt and debt servicing. Five developments serve as the necessary backdrop.

First, in the face of domestic pressures and international economic confusion, many *developed countries pared down their aid and lending* to the developing world. As a percentage of GNP, bilateral aid and loans have declined in the United States and elsewhere. Creditor clubs have continued to enforce relatively strict debt servicing, but Sweden, Great Britain, Canada, and, most recently, Japan have embarked on programs of limited debt forgiveness that may undermine developed country unity in future debt renegotiations. It seems likely that official creditors may, in the future, concentrate on the needs of the least developed nations and leave most financing of richer developing nations to the private sector.

Second, there has been a marked *intensification of private bank competition* in the international economy in the 1960s and 1970s. Small U.S. banks, seeing that the giants were making more and more of their profits abroad, expanded to assure their access to the Euromarkets. Simultaneously, European banks moved into each others' markets, and Japanese banks moved rapidly into international money markets. By November 1977, 285 foreign banks were represented in London alone. In sharp contrast to earlier eras, large banks cooperate freely across national boundaries regardless of nation of origin, but may resent smaller interlopers from their own nations trying to break onto the international scene.

Once abroad, the pressure to prosper is great. Withdrawal is unacceptable to most newcomers. Therefore, to establish quick profits and global stature, smaller banks have cut loan margins, extended credit for longer periods, relaxed credit standards, and sought new profit-generating activities when they realized that the larger banks had already taken the best business. Large banks were forced to match the terms of smaller banks or lose customers. They followed reluctantly. When profits rose, "gogo" bankers replaced their more conservative colleagues at the forefront of the financial hierarchy.

Spirited competition created a buyers' market. Banks reacted by seeking new profit centers. Foreign exchange, a service center under a fixed rate system, became vital as a profit center by the early 1970s. Bank loyalty to fixed exchange rates evaporated as profits sloshed in. London newcomers *planned* to support their expensive new operations from foreign exchange profits until they established a solid lending base. Frequently, banks with domestic difficulties tried to gamble their way out of trouble in the foreign exchange crap shoot. Inevitably somebody had to lose. Not until the collapse of the Franklin National Bank and the Bankhaus Herstatt in 1974 did blind speculation abate.

Third, bank competition was further increased because *banks were impelled to increase their loans outstanding.* Large private banks became petrodollar recyclers. Arab OPEC nations invested a large portion of their funds in short-term Eurodollars, deluging the soundest banks in liquidity which they needed to put profitably to work. To maintain system stability and to safeguard their own solvency, banks sought new borrowers. Non-oil-exporting LDCs were one obvious source of eager borrowers.

In the rush to lending, banks discovered that since no reserve requirements existed to slow Eurocurrency interbank borrowing, banks could become major lenders without large capital exposures. Increasingly, banks borrowed short to lend long. New Eurobanks could build up sizable positions without acquiring a large deposit base. Although this mechanism helped reallocate petrodollars flowing into the largest banks, it also bloated the system's liquidity and pushed smaller banks into questionable lending positions. Since interbank funds were always available and the loss experience before 1975 was excellent, smaller banks built up major commitments that forced them to remain active in the markets even after the situation deteriorated.

Fourth, traditional transnational enterprise and governmental *loan demand stagnated.* Facing the worst recession since the 1930s, many transnational enterprises (TNEs) restricted their new investments or financed them internally. Large enterprises also began financing each other through the commercial paper market, depressing the banks' commission income. About the same time, major TNEs and government agencies found they could obtain funds in the more predictable, fixed rate Eurobond market without resorting to the variable rate Eurocurrency realm.

Finally, as private loan repayments began to fall into arrears, the private banks sought help first from their own governments and then directly from the International Monetary Fund. The *IMF's position strengthened* significantly. Private banks found that, although they had become political actors on the international economic scene, they were unable to exercise firm power over their debtors. Private banks' bargaining positions vis-

à-vis debtor nations deteriorated when their exposures became
so large that they could not write them off without severe
consequences for their earnings. The IMF, therefore, became an
instrument that private as well as official lenders could work
through to ensure their eventual repayment.

The final four essays explore different aspects of debtor-
creditor renegotiations in the light of these developments.
Barbara Stallings's analysis of the relationships between Peru
and its private American creditors serves as a link between this
and the previous section. Starting from an interest in the impact
of external debt on Peruvian development, Professor Stallings
examines how the pressures on the Peruvian government to
meet the servicing of its external debt influenced the ability of
the government to meet the developmental needs of its population. She suggests that even well-intentioned governments, when
shackled by unyielding external creditors, may prove unable to
move their nations toward development and distribution. The
difficulties of one nation with its foreign creditors are spelled
out in detail.

John S. Odell and Jonathan David Aronson start from the
same sort of difficulties that Barbara Stallings analyzes for Peru
and move to a wider perspective. John S. Odell looks for common elements in debt renegotiations between official, developed country creditors and Brazil, Ghana, and Chile. He examines the bargaining relationship between debtors and creditors
and identifies factors that influenced differences in renegotiation outcomes in these nations. He suggests ways that future
debt renegotiations could be assessed to predict possible outcomes.

Jonathan David Aronson looks at the same problems in renegotiations involving private creditors and the governments of
Zaire, Indonesia, and Turkey. He also analyzes the political influence of private banks on the international debt scene and
tries to indicate the dimensions of their possible power in dealing with developed and developing states. Past experience is
used to assess the prospects of debt renegotiations and disrup-
tions involving private creditors dealing with Mexico and Brazil.
The analysis suggests that at least the richer developing nations
may be in a stronger bargaining position with the banks than

other authors in this section suggest. The possibility of future cooperation between commercial banks and the richer developing nations, even in the face of developed country opposition, is proposed.

Finally, Charles Lipson carries the analysis of debt renegotiations onto the international scene and looks at the changing role of the International Monetary Fund in debt renegotiations. He raises the possibility that, as creditor-club negotiations between governments or between private banks and governments fail to find acceptable solutions to debt difficulties, the IMF and other international institutions may be called on to enforce the will of the creditors and to provide the creditors with sufficient confidence in the borrowers to continue their lending.

—J.D.A.

9
Peru and the U.S. Banks: Privatization of Financial Relations

Barbara Stallings

The dominant trend in U.S.-Third World financial relations during the 1970s has been "privatization." After forty years of hovering in the wings, while bilateral and multilateral agencies took front stage, the private bankers have once again assumed the dominant role in providing funds to the governments of Third World nations. Those governments have borrowed large sums from the private capital market, and they have also begun to float international bond issues. At the same time, multilateral aid has risen only slowly, and U.S. bilateral aid has fallen off, so that private bank funding now constitutes over 50 percent of total development finance, more than twice as much as it did a decade ago. In addition, bilateral and multilateral funding agencies, by bringing private banks into their loan arrangements, have privatized public sector loans themselves.

This trend toward privatization in Third World finance has been characterized by three main features:

1. Privatization has enabled the banks to maintain and even bolster their profits during the most serious global recession

The author wishes to thank the following people for comments on earlier versions of the manuscript: Jonathan Aronson, Julio Cotler, Jessica Einhorn, Stuart Fagan, Richard Fagen, Richard Feinberg, E. V. K. Fitzgerald, Harry Magdoff, Cheryl Payer, Clark Reynolds, Janet Shenk, and especially Tom Seidl.

since the 1930s; this has occurred in spite of the so-called country risk problem. The banks are taking whatever steps they deem necessary in order to protect and extend these profits, including reliance on public institutions.

2. Privatization, while certainly not eliminating public sector loan activity, has produced a shift in emphasis. Thus, U.S. government agencies, the World Bank, the IMF, and similar institutions now place more stress on supporting the private sector than on taking the lead in providing funds. This support, when necessary, includes support for the stability of the financial system as a whole.

3. Privatization has squeezed Third World countries—and especially their working classes—rather than benefiting them. Terms on private loans are more stringent than on loans from public institutions, and private lenders are less patient about repayment. The hope, or fear, that was present two years ago, that governments would gain new leverage as a result of their indebtedness, is being proved a myth.

One of the countries in which these trends can be clearly observed is Peru. There, in 1976, a consortium of six U.S. banks imposed a set of conditions for the management of the economy and undertook to monitor their implementation. In return, the banks extended a $200 million loan to tide the beleaguered Peruvian government over a growing balance-of-payments crisis. The following year, in response to widespread criticism, the banks retreated from such direct intervention and called in their ally, the International Monetary Fund. The policies imposed have left the Peruvian working class with only a fraction of its former purchasing power as the two sets of lenders—with the help of the Peruvian government itself—strive to make sure that Peru pays its debts.

This study focuses on the Peruvian debt situation. The economic policies of the current miltary regime are described, showing the buildup of the crisis that faced the country in mid-1976. The agreement with the banks is then discussed, together with the effects of the bank measures for Peru. One result was the entry of the IMF into Peruvian policymaking when, in 1977, the banks imposed this as a requirement for refinancing their loans. An attempt is also made to explain the bankers' decisions—why did they move in to monitor the Peruvian economy in 1976 and, equally important, why did they then step back and call in the Fund in 1977? The final section offers some tentative conclusions on the meaning of the growing role of the private banks in Third World financing—for the countries and for the banks themselves.

1. Economic Background: 1968-1975

In October 1968, Genéral Juan Velasco Alvarado led a coup that overthrew the civilian government of Fernando Belaúnde Terry. The military government that was established broke with the tradition of military governments in Latin America by not supporting the established socioeconomic structure, but rather proposing to radically restructure Peruvian society. Under an ideology that promised a "third way" between capitalism and communism, the new government undertook an extensive agrarian reform centering on the creation of co-ops, an industrial and mining reform introducing worker participation and profit sharing, and the nationalization of some key foreign firms including branches of Standard Oil of New Jersey, ITT, W. R. Grace, Cerro, and Chase Manhattan Bank. The government was not anti-foreign capital, but it did want to change the nature of foreign investment. On the one hand, it wanted to decide what types of investment were desirable. On the other hand, it planned to have the state itself become the principal investor and, therefore, looked more to foreign loans than direct investment. Despite the redistributive rhetoric, the reforms actually benefited only a small part of the population. Moreover, even those groups did not wholeheartedly support the military government which, being unable to consolidate a strong political base, remained very much an attempt at modernization from above.[1]

During the first five years, in spite of the changes going on and the lack of political support, the Velasco government managed to maintain a strong economy. Growth in gross domestic product (GDP) between 1969 and 1973 averaged 5.5 percent; industry grew by an average of 7.1 percent annually. Unemployment fell from 5.9 percent in 1969 to 4.2 percent in 1973. Real wages and salaries both increased by an average of 6.6 percent, while inflation was held to an average of 7.2 percent. The trade balance was positive and, even though the service balance generally dragged the current account into deficit, the latter was not large enough to cause any serious problems with financing. Net reserves, in fact, increased from $131 million in 1968 to $411 million in 1973.[2]

Under this prosperous surface, however, potential problems lurked. The threat of accelerating inflation existed. Real wages were increasing faster than the food supply. The budget deficit which averaged between 15 and 20 percent of total central government expenditure between 1971 and 1973 was also ominous. Such a deficit was not surprising, of course, for a government taking a greater role in the economy. Expenditures increase but the political resistance of the local landowners and bourgeoisie prevent taxes from being increased enough to offset the expenditures.

More serious from the government point of view were potential problems with the balance of payments. The outlook appeared to be favorable, but this was because of very optimistic forecasts about mineral exports. Although few went so far as the state oil-company spokesman who declared that "Peru's economic future is now assured" when Petroperú struck oil in 1971, Peruvian and foreign analysts alike put an increasing emphasis on oil. Great stress was also placed on the expectation of major volume increases which would raise the value of copper exports. The traditional volatility of prices for primary products was ignored.

At the same time, plans were being laid for an industrial development strategy that relied heavily on capital-intensive technology. This type of strategy not only reduces the job-creating potential of industrialization, but it also necessitates large amounts of imported capital goods and intermediate inputs. Simultaneously, the Peruvian military were importing large amounts of expensive Soviet and Western military equipment. These imports, together with debt service payments which will be discussed below, threatened to drive Peru into a balance-of-payments crisis if the export boom failed to materialize.

In the meantime, the question arose of how to finance the industrialization program and the equipment necessary to produce the additional exports. The United States and its allies in the multilateral agencies refused to supply funds, since the Velasco government had incurred their wrath through nationalization of Standard Oil's subsidiary, International Petroleum Company, and through other actions. In concrete terms, this meant that foreign investment dried up and Peru received almost no loans from AID or the Export-Import Bank between 1969 and March 1974 (although the Hickenlooper amendment was never formally invoked). Loans from multilateral agencies were also conspicuously absent. Between 1968 and late 1973, Peru received only one World Bank loan. Credits were slightly more available from the Inter-American Development Bank (IDB), but a significant portion of their loans were in response to a serious earthquake in Peru in 1970.[3]

Only one source to which the government could turn to finance its investment projects remained—the international capital market. Realizing that Peru was going to need good relations with the private bankers, the government took early steps to prepare the ground. When it took control of the domestic banking sector (including Chase Manhattan's Banco Continental), it sought favor with Chase—and presumably the rest of the financial community—by buying its shares for three times their book value.[4] Thus, Peru was able to escape the official credit blockade by raising $147 million on the Eurocurrency market in 1972 and $734 million in 1973. In the latter year, Peru was the third largest borrower among Third World nations.[5]

In spite of its leftist rhetoric, the banks saw Peru as a good credit risk because of its copper and oil. Moreover, Peru's need for finance coincided with a drop in loan demand among large U.S. and European corporations, the banks' traditional clients. The resulting excess liquidity was exacerbated by the petrodollar glut after 1973, when the OPEC governments deposited their huge new revenues with the major international banks. Consequently, what appeared to be mutually advantageous deals between Peru and the banks were possible.[6] These loans almost doubled Peru's debt burden between 1968 and 1973 and nearly

Table 1
Peruvian Debt and Debt Service, 1968-1978 ($ millions)

	Public Debt[a]	Service Payments[b]	Service Ratio[c]
1968	$1,100	$146	14.6%
1969	1,132	126	11.8
1970	1,196	168	13.7
1971	1,309	209	19.6
1972	1,606	213	18.5
1973	2,155	434	32.2[d]
1974	3,008	449	24.4[d]
1975	3,466	402	23.0
1976	4,383	505	29.0
1977	N.A.	811	49.5
1978[e]	4,800	1,000	55.0

Source: World Bank, "Peru:Informe Socioeconómico," January 1978, and television speeches by Peruvian President and Finance Minister.

a Disbursed and undisbursed public and public-guaranteed debt

b Interest plus amortization

c Service payments exports

d Includes prepayments without which ratios would be 23.6% (1973) and 18.1% (1974)

e Public debt figures are for mid-1978; service payments and ratio are those that would result if Peru paid full amount owed during 1978.

tripled it between 1968 and 1974. Debt service (interest plus amortization) surpassed 20 percent of export earnings by 1973. (The growth of Peruvian debt is shown in Table 1.) Neither borrowers nor lenders were concerned, though, since it was presumed that Peru's mineral wealth would provide repayment.

By 1974, potential problems outlined above began to appear. Although growth rates continued to be high and unemployment low, the inflation rate shot up to 17 percent, causing real wages to fall. Moreover, for the first time since the military took power, the trade balance went into deficit; while exports increased 35 percent between 1973 and 1974, imports almost doubled. In percentage terms, the main culprit was the oil price increase: the cost of Peru's fuel and lubricant imports nearly tripled. Of greater significance in absolute terms, however, were volume and price increases of inputs and capital equipment for industry.

Between 1969 and 1973, capital formation by the public sector had increased by an average of 15.6 percent per year; in 1974, this figure jumped to 56.5 percent. Major increases included central government investment in agriculture (44 percent) and public enterprise investment in Petroperú (88 percent), Mineroperú (139 percent), Sideroperú (1016 percent), and Pescaperú which increased from nothing to over $32 million.[7] Most of the equipment involved in this investment spurt was produced abroad, thus the increase in imports. This marked a qualitative change in the government program. The cheap phase of the reforms (expropriation of agriculture and some industrial enterprises) was over; the expensive phase (creating new heavy industry) was beginning. In addition to the trade deficit, the deficit in services also increased, such that the current account deficit in 1974 totaled $725 million (up from $174 million in 1973). This deficit was financed by going to the Euromarket for another $366 million in medium-term loans, plus a large amount of short-term money. In addition, AID, the Export-Import Bank, and the international agencies poured in large sums when the credit blockade was lifted after the signing of the so-called Greene Agreement in February 1974.[8]

In 1975 the budget deficit doubled, and both the inflation and the balance-of-payments problems became more acute. Emergency measures were introduced at the end of June. The average price of basic consumer goods was raised by 20 to 30 percent, as many subsidies were lowered, in an attempt to cut the budget deficit and thus, eventually, the inflation rate. In an attempt to forestall opposition from workers and to partially offset the fall in demand, the government announced a general wage increase. The minimum wage, however, was increased by only 20 percent, and the poorest groups (the unemployed and the "informal" sector) did not benefit.[9] As a result of the June measures, the growth rate faltered, demand fell, and unemployment rose.

The growing economic crisis provided justification for the August 1975 coup within a coup. General Francisco Morales Bermúdez, Velasco's prime minister, took over as president. Although Morales Bermúdez characterized his regime as a continuation of the Velasco Alvarado government, it was obvious that the change meant a move to the right. Repression increased, leftist military officers were forced to retire, and more orthodox economic policies were introduced. Balance-of-payments problems nevertheless remained, in spite of $433 in loans from the Euromarket and the World Bank, and net reserves fell from $693 million to only $116 million by the end of 1975.

A further round of austerity was introduced in January 1976, when the new finance minister, Luis Barúa Casteñeda, announced a series of changes similar to those of the previous June. Further price increases on basic consumer items were introduced. Again, wage increases were authorized to try to limit the opposition and to maintain demand. A second set of measures, tax increases and budget cuts, were designed to reduce the government deficit. Attempts were also made to lower imports by a system of licensing, and a set of production incentives was promised.

The aims of the measures were threefold: to increase production, to control inflation, and to keep the balance-of-payments deficit from getting out of hand. If the economy could manage to limp through 1976, it was hoped that the balance of payments would improve through increasing copper and oil exports and that other difficulties would thus be mitigated.[10] Meanwhile, further international credit would be needed to cover the deficit.

2. The Bankers Intervene: 1976

By early 1976, then, the Peruvian economy faced a serious crunch, owing to a combination of bad luck, bad planning, and the inevitable dilemmas of dependent capitalist development. The bad luck had to do with the failure of the expected oil bonanza, the disappearance of the anchovy schools which had provided a major Peruvian export, and the fall of copper prices. Bad planning reinforced these problems through overfishing and borrowing money to build a billion-dollar pipeline before the extent of the oil reserves was known.[11] As mentioned earlier, however, fluctuations of export revenues are always inherent in the economic situation of small dependent countries.

Again, the government saw the main problem as the balance of payments which could not be brought into equilibrium in the short run because exports could not be increased and imports could not be cut without bringing the economy to a standstill. Only the debt service payments (which were about $500 million compared with the trade deficit of $740 million) seemed flexible. Outright suspension of payments would end access to the international capital market, so refinancing was necessary.

The traditional way to solve a balance-of-payments crisis would be for Peru to go to the IMF and sign a letter of intent. This would give access to certain IMF funds and further bilateral, multilateral, and private banking sources. The problem was that the IMF would demand a drastic stabilization program which even the Morales officials neither could nor would accept. They realized that the results would alienate workers through wage and employment cuts, industrialists through a fall in demand (and thus profits), and the military through curbs on the purchase of arms. Given the regime's lack of existing support, the potential was too explosive: they feared that the government might be brought down.

The Peruvians therefore approached the major U.S. banks in March 1976 and asked for a large balance-of-payments loan *without* having signed a prior agreement with the IMF. The bankers ultimately accepted the Peruvian position because the outcome, if the crunch were to come, was not clear enough to take the risk. General Jorge Fernandez Maldonado and the left-wing faction of the government could conceivably come out on top in a confrontation, thus leading Peru back toward a radical nationalist position. It seemed safer to support the Morales government, with its new rightist tendencies, rather than risk such a leftist outcome. One New York banker involved in the negotiations put the point very clearly. He said the "main reason" for the loan was "to perpetuate Morales Bermúdez in power" since the banks considered this the best bet for getting their money back.[12]

The banks also wanted to refinance the Peruvian loans for several additional reasons. First, Peru was important both in itself and in symbolic terms. Its debt, $3.7 billion at that point, was one of the largest in the Third World. Half of it was owed to private banks, including $1.5 billion to U.S. banks alone. Second, a Peruvian default might have triggered a chain reaction among other Third World countries in trouble with their foreign debts. Third, default would have created animosity among the smaller U.S. banks and the international banks which had been involved in the syndicates for Peruvian loans arranged by U.S. institutions in the past. These banks might then refuse to participate in future Third World loan syndication generally, having been badly burned in Peru.

Nevertheless, the banks had no intention of making it easy for the Peruvians. For one thing, they had to save face and to keep from getting a reputation of being a "soft touch." Thus they needed to construct a set of requirements that would provide their pound of flesh. This was especially the case since Peruvian officials had paraded around the world denouncing imperialism and capitalism for the last seven years. Also some formula had to be devised to mollify the banks' clients who were at that time being threatened by the Peruvian government. These included Marcona Mining Company (still negotiating compensation for its iron mine nationalized in mid-1975) and Southern Peru Copper Corporation (which faced problems over depreciation allowances and tax delinquency). Finally, a way had to be found to assure that Peru would generate sufficient foreign exchange to be able to pay the service on its past loans without resorting to further international credits for this purpose in the future.

The resulting deal between Peru and the banks was a three-part program which dealt with all the banks' problems. It included:

1. an orthodox stabilization program, though of a milder sort than the IMF would have imposed, involving a 44 percent devaluation, price increases, and minor budget cuts;

2. more favorable treatment of foreign investment, including reopening the jungle and coastline to private oil companies, agreement with Marcona on a price to be paid for its mine, and agreement with Southern Peru on payments due;
3. partial withdrawal of the state in favor of local private enterprise, which began with the sale of Pescaperú's anchovy fleet to private interests and changes in labor legislation to attract more private investment.[13]

All of the loan conditions, of course, were described by the bankers as essential for guaranteeing Peru's economic future. They argued, for example, that Southern Peru's immediate repayment of the $50 million in back taxes, depreciation allowances, and penalties would have meant postponement of completion of the Cuajone mine and, therefore, Peru's loss of an estimated yearly output of $250 million of copper, a key foreign-exchange earner. In the Marcona case, they rationalized that, if the company were not compensated, the Hickenlooper amendment could be invoked, cutting off essential U.S. aid and other funds. Finally, the bankers expected more favorable treatment of the private sector to increase private investment so that the government would not have to run up huge deficits and borrow abroad to finance its projects.[14]

The most controversial aspect of the program was that the banks were to monitor the Peruvian economy to make sure that the agreed-upon inflation, budget, and other targets were met. Not since the 1920s had private banks become so involved in the domestic affairs of a Latin American government. The loan was divided into two equal tranches; the first was released immediately, the second was held for several months. Authorization to draw the second tranche was to be contingent on 75 percent of the lenders (by dollar participation) agreeing that Peru was making satisfactory economic progress. Even the bankers admitted the weakness of this arrangement in comparison to the more-detailed IMF monitoring. As one stated, "We won't be seeing any major changes. This second drawdown is just something to keep *some* sort of control."[15]

The package was put together by Citibank, with the participation of Bank of America, Chase Manhattan Bank, Manufacturers Hanover, Morgan Guaranty, and Wells Fargo. Those six composed the "steering committee" for the loan, since no bank was willing to take total responsibility as lead manager. Bankers Trust and Continental Illinois were also invited to join but refused because they disagreed with the banks assuming the monitoring function.

The steering committee banks agreed to provide $200 million, contingent on a further $200 million to be raised from private banks in Western Europe, Canada, and Japan. The steering committee banks would themselves place half of their share with smaller U.S. banks, with the aim of spreading Peru's debt and their risks as widely as possible. Beyond the special conditions, the terms of the loans were quite stiff. The interest rate was 2.25 percent above the interbank rate, and the maturity was only five years.[16]

The effects of these policies on the Peruvian economy were dramatic and negative, but determining who was responsible for them becomes complicated. The banks imposed a set of conditions, but Morales and his top economic officials wanted to move in that direction in any case. They definitely favored private enterprise and foreign capital more than had the Velasco regime. Furthermore, they had announced stabilization measures before loan negotiations were even begun (in January 1976), and it must be remembered that Morales was de facto head of government when the first such measures were introduced in June 1975. Thus, it seems likely that many of the changes would have been made, with or without the banks' intervention, although the intervention was certainly useful in helping overcome internal opposition to austerity measures. Some of the blame could be shifted to the bankers who also provided access to extra funds which somewhat softened the austerity program.[17]

One result of the banks' policies was a drop in production.[18] The drop had already begun in 1975, in part due to extremely poor performances in the fishing and mining sectors. There were also important declines in industry and services as a result of the 1975 emergency measures. Thus the GDP growth rate fell from an average of 6.3 percent in 1972-1974 to only 3.5 percent in 1975. The bank measures further depressed the economy, and it pushed down to 2.8 percent in 1976, despite a strong recovery in fishing, mining, and agriculture (sectors essentially unrelated to government demand policy). Sharp declines in 1976 occurred in those sectors that were most susceptible to changes in internal demand—industry, construction, and services.

The employment situation also suffered reverses. In a pattern similar to that of production, open employment had already increased in 1975, going up from an average of 4.1 percent during 1972-1974 to 5.2 percent in 1975. This figure increased only very slightly to 5.3 percent in 1976, but underemployment increased from 41 percent to 45 percent between 1975 and 1976. The biggest effect of the 1976 measure was on wages and salaries. According to an OAS study, real wages and salaries for the Lima area reached a peak in 1973, 33 percent above their 1968 level. They then fell in 1974 and remained at the same level in 1975. During 1976, the drop was so serious that average remunerations were back to their 1968 level.[19] In addition to these negative effects in terms of growth, employment, and remunerations, structural changes also resulted from the banks' conditions. Specifically, private enterprise, in general, and foreign capital, in particular, began to regain much of the economic and political power lost during the Velasco years.

3. Enter the IMF: 1977-1978

The Peruvian drama repeated itself in 1977, but with an important change in the cast of characters. Though the balance of payments was expected to improve, a huge trade deficit still threatened, and service payments on the debt remained oppressive. Thus, Peru sought foreign financing once more. This time, however, the banks refused to negotiate without IMF participation. Why did the bankers change their minds? The reasons for their switch are easier to understand than the explanation for their original decision to monitor the situation themselves. Many factors were at work; all pushed in the same direction.

The first set of factors was negative from the banks' point of view and concerned problems arising from the direct intervention. Most important was the opposition to the new monitoring role. Opposition from the left had been expected, but the banks were probably unprepared for the opposition from within their own ranks. Bankers Trust and Continental Illinois, both major U.S. institutions with heavy involvement in Peru, had refused to join the steering committee or to participate in the new loans. They objected to the damage to the banks' image which could result. As Alfred Miossi, executive vice-president of Continental Illinois, put it: "For a private bank to police the actions of a sovereign government puts it into a difficult position. International agencies have a more neutral role and are better suited for this."[20] Another banker, whose own institution was a steering committee member, said, "I don't think the banks can play the role of appearing to intervene in the affairs of a country. Whether they like it or not, it could be considered Wall Street imperialism."[21] European bankers likewise expressed concern, speaking of the "politicization" of the deal. They pointed out that banks identified with the stabilization program ran the risk of becoming scapegoats for the unpleasant results.[22]

Bankers also expressed doubt that they would have as much clout as the IMF because of their commercial ties to Peru. As one critic suggested, "The banks have a vested interest in Peru, and they've got to think of their commercial lending relations in that country. What are the Peruvians going to think if they start snooping around and delving into the books?"[23] Presumably, G. A. Costanzo, Citicorp's vice-chairman, spoke for the other banks when he said: "The reaction to this loan was a signal to me that I want *no* part in deals with this kind of discipline in the future."[24]

The second set of factors explaining the banks' decision focused on the advantages of working more closely with the IMF. First of all, bringing in the Fund would end the criticism leveled at the steering committee banks and would reunify the banking community. Those bankers who had opposed the 1976 operation had all advocated closer relations with the IMF. It would provide a more "neutral" facade for imposing conditions on Peru, but appearance was not the only advantage. The banks would also be able to profit from the Fund's experience in dealing with Third World governments, its access to data on the economies, and its capacity to set up and implement a monitoring procedure.

Closer cooperation with the IMF would also jibe with the wishes of the Federal Reserve Board, the U.S. government agency charged with regulating the banks' overseas operations. The then chairman of the Federal Reserve, Arthur Burns, had been advocating more cooperation for some time, pressuring the banks to stop acting independently with respect to the debt problem. In a February 1977 speech, he made this position public, declaring, "We need to develop the rule of law in this field, and the only instrument for this is the IMF. Unless we have the rule of law, we will have chaos."[25] The exact nature and extent of bank-Fund cooperation was undetermined. Proposals varied from greater sharing of information to joint loans.

The third factor behind the reversal of the banks' position was what enabled them to work more closely with the Fund. That is, they knew that the IMF economists would demand more stringent conditions than they themselves had imposed the previous year, but such conditions now seemed more viable. In 1976, the bankers had been fearful of forcing the government to the wall, but intervening events had made them more confident that the outcome would produce a shift to the right rather than the left. The most important indication was the July 1976 ouster of the leftist-leaning cabinet ministers; public protest resulted. In addition, the government's ability to disperse the demonstrations and break the strikes protesting the mid-1976 stabilization measures was comforting to the bankers. They drew the conclusion (soon to be severely challenged) that the Peruvian political climate was not as explosive as they had believed the previous year.

Given the banks' insistence on involving the IMF, the Peruvian government acquiesced, and a Fund mission arrived in Lima in March 1977. The mission decided that Peru should reduce its 1977 inflation rate to 15 percent, its budget to no more than 20 billion soles,[26] and that its balance of payments should be equilibrated with no new loans. In a typical set of demands, the IMF "suggested" that Peru:

- cut all subsidies to public enterprises, leaving them to acquire necessary financial resources through price increases;
- raise gasoline and other fuel prices sufficiently to eliminate

the Petroperú deficit (16 billion soles) and to provide a surplus for the central government;

- cut another 10 to 20 billion soles from the deficit by eliminating the purchase of capital goods for public sector investment and selling off firms to the private sector;
- tighten up the tax system by eliminating all tax exemptions (including those on traditional exports), creating an emergency "wealth tax," and indexing tax payments;
- eliminate noneconomic restrictions on imports (e.g., quotas);
- devalue the sol by 30 percent (i.e., to 90 soles per dollar)
- limit wage and salary increases to 10 to 15 percent.[27]

The political implications of this program were intolerable even to Peru's conservative financial officials. The central bank's president, Carlos Santistevan, and several of its directors sent a letter to Finance Minister Barúa, threatening to resign if the IMF program were accepted. The latter stated that the Fund was "seeking to balance the economy in an extremely short term, and its measures would have excessive and unnecessarily depressive effects which can, and should, be avoided."[28]

Santistevan and the central bank countered the IMF with a more flexible set of proposals, but at the same time other members of the government (especially Industry Minister General Gastón Ibañez) proposed measures to *expand* the economy. They wanted to increase government spending, to peg the exchange rate, to reinstate food subsidies, and to cut the price of gasoline. Caught between these opposing pressures, Morales Bermúdez made no decision, and, in May, Finance Minister Luis Barúa resigned in frustration.

· The new minister, Walter Piazza, was the first private businessman appointed to a cabinet post by the military government. His proposals resembled those of the IMF, the main exceptions being a higher budget deficit and a higher expected-inflation rate. On the basis of this program, Piazza managed to negotiate a deal with the Fund, but it was rejected by the cabinet and he, too, resigned.[29] Nevertheless, certain elements of his program—mainly price rises—were put into effect, arousing strong popular opposition including the first general strike since 1919. The government response was two-edged. On the one hand, it imposed a curfew and sent in police and army troops. Hundreds of workers were arrested, and at least nine people were killed. Subsequently, laws were suspended to allow factory owners to fire strike participants; some six thousand lost their jobs. On the other hand, the government also tried to mollify the strikers by raising wages and salaries. The increases, however, were not enough to cover increases in food and transportation.[30]

Three months later, the Peruvian government finally signed an agreement with the IMF which was very similar to the Piazza proposals. Under this accord the real crunch would come in 1978 when the government was to cut the budget deficit to one-third the 1977 total and inflation by one-half. This implied a further increase in unemployment and a further reduction in the purchasing power of wage earners. In return, Peru was to receive $100 million to be disbursed in bimonthly installments over two years.

The first installment of the IMF loan was released in December, but in February the Fund's mission returned and declared Peru in massive violation of the agreement. In refusing the second and all further drawdowns, it focused special attention on the budget deficit (reportedly already over the yearly total agreed upon), Peru's pegging of the sol at 130 per dollar, and some dubious accounting procedures designed to help cover up the shortfalls.[31] When the banks learned of the report, they immediately halted loan negotiations meant to provide an additional $260 million. The U.S. government also refused further assistance; the only debt relief still on line was the Soviet Union's agreement to postpone 80 percent ($100 million per year) of the payments due for arms purchases between 1978 and 1980.

The weakness of the Morales government at this point was dramatic. The Peruvian public sector foreign debt was $4.8 billion (private debt added another $3.4 billion), on which Peru was scheduled to repay over $1 billion in interest and amortization during 1978 alone. This sum constituted 55 percent of export revenues, and the government estimated that the figure could rise to 70 percent by 1980. The central bank had virtually no foreign exchange, and lines of credit were shut off.[32] In practical terms, this meant that, without quick action, Peru's imports would have to be drastically cut, throwing tens of thousands of people out of work and cutting the food supply.

The banks and the IMF nevertheless insisted on further austerity measures as the sine qua non before extending any relief. Some officials in the Carter administration were slightly more hesitant—although they did nothing—because they recognized the obvious contradiction between the need for repression implied in further austerity measures and the Morales plan to return the government to civilian control. Although certain Peruvians—including members of the local bourgeoisie as well as the left—suggested a moratorium on debt payments rather than further austerity, there is no indication that Morales or any of his top economic officials seriously entertained this idea. Their own inclinations and the overwhelming financial power of the banks and the Fund pushed in the same direction. Thus, on May 15, prices were doubled on fuel, public transportation, and basic foodstuffs as government subsidies were eliminated in order to cut the budget deficit.

Coming after workers had already lost one-fourth of their purchasing power to inflation in the first quarter of the year, the measures quickly produced clashes in the streets of Lima and strikes in provincial cities. After more than a dozen persons were killed, the government placed the country under martial law, jailed hundreds of leftist labor leaders, and postponed elections scheduled for June 4. This did not stop a two-day general strike on May 22-23. The strike was almost total in many parts of the country, but the power of the workers was simply not sufficient to outweigh that of the international financial community. This was especially true since the government was, at most, mildly against the austerity measures and possibly wholeheartedly in favor.[33]

What did Morales gain from the price increases in addition to the heightened enmity of the vast majority of the population? Apparently, he gained the support of the IMF, the banks, and the U.S. government in his search for debt relief. Within days of the new austerity measures, and with the sound of strikes and rioting still echoing in the streets, the international banks tentatively agreed to roll over some $200 million in amortization owed them during the rest of 1978. Interest was still to be paid, however, and the deal was tied to a new agreement to be signed with the IMF by September.[34] Such an IMF agreement could pave the way for a complete rescheduling of the foreign debt as the Peruvians requested. The U.S. government also promised minor aid in the aftermath of the May events in the form of a $15 million agricultural credit.[35]

But the relief is only temporary and partial; the basic question still remains. Can the Morales government implement an austerity program that calls for further cuts in workers' incomes, plus a drop in military imports and in inputs for local industry? The task may be even more difficult this time around since opposition has now been institutionalized in the Constituent Assembly just elected to prepare for Peru's return to civilian rule. The left won 28 percent of the one hundred seats, and even the right-wing Popular Christian party has said it will oppose the military government. Thus, the only way that an austerity program can be implemented is by greatly stepping up the existing level of repression and probably closing the Constituent Assembly. The process will provide an exceptionally clear test of the Carter human-rights policy. Are human rights in Peru more important than support for the IMF?

4. Conclusions

The Peruvian case is important in itself, but it also sheds light on a number of more general problems and questions about private bank financing in the Third World. These problems and questions can best be seen by returning to the three characteristics of privatization of finance mentioned at the beginning of the chapter. The first characteristic of the privatization process is its role in helping to sustain the growth of bank profits. In the early 1970s, the banks' U.S. and European loan demand began to falter; in response, they began to look to a group of Third World countries as desirable clients. Although adequate published data are lacking to verify the importance of these loans, some indication is suggested by the fact that the international share of the profits of the top dozen U.S. banks rose from 17 percent in 1970 to 49 percent in 1977. To take the example of Citibank, its South American profits went from less than 2 percent of the total profits in 1971 to 27 percent in 1977. Brazil alone accounted for 20 percent of Citibank's profits in the latter year and for 13 percent of Chase's.[36]

Peru was an early participant in the new loan market, entering in 1972. A year later, it represented 8 percent of all loans to Third World countries, surpassed only by Mexico and Algeria.[37] The importance the banks attributed to the Peruvian loans can be deduced from the fact that they broke the informal blockade that the U.S. government and the multilateral agencies had established against the Velasco government. The prospect of profits—both immediately and in the longer run—outweighed political factors. In fact, descriptions of the situation in Peru in the early 1970s are reminiscent of Latin America in the 1920s. One top officer in a big private Lima bank (who opposes the military government) says: "The foreign bankers came down here lending money as if there were no tomorrow. Of course the government took their money. How would it refuse? Why should it?"[38]

When problems arose with the Peruvian loans, the banks' initial inclination was to intervene directly, but the adverse reaction has probably eliminated direct intervention as a future option. The criticism that arose, especially inside the financial world, was decisive. The banks do not want the publicity and controversy that came with setting macroeconomic conditions for loans and monitoring their implementation. They are still inexperienced in dealing with countries as clients. Not only do such clients differ from individuals and private corporations in size, sources of income, and political considerations, but the setting is different as well. Rather than behind-the-scenes negotiations with no one knowing the details, the new-style negotiations become front-page news when the press and political opponents dig for information. After the Peruvian experience, it became clear that some official agency would have to be brought in; the IMF was the obvious choice.

The second characteristic of the privatization process of the 1970s refers to the new role of the public institutions. Rather than being the key actors themselves, as they were during the

1950s and 1960s, they began to put more emphasis on supporting the private banks. An especially close collaboration has
developed between the banks and the Fund—although they are
not always in agreement, nor is the simplistic view of the latter
as the "tool" of the former correct. The Fund has its own ideas
about how an economy should be run and does not need any
coaching from the banks. In fact, one of the disagreements
between the two seems to center on the banks' view that the
Fund is too rigid in its prescriptions.[39]

The new supportive relationship is also evidenced by cofinancing of loans by bilateral or multilateral agencies and one or
more private banks. Cofinancing was first introduced by the
Export-Import Bank in 1970. Today, Exim frequently provides
only part of the credit for an export financing deal, dividing the
package between itself and the private banks. In addition, for a
small fee, Exim provides a guarantee that covers all commercial
and political risks and guarantees full repayment plus most
interest payments.[40] In 1976, cofinancing was extended to the
World Bank and the Inter-American Development Bank.

Opinions within the U.S. government about support for the
banks varies. Certain senators and congresspeople, for example,
are intent on imposing controls to prevent the government from
"bailing out the banks," but Treasury officials are more supportive of the privatization trend. As C. Fred Bergsten (now assistant secretary of the Treasury for International Affairs) said
at the time of the banks' Peru operation: "I think it is better in
international political terms that a Morgan Guaranty—or hope-
fully a consortium of international banks—makes the loan. It's
better for them to put tight controls on than to have a national
government have to do that. It can then be portrayed as coming
through market pressures, and judgements on the economic
merit of the country's position, rather than being laden with
political overtones."[41] In the Peruvian case, the government
gave less help than the banks and Peruvian officials advocated.
Both the State Department and the Treasury stressed, however,
that if the situation became critical, they would reevaluate.[42] A
major question, now that Peru wants to reschedule its debt, is
who will have first claim on the available resources—the public
lenders or the private banks?

Support for the private banks also implies support for the financial system as a whole. One of the key issues raised by the subject of private loans to Third World countries has revolved around the question of stability, with some arguing that, sooner or later, an important country will default on its debts. Others may then follow—a new version of the domino theory—but, even if they do not, a single default may bankrupt some of the weaker banks and trigger a chain reaction throughout the banking system. In historical terms, the analogy goes back to heavy Latin American borrowing during the 1920s and a crash similar to that of the 1930s.

Such a scenario does not seem likely, however, for at least two reasons. First, the institutional changes brought about partially because of the upheaval of the 1930s—creation of the IMF and the World Bank as well as the greatly increased economic role of capitalist governments—militate against a repeat of the chain defaults. Second, the bankers themselves are aware of the potential problems and are taking steps to avoid them. Specifically, they refuse to accept a default. Rescheduling has replaced default as the worst possible scenario from the banks' point of view, with both banks and countries (for different reasons, to be sure) wanting to avoid even rescheduling in order to maintain the countries' creditworthiness. Refinancing loans provides one alternative. Another alternative is increased funds from the U.S. government, and herein arise the foreign policy implications of the debt problem. Will the U.S. government sit by and watch some of the major U.S. banks endanger themselves—and thus the system as a whole—because of repayment problems on loans? Or will it come to their rescue, either positively (public loans to Third World governments so they can repay their private loans) and/or negatively (forcing the governments to pay, through a credit blockade or other means)?

The third characteristic of the privatization process has to do with the price paid by Third World countries. The most concrete change has to do with the worsening terms of the loans they receive. Even leaving aside grants and soft loans, there has been deterioration of two kinds. The maturity of hard loans from multilateral agencies was usually about ten years, while the new Euroloans average from eight to ten years. Also, the new loans carry floating interest rates which create planning problems and probably make overall payments more costly than the old fixed rate system. In addition, the profit-making character of the banks makes them less patient with repayment problems than were AID, the World Bank, and the IDB.

Ultimately, both public and private loans have tended to lead to IMF austerity programs. Just as the IMF seal of approval was the linchpin of the system of public development finance in the 1950s and 1960s, so it has come to be under the privatized system in the 1970s. In both cases, the political and economic costs imposed on the beleaguered countries are tremendous, as the Peruvian case illustrates very well.

In economic terms, stabilization programs play utter havoc with domestic economies. A few groups profit—those connected with the banking and primary-exporting sectors—while the vast majority pays the price. Those who suffer most are workers who see their wages cut or who lose their jobs. In Peru, even official statistics admit that average incomes in real terms are now only 60 percent of their 1973 level and that less than half the work force has "adequate employment."[43] In structural terms, the industrial sector as a whole seems to be in danger. On the one hand, credit and demand have fallen as a result of the stabilization measures. On the other hand, if imports are cut to provide foreign exchange to service the debt, those cuts must fall heavily in capital goods and inputs for domestic industry. In any case, growth will have to be much slower than in the past as increasing proportions of export earnings go for debt service.

The political consequences of stabilization programs are equally dramatic. Such programs have proved impossible to implement in the Third World countries without highly authoritarian regimes. The growing repression in Peru since 1976—curfews, arrests, deportations, deaths, supression of strikes and demonstrations, dissolution of workers' organizations—is not mere coincidence. It is an integral part of stabilization as workers refuse to passively accept the burden of maintaining the banks' profits. Under these circumstances, many doubt that Morales's plan to return Peru to democratic rule by 1980 will prove feasible.

A couple of years ago, some hoped and others feared that

private loans would give Third World governments increased leverage in dealing with the banks because the threat of default could be used to gain concessions. Peru provides some rather dramatic evidence on the lack of realism of such a notion: the government has now capitulated to all of the IMF/bank demands. Available evidence indicates that new leverage exists only if the country in question is of key importance in political and economic terms *and* is under clear and present danger from a credible leftist force. In the Latin American context, there are probably only two countries of sufficient importance to threaten the banks—Brazil and Mexico. In neither case, however, is there any immediate leftist threat nor any desire by the governments to use their potential power, so the question is still a moot one. Looking further afield, two European cases are instructive. In Italy, the IMF and the banks failed to gain any major concessions in terms of economic policies because of Italy's importance to the EEC and NATO, and because the Communist party has a real chance to take control of the government. In Britain, on the other hand, the IMF did manage to wring major concessions, in spite of the U.K.'s international importance, because no serious threat existed.[44]

In summary, the Peruvian case (and other, less-detailed evidence) indicates that the banks have been the primary beneficiaries of the privatization of development finance in the 1970s. This has occurred directly through protecting and expanding their profits and, indirectly, through obtaining increased support from public sector institutions. The Third World countries —and especially their working classes—have borne the brunt as living standards have decreased and repression increased in order that available resources can go to service the foreign debt. Those of us who find such a situation unacceptable must turn our attention to looking for alternative solutions, not just for the immediate crises but for the long run as well. Many of us doubt that such a solution can be found within a capitalist framework, but this is the subject for another paper.

Notes

1. For background information on Peru and the military, see Abraham

Lowenthal, ed., *The Peruvian Experiment* (Princeton: Princeton University Press, 1975); E. V. K. Fitzgerald, *The State and Economic Development, Peru since 1968* (Cambridge: Cambridge University Press, 1976); Aníbal Quijano, *Nationalism and Capitalism in Peru* (New York: Monthly Review Press, 1971); and *Latin American Perspectives* 4:3 (1977). The most complete political-economic history of recent Peru is E. V. K. Fitzgerald, *The Political Economy of Peru, 1956-77* (Cambridge: Cambridge University Press, forthcoming).

2. Figures from Peruvian Central Reserve Bank documents.

3. See annual reports for all four organizations over this period. For a general analysis of U.S.-Peruvian relations during this period, see Jessica Einhorn, *Expropriation Politics* (Lexington, Mass.: Lexington Books, 1974).

4. Shane Hunt, "Direct Foreign Investment in Peru," in Lowenthal, *The Peruvian Experiment*. Two years later, Chase returned the favor by agreeing to lead an international syndicate to find funds for the Cuajone copper mine—a key project whose financing had been stalled for two years.

5. Organization for Economic Cooperation and Development, Development Advisory Committee, *Development Cooperation, 1976* (Paris, 1976).

6. For a discussion of the origin of these loans in terms of differently timed cycles in the advanced and Third World nations, see Michael Kuczynski, "Semi-Developed Countries and the International Business Cycle," *BOLSA Review*, January 1976. For data on the OPEC deposits, see Karin Lissakers, *International Debt, the Banks, and U.S. Foreign Policy*, staff report prepared for U.S. Congress, Senate, Committee on Foreign Relations, Subcommittee on Foreign Economic Policy (Washington, D.C.: U.S. Government Printing Office, 1977).

7. Calculated from Banco Central de Reserva, *Memoria Anual*, 1975.

8. The Greene Agreement between Peru and the United States was negotiated by James Greene, former official of Manufacturers Hanover. In a feat of economic diplomacy, it resolved the long-standing disagreement between the two countries over compensation for Standard Oil's subsidiary, International Petroleum Company. A lump sum was agreed on as compensation fo *all* companies nationalized by Peru, with separate lists of recipients presented by the United States and Peru (see discussion in *Latin American Economic Report*, March 1, 1974).

9. See accounts in *Latin American Economic Report*, July 11, 1975.

10. *Andean Report*, January 1977.

11. Another interpretation of the pipeline decision, however, says that it was not made on economic but on military grounds. That is, for reasons of national defense, the military decided to build the pipeline rather than

use the cheaper means of shipping oil by way of Brazil.

12. *Washington Post*, March 14, 1978.

13. Accounts of the package can be found in various places. See, among others, *Andean Report*, August 1976; *Latin American Economic Report*, July 30, 1976; *New York Times*, July 24, 1976, and August 4, 1976; *Financial Times*, July 27, 1976; and Nancy Belliveau, "What the Peruvian Experiment Means," *Institutional Investor*, October 1976.

14. Belliveau, "What the Peruvian Experiment Means."

15. Ibid.

16. Completing the negotiations proved difficult. One of the complications was the disclosure in mid-August that the Peruvians had purchased a large number of Soviet aircraft worth approximately the same amount as the U.S. loans. Rumors that the loans would therefore be withdrawn proved groundless, but the bankers were not pleased (see *Financial Times*, August 1, 1976).

17. The relationship between banks and the Peruvian government was similar to that which often exists between the IMF and governments seeking loans. Like the banks, the Fund has its views of how an economy should run, and they often coincide with the views of one faction of the government. This faction, however, may not have sufficient power to impose its policies without outside help.

18. Figures from Peru's Central Reserve Bank as reported in World Bank and IMF documents.

19. *Caretas* (Lima), April 5, 1977.

20. Belliveau, "What the Peruvian Experiment Means," p. 34.

21. Harvey D. Shapiro, "Monitoring: Are Banks Biting Off More than They Can Chew?" *Institutional Investor*, October 1976, p. 2.

22. Belliveau, "What the Peruvian Experiment Means," p. 34.

23. Ibid.

24. Ibid.

25. *Business Week*, March 21, 1977.

26. In 1976, the sol was valued at 65 per dollar.

27. Details are presented in the Lima weekly, *Caretas*, April 5, 1977, pp. 11-15.

28. *Latin American Economic Report*, April 22, 1977.

29. For a more extensive account of the contradictory sequence of events surrounding the IMF negotiations, see Nicholas Asheshov, "Peru's Flirtation with Disaster," *Institutional Investor*, October 1977.

30. Bill Bollinger, "Workers' Militancy Grows in Peru," *Guardian*, April 26, 1978.

31. *Latin American Economic Report*, March 10, 1978.

32. Information comes from television speeches by Morales Bermúdez

and Finance Minister Javier Silva Ruete (see *Wall Street Journal*, May 22, 1978, for the former and *Latin American Economic Report*, June 23, 1978, for the latter).

33. Bill Bollinger, "Peruvian Workers Stage General Strike," *Guardian*, May 31, 1978.

34. *New York Times*, June 10, 1978. The Chase Manhattan Bank, lead bank for the huge Cuajone copper mining project, held out on this latest agreement. Chase sent a telex to the Peruvian government, demanding that a law be approved immediately guaranteeing continuation of the current practice of setting aside money from copper sales to service the Cuajone loans. Retaliation, in the form of interfering with new loans, was threatened if such a law were not forthcoming (see *Financial Times*, May 24, 1978, and June 1, 1978).

35. *Wall Street Journal*, June 2, 1978.

36. Information from the annual reports of the banks.

37. Organization for Economic Cooperation and Development, Development Assistance Committee, *Development Assistance, 1973* (Paris, 1973).

38. Asheshov, "Peru's Flirtation with Disaster," p. 38. See similar comments in *Business Week*, September 5, 1977, pp. 31-34.

39. For an anaylsis of differences of opinion between the banks and the Fund, see Cary Reich, "Why the IMF Shuns a 'Super' Role," *Institutional Investor*, September 1977.

40. On Export-Import Bank cofinancing, see Richard Feinberg, "The Political Economy of the Export-Import Bank" (Ph.D. dissertation, Stanford University, 1978).

41. Shapiro, "Monitoring," p. 2.

42. Interviews with State Department, Treasury Department, and private bank officials.

43. From a television speech by Finance Minister Javier Silva Ruete.

44. On the Italian and British experiences with the IMF, see Barbara Stallings, "The IMF in Europe: Inflation Fighting in Britain, Italy, Spain, and Portugal," in *Inflation and Political Change*, ed. Leon Lindberg (New York: Pergamon Press, forthcoming).

10
The Politics of Debt Relief: Official Creditors and Brazil, Ghana, and Chile

John S. Odell

International debt policies have become prominent elements in relations between rich and poor nations. In most years since the 1950s, the majority of less developed states has kept up public debt repayments according to schedule while increasing borrowings. Nonetheless, states have periodically fallen into trouble. Some have avoided an explicit renegotiation of their existing debt, but such renegotiations have become a fairly regular feature of North-South relations. Since 1956, there have been thirty-eight official multilateral debt renegotiations involving twelve less developed states.[1] During the 1960s and early 1970s, LDCs whose debt was more than half the total LDC debt had official refundings.[2] In multilateral discussion, the Group of 77 Third World countries have proposed debt cancellation for the poorest states and changes in procedures used for dealing with debt. More reschedulings or refinancings seem likely.[3]

This essay analyzes the outcomes of debt renegotiations between less developed states and official creditors. Debtor-creditor bargaining prior to a request for a refunding will be discussed only as necessary for this purpose. One view of debt renegotiations, expressed by a number of interviewees in the U.S. government and the International Monetary Fund, is that they are largely technical affairs, handled at middle levels of the

The author is pleased to acknowledge the generous support of the Harvard University Center for International Affairs and the excellent research assistance of Richard Burkholder. He is grateful for critical comments by Jonathan Aronson, David Denoon, Jorge Dominguez, Jessica Einhorn, Lawrence Franko, Stephen Kobrin, Cynthia McClintock, and Robert Paarlberg.

bureaucracy, and governed by financial criteria. Relief is given when it is "needed," but only then and only to the degree needed. Noneconomic conditions and policies are considered to have little significance in influencing these events. On the contrary, though the politics of debt relief may be secondary to the economics, the cases of the three countries examined here show that the effects of noneconomic factors on the outcome can be decisive.

This essay first suggests several financial conditions as causes of imminent or actual default and renegotiation. Second, it will argue that domestic political conditions in debtor states are critical variables in the medium term. As domestic politics shift, the state's orientation toward East and West, its inclination to request debt relief, and its willingness to accept foreign creditors' conditions may shift in response. Thus, in the medium term, these international relations may be volatile for reasons not controlled by the primary actors. It is clear, conversely, that external creditors can affect debtors' domestic politics in several ways.

Creditors often contend that most debtor states will avoid open default or repudiation of debts to protect their creditworthiness. In contrast, some prominent Third World advocates claim that the North-South distribution of power is changing and that LDC collective bargaining techniques, presumably backed by a threat of joint withholding of payments, could force a more favorable settlement of past debts.[4] The essay's third point is that most debt relief experience is consistent with what one would expect from a great international inequality of power and dependence, or a neo-colonial relationship, despite the much-proclaimed decline in the utility of military force in some international relations since the early twentieth century. Typically, a debtor state whose reserves are approaching exhaustion sits alone across the table from much stronger, rich states which have reached a coordinated position. In the longer run, perhaps after an intervening period of volatility, most debtor states yield to the creditors' demands for a contractionary program to restore external creditworthiness. Nevertheless, the weak party is not totally without any basis for maneuver even then; the strong parties have far from perfect control. Indeed, the case of Ghana suggests conditions under which some debtors might choose repudiation and improve their bargaining position.

Fourth, and finally, debt relief outcomes are sometimes affected by differences among creditors. Although creditor governments have tended to move in parallel, reflecting their agreement on the need to preserve the sanctity of the contract, several exceptions have occurred in the 1970s. Creditor disagreement may arise from different financial stakes in a given case, or it may be an expression of different ideologies and political objectives among creditor governments. If they are unable to arrive at a common policy, their division may delay a settlement, or it may increase the debtor government's leverage and capacity to resist. The increase in private bank lending to developing countries in the 1970s adds another axis to creditor bargaining in renegotiations, as evidenced by the cases of Chile, Peru, and Zaire.[5]

1. Common Financial Conditions
Associated with Requests for Debt Renegotiation

Several recent studies attempt to identify the factors distinguishing the situations where renegotiations have occurred from those where they have not. Pierre Dhonte compares financial data for thirteen renegotiation cases with a sample of sixty-nine other less developed countries, using a benchmark of 1969.[6] He concludes that renegotiation of debt repayments occurs when heavy involvement in foreign debt is accompanied by unfavorable borrowing conditions (terms and roll-over ratio). These are often cases in which a heavily involved state resorts to medium-term and commercial credits to the extent that its repayment needs come to exceed its capacity to obtain and absorb new loans. They are also cases with greater-than-normal problems of "bunching," the concentration of repayments in the space of a few years. Dhonte further suggests that the growth of debt is best kept in line with the growth of exports, especially for large debtors.

What are the underlying reasons for these financial trends? Creditors conventionally place the primary blame on faulty economic policies by the debtor government.[7] This government makes inefficient investments and maintains large budget deficits while expanding the money supply rapidly, accelerating inflation. These policies, combined with an overvalued exchange rate, encourage imports and discourage exports and savings, leading to continued payments deficits, depletion of reserves, and, eventually, inability to repay debt.

Unquestionably, this is an important influence, particularly for some cases. Brazil's obligations were renegotiated in 1961 and again in 1964. During the interim, the central government's deficit increased substantially, and the rate of price inflation doubled, compared with the late 1950s. From 1965 to 1969, the new government held the deficit much below the level of the late 1950s, and the inflation rate returned to a more moderate level, though at the expense of recession. Thereafter, exports expanded, and Brazil received increased access to private capital markets and official aid; no further debt reschedulings have been requested.[8]

Under Nkrumah, Ghana spent heavily for prestige construction projects and built a set of industries that relied heavily on imported raw materials and spare parts. Even though imports were rationed, payments deficits became regular and international reserves were depleted. There was no central machinery to control borrowing by public entities. Import licensing administration became infected by corruption, facilitating an import binge in 1965 financed by rapidly accumulating medium-term suppliers' credits. Arrears also accumulated, and suppliers began to balk at further shipments; reserves sank to £3.5 million. Under these conditions, Nkrumah was overthrown in February 1966, and the new military government announced that Ghana could not service its debts.[9]

One of the first acts of the Allende government in Chile in 1970 was to raise the wages of the poorer sector by about 50 percent. This stimulus of the economy produced a year of prosperity, but, thereafter, policy began to contribute to shortages, great inflationary pressure, and a payments deficit which all but exhausted Chile's international reserves. Allende refused to impose import controls, and for a time refused to devalue, but he accelerated the printing presses. The money supply increased

119 percent in 1971, another 139 percent in 1972, and 330 percent in the year ending September 1973. Meanwhile, both domestic agricultural and domestic industrial production fell. In November 1971, Allende requested a debt renegotiation; some relief was granted in 1972, and then again after the military coup, in 1974 and 1975.[10]

Other analysts, however, emphasize the role of "donor" and creditor countries' policies in producing debt servicing crises. Obviously debt problems would be less severe if the resources had been transferred on easier terms in the first place. The terms of official, bilateral development loans eased somewhat during the 1960s, but the proportion of assistance extended as loans increased. The bilateral grant proportion of total aid fell from 74 percent in 1962 to 48 percent in 1970.[11] Interest rates on multilateral loans rose along with market interest rates. Moreover, during the middle 1960s, Western governments expanded the relatively expensive programs of export credit they operated to promote their own exports. Overpricing of goods purchased with these credits is common.[12] Private creditors have extended new commercial loans eagerly, even after the debtor's economic trouble signs have begun to appear, usually charging premium rates. For example, suppliers' credits to Nkrumah grew after the IMF had repeatedly called for drastic curtailment. Bank lending to Zaire in the early 1970s and to Pertamina of Indonesia after 1972 could also be mentioned.[13]

If new aid flows do not parallel the growing debt service obligations, then the net transfer of resources will decline and perhaps even turn outward. India's request for debt relief in 1967 arose not from a reliance on short-term export credits or an abrupt balance-of-payments crisis, but because of a sharp drop in gross aid flows, chiefly on the part of the United States.[14] Net transfers to Chile during the last three years of the Frei regime averaged $84 million. In 1971, it swung to *minus* $46 million as new loan disbursements from OECD governments nearly dried up. At the end of that year, Allende called for debt relief.[15] Finally, to the extent that creditor governments impose trade barriers to the exports of their debtors, they make it more difficult, as the United States found in the interwar period, for the debtors to repay.

A third major influence contributing to cases of financial distress has been the condition of the world economy, especially the commodity market of greatest interest to the debtor. Often, payments deficits can be partly attributed to a collapse in the country's principal export market and a deterioration in its terms of trade. The international price of Brazilian coffee, for example, declined from 57 U.S. cents per pound in 1955 to 34 cents in 1963. Ghana in the early 1960s relied on cocoa for two-thirds of its export earnings, but its price fluctuated from 27 U.S. cents in 1956 to 44 cents in 1958 and then dived to a low of 17 cents in 1965.[16] Brazil and Ghana both experienced declines in their terms of trade during this period, costing Ghana lost foreign exchange earnings equivalent to 46 percent of its trade deficit on average.[17] The copper price also undermined Allende. From 1970 to 1971, the London price dropped by 23 percent, though it rose sharply in 1973.

Whether debts are renegotiated and the degree of relief, then, depend first on the severity of the financial situation and the prospects for the future. Creditor governments have always denied that an international regime for debt relief exists, hoping to discourage requests. They respond to requests "with extreme distaste and a great deal of sanctimonious talk about the breakdown of financial discipline, the risk of contagion and 'Kontrakt ist Kontrakt.' The result is usually some grudging stretching of debt service for a few years."[18] Typically in official refundings, the debtor is brought before an ad hoc, multilateral creditor club. The terms often have been commercial, sometimes allowing the creditor agency actually to profit from the renegotiations.[19] Frequently, relief has been limited to service payments due over a period of one or two years (the consolidation period), though in some cases relief was repeated several times.[20]

These common outcomes are exemplified by Brazil's renegotiations in 1961 and 1964 which will be considered next. The essay's arguments will then be further developed through examinations of Ghana's and Chile's experiences. These latter cases were chosen in order to illustrate outcomes that depart from the more common pattern, and not with the intention of rigorously testing hypotheses.

2. The Case of Brazil: 1958-1964

Brazil had a long history of defaults, refundings, and political instability prior to the 1950s. During the term of elected president Kubitschek (1956-1961), Brazil accomplished remarkable overall growth, but problems began to appear. Inflation accelerated in 1958, and Brazil's terms of trade were declining. After the 1958 elections, Kubitschek authorized a stabilization program, though more gradual than the shock treatment recommended by the IMF whose approval was a condition for a major American bilateral loan. But each turn of the screws brought to the surface domestic political protest by affected groups. Industrialists succeeded in frustrating the credit cutback; coffee growers denounced the restrictions on the coffee support program. The Kubitschek government was stung by charges from the left that its officials were stooges of Wall Street and the IMF. The domestic political conflict became quite shrill and bitter. In June 1959, Kubitschek decided on a bold shift in strategy: he broke off negotiations with the IMF, making Brazil the first country to reject an IMF program outright, and he abandoned the stabilization program. He declared in a speech before the Military Club, "Brazil has come of age. We are no longer poor relatives obliged to stay in the kitchen and forbidden to enter the livingroom. We ask only for collaboration of other nations. By making greater sacrifices we can attain political and principally economic independence without the help of others."[21] This gesture of defiance won him considerable support both at home and abroad,[22] but it did not stop the inflation, check the decline in terms of trade, or help Brazil diversify its exports. The deficit was covered with greater short- and medium-term commercial borrowing.

The outcomes of the next four years, including debt relief, also reflected changes in Brazilian domestic political conditions, though in the end the debtor submitted to the creditors' demands. The new president, Janio Quadros, was a charismatic figure who drew his greatest support from Brazil's upper classes while giving the impression that he was sympathetic to Castro's socialism. Upon his inauguration in January 1961, Quadros denounced Kubitschek for overspending and announced that the nation faced an alarming foreign debt problem. He quickly instituted a more severe anti-inflation program, which included dismissal of public employees, cuts in import subsidies, devaluation, a wage freeze, and a credit squeeze.[23] The IMF gave its approval, the creditors were relieved, and they agreed then to a package of debt relief and new aid totaling $2 billion. The U.S. announcement made clear that the Kennedy administration regarded Brazil's economic development as vital for maintaining democratic government in Latin America.

Suddenly, in his eighth month and under pressure at home for his independent foreign policy vis-à-vis. Cuba, Quadros submitted his resignation, perhaps as a domestic bargaining ploy, but Congress quickly accepted. Joao Goulart, the vice-president, was a populist whose political base was in the labor unions. Goulart eventually became president, and soon, like his predecessors, he found himself caught between the pressures of foreign creditors and the protests of domestic opponents. Goulart vacillated, attempting in successive moves to placate first one and then the other, and succeeded only in displeasing nearly everyone. During a trip to Washington in the spring of 1962, he tried to reassure the United States and the IMF by declaring his opposition to Castro and promising to treat foreign investors reasonably. The United States released aid funds which had been held up because of unfulfilled demands for reducing government spending. Nevertheless, the economy deteriorated during 1962 with inflation accelerating. Food riots and a general strike took place in July.

In early 1963, the government adopted a new stabilization program of the sort Quadros had effected. The finance minister also tried to persuade the Americans to refinance Brazil's large foreign debt to allow imports to continue, but Washington was becoming disillusioned and concerned about Communist infiltration. A new aid commitment was made, but disbursement was conditioned on policy performance, including restrained wage increases. The Goulart advisers reasoned that Brazil could not afford another Kubitschek gesture of independence.[24] Just after an IMF mission arrived in Brazil, however, the cabinet knuckled under to demands for a 70 percent salary increase for the civil servants and the most powerful political group, the military.[25] Ministers who favored the anti-inflation program were unable to mobilize domestic political forces to carry the day. The IMF did not make the loan. In June, there was active but inconclusive consideration in Brazil of a plan to declare a unilateral debt moratorium. Goulart had turned away from the stabilization plan in response to objections from the extreme left, and then was without a program for dealing with the insistent inflation and debt problems. He replaced his chief economic policymakers, and, in January 1964, he implemented a new law restricting the level of profits foreign investors could repatriate.

Economic conditions continued to deteriorate, and the domestic political struggle increasingly came to be dominated by the extremes of left and right, while Goulart failed to organize a mass political base to defend his regime. In the absence of a strong anti-inflation program, foreign creditors continued to refuse more than minor and very short-leash help. In addition, they objected to the profit remittances law, and the United States was becoming more and more concerned about leftist tendencies in the federal government. U.S. aid was given, however, to favored state governors. The U.S. embassy was aware after late 1963 that conspiratorial activity was growing rapidly.[26]

The shift in Brazil's foreign economic policy came on the heels of the dramatic overthrow of the Goulart regime and the democratic institutions at the end of March 1964. In mid-March, Goulart had decreed new land reform and nationalization policies at a major political rally, which indicated to the military that he had adopted the advice of his most radical advisers to rally the "popular forces" and perhaps suspend the constitutional regime. After Goulart also sided with rebels in the navy who were challenging senior officers and after he rejected last-minute warnings from moderate officers, he was deposed. With lightning speed, the United States sent its "warmest wishes" to the new head of state within two days.[27] The military government moved decisively to meet the foreign creditors' conditions, and, in turn, Brazil was granted debt relief and new credits. The generals abolished import subsidies for wheat and oil, revoked the profit remittance law, simplified the exchange system, and clamped down on credit, putting the economy into recession. The mass public was, of course, "denied its voting power, and strong labor unions were dissolved."[28] The generals repudiated the independent foreign policy of their predecessors and shifted to an unequivocal pro-American position.[29] The 1964 Hague Club Agreement refunded the arrears accumulated since 1961 and 70 percent of the payments due in 1964 and 1965 on relatively hard terms. Private American and European banks provided an additional $138 million in new credits.[30] A Brazilian regime with a different power base and different domestic priorities found it much easier to agree with foreign advice. During this stage of its history, Brazil's politics contributed to volatile financial relations in the medium term, followed by compliance with the vision of the dominant powers. In this case, there is little evidence of either creditors' division or debtor solidarity.

3. The Case of Ghana: 1966-1974

Ghana's case, like Brazil's, shows the intimate two-way relationship between debtor politics and international debt relations. But it also provides a glimpse of one attempt to escape from an unequal international bargaining situation, the rare tactic of unilateral repudiation. When Nkrumah's regime was overthrown in 1966, it left behind a medium-term debt that has been variously placed between £100 million and £400 million.[31] The repayment obligations were beyond Ghana's capacity, and the National Liberation Council (NLC) declared a debt moratorium but accepted the obligations and began negotiations with the IMF. Fearing that Nkrumah might be able to enlist Soviet support for a countercoup, the NLC officers quickly expelled Soviet and Chinese technicians from Ghana and shifted foreign policy decisively toward the West. The United States, though it had little stake in the medium-term debt, enthusiastically sent military aid, soft development loans, and PL480 food shipments. Western donors refused Nkrumah's requests for aid.[32]

To restore the confidence of foreign suppliers, the NLC accepted IMF conditions for a stabilization program and received a standby credit. The Fund sponsored a meeting of major creditors to arrange debt relief. Britain held the largest share of the suppliers' credits; West Germany was the only other major creditor holding a substantial share.[33] The British had the most to lose from a soft settlement, and they took the toughest stance among the creditors. The less involved the creditor, and the softer the terms of its loan, the more likely it is to tolerate a generous debt relief exercise. The United States was more lenient for this reason, for political reasons, and also because tough terms would have, in effect, transferred much of the benefit of its soft loans back to the harder lenders.[34] The agreement reached in December 1966 consolidated 80 percent of the medium-term debts falling due in the two and a half years after June 1966. These amounts were to be deferred until 1971, then repaid in eight years. In 1968, a similar agreement was reached covering payments falling due in 1969-1972. Without rescheduling, Ghana's 1969 debt service would have been £45 million, slightly less than half its export earnings.[35] But these agreements also provided for new interest charges of up to 6 percent during the moratorium. According to the government of Ghana, the addition of moratorium interest increased Ghana's nominal obligations by 38 percent.[36]

In 1969, the military government held elections and returned power to a civilian government. The new finance minister, J. H. Mensah, took a harder line in negotiations with creditor governments, arguing in 1969 and 1970 for a longer-range settlement to facilitate planning, and proposing that they refinance the credits of their exporters with official loans on soft terms (40 years maturity, 10 years grace, 2 percent interest) so that the balance of foreign exchange receipts could be used for development rather than debt repayment. Mensah also wanted moratorium interest and contractual interest under earlier agreements dropped.[37]

Most creditor countries were sympathetic in view of Ghana's continuing tight situation, but the British rejected the proposal, adamantly opposing the waiver of moratorium interest. If the other creditors had been able to bring the British around to their view, a final settlement probably would have been reached in July 1970. Instead, Ghana's negotiations with the British broke down. Britain was determined to avoid setting a precedent that other Commonwealth countries might cite to escape from their own contracts.[38] When another two-year consolidation was finally agreed in July 1971, over Mensah's objections, he complained testily, "The agreement we are signing not only threatens to sanctify, with the concurrence of our Government, the principle of relieving debts by increasing them, but also, embodies a particularly harsh application of that principle."[39] He pointed out that Western creditors imposed harsher terms than Ghana's Eastern creditors.

During 1971, Ghana's balance of payments took a turn for the worse. After Mensah lifted import controls and set an expansionary budget in 1970, imports surged upward. Furthermore, the cocoa export price, which had rocketed from 17 cents to 46 cents per pound in 1969, plunged again in 1971 to 27 cents.[40] With their international reserves approaching exhaustion, Ghanaian leaders differed sharply over whether to accept creditor and IMF demands for painful austerity measures to deal with inflation and payments deficits. Mensah argued that the payments problem was cyclical and that such a stringent program would have unacceptable development and political effects.[41] Creditor governments refused to make further aid commitments until Ghana came to terms. The prime minister and the cabinet eventually decided in December 1971 to enact an extremely large devaluation, one that immediately raised import prices 78 percent. The political effects became apparent almost as quickly as the economic. Many imported consumer goods nearly doubled in price or disappeared from the shelves, and public discontent flared. On January 13, 1972, military officers, partly motivated by long-simmering dissatisfaction with the way the government was treating the military, again overthrew the elected government.[42]

By failing to anticipate accurately the domestic political consequences of their demands and internal conflicts, the creditor governments apparently helped pull the rug from under themselves. The National Redemption Council (NRC) led by Colonel Acheampong shifted external policy abruptly toward a much harder line, despite the extremely serious financial situation. They decided to make explicit the ability of a desperate debtor to rupture financial relations. The NRC sought public support by rescinding half the devaluation immediately. They declared a moratorium on payment of short-term foreign debts, including substantial arrears. After a month, the new government repudiated outright £35 million in "corrupt" Nkrumah medium-term debts to four British firms, over half of Ghana's debts to Britain. The NRC announced, moreover, that all other supliers' credits would be honored only if it were determined that they were linked to economically viable projects and were not "vitiated by fraud, corruption or other illegaility."[43] Further, legitimate suppliers' credits would then be repaid on IDA terms (10 years grace, 50 year amortization); this unilateral step would mean the credits then had a grant element of 90 percent, effectively repudiating most of them. It was announced that the earlier rescheduling agreements, including moratorium interest, would not be honored and that Ghana henceforth would meet with its creditors only bilaterally. No U.S. debt was repudiated. New efforts to discipline imports and restrict smuggling, together with an "Operation Feed Yourself," were begun.[44]

In the end, the NRC failed to sustain all their demands, but the final settlement was considerably more favorable to Ghana than anything the creditors had accepted before the repudiations. The British initially suspended export credit guarantees and, in 1973, exerted strong and successful pressure to delay approval of a World Bank loan.[45] The United States was initially more sympathetic, but its position hardened as the expropriation and debt dispute with Chile became more acrimonious.[46] For a time, the repudiation did make it difficult for Ghana to get import credit, but in 1972 Ghana's balance of payments began to benefit from another sharp upswing in raw-materials markets. In 1972 and 1973, Ghana registered payments surpluses, began repaying its short-term debts, and got import credit flowing again, though under Ghanaian restraints.[47] To emphasize the independence of their bargaining position, the NRC also resumed aid and trade ties with the Soviet-bloc countries. But new Western aid was being delayed, and in March 1974 a final settlement of the medium-term debts was agreed multilaterally. In one of the most generous debt relief operations to date, the medium-term Nkrumah debts were rescheduled over eighteen years, beginning after ten years grace, with an interest rate of 2.5 percent beginning with the moratorium period. Ghana was not forced to make performance commitments, as Indonesia had been in 1970. A precedent-setting feature of the agreement allowed the government of Ghana three months in which to repudiate certain "corrupt" loans if sufficient documentation could be supplied. Five contracts were challenged under this procedure, but the creditor representatives did not consider the documentation sufficient, and the government of Ghana quietly dropped the matter.[48]

Between 1966 and 1974, then, the leadership of Ghana changed three times, reflecting both domestic concerns and foreign influence. The 1972 coup by the NRC in particular brought about a notable change in Ghana's policy toward foreign debt, though the direction of the change was hardly predictable from the Brazilian military coup of 1964 or others. The outcome of Ghana's debt renegotiation shows the difficulty of escaping from the underlying international position of weakness, and some scope for maneuver within that position. The debtor government improved its bargain by national action without assistance from other debtor states. Divisions among creditors in this case did not lead to separate conflicting settlements, but they did delay the eventual multilateral settlement by several years.

4. The Case of Chile: 1970-1977

The case of Chile in the 1970s shows again how dramatically the policy of the debtor country may depend on domestic political developments. Creditor responses to Chile also illustrate how policies may differ according to political values in the creditor states as well as relative financial stakes, giving the debtor some leeway. But considering the strategies of the Allende and Pinochet regimes indicates also the difficulty of eluding foreign creditors' demands over the long run.

Prior to the Allende regime, Chile suffered recurring debt problems related to pesistent inflation and payments deficits. At the end of 1964, the new government of Eduardo Frei requested debt relief; export credits due in 1965 and 1966 were consolidated and refinanced or rescheduled on a commercial basis. In its last three years under Frei, Chile obtained substantial new foreign loans, thereby avoiding overall payments deficits.[49] In addition, despite the inflation and Chile's stagnant growth rate, private banks were willing to risk short-term trade credit, normally around $300 million from all sources, in order to gain a foothold in this market.[50]

Upon taking office in November 1970, Allende therefore inherited a heavy involvement in foreign debt, and thus a strong underlying susceptibility to foreign creditor influence over policy. But Allende chose not to risk the repudiation strategy tried by Acheampong. In fact, the Popular Unity government made strenuous efforts during its first year to keep up payments to foreign banks; it also continued to repay on schedule all debts to international organizations, all debts incurred under Allende, and payments due under the debt consolidations of 1948 and 1965.[51] Chile and Brazil, with considerably more modernized economies than Ghana, had correspondingly more to lose in private foreign credit forgone as a result of repudiation. But, of course, Popular Unity was also committed to a thoroughgoing restructuring of the domestic economy along socialist lines, including nationalization of banks, mines, industries, and farms. The expropriation of the U.S. copper properties was the centerpiece of the program, and decisions were made in mid-1971 that the two major companies would receive no compensation.

Very soon after Allende's inauguration, U.S. creditors began what became an almost total withdrawal of the short-term credit they had extended to the Frei regime. Loss of creditworthiness was given as the reason,[52] despite the debt repayments and the economic boom with low inflation that Chile experienced until the end of 1971, and even though alternative Western sources continued to lend. President Nixon and Secretary of the Treasury Connally decided on a tougher U.S. policy toward expropriations in 1971. Soon after the copper-compensation announcement, the Export-Import Bank, citing the copper dispute, refused a Chilean request for a loan to buy three Boeing planes, a move denounced as interference even by the Christian Democratic opposition in Chile. Evidently the

State Department resisted, but sources there reported that the decision had been made "at White House level" in response to strong pressure from U.S. business.[53] In addition, no more loans were made to Chile by the World Bank after June 1970 or by the Inter-American Development Bank (IDB) after January 1971, even though the IDB did make new loans during that period to Argentina and Uruguay, which had comparable inflation rates in 1972. Chile's net transfer turned negative in 1971. Meanwhile, copper prices and export receipts dropped in 1971 while imports increased slightly, so that the current account deficit increased sharply as the capital account surplus was evaporating.[54] Reserves declined seriously.

In November 1971, the government suspended payments on most of its foreign debts and asked to renegotiate payments due through 1974. The United States held over half the debt, but Allende's strategy was evidently to maintain good relations with the Europeans, Chile's major customers for copper, and to isolate the American opposition. Like Britain in Ghana's case, the United States adopted the hardest line in the Paris Club meetings, holding out against relief unless Chile accepted IMF supervision of its economy and paid adequate compensation to U.S. copper companies. Other major creditors sharply opposed the latter condition, and the Chilean government insisted on autonomy in domestic economic policy.[55] During the negotiations in March 1972, documents describing the plotting of International Telephone and Telegraph at the time of Allende's election were published, which may have weakened the United States and strengthened Allende in the debt bargaining.[56] Other creditor governments agreed to debt relief, perhaps preferring not to be identified with an effort to bail out American companies. In April 1972, the United States acquiesced to a multilateral agreement to defer 70 percent of payments, but only payments due in late 1971 and 1972 and on relatively hard terms. On the expropriation question, Chile agreed to an ambiguous formula, specifying that "just" compensation should be paid according to "Chilean and international law," but Chile did not have to submit to an IMF standby.[57] Chile was given a short breather, and was told to return a year later to discuss relief for 1973. The U.S.-government effort to prevent debt relief may also have been weakened by Chile's success in January 1972 in renegotiating most of its 1972 and 1973 obligations to the private banks.[58] In any case, the U.S. government refused to agree to relief on its own credits until after Allende was overthrown.

In 1972, the Popular Unity government pursued its strategy of using other powers to strengthen itself against the United States. In November 1972, the finance minister announced that Chile had been able to increase its foreign borrowing, mentioning short-term credits amounting to $250 million from Canada, Argentina, Mexico, Australia, and Western Europe and $103 million from the USSR. Long-term loans came from the USSR, Eastern Europe, and China ($446 million) and from other Latin American countries ($70 million). Many of the loans were tied to purchases in the donor country.[59]

But after 1971, the Chilean economy deteriorated steadily and severely, partly because of the government's own policies and partly because of factors beyond its control. As a result of the nationalizations and efforts to sabotage them, both agricultural and industrial production had fallen drastically by October 1972, many basic foods and industrial spare parts were missing from the shelves at times, and inflation stood at about 115 percent for the year.[60] Shortages forced a sharp increase in food imports and a drain on foreign exchange. A twenty-three-day general strike in October 1972 posed a severe political challenge to the government. Truck owners, who started this campaign, evidently received financial support from the CIA.[61] Moreover, Kennecott seriously hurt foreign exchange earnings by legal action preventing European customers from paying for copper shipments. The Soviet government reportedly declined to give more aid after 1972 until Chile got its house in order and credit from the World Bank had been reopened, probably reflecting unwillingness to take on the cost of another client like Cuba.[62]

In 1973, the Allende government lost further control of both the economy and the polity. It continued rapid nationalizations, in defiance of the congress and the courts, and accelerated the runaway creation of currency. The consumer price increase for the twelve months ending in August 1973 has been estimated at over 300 percent.[63] The government maintained that the country's troubles were caused by domestic and foreign opponents. In July 1973, Chile returned to the Paris Club to ask for debt relief for 1973 and 1974.[64]

A military coup crushed Popular Unity and Chile's democratic institutions on September 11, 1973. The new Pinochet junta reversed nationalizations and Allende's anti-U.S. foreign policy, and adopted stringent economic policies designed to return the country to a free market system, attract foreign investment, and end the inflation and payments deficit. The junta pledged to honor Chile's debts and agreed to reopen the question of compensation for U.S. copper firms.

Quickly, the United States and some European creditors exchanged policies toward Chile. The United States dispatched relatively large loans for wheat and corn. The Inter-American Development Bank soon made two more-substantial loans, one of which was processed with unusual speed. The Eximbank reconsidered the suspension of its programs for Chile.[65] By November, there was "a dramatic turnaround in the availability of private United States (short-term) bank loans."[66] In November, the U.S. government dropped the demand that copper compensation be paid as a precondition for renegotiating Chile's debts.[67] The Pinochet government satisfied IMF terms for a standby loan, and in March 1974 it succeeded in negotiating debt relief for 1973 and 1974 on relatively hard terms.[68]

European members of the Paris Club went along, though some had already expressed opposition to the regime on moral and ideological grounds. These objections to the junta's brutal domestic repression surfaced in December 1973, when West Germany held up IDB loans to Chile. "In the World Bank there was very strong opposition to the new government on the part of a number of West European countries."[69] And, in 1975, Britain, Italy, Belgium, the Netherlands, Sweden, Norway, and Denmark refused on human-rights grounds to renegotiate the 1975 debt service. One U.S. official said, without a smile, "We expressed displeasure that, broadly speaking, some countries put political aspects above technical considerations."[70] The United States was joined by France, West Germany, Spain, and Canada in renegotiating on a bilateral basis that year. The

German delegation told these other creditors that, for human rights and domestic political reasons, the delegation was unable to agree to terms more generous than those extended to Allende; that position limited 1975 debt relief.[71] Reportedly because of the human-rights issue, the Pinochet government decided in 1976 and 1977 not to seek further debt renegotiation.[72] Nevertheless, by early 1976, Chile had received some $2 billion in foreign credits since the coup, even though its inflation rate was still the highest in the world.[73]

5. Conclusions

Considering cases other than these three would cast light on different relations and phenomena. Military conflict as a precipitating or contributing factor in debt renegotiations is indicated by the cases of Pakistan (1972) and Zaire (1975-1978). Indonesia's experience in the late 1960s confirms that sometimes the debtor can get help from one creditor (the United States) in bargaining over the terms of new aid from another (Japan).[74] Meetings concerning India show that intercreditor bargaining can cause a shift in the shares of the burden accepted by specific creditors.[75] India's experience also demonstrates that debt relief is sometimes given deliberately as a form of development assistance in the absence of a debt servicing emergency. The cases of Mexico and Argentina provide a basis for investigating the conditions under which a heavy borrower can avoid explicit renegotiation of obligations, even when its economy is faltering.

The cases of Brazil, Ghana, and Chile examined here show, first, the effects of cyclical changes in the world economy, economic and financial practices of debtor governments, and policies of creditor governments in bringing about occasions of imminent or actual default and renegotiation. Second, after debt relief has been requested, creditor governments are likely to form a united front, but in some cases their political values and differing economic interests may divide them. Such divisions may strengthen somewhat the bargaining leverage of the debtor government. In Ghana in 1966, the United States was prepared to reward the new Western-oriented government with

long-term assistance even though it was in default to other
creditors on medium-term debts. A credit boycott was not possible. On the other hand, in the 1970 talks concerning the
Nkrumah debts, the creditors with smaller shares did support
the British refusal to accept a softer relief agreement. Thereafter, to the extent that Ghana's leverage was enhanced, the
reason was other than creditor division.

Allende was able to continue to obtain debt relief and loans
after 1971, while Chile was defying U.S. demands; conceivably
this leeway could have helped his regime withstand U.S. pressure and interference if domestic economic and political policies
and conditions had been more favorable. While Chile had a
socialist government, it was able to obtain some help from prosocialist governments elsewhere. Then when the junta took
power, it was able to call on the relatively favorable regime in
Washington and U.S. banks while prosocialist regimes attempted
a hard line. In both periods, the underlying international structure of power favored the American policy. Reportedly, Zaire's
more recent difficulties elicited limited competition in gener-
osity between France and Belgium over postcolonial influence
in Kinshasa.[76] Divisions among creditor governments were not
apparent in the case of Brazil in the early 1960s.

Third, all three cases demonstrate the medium-term volatility
of debtor government policy in response to shifts in domestic
politics. In Brazil, more nationalistic and leftist groups seemed
to alternate with financially more-orthodox groups in influencing the calculations of political leaders regarding debt and
relief conditions in 1958, 1961, 1963, and 1964. Changes of
regime in Ghana in 1966, 1969, and 1972 each led to changes in
Ghana's policies in debt negotiations, as did the coup in Chile in
1973. Conversely, action by creditor governments can certainly
influence domestic politics in debtor states, Chile being the
most deliberate example. Also, foreign demands for orthodox
austerity measures can give political leaders a tool for increasing
their domestic support, if they reject the demands (Kubitschek
1958, Goulart 1963, Acheampong 1972). Or, whether they
reject or accept, the foreign demands can enhance conditions
under which their opponents can increase social instability or
oust the leadership (1964 junta in Brazil, the NLC in Ghana in

1966, Acheampong in 1972, Pinochet in Chile in 1973). It would be valuable to study a larger number of cases to determine which of these domestic effects of creditor policy is more common. These three cases suggest, in any case, that a military coup can produce either a more accommodating or a more intransigent debtor. The implication for lender and creditor governments, to say the least, is that their policy decisions require continuing specific analysis of domestic political conditions in borrowing and debtor countries. Withholding aid without regard to domestic political developments can rebound to the creditor's disadvantage.

Finally, after intervening domestic turbulence, the great underlying imbalance of power and vulnerability between creditors and debtor commonly expresses itself in the eventual compliance of the weak with the demands of the strong. If the past is a fair indicator, the implications for most Third World nationalists are sobering. But are there no processes or strategies that might aid less developed debtor states in escaping from this type of unequal dependence? One might speculate that three such escapes that have been effective on other issues will not operate on debt questions.

First, in bargaining with foreign investors in extractive industries, LDC governments have benefited from a long-run process that erodes the power of the multinational firm, known as "the obsolescing bargain."[77] As the perceived risk of the successful investment declines, the host country's expertise for operating the industry itself rises, and the government's experience in extracting concessions from the firm accumulates, the government makes bolder demands and increases the state's share of the return from the enterprise. In the case of foreign lending to sovereign borrowers for general purposes, successful economic development itself should similarly operate to make the state a more attractive borrower and thus to erode private lenders' bargaining power over terms. But "moving up a learning curve," in the sense of mastering the development problem itself, is much more problematic than mastering the techniques of producing and selling copper ore, so the process by which the credit bargain with private lenders might obsolesce seems less natural. For states encountering difficulties, the risk increases and the bargaining position of the state deteriorates. Official lenders operate according to different calculations. Economic progress should have the opposite effect there, diminishing the state's ability to acquire concessional loans, while countries experiencing stagnation or failure do not seem to elicit great sympathy regarding their debts to official creditors, until they reach sight of the point of insolvency. As a debtor state approaches that extreme point, its bargaining power on debt questions may again turn upward.

Second, the strategy of forming an international coalition of the weak has boosted the position of the OPEC countries and has been felt in voting in larger international organizations. But this strategy is unlikely to aid debtors in trouble. The debtors with the largest shares of the total debt owed to private lenders are most unwilling to frighten away their bankers by discussing a joint moratorium or repudiation. Even a combination including most LDC debtors would be unable to cause serious harm to the treasuries of creditor governments by withholding debt service payments. In any case, the chances of building such a coalition are very slim here as well. Of the seven states owing the largest amounts to official creditors, five are also actively seeking private financing.[78]

A third strategy would be to repudiate economic ties with the West and turn to the Soviet Union for support on the Cuban model. The Popular Unity regime in Chile received some support from the Eastern states in 1972, but the Soviet Union reportedly closed its purse thereafter. The Soviets themselves hold enough foreign debts to give them an interest in upholding the sanctity of contracts. So turning to the Soviet Union would have to be considered a limited strategy and a risky one, except perhaps in the form of a mild gesture to impress Western negotiators.

Ghana's case shows, nonetheless, that the desperate debtor is not without some souces of influence over the financial outcome. After repudiating some debt and sharply raising its demands concerning the balance in 1972, Ghana negotiated a more favorable settlement on the Nkrumah debt than creditors had been willing to accept before. Thus, it may be that once a debtor has passed a certain point, the additional cost of repudiating debt drops below the cost of continuing to honor it. In those circumstances, creditors are likely to reason that one cannot draw blood from a stone, causing them to value the debtor's promise to resume some payments in return for concessions. Past that point, the foreign creditor is the one who must worry about a disintegrating bargain. Perhaps no debtor is likely to place himself beyond that point deliberately as a matter of strategy. But the Ghana of 1972 through 1974 found itself in that condition with little to lose in access to capital markets, in contast to Brazil and Chile. In a sense, Ghana was then weak enough to drive a better bargain. At the same time, during the period when the final debt settlement was being negotiated, Ghana's bargaining position benefited from an improvement in its export markets. A sharply rising cocoa price and a payments surplus helped keep Ghana afloat. These two conditions may enhance the likelihood of both the attempt and the success of a debtor government strategy including selective repudiation. Nevertheless, as long as the underlying inequality of dependence persists, it is that international condition that can be expected to shape the main outlines of debt relief outcomes.

Notes

1. See Brian G. Crowe's article (Chap. 2) in this volume for a complete listing of official bilateral and multilateral debt renegotiations that have taken place since 1956.

2. Henry J. Bittermann, *The Refunding of International Debt* (Durham, N.C.: Duke University Press, 1973), p. 6.

3. It is true that the growth of aggregate LDC debt in real terms has been much less than the nominal rate. Also, a state may escape default by virtue of strong performance in exports, tourism, or capital inflows. But even those who are relatively optimistic about the future concede that the debt buildup in recent years has been quite large in particular cases, and that more refinancings or reschedulings might well be needed to avoid defaults (see Morgan Guaranty Trust Company, *World Financial Markets*, June 1977; and Gordon W. Smith, *The External Debt Prospects of the Non-Oil-Exporting Developing Countries: An Econometric Analysis* [Washington, D.C.: Overseas Development Council, 1977]).

4. Mahbub ul Haq, *The Poverty Curtain: Choices for the Third World*

(New York: Columbia University Press, 1976), p. 143.

5. See *New York Times*, August 4, 1976; *Business Week*, March 21, 1977, p. 117; *Latin America Economic Report*, 1976-1978, passim; and Nancy Belliveau, "Heading Off Zaire's Default," *Institutional Investor*, March 1977, pp. 23-28. Jonathan David Aronson's article (Chap. 11) in this volume deals explicitly with this matter.

6. Pierre Dhonte, "Describing External Debt Situations: A Roll-Over Approach," IMF Staff Papers, March 1975, pp. 159-87; also see Gershon Feder and Richard E. Just, "A Study of Debt Servicing Capacity Applying Logit Analysis," *Journal of Development Economics* 4, 1977, pp. 25-38.

7. See for example Robert Bee, "Lessons from Debt Reschedulings in the Past," *Euromoney*, April 1977, p. 33.

8. UNCTAD, *External Debt Experience of Developing Countries: Economic Developments following Multilateral Debt Renegotiations in Selected Developing Countries*, report by the UNCTAD Secretariat (TD/B/C.3/AC.8/9), November 19, 1974, pp. 9-12, 19; Bitterman, *Refunding of International Debt*, pp. 122-28.

9. "Ghana's 20 Years," *New African Development*, March 1977, pp. 184-89; David Denoon, "Aid: High Politics, Technocracy, or Farce?" (New York University, Department of Politics), Chap. 5; Ghana, *Economic Survey*, 1966, pp. 25-27.

10. Edward Glab, Jr., "A Political and Economic Overview of the Popular Unity Government," in *Chile: The Balanced View*, ed. Francisco Orrego Vicuna (Santiago: University of Chile, 1975), pp. 167-88; Cheryl Payer, *The Debt Trap* (New York: Monthly Review Press, 1975), pp. 184-99.

11. David Wall, *The Charity of Nations* (New York: Basic Books, 1973), p. 22.

12. *Partners in Development*, report of the Pearson Commission on International Development (New York: Praeger, 1969), pp. 119, 153-67.

13. See Philip A. Wellons, *Borrowing by Developing Countries on the Eurocurrency Market* (Paris: OECD, 1977), Chaps. 2 and 6.

14. Goran Ohlin, "Debts, Development, and Default," in *A World Divided*, ed. G. K. Helleiner (New York: Cambridge University Press, 1976), pp. 212-13.

15. Despite net transfers in 1972 and 1973 of $138 million and $104 million, Chile was still not able to get its accounts in order (IBRD, *World Debt Tables*, Report EC-167/76, 2 vol., October 31, 1976, vol. 2, p. 28).

16. IBRD, *Commodity Trade and Price Trends*, 1977 ed., Report No. EC-166/77, August 1977, pp. 30-33, 84-85.

17. UNCTAD, *External Debt Experience*, pp. 4-5. Changes in terms of trade were relatively unimportant to the debt renegotiations of Indonesia

(1966), India (1968), and Pakistan (1972).

18. Ohlin, "Debts, Development, and Default," p. 210.

19. Letter from the president of the U.S. Export-Import Bank to Senator William Proxmire, (U.S., Congress, Committee on Banking, Housing, and Urban Affairs, Subcommittee on International Finance, *International Debt*, Hearings, August 29, 1977 [Washington, D.C.: U.S. Government Printing Office, 1977], pp. 107-9).

20. The magnitude of relief (the proportion of payments due that are deferred) has varied noticeably among countries, as have the terms. But, in a number of cases, the period allowed for repaying the deferred amounts has been no more than four to eight years with a grace period. The interest rate on the consolidated debts is determined in bilateral negotiations with each creditor and varies among creditors. The debtor's obligations may be increased by charging additional interest during the moratorium period. The debtor is normally required to submit to certain "undertakings," such as restrictions on medium-term foreign borrowing and domestic demand, which have often been arranged by means of negotiations with the IMF for a standby credit. Most agreements contain a most-favored-nation clause for creditors to prevent the debtor from offering more favorable terms to one creditor than to another (UNCTAD, *External Debt Experience*; UNCTAD, *Present Institutional Arrangements for Debt Renegotiations* [TD/B/C.3/AC.8/13], February 26, 1975; IBRD, *Multilateral Debt Renegotiations: 1956-1968*, Report No. EC-170 prepared by Patrick de Fontenay, April 11, 1969).

21. *New York Times*, June 28, 1959, quoted by Thomas E. Skidmore, *Politics in Brazil, 1930-1964* (New York: Oxford University Press, 1967), p. 181.

22. Skidmore, *Politics in Brazil*, Chap. 5; and Payer, *Debt Trap*, pp. 148-49. For another interpretation, see Nathaniel H. Leff, *Economic Policy-Making and Development in Brazil, 1947-1964* (New York: Wiley, 1968), pp. 66, 105-6.

23. Skidmore, *Politics in Brazil*, pp. 194-95; *New York Times*, February 23, 1961, p. 8.

24. Skidmore, *Politics in Brazil*, pp. 240-41.

25. *New York Times*, May 19, 1963, p. 20.

26. Skidmore, *Politics in Brazil*, pp. 234-76; *New York Times*, August 30, 1963, p. 28.

27. *New York Times*, April 3, 1964, p. 1; Skidmore, *Politics in Brazil*, pp. 284-302.

28. Payer, *Debt Trap*, pp. 153-57; *New York Times*, May 1, 1964, p. 2.

29. Skidmore, *Politics in Brazil*, p. 329.

30. Bittermann, *Refunding of International Debt*, pp. 124-25.

31. Ghana, *Economic Survey 1966*, August 1967, p. 27, lists suppliers' credits outstanding at the end 1965 totaling NC301 million, equivalent to £150 million at prevailing exchange rates; see also *West Africa*, March 25, 1974, p. 329.

32. J. D. Esseks, "Economic Policies," in *Politicians and Soldiers in Ghana, 1966-1972*, ed. Dennis Austin and Robin Luckham (London: Frank Cass, 1975), pp. 37-44; Christopher Prout, "Finance for Developing Countries," in *International Economic Relations of the Western World, 1959-1971*, ed. Andrew Shonfield, vol. 2 (London: Oxford University Press, 1976), p. 398.

33. IBRD, *Multilateral Debt Renegotiations*, Table 6.

34. *West Africa*, April 1, 1974, p. 365; and Prout, "Finance for Developing Countries," p. 397.

35. Bittermann, *Refunding of International Debt*, pp. 168-71; *Financial Times*, October 23, 1968, p. 4.

36. *Financial Times*, July 7, 1970, p. 9.

37. Ibid.; Ghana, *Budget Statement for 1970-1971*, August 25, 1970, pp. 32-34.

38. Prout, "Finance for Developing Countries," p. 398; Ronald T. Libby, "External Co-Optation of a Less Developed Country's Policy-Making: The Case of Ghana, 1969-1972," *World Politics*, October 1976, pp. 74-75.

39. *Financial Times*, August 21, 1971, p. 23.

40. Denoon, "Aid: High Politics, Technocracy, or Farce?" Chap. 5; IBRD, *Commodity Trade*, p. 30.

41. Libby, "External Co-Optation," pp. 67-86. In retrospect, the key cocoa price was on an upward track interrupted by a decline between 1969 and 1971. From 1971 to 1976, the price quadrupled, supporting Mensah and astounding his foreign advisers.

42. Denoon, "Aid: High Politics, Technocracy, or Farce?" Chap. 5.

43. *Financial Times*, February 16, 1972, p. 9.

44. *West Africa*, April 29, 1974, p. 482; Libby, "External Co-Optation," pp. 86-87; *Economist* (London), February 12, 1972, p. 39; Esseks, "Economic Policies," p. 55; Prout, "Finance for Developing Countries," p. 399; and Bittermann, *Refunding of International Debt*, p. 173.

45. Denoon, "Aid: High Politics, Technocracy, or Farce?" Chap. 5.

46. *West Africa*, April 1, 1974, p. 367.

47. Libby, "External Co-Optation," p. 87; Ghana, *Budget Proposals for FY 1974-75*, by Col. I. K. Acheampong, August 23, 1974, p. 1.

48. *West Africa*, April 29, 1974, pp. 485-89; Denoon, "Aid: High Politics, Technocracy, or Farce?" Chap. 5; *New African Development*, March 1977, p. 189. The final settlement of the Nkrumah debts has still

not, however, brought Ghana to economic and financial happiness. In 1974, the balance of payments returned to deficit. The problems were traceable to the rise in the cost of oil and other imports, soaring import volume, the recession in advanced countries, plus a continuing decline in production of cocoa for export (related to smuggling and weather) despite the elevated world price. Soaring food prices and shortages confronted the Acheampong government with a grave political crisis in 1977 (*West Africa*, August 1, 1977, pp. 1576-77, and September 26, 1977, pp. 1973-75; *New York Times*, December 13, 1977, p. 6, and December 15, 1977, p. 2).

49. IMF Balance of Payments Yearbooks, quoted by Jonathan E. Sanford, *The Multilateral Development Banks and the Suspension of Lending to Allende's Chile*, study published by Congressional Research Service, Library of Congress, 1974; reprinted in Orrego Vicuna, ed., *Chile: The Balanced View*, Table 5, p. 149.

50. NACLA, *Latin America and Empire Report*, January 1973, p. 16; *New York Times*, November 12, 1973, p. 53.

51. See testimony of James R. Greene, Manufacturers Hanover Trust Company, U.S., Congress, Senate, Committee on Foreign Relations, *Multinational Corporations and United States Foreign Policy: Hearings*, March 28, 1973, Part I, pp. 361-64; *Financial Times*, July 31, 1973, p. 4; and *Latin America*, July 9, 1971, p. 223.

52. U.S., Congress, Senate, Committee on Foreign Relations, *Multinational Corporations*, pp. 360, 367; *New York Times*, November 12, 1973, p. 53.

53. *Latin America*, August 20, 1971; *New York Times*, August 14, 1971, cited by Paul E. Sigmund, "The 'Invisible Blockade' and the Overthrow of Allende," *Foreign Affairs*, January 1974, reprinted in Orrego Vicuna, ed., *Chile*, p. 115.

54. Sanford, *Multilateral Development Banks*, p. 149.

55. *New York Times*, November 10, 1971; Payer, *Debt Trap*, pp. 192-94; Economist Intelligence Unit, *Quarterly Economic Review of Chile*, No. 1, 1972, pp. 5-6; *Wall Street Journal*, January 10, 1972, p. 12; and *Business Week*, January 1972, p. 37. Britain and Germany reportedly supported the United States on expropriation (*Latin America*, September 15, 1972, p. 289).

56. *Latin America*, March 31, 1972, p. 101; *Quarterly Economic Review of Chile*, No. 2, 1972, pp. 5-6.

57. *Economist*, April 22, 1972, p. 101; *Latin America*, April 28, 1972.

58. Sigmund, "Invisible Blockade," p. 118; *Quarterly Economic Review of Chile*, No. 1, 1972, p. 6; NACLA, *Latin America and Empire Report*, January 1973, p. 19.

59. Sigmund, "Invisible Blockade," p. 119.

60. Glab, "Political and Economic Overview," pp. 186-91.

61. *Time*, September 24, 1973, quoted in NACLA, *Latin America and Empire Report*, October 1973, pp. 6-12; *New York Times*, September 24, 1974, p. 2. There is no doubt that the president of the United States intervened directly in Chilean politics to thwart Allende (see Richard Nixon, *RN: The Memoirs of Richard Nixon* [New York: Grosset and Dunlap, 1978] , p. 489).

62. *Latin America*, October 13, 1972, October 20, 1972, and March 23, 1973; *Financial Times*, March 27, 1973, p. 5.

63. Glab, "Political and Economic Overview," Table 12, p. 179.

64. *Journal of Commerce*, July 12, 1973, p. 9; *Financial Times*, July 31, 1973, p. 4.

65. *Washington Post*, October 6, 1973, p. 1; *Journal of Commerce*, October 17, 1973, p. 1, cited by James Petras and Morris Morley, *The United States and Chile: Imperialism and the Overthrow of the Allende Government* (New York: Monthly Review Press, 1975), p. 141; Sanford, *Multilateral Development Banks*, pp. 135-41; *Journal of Commerce*, January 10, 1974, p. 1.

66. *New York Times*, November 12, 1973, p. 53. This turnaround came while the Chilean economy and balance of payments were still in chaos, and before the government had settled the disputes with the U.S. government. However, Chilean policies had been changed, and copper production and copper export prices were on an upswing (*Bank of London and South America Review*, February 1974, pp. 101-2; *Financial Times*, April 24, 1974, p. 5).

67. *Latin America*, November 16, 1973, p. 362.

68. *Journal of Commerce*, January 31, 1974, p. 3; *Latin America Economic Report*, March 15, 1974, p. 41, and May 10, 1974, pp. 71-72.

69. Interview by Petras and Morley, *The United States and Chile*, pp. 146-49.

70. *New York Times*, May 17, 1976, p. 43.

71. *Financial Times*, June 5, 1975, p. 4; *Latin America*, March 7, 1975, p. 73; March 28, 1975, pp. 100-101; May 23, 1975, p. 158; interview with a U.S. official.

72. *Latin America Economic Report*, November 5, 1976, p. 170.

73. *New York Times*, February 20, 1976, p. 1; and March 15, 1976, p. 1. In 1975 and 1976, U.S. leaders also began to express their concern over the regime's harsh methods. In June 1977, the Carter administration brought human-rights considerations to bear on financial decisions, holding up two loans for Chilean farmers (*Latin America*, May 14, 1976, p. 150; *New York Times*, June 29, 1977, p. 3).

74. Franklin B. Weinstein, *Indonesian Foreign Policy and the Dilemma*

of Dependence (Ithaca, N.Y.: Cornell Unversity Press, 1976), p. 235.

75. See U.S., General Accounting Office, *Developing Countries' External Debt and U.S. Foreign Assistance: A Case Study*, report by the Controller General to the Congress, May 11, 1973; and IBRD, *Multilateral Debt Renegotiations*, pp. 17-18, 36.

76. Interviews with U.S. officials.

77. Raymond Vernon, *Sovereignty at Bay* (New York: Basic Books, 1971); Theodore H. Moran, *Multinational Corporations and the Politics of Dependence: Copper in Chile* (Princeton: Princeton University Press, 1974); Franklin Tugwell, *The Politics of Oil in Venezuela* (Stanford: Stanford University Press, 1975).

78. The other two, India and Pakistan, hold over $16 billion of the official credit, but their combined share is only 31 percent of the total (U.S., Department of the Treasury, "Report on the External Debt of Developing Countries and on Debt Relief Provided by the United States," January 1978, p. 26).

11

The Politics of Private Bank Lending and Debt Renegotiations

Jonathan David Aronson

It is better to have loaned and lost than never to have loaned at all.
—Leon Frazer[1]

Manias of foreign lending exploded on to the international economic stage in 1808-1810, 1823-1825, 1856-1865, 1885-1890, 1910-1913, and 1924-1928. Most of those booms were sparked by some exogenous shock that drew attention to new opportunities for profit, matured into a wave of euphoric over-lending, and ultimately subsided into "revulsion" and "discredit." Charles Kindleberger argues that cyclical borrowing was usually followed by cyclical default, primarily because the debtors' development never got thoroughly underway.[2] He contends that "productive loans in developing countries are not very productive and do not stay long out of default."[3]

Memory is short. Depression, default, and repudiation buried the foreign bond market without honor in the 1930s. In the two decades after World War II, official bilateral and multilateral aid and loans accounted for an overwhelming proportion of international capital transfers to LDC governments. The Interest Equalization Tax and the Voluntary Foreign Credit Restraint guidelines may or may not have steadied the U.S. balance of payments and delayed the dollar's devaluation; their implementation in the mid-1960s certainly accelerated the growth of the Eurocurrency and Eurobond markets and stimulated the expansion of U.S. banks abroad.[4] Exhumed and reincarnated, foreign private lenders rushed to service the expanding international borrowing needs of their corporate customers.

This chapter draws heavily on Chap. 7 of my *Money and Power: Banks and the World Monetary System* (Beverly Hills, Calif.: Sage Publications, 1978). John S. Odell generously provided me with insightful comments on an earlier draft.

They increasingly returned to governmental borrowers in 1971 and 1972 when President Nixon depressed U.S. interest rates in an effort to rejuvenate the American economy by November 1972. The quadrupling of oil prices further stimulated the 1970s private lending boom. Petrodollar recycling coupled with stagnant loan demand from traditional borrowers saturated banks with liquidity. Non-oil-exporting developing countries needed external funds to meet their higher oil costs and to continue their development programs. A perfect match!

Soothed by the relatively benign repayment experiences of the past thirty years, bankers ignored Santayana's warning. However, in the 1970s, as private banks replaced official institutions as the primary creditors of many richer, developing nations, private renegotiations became necessary with ever greater frequency. Moreover, as bunched debt-servicing payments come due between 1979 and 1981, such renegotiations could proliferate. Depression or even moderately severe global recession could provoke massive, domino defaults and undermine the solvency of the international banking and monetary systems and the stability of international economic relations.

Other chapters in this volume explore the national and international implications of official and private lending to LDCs. Here, three areas are examined. First, what are the mechanisms and what are the limits of private banks' political power over governments, particularly governments of developing nations? How has this influence evolved over time? Second, what do the experiences of five debtor nations contribute to our understanding of the relative bargaining power of private creditors and official debtors? Is there any credence to the hypothesis that as large, wealthier developing nations increase their private borrowing, their bargaining power improves vis-à-vis their creditors? Third, can private creditors assume explicitly political roles in the world economy thereby effectively diminishing the likelihood of a major economic collapse, or must the pattern of boom and bust eternally repeat itself?

1. The Mechanisms and Limits of Banks' Political Influence

British, French, and, to a lesser extent, German banks girdled the globe by 1870. Their operations and influence were linked to their home nations' policies; they lent mostly to their home nations' allies and colonies. Banks in each home country co-operated on loans. Each nation's banks concentrated on domestic clients, allies, and colonies for their overseas business, not on foreign competitors' markets.[5] Today, the largest international banks often work together on huge syndicate loans to third countries and compete actively in each others' home markets. The biggest banks have more in common with each other than with smaller financial institutions in their own nations. Indeed, the global integration of financial markets and institutions has altered the mechanisms of banks' political influence in the last twenty years.

Bank Power and Developed Nations

How might banks influence governments? In developed nations, banks lobby their home governments for their preferred policies. Traditional studies of corporate influence tend to focus on this direct mechanism.[6] However, large, international banks and insular, local and regional banks often have different interests on international banking issues and frequently counterbalance each other in their lobbying. Even when the banking industry is united, bank interests are frequently undercut by hostile government officials and by rapidly growing, countervailing "public interest" lobbies. Indeed, the politicization and publicity surrounding banking issues almost assure that leading bankers' public advocacy of major policy changes, particularly in the United States, will be rebuffed. No government official facing early elections will willingly put himself in the position of seeming to be in the banks' collective pocket.[7]

The decline of the banks' lobbying effectiveness in developed nations has not left the financial institutions powerless. They have simply been forced to rely on more subtle mechanisms of influence which developed as their market and structure became more global. When government regulations restrict bank freedom, banks' global flexibility allows them to slip through existing loopholes. Thus, banks were unable to persuade U.S. authorities to remove exchange restrictions between 1963 and 1974, but legally evaded their intent. Regulatory efficiency suffered.[8] In addition, the growth of the unregulated Euromarkets was vastly stimulated, making it more difficult for authorities to control global money supply and manage exchange rate stability.

The banks' ability to indirectly influence government policies also grew with the growth of the Euromarkets. Although bank and other market participants were unable to dictate specific policies on developed country governments, their control of vast liquidity, far surpassing governments' reserves, allowed them to limit governments' choice of viable options. Thus, when the private sector determined that the structure of the monetary system was unacceptable after the second devaluation of the dollar on February 12, 1973, private actors used the market to shut down the system and forced floating exchange rates on reluctant government officials. This was done even though banks and corporations considered the second devaluation sufficient in economic terms.[9] Euromarket flexibility and market participants' wariness of national economic policies suggest that commercial banks will indirectly influence the content and effectiveness of nations' economic and monetary policies. Money's fungibility and the growth of bank resources in the future may allow banks even greater latitude in neutralizing government policies they oppose.

It is striking, however, that to date many banks have used their indirect influence unconsciously rather than intentionally. Remarkably, most bankers cling to the notion that their operations are entirely economic and never political.[10] They have not admitted, apparently even to themselves, that their narrow pursuit of private interests may sidetrack government policies. Apparently, this blind spot has slowed the effective use of banks' indirect influence in international relations among developed nations and also their influence on relations between developed and developing nations. If banks choose to exercise their full power, subtly and without publicity, their potential political influence is great.

Bank Power and Developing Nations

Bank influence over policies in developing nations is more direct. The demand for funds to continue development policies is so great in most LDCs that private banks derive considerable power from their ability to grant and withhold credit. By announcing the conditions under which they will lend, banks can influence the direction and pace of development and economic policies. As long as a government's demand for external credit exceeds banks' willingness to supply additional credit, the banks hold substantial leverage. In practice, banks' influence over developing countries varies considerably from country to country. In general, private bank influence on the least developed countries is minimal because governments and international financial institutions provide most of the funds for those nations on a concessionary basis. Bank influence over LDCs just beginning to turn to private sources for funds is rather substantial because the country is willing to go to some lengths to generate an inflow of funds. On the other end of the spectrum, the wealthier developing countries which already have established themselves as prime borrowers may be able to reduce banks' influence over their policies by creating competition among would-be lenders, particularly if those lenders "need" to lend money. Bank power over LDC borrowers also depends on the ability of lenders to utilize their funds profitably elsewhere. Predictably, banks saturated with liquidity in the mid-1970s eagerly lent to "safe," richer LDCs.[11]

The institutional drive for business is often misunderstood outside the banks. Myth has it that "banking is the art of lending money and getting it back." Untrue. When loans are repaid, creditors must find new debtors or shrink in size. Large lenders prefer borrowers who roll over their debts while religiously meeting their interest payments. When loan demand is slack, banks must maintain existing loan levels or face declining profits and edgy stockholders.[12] Today, a renewable loan to AT&T on very thin margins may be less desirable than a profitable Mexican government loan.

As a result of these profitability considerations, bank influence could diminish in many LDCs. Prior to 1970, short maturity credits dominated private lending to LDCs. Longer-term credits became more common in the early 1970s and are now reaching maturity at an ever-increasing rate. The banks want to assure relatively prompt loan servicing, but they do not want to withdraw from Third World lending. Indeed, banks are aware that if they chose to withdraw, they would risk provoking costly defaults.[13] As a result, in those nations where private banks have large, profitable exposures, their ability to force major policy shifts on governments without official support from the developed countries and the international financial institutions is apparently declining. Since commercial banks need LDC loans to maintain their current profitability, they are eager for their LDC borrowers to prosper.

Moreover, major LDC defaults could threaten the solvency of banks worldwide. If direct bank influence over their major LDC clients is declining and if banks' indirect influence over developed nations is growing, is it possible that private banks could enter the international political arena to protect their interests and, in the process, substantially influence the negotiations between the developed and developing nations on the issue of the New International Economic Order? These questions are examined in the next two sections.

2. Debt Renegotiations between
Private Banks and LDC Governments

Lending is a two-way street. Banks influence LDCs by extending or denying credit. Their lending policies affect nations' economic policies and development. However, once substantial funds are extended, banks are committed. When large sums are involved, banks are unlikely to cut their losses and run. Usually, nations unable to service their external debts have rescheduled their public borrowings and refinanced their private ones. Lenders are strict because they control the borrower's creditworthiness, but understanding because default or repudiation would be calamitous. In the game of brinkmanship, however, the threat of national debt repudiation gives the borrower an advantage.

Despite the LDC private debt explosion of the 1970s, the lack of repayment of the principal of Eurocurrency loans and the shifting composition of debt adumbrates major shifts in debt renegotiations. The nature and outlook for official debt renegotiations are described elsewhere in this volume. Private renegotiations follow a similar, but not identical, pattern.

While official creditor clubs almost always occupy center stage, private renegotiations frequently take place in separate, though sometimes parallel, meetings. In addition, the differing bargaining positions between public borrowers and private creditors sometimes preclude the actual calling of meetings of private creditor clubs and force debtors and creditors to work out their differences in other frameworks.

The growing volume of private lending to LDCs has made it necessary to consider mechanisms for handling overdue private debt. In the past, private creditor clubs have often mirrored the results of their official brethren, but usually have relied more on refinancing than on rescheduling. What common roots do formal and informal renegotiations between private creditors and official debtors share? How might these interactions affect the relations between industrialized and developing nations? By examining five major cases of creditor-debtor interactions, wider conclusions can be drawn.

Loans and Negotiations with Zaire

Zaire was a major test case and prime irritant for commercial banks. Its rich copper bounty and seemingly unending mineral wealth promised to make Zaire "the Brazil of Africa." However, its people are poor, its infrastructure primitive, and its birthrate high. Still, Zaire's government had maintained stable control over a country blessed with abundant copper, cobalt, and zinc deposits. Commercial banks, particularly from nations needing Zaire's minerals, decided to participate in the financing of Zaire's growth. Banks' massive post-1973 liquidity also persuaded them to experiment with lending to Zaire.

Table 1 indicates that in 1973 fifteen Japanese banks entered into thirty-three Eurocurrency syndicate participations to Zaire. No other nation's banks were nearly as active. American and European banks quickly entered the competitive fray. Belgian banks that had maintained their colonial ties were also active. Indeed, any foreign bank with an office in Zaire was dragged into Zaire's money-raising efforts.[14] U.S. and European banks continued to lend to Zaire in 1974 and 1975, but Japanese banks, shackled with liquidity problems after Herstatt's collapse in mid-1974, stopped all publicized lending to Zaire after 1973.

Table 1
Publicly Announced Private Bank Lending to Zaire by the Largest 300
in the World: 1973 - 1976 [a]

Bank's Origin	# In Top 300	1973		1974		1975		1976	
		Man	Par	Man	Par	Man	Par	Man	Par
Canada	7	0	9	0	4	0	3	0	0
Europe	10	5	14	1	2	0	0	0	0
Japan	15	2	33	0	0	0	0	0	0
U.K.	7	1	13	0	1	0	1	0	0
U.S.	13	2	14	3	2	2	6	0	0
Total Top 300	52	10	83	4	9	2	10	0	0
Other Smaller Banks	24	5	30	0	2	1	4	0	0
Total All Banks	76	15[b]	113	4	11	3	14	0	0
Ratio T300/All Banks	.68		.73		.82		.71		--
Ratio Par/Man			7.53		2.75		4.67		---

Source: Amex Euromoney Syndication Guide

[a] These contain publicly announced loans only and are not complete. The author
has attempted to aggregate loans and participations extended by two or more
units with identical ownership. Thus if U.S. headquarters and a London subsidiary of the same bank each participate in the same loan, only one participation
is counted. When a subsidiary or consortia bank has multiple stockholders,
they are counted as individual banks. Difficulty in identifying exact ownership
of some smaller banks may slightly distort the numbers in the table but should
not change their overall distribution greatly.

Man = Managed, Par = Participated. Banks often manage or participate in multiple
loans to a country in a single year. Syndicate loans can have multiple managers
and varying numbers of participants.

[b] In 1973 the publicly announced credits to Zaire were managed by five European,
five American, two Japanese, two consortium, and one British bank.

When repayment difficulties surfaced, much of the Japanese
bank debt was senior to the debt of banks from Europe and the
United States.

By 1974, Zaire's total external debt reached $2.5 billion.
Quadrupled oil prices increased the prices of essential imports
even as Zaire's economy was disrupted by the Angolan civil war
which crippled the transport of copper. The war also impoverished Zaire since it was sending material aid to one faction.
Falling copper prices in 1974 and 1975 and Zaire's inept
handling of newly nationalized industries siphoned away foreign
exchange and left the economy in a shambles. In 1970, Zaire's
current account deficit was only $25 million. The deficit
jumped to $200 million in 1973, $500 million in 1974, and
approximately $800 million in 1975. Simultaneously, Zaire's
international reserve position, which had increased from $186

million in 1970 to $234 million at the end of 1973, dropped to $140 million at the close of 1974 and to $58 million at the end of 1975.

By the end of 1975, commercial banks were concerned about their Zairian debts. Many syndicate loans were in arrears on their interest and principal for as long as nine months. Furthermore, Zaire seemed to be giving preference to some banks at the expense of others and was not providing appropriate explanation or information. Since a single bank calling for default could have jeopardized the position of all external private lenders and official creditors as well, joint action was needed. Banks refused to enter into new agreements and cancelled a previously negotiated, but unsigned, loan in early 1976 when foreign investors in a new mining project abandoned it.[15] Private banks were left holding approximately $400 million in loans to Zaire which the government was unable to repay.

In the spirng of 1976, following extensive IMF technical assistance, Zaire announced an economic stabilization plan, requested an official creditor club for the purpose of general debt rescheduling, and expressed willingness to meet with its private creditors. In late April 1976, agent banks met in London and began to work toward a unified approach. In June, Zaire persuaded its official creditors to reschedule its official debts at Paris Club meetings, and declared its intention of treating private debts on the same terms as its official debts. In mid-July, the U.S. Export-Import Bank persuaded Zaire to agree in principle to a preferential-payments mechanism for its governmental debt, angering private debtors who saw this move as a clear violation of the spirit of a unified approach. Prompted by the government initiatives, the private banks began to achieve a more unified position in which thirteen agent banks, under the leadership of Citibank's Dr. Irving Friedman, represented the interest of all private creditors.

Meetings among the banks and between the agent banks and the Banque du Zaire resulted in a memorandum of understanding signed in London on November 5, 1976. According to Dr. Friedman, the agreement was not meant to restructure or stretch out Zaire's debt repayments on loans where Zaire was in default, but to restore the creditworthiness of the nation by taking steps to convince private lenders that Zaire was a good risk again.[16] The memorandum called on Zaire to immediately pay $40 million in interest in arrears on its loans and to begin paying money into a special fund to cover all arrears on principal payments. In addition, Zaire agreed to begin negotiating with the IMF for eligibility to draw $110 million in standby credits, thus opening the door for the IMF to exert relatively stringent control over Zaire's economic policies. In return, Zaire was allowed to postpone payment of 85 percent of its 1975 and 1976 source loans for three years and then stretch repayment for another seven years. The remaining 15 percent would be stretched over a three-year period. Citibank also agreed that, once other steps were taken, it would use its "best efforts" to assemble a $250 million short-term loan, to be used to speed Zaire's industrialization and not to repay the funds due to private banks.

Once the agreement was reached to refinance rather than reschedule, Zaire's government changed tactics. The government insisted that the $250 million be a medium-term, five- to seven-year loan rather than the originally negotiated six-month trade credit. Zaire paid its interest, but placed the owed principal into a blocked account at the Bank for International Settlements and refused to release it until the $250 million was delivered. Organization of the loan was proceeding slowly when it was disrupted by the invasion of Shaba Province in March 1977. In late 1977, Irving Friedman commented that Zaire was "broke, as broke as any country in the world."[17] However, by late February 1978, Citibank was on the verge of finalizing a $220 million credit contingent on IMF involvement in Zaire's economy that would have carried an interest rate of 2.25 percent over the London interbank rate and would have flowed to Zaire's suppliers "through a letter-of-credit mechanism" and not directly to the country.[18] The loan was delayed and went back on the shelf when, in May 1978, rebels based in Angola invaded Zaire's mineral-rich Shaba Province for the second time in little more than a year.

Efforts to bail out Zaire immediately returned to the official sphere. In mid-June, the United States, West Germany, Italy, France, Britain, Belgium, the Netherlands, Canada, Japan, and

Iran met in Brussels to patch together a financial aid plan to see Zaire through 1978 and to attempt to solidify its debt position. In return for stepped-up official aid and for relief on the estimated $1.2 billion that Zaire would have been in arrears by the end of 1978, Zaire accepted foreign control over its central bank and finance ministry.[19] In August, Erwin Blumenthal, a retired Bundesbank official, arrived in Kinshasa to represent the IMF and take effective control of the Banque du Zaire. In November, Blumenthal forbade banks from doing further business with fifty Zairian companies that had overextended their credit. Private lenders moved to the background, hoping for an eventual way out.

Surprisingly, Zaire's difficulties have had little influence on the rate and nature of lending to other non-oil-exporting developing countries. Banks perceived Zaire as a possible new profit source with unique prospects and problems. Significantly, despite provocation, commercial banks have not declared Zaire to be in formal default. Banks recognized that, once they were committed, a declaration of default would close some of their options. They prefer to ignore short-term reversals and hope for a brighter future. Indeed, Citibank has even attacked the notion that loans to non-oil-exporting developing nations are likely to decline.[20]

Loans and Negotiations with Indonesia

On November 4, 1976, the day before the Zaire package was announced, Morgan Guaranty indicated that Indonesia might be in technical default on two loan agreements totaling $850 million.[21] While no payments to American-led syndicates were omitted, the world's commercial banks shivered collectively.

Indonesia, an original member of OPEC, has led a checkered international monetary existence in the past two decades. Under President Sukarno, Indonesian debt soared, but, rather than meet all international obligations, Indonesia withdrew from the IMF in August 1965. Prices rose by over 600 percent in 1965 and 1966 while the currency depreciated sharply. By early 1967, General Suharto assumed effective control of the government, turned to the IMF and the World Bank for stabilization and rehabilitation advice, and rejoined the IMF in February 1967. Debt renegotiations began. Four separate creditor clubs culminated in the consolidation of $2.1 billion of Sukarno's debt in 1970, by far the largest single amount renegotiated between 1956 and 1978. Terms were quite generous, allowing Indonesia to stretch repayment over a thirty-year period.[22]

Still, Indonesia's oil wealth attracted the attention of private lenders. Morgan Guaranty, along with Citibank, a traditional lead bank for Indonesia, estimates that at the close of 1976 Indonesia had medium- and long-term private debts of approximately $3.44 billion, about 65 percent owed to U.S. banks.[23] Significantly, approximately $1.5 billion was owed to the nine largest U.S. banks which held 43 percent of Indonesia's private bank debt and nearly 15 percent of its total external debt of $10 billion as of June 30, 1977.[24] Table 2 indicates that U.S. banks have dominated the Indonesian external debt scene since 1973. While banks of other nations participated and even comanaged Eurosyndicates, particularly in 1975, they were secondary actors. Japanese banks were the only real competition to U.S. banks in Indonesia. Some of their dealings do not show up in lists of publicly announced credits. Given the con-

Table 2
Publicly Announced Private Bank Lending to Indonesia by the Largest 300 Banks in the World: 1973-1976[a]

Bank's Origin	# In Top 300	1973		1974		1975		1976	
		Man	Par	Man	Par	Man	Par	Man	Par
Canada	7	1	3	0	3	6	18	5	14
Europe	26	0	0	1	9	7	25	2	11
Japan	17	0	4	0	11	5	20	1	2
U.K.	8	0	2	0	2	2	10	3	6
U.S.	34	2	5	4	14	16	43	33	62
Asia	7	0	0	0	2	0	7	1	6
Total Top 300	99	3	14	5	41	36	123	45	101
Other Smaller Banks	68	1	3	1	25	9	35	5	43
Total All Banks	167	4	17	6	66	45	158	50	144
Ratio T300/All Banks	.59		.82		.62		.78		.70
Ratio Par/Man			4.25		11.00		3.51		2.88

Source: Amex Euromoney Syndication Guide
[a] See note on Table 1.

centration of American bank lending to Indonesia, the possibility that the relationship between borrowers and lenders will remain apolitical is remote.

Pertamina, the state oil company, accounted for 72 percent of Indonesia's export earnings in 1975 and for 40 percent of total government revenues. It was a power unto itself, largely unhindered and unchecked by the central government. Pertamina engaged in a wide range of activities including hotels, steel, tankers, and rice estates. For a time, it even acted as an autonomous development agency financing its own investments from foreign loans and its own earnings. However, to develop its oil reserves it required outside, private sources.

The denouement began in the spring of 1975 when the Indonesian government was forced to revise its estimates of Pertamina's total debts from $3 billion to $10 billion. The government was apparently unaware of the extent of Pertamina's shipping, real-estate, and manufacturing activities. When Pertamina failed to repay $100 million to two different foreign bank syndicates, the government investigated and found Pertamina's actual debts were $10.5 billion, an amount beyond the company's servicing capacity. Relations between lenders and Pertamina were at times so strained that the company refused to disclose details of its cash flow and repayment capabilities. Reputations were tarnished all around. If Pertamina were improvident in its borrowing, were the banks any less improvident in their lending? Perhaps the Indonesian government should have supervised more closely the nation's most important company. But shouldn't bank regulators have known how much Pertamina had borrowed? Surely, examiners' reports indicated that credit documentation was inadequate?

After these revelations surfaced, the banks, assisted by the U.S. embassy, negotiated a Bank of Indonesia assurance that Pertamina's foreign creditors would be paid. Indonesia immediately borrowed $300 million from a ten-bank syndicate led by Morgan Guaranty to meet some of its outstanding obligations. For 1975, Indonesia's publicly announced Eurocurrency credits totaled $1,348 million, double the $669 million loaned in 1974. In 1976, however, Indonesia's Eurocurrency loans dropped to $470 million.

In 1976, the Indonesian government, to retain its creditworthiness, assumed Pertamina's debts. Strict controls were
instituted over Pertamina's borrowings and many non-oil
projects were cancelled or channeled into other government
departments. Reporting standards were improved immensely.
Furthermore, to soothe creditors and unravel Pertamina's
dealings, Indonesia hired Arthur Young Associated to make a
complete financial accounting and retained three investment
banks as financial advisers to the Bank of Indonesia. Eventually,
Pertamina's debts were pared to $6.2 billion, and Indonesia was
able to obtain the nearly $1 billion it required in 1977.

Aside from Pertamina's debts, tanker loan problems plagued
Indonesia, causing severe difficulties with its international
backers. In July 1976, Bruce Rappaport, of Inter-Maritime Management, filed suit for payment of $1.25 billion owed to him
for providing Indonesia with oil tankers. Banks feared that
Pertamina's failure to pay this debt could throw Indonesia into
technical default on many more loans. Morgan Guaranty and
Citibank suggested that Indonesia might already be in technical
default on its borrowings.[25] Neither side wished that. In the fall
of 1977, the Rappaport cloud finally lifted when he accepted
payment of $150 million spread over three years.[26]

During the Pertamina and Rappaport uproar, commercial
banks chose to ride out the storm without demanding formal
rescheduling. Even with the Zaire model fresh in their minds,
private creditors preferred to avoid formal confrontations. Indonesia's immediate prospects were brighter than Zaire's, and the
amounts at stake were far greater. Banks wanted to retain the
ability to lend to Indonesia, and believed that waving the IMF
in front of the Indonesians would have proved counterproductive. Banks and the Indonesian government were pleased to avoid
the antagonism and uncertainty of renegotiations. The politicization and increased media coverage such a negotiation would
have spurred were undesirable for all parties. By giving in to the
banks' belated demands for closer supervision, Indonesia was
able to persuade the banks to consider future loans. By remaining patient with Indonesia, the banks were able to work with
and retain a good and profitable customer.

Loans and Negotiations with Turkey

In early 1978, Turkey found it necessary to reschedule approximately $1.1 billion of its external debt. Although several times larger than the Zaire episode, the negotiations received relatively little attention outside the financial community, perhaps because of its "developed" status. Private banks, heavily involved in Turkey, approached its problems somewhat differently than they had in Zaire or Indonesia. Their strategy of linking their debt's future explicitly to official debt is striking. In effect, the banks have formed an unspoken alliance with the IMF. They will not lend to Turkey (or other troubled nations) until the IMF imposes a hard financial line. Neither, in light of the Peru and Zaire experiences, will they impose conditions on Turkey or other troubled borrowers themselves.

From the declaration of the Turkish Republic in October 1923 until August 1958, all payments of principal and interest on external debt were made when due.[27] By 1958, Turkish external debt mounted to about $1 billion and payments due were $371 million, an amount larger than Turkish exports in 1957 or 1958. From August 1958 until May 1959, when it signed agreements with the United States and fourteen members of the Organization for European Economic Cooperation, Turkey suspended payment on public and private debts and overdue commercial bills.[28] Problems recurred in 1964, requiring Turkey to reschedule $220 million in 1965. External public debt continued to grow from $1.38 billion at the end of 1965 to $2.76 billion at the end of 1971, $3.51 billion at the end of 1973, and $4.11 billion at the end of 1975. External public debt owed to private creditors increased more slowly, from $72.9 million at the end of 1965 to only $144.2 million at the end of 1975, before ballooning to $659.8 million as of April 20, 1976.[29] Private debt continued to increase through 1976 and early 1977 at a rapid rate and was, as indicated in Table 3, largely held by American banks. By the end of 1977, the foreign commercial bank debt of Turkey was about $6 billion of which $1.465 billion was held by American banks.[30] Much of it was for short maturities.

Table 3
Publicly Announced Private Bank Lending to Turkey by the Largest 300 Banks
in the World: 1973-1976 [a]

Bank's Origin	# In Top 300	1973 Man	Par	1974 Man	Par	1975 Man	Par	1976 Man	Par
Canada	3	0	0	0	0	0	1	0	2
Europe	6	0	0	0	0	1	4	0	2
Japan	0	0	0	0	0	0	0	0	0
U.K.	4	0	0	0	0	1	4	0	1
U.S.	10	0	0	0	0	3	5	5	8
Total Top 300	23	0	0	0	0	5	14	5	13
Other Smaller Banks	22	1*	1	0	0	7	14	1	11
Total All Banks	45	1	1	0	0	12	28	6	24
Ratio T300/All Banks	.51	0	0	0	0		.50		.54
Ratio Par/Man		1.00		----		2.33		4.00	

Source: Amex Euromoney Syndication Guide

[a] See note on Table 1. In 1973, 1975, and 1976 the International Financial Corporation, a World Bank affiliate, managed and participated in one loan.

In 1977, Turkey's balance-of-payments deficit plunged to $2.84 billion. The cost of imported petroleum, $1.85 billion, exceeded total Turkish export revenues by $100 million.[31] Official reserves fell from a maximum of $2.25 billion at the end of 1973 to a paltry $500 million four years later. Iraq was owed $250 million for petroleum, and total official arrears amounted to $3.75 billion of a total debt of $15 billion. Over $350 million of payments on convertible lira deposits was late to private lenders. Private creditors met in February 1978 in Paris and decided not to take a hard line, but to wait for official renegotiations to work things out. The banks carefully accepted the need to "stretch out" repayment of Turkish interest and principal without referring to renegotiations, reschedulings, or refinancings. One leading financial journal concluded that in Peru, Zaire, Turkey, and elsewhere "the banks involved appeared to have striven to avoid enforcing default, almost at any price. Instead, some of the countries have been allowed to fall into serious arrears of interest and principal."[32]

The Turks fell prey to two serious policy errors. In 1975, they restored convertible lira accounts which provided needed funds, but at high interest for short terms. To get over a short-term political crisis, the Turkish government planted the seeds for long-term economic difficulties. Even more serious, the money supply was allowed to increase by 86 percent in 1976 and 1977, allowing the state economic enterprises, which account for 40 percent of Turkish industrial output, to embark on inflationary spending programs.[33] Central bank independence was eroded, and politics took precedence over economics.

When the Ecevit government replaced the Demirel regime in January 1978, it inherited a convertible lira debt of nearly $2 billion, over half of which was due within the year, exclusive of the overdue $350 to $400 million. The IMF pressed for an immediate devaluation of the lira. The government has so far resisted, cognizant that, after devaluation in 1959, there was a revolution and, after devaluation in 1970, the commanders of the armed forces threatened to take the country into military dictatorship.[34] Nonetheless, the government seems to be slowly giving in to the IMF demands. It introduced a strict, new import regime in 1978 in line with IMF suggestions and remains in close consultation with both the IMF and the commercial banks.

The commercial banks have remained patient, believing that, eventually, they will get their money and interest. They are content at this time to let the IMF and the official creditors make the effort to find a renegotiated solution. Turkey's relatively developed status and its NATO connections reassure the banks that in the end they will come out ahead.

The Outlook for Lending to Brazil and Mexico

American Express has estimated that one out of four dollars borrowed in 1977 by non-oil-exporting developing countries will go for debt servicing and that, by 1980, one out of every two dollars will be used to repay old debts.[35] Brazil and Mexico are by far the largest LDC borrowers, accounting for 66 percent of all outstanding loans by banks to non-oil-exporting developing countries. If these nations were to encounter serious repayment difficulties, the impact on the private banking system could be major. Therefore, it is necessary to look at the relative bargaining strength of the banks and of these two major borrowers.

Brazil's total external debt at the end of 1977 reached about

$31.5 billion, 85 percent of which was held privately. Of this, almost $12 billion was held by American banks. Brazil's 1977 debt service was approximately $5.3 billion, 40 percent of its total export earnings. Even with the increases in coffee prices, Brazil must continue to raise huge amounts of external funds to finance its growth and balance-of-payments deficit.[36] Mexico's debt is only marginally smaller, around $24.8 billion at the end of 1977, of which $21.8 billion is held by private creditors including $11.2 billion by U.S. banks.[37] Its debt service eats up about 30 percent of its total export earnings. In addition, the 40 percent devaluation of the peso substantially increased Mexico's servicing obligations because most of its external debt is denominated in strong currencies.[38]

American banks claim that risk splitting would minimize the losses in even a major national default. Except for those few giant banks that maintain global networks and exposures, this assumption is questionable. But even the largest banks are making a disproportionate share of their profits in Mexico and Brazil. Citibank made 20 percent and Chase Manhattan made 13 percent of 1977 profits in Brazil and only a slightly smaller percentage of their earnings in Mexico. In addition, some banks have placed more than 10 percent of their capital, the U.S. legal lending unit limit, into these nations by extending credit to several ostensibly separate government agencies or government controlled companies. Should either country suddenly repudiate its debts or be completely unable to meet its payments, the entire U.S. banking structure would be shaken. Therefore, although nobody seriously expects catastrophic problems, banks watch Brazilian and Mexican developments closely even as they continue to extend them credit.

Brazil and Mexico have had different debt histories. Brazil was unable to meet its sterling bond interest payments in 1898 and defaulted on the bulk of its debt in 1930-1931. From 1936 through 1960, Brazil walked a thin line, often teetering on the brink of insolvency before consolidating much of its debt with the IMF and the United States in 1964. Hague Club negotiations and bilateral negotiations with the Export-Import Bank failed to solve the problem, so new consolidation efforts were made at a second Hague Club in 1963-1964, in which the United

Table 4
Publicly Announced Private Bank Lending to Brazil by the Largest 300 Banks
in the World: 1973-1976[a]

Bank's Origin	# In Top 300	1973		1974		1975		1976	
		Man	Par	Man	Par	Man	Par	Man	Par
Canada	7	1	31	2	31	20	61	10	31
Europe	54	8	36	10	40	20	76	38	91
Japan	19	5	80	3	35	0	16	0	7
U.K.	9	1	15	3	10	8	34	11	14
U.S.	65	9	57	14	47	66	188	48	95
Other Top 300	7	2	6	2	14	9	29	6	16
Total Top 300	161	26	225	34	177	123	404	113	254
Other Smaller Banks	210	16	71	25	79	44	238	29	216
Total All Banks	371	42	296	59	256	167	642	142	470
Ratio T300/All Banks	.43		.76		.69		.63		.54
Ratio Par/Man			7.05		4.34		3.84		3.31

Source: Amex Euromoney Syndication Guide

[a]See note on Table 1

States participated. Since assumption of military rule in 1964, Brazil has managed to meet the service requirements on its debts. In striking contrast, Mexico has consistently repaid its principal and interest due on external loans since the revolution was "institutionalized" in 1924.[39] As a result, until recently, it was easier for Mexico to obtain medium- and long-term private credits than it was for Brazil.

Tables 4 and 5 demonstrate the dominance of American banks among recent lenders to Brazil, and even more to Mexico. Whether banks can or wish to curtail their lending to non-oil-exporting developing countries is a major question. An August 1977 Senate committee report concluded, "The fact is, the big banks are now so deeply enmeshed in the whole deficit financing process that they cannot afford to say 'no,' either to their major depositors or to their major borrowers."[40] If anything, banks have been squeezed somewhat as LDC borrowers prepaid some of their high-interest loans and refinanced them, with ease, at lower spreads.[41] Although many banks have reached or have almost reached their lending limits to non-oil-exporting LDCs, they need to continue to slowly expand their lending to these nations or face the strong possibility of internal profitability problems and/or the threat of severe repayment problems

Table 5
Publicly Announced Private Bank Lending to Mexico by the Largest 300 Banks
in the World: 1973-1976a

Bank's Origin	# In Top 300	1973		1974		1975		1976	
		Man	Par	Man	Par	Man	Par	Man	Par
Canada	7	1	6	5	31	8	37	20	35
Europe	45	0	10	7	40	9	48	25	60
Japan	18	5	51	4	30	0	11	4	22
U.K.	7	0	0	2	17	5	27	5	13
U.S.	67	2	14	11	58	31	128	60	136
Other Top 300	8	0	0	1	5	3	12	2	12
Total Top 300	152	8	81	30	181	56	263	116	278
Other Smaller Banks	203	2	9	15	79	31	143	44	207
Total All Banks	355	10	90	45	260	87	406	160	485
Ratio T300/All Banks	.43		.90		.70		.65		.57
Ratio Par/Man		9.00		5.78		4.67		3.03	

Source: Amex Euromoney Syndication Guide

aSee note on Table 1

in a limited number of nations. The problem is heightened by the existence of cross-default clauses that throw a borrower in default against a single creditor into automatic default on almost all its loans. Often some creditor can call its outstanding loans for immediate repayment. If the borrower is unable to repay or other other banks cannot be found to pick up the difference, a nation's credit structure could face possible collapse.[42] This was one reason banks were extremely cautious not to declare Zaire, Indonesia, Peru, Turkey, or other nations to be *officially* in default.

Neither Brazil nor Mexico has requested or desired rescheduling of their loan obligations during the 1970s. Indeed, their international borrowing has continued to climb. When many developing nations advocated some form of general debt forgiveness in the Manila Declaration and at the Conference on International Economic Cooperation in Paris in 1976 and 1977, these two nations quietly but forcefully opposed the initiative. Brazil and Mexico feared that if forgiveness declarations were pressed too hard they might become isolated from their private creditors. Richer LDC borrowers saw debt forgiveness as an extreme that would benefit mainly India and Pakistan, and several other nations with large public debt but almost no private loans outstanding.[43] Richer borrowers feared that an exclusively official rescheduling would discourage further private lending.

Private banks believe Mexico and Brazil will continue to be attractive borrowers. Mexico has two great advantages. Its newly discovered petroleum reserves promise to make it the world's third largest oil exporter. If the petroleum fields can be developed at a reasonable price,[44] Mexico will have little difficulty repaying its vast borrowings. American lenders are also attracted by Mexico's contiguous border with the United States. Most creditors feel that the U.S. government is so involved with Mexico's economy that it would aid the Mexican government and U.S. lenders if disaster threatened. As a result, Mexico is almost always the first developing nation in which newly international U.S. banks become involved. It is the gateway to Central and South America and the testing ground for novice lenders.

Still, international creditors are concerned about Mexico's recent economic performance, its lopsided reliance on future oil wealth, and its potentially explosive social problems. Banks are uneasy about its financial officials and perceive the government planning mechanism as overly rigid. Social and economic disarray could scuttle the economy, distract the government, and make it difficult to continue servicing foreign debts.

Commercial banks are not totally reassured about Mexican prospects. Their high liquidity levels, however, induce further lending. Although margins have narrowed in the past three years, banks have refused to lengthen terms excessively. For example, in mid-1977 when Nacional Financiera, Mexico's development agency, wished to raise at least $200 million, it chose a "renewal" technique. The agency wanted ten-year money, realized it would be difficult to obtain, and therefore offered potential lenders the option of withdrawal or roll-over of the loans every two years. In effect, the agency negotiated a two-year loan that could be renewed four times.[45]

Brazil faces different problems and opportunities. It lacks Mexico's proven oil reserves, but is nevertheless extremely rich in resources and increasingly diverse in output. While it has borrowed more than Mexico, the maturities of its debts are spaced carefully to assure that they do not bunch too heavily in one short period.[46] In addition, Brazil publishes its global debt and not just its external public or state-guaranteed debt. Foreign banks are pleased by Brazil's conscientious willingness to disclose its debt position and to work with creditors to rationalize its debt position, and also by the openness and accessibility of Brazilian officials.[47] Minimal red tape clogs negotiations surrounding lending syndicates which makes Brazil more attractive to lenders. Brazil also is working to control its domestic economy and has experimented with six-month, renewable bankers' acceptances. So far, the major issue of renewable acceptances for Petrobras has been rolled over without any difficulty.[48] Indeed, despite problems of domestic distribution, most banks like the "feel" of the Brazilians and slightly prefer to lend to Brazil than to Mexico.

Although private lending to Brazil and Mexico is unlikely to continue growing as rapidly in the future, banks remain willing to finance these nations. Their prospects remain strong. However, creditors spread risks as widely as possible, work to keep maturities moderately short, and take as much of their profit up front as possible. Thus, despite the incomplete data encompassed in Table 4 and 5, it is clear that, since 1973, the ratio of participants to managers of Eurocurrency loans to Mexico and Brazil has fallen substantially and steadily. Fewer banks will participate in syndicates without receiving some share of the lucrative management fee. As a result, the average number of managers required to raise a fixed sum of money has increased in recent years.

However, commercial banks apparently have separated their experiences in Zaire, Indonesia, and Eastern Europe from their Latin American lending. This is partially accounted for by geographic divisions within banks amd the banks' perceptions that Zaire was a failed experiment and Indonesia a special, oil-laden case. U.S. banks are also familiar with Latin American business practices. Their experience is longer, and their confidence remains, perhaps unjustly, high.

Nonetheless, in all five countries examined here, banks have been hesitant to exert too much direct influence on internal politics, while simultaneously building a base from which they might indirectly exert critical impact. Vast loans to these and other, richer nations have created a system of mutual hostages. Without continued private, external support, many nations' economies could suffer severe reversals. Without borrowers' cooperation, industrial nations' economic stability and numerous large banks' survival would be endangered. This reciprocal hostage situation suggests important potential implications of banks' actions for international political relations among developed and developing nations in the next decade.

3. Lending, Debt, and Banks' Political Influence

Until very recently, the constant threat of debt difficulties has been paraded through the financial and business journals. Actually, there were more formal debt renegotiations, albeit among official creditors, from 1967 through 1972 than since then. However, as private creditors took over the burden of lending to richer non–oil-exporting developing countries in the 1970s, their potential political influence became more complex. Private banks and the heavier borrowing, non–oil-exporting LDCs each hold the power to undermine the other's goals and stability. Both groups are aware that it is in their interest to continue to cooperate. Bank influence arises from the need of wealthier LDC borrowers to continue to dip into the international capital markets.

For their part, private banks have committed so much money that most of them cannot cut their losses and abandon the Third World. When pressed, most international bankers admit that their non–oil-exporting LDC loans will continue to rise.[49] The abundance of petrodollar liquidity requires banks to constantly search for willing borrowers. The LDCs remain favored recipients. Banks are likely to continue to lend to the wealthier LDCs as long as they continue to service their loans with some regularity.

The critical questions remain: (1) How will banks employ their *direct* influence, based on their ability to grant and withhold credit to LDCs, and their *indirect* influence over developed countries, based on their domination of the Euromarkets, to safeguard their debt in developing countries and to ensure the safety of future loans? (2) If future bank profit potential lies solidly in the LDCs, could and might banks use their indirect influence to tilt the outcomes of North-South disagreements toward the LDCs? In essence, these two questions focus on the actual or potential political role of banks in dealing with developed and developing countries.

Bank Power and LDC Debtors

Other chapters in this volume note that, in the past, debtor governments, particularly LDC debtor governments, have eventually been forced to capitulate to terms dictated to them by their official and private creditors. Frequently, such solutions further impoverished and pressed the lower classes in the borrowing nations. Does the same fate await major LDC debtors that are now falling deeper and deeper into arrears? The five cases reviewed here suggest that a new structure of bank-borrower relations may be emerging. The banks have become so involved in LDCs that they cannot easily withdraw. Simultaneously, the dependence of the larger banks on LDC lending for continued profits is striking. Even should global liquidity begin to decline and corporate and developed country borrowing demands rebound, the LDCs are likely to remain a profitable outlet for private bank funds.[50]

At the same time, the elites, who control governmental borrowing in the developing world, remain vulnerable to the traditional pressures to which they are subjected by official and private creditors. They realize that substantial increases in their external borrowing capacity require some reasonable attempt to meet repayment commitments, even if the result is the squeezing of the lower classes.

As a result, bankers and their borrowers find themselves in the position of mutual hostages. Each can do mortal damage to the other, but together they can continue to support and work with each other for their own benefit. Even the lower classes might benefit because the banks are slowly becoming sensitive to the threat that social unrest could undermine autocratic governments and result in new leaders unwilling to meet their past commitments. They, therefore, are beginning to take distributional questions into consideration on their loans along with cash flow and other economic factors. At least in the short- and medium-term, there appears to be considerable flexibility for further cooperation if each side will make explicit efforts to reassure the other of the sanctity of contracts. Rather than bemoaning the inevitability of future debt renegotiations and the possibility of massive defaults, it may be possible to find positive, cooperative methods to fortify the lenders, contribute to the development of the LDCs, and also strengthen the delivery of basic human needs to the masses of the population.

From the banks' perspective, nations become viable candidates for loans when they demonstrate the political will as well as the economic capacity to service their debts. However, banks' ability to exercise direct influence over LDCs with sizable existing debt by threatening to withhold future credit is of minimal value when banks are overflowing with liquidity. Similarly, banks were dismayed with the effects of their efforts to influence Peruvian policy and are unlikely to try again to exert direct influence over borrowers to channel their economic policies in conservative directions. Indeed, direct bank influence is only likely to be useful in inducing countries that have not yet borrowed substantial amounts from the Euromarkets to show a positive record in order to attract future funds.

By the same token, the banks' indirect potential to undermine a nation's economy and isolate it from world money markets is only effective to the extent that banks are willing to write off their previous loans. Unless the debtor nation nationalizes foreign bank branches and subsidiaries without compensation and refuses to meet its external obligations, banks are likely to seek a compromise solution rather than take a completely hard line.[51] At least part of the weakness displayed by LDC debtors in past cases has been their all-or-nothing attitude. Only by taking the initiative and forcing the banks and official creditors into a more defensive position are debtor nations likely to effectively bargain with their creditors. Only by accepting the necessity of finding some middle compromise can debtors exercise their influence to renegotiate loan agreements while retaining future creditworthiness. Many LDCs now can offer their creditors the carrot of repayment rather than be forced to submit to the stick of threatened uncreditworthiness.

Recognizing their own weakness in negotiations, banks have more and more tried to enlist the aid of the IMF and the industrialized nations in their loan difficulties. In Zaire, Indonesia, and Turkey, the private banks have ventured aggressively into renegotiations only to retreat to the protective help of the IMF and the creditor governments. In Brazil and Mexico, their lending exuberance continues, but their demands for fuller economic data and their recommendations of appropriate economic policies have also increased. Should these nations be forced to renegotiate their loans, or some portion of them, the banks, in all likelihood, would work to involve the U.S. government and the IMF as quickly as possible. But since the private banks have come to dominate lending in these countries, official creditors may be more hesitant to enter the fray, leaving these nations with a better bargaining position.

If the bank bargaining position is no longer as dominant vis-à-vis the LDC debtor as before, how can LDC governments persuade banks to continue and even increase their lending? Similarly, how might LDCs, which have traditionally been unable to attract private lenders because of their extreme poverty, do so? Excess bank liquidity does prompt banks to search for new borrowers, but is hardly likely to persuade banks to throw money away. It is necessary, therefore, for would-be borrowers to diffuse the politics of external, private borrowing and, at the same time, reassure the lenders of their willingness and ability to repay. It would be particularly useful if debtor nations explicitly disaggregated public and private debt forgiveness and even dropped the demands for forgiveness. New International Economic Order rhetoric on the issue of debt discourages the expansion of private lending.[52] By concentrating on other issues, many of which would not threaten the external lenders, the LDCs might help their creditworthiness. Zaire has certainly harmed the chances of others of the poorest LDCs to borrow privately, but has not closed the door completely.

Even more important to the banks is the attitude of LDC debtors toward external economic advice and management and their willingness to provide sophisticated and accurate economic statistical data to the creditors. Some countries will choose to strike out on their own independent economic path. In rejecting

IMF advice, they limit their chances of attracting new private loans.[53] On the other hand, if, with full knowledge of the consequences, LDCs are willing to accept IMF advisers and advice on the management of their economy, even if it means some curtailment of their independence, they are likely to be able to induce private banks to lend to them. Similarly, as in the case of Brazil, if countries will make their economic and financial statistics freely available to the banks and allow banks full access to debt figures, the banks will tend to respond with enthusiasm.

On the surface, this potential cooperative liaison between the banks and those LDC governments wishing to attract their funds omits all mention of the masses in those LDCs. The banks, of necessity, negotiate with the elites in government and industry within the LDCs. It has been charged that the measures necessary to attract bank loans, as well as the uses to which external funds are put, will exacerbate the economic differences between classes in the LDCs and impoverish those already below the poverty line. Unfortunately, this negative impact of bank lending and loan requirements all too often is still present. However, there is some reason for encouragement. The banks are becoming increasingly aware of the possibility of instability arising from the lower classes and are beginning to consider these factors. Indeed, since the banks' interest is rooted to the future of an entire nation and not just to the success of a single government industry or project, it is in the banks' interest to think in wider terms than other types of transnational enterprises. Although this has not been immediately translatable into terms favorable to the masses, some progress seems possible. Similarly, both the developing countries and the IMF have received so much criticism from outside observers that they are beginning to worry explicitly about basic human needs and not just overall economic performance in their assessments. In the future, if bank lending can be fortified in developing nations, all elements of the population may have the opportunity to benefit.

Bank Power and Industrial Nations and the New International Economic Order

Assessing potential bank direct and indirect influence on the relations among industrialized nations and on the interactions between the developed and developing world remains problematic. Bankers remain eager to lend to the most stable, industrial nations, but are unlikely to grant or withhold credit explicitly to manipulate these nations' economic policies.

Banks are still a significant political force, however. The simple denomination of business in a particular currency can influence a nation's economic prosperity. Bank activities can disrupt national monetary policies. Banks' foreign exchange activities can undermine exchange rates, domestic economic stability, and even the stability of the international monetary structure. Indeed, indirect bank influence over OECD nations is growing.

Since international banks are more global in outlook than ever before and will ally themselves with nations or borrowers to bolster their positions, it is not unseemly for U.S. banks to praise Germany and Japan while decrying American policies. While most nations' banks believe in the long-term strength of the American economy, they are disillusioned and predict continued weakness for the dollar. If surplus OPEC nations come to concur in this conclusion, such predictions could become self-fulfilling.

When direct influence fails, indirect bank influence remains. By moving funds or business from country to country and currency to currency, private enterprises can undermine industrialized countries' payments positions. Thus, although the United States has explicitly chosen to stabilize the monetary system by running sizable deficits, bankers are uneasy with this approach because Japan and Germany continue to run massive surpluses.[54] Until U.S. policy changes, it is likely that banks will indirectly pressure the government to stop "benignly" neglecting the dollar. Significantly, the internationally oriented private sector generally opposes greater protectionism but supports policies of international economic restraint. In the medium term, their voice (direct and indirect) will delimit the boundaries within which the United States and other OECD nations can effectively act.

Such indirect bank power also presents the possibility of private influence on the evolution of North-South relations in the next decade. Banks will resolutely oppose any major move toward private forgiveness of debts owed by the LDCs. In the same vein, they will fight any attempt at the creation of a New International Economic Order that is primarily a power grab by the LDCs. On the other hand, a New International Economic Order designed to enhance the economic prosperity of the LDCs without completely undermining the industrialized nations' control of the economic system might find substantial support among private creditors in the developed nations. Banks would certainly support almost any basic commodity scheme that raised or at least stabilized the foreign exchange earnings of major debtor countries, even if the governments and the peoples of the developed world had to pay somewhat higher prices. Similarly, banks would approve stronger currencies in th LDCs and would not favor moves by industrial nations that impoverished major debtor nations. Indeed, banks might be far more supportive of LDCs than foreign extractive or manufacturing corporations which are involved in a more-limited portion of LDC economies. Near total economic prosperity is needed in the LDCs for the banks to fortify their medium- and long-term profit outlook.

4. Brief Concluding Thoughts

Trends in international banking suggest that, in the future, banks may often find their interest identical to their major LDC borrowers. Although the ability of banks to directly influence government decisions may have declined in recent years, their ability to influence relations among nations through their control of markets has climbed. However, most bankers remain unaware of their indirect power or are hesitant to employ it. Perhaps, as banks gain understanding of the changing nature of their political roles in the international economic system, they will begin to use their monetary clout to indirectly influence the types of settlements reached by nations on international economic issues. Their power is likely to be most visible and effective in the relations among industrialized nations seeking common policies for their negotiations with the developing world. They are also likely to help LDCs continue to borrow on the international capital markets if they can be assured of the

borrowers' intention and ability to meet their servicing pay-·
ments.

Multinational banks have become political actors of the first
rank with a major impact on the relations among nations.
Unless banks gain a greater understanding of the nature and
limits of their power, they are likely to misuse it. Unless governments accept private actors as the political forces they are, government policies are doomed to inefficiency.

Notes

1. Leon Frazer was with the First National Bank of New York and
served as president of the Bank for International Settlements. Cited in
Charles P. Kindleberger, "Debt Situation of the Developing Countries in
Historical Perspective," Paper for a symposium at the Export-Import
Bank, April 21, 1977, p. 14.

2. Kindleberger, "Debt Situation," p. 9. For a fuller exposition of this
cyclical theory, which is largely based on the work of Hyman P. Minsky,
see Charles P. Kindleberger, *Manias, Panics, and Crashes* (New York: Basic
Books, 1978).

3. Kindleberger, "Debt Situation," p. 8.

4. For a fuller exposition of the impact of U.S. exchange restraints on
bank expansion, see Jonathan David Aronson, *Money and Power: Banks
and the World Monetary System* (Beverly Hills, Calif.: Sage Publications,
1978), chap. 4.

5. See Herbert Feis, *Europe, the World's Banker: 1870-1914* (New
York: W. W. Norton, 1965).

6. See E. E. Schattschneider, *Politics, Pressure, and the Tariff* (New
York: Prentice Hall, 1935); and Raymond Bauer, Ithiel Pool, and Lewis
Dexter, *American Business and Public Policy: The Politics of Foreign
Trade* (Chicago: Aldine-Atherton, 1972).

7. At the Nairobi IMF meetings in 1974, Bank of America President
A. W. Clausen suggested that the United States might be more forthcoming
in aiding developing countries. Treasury Secretary Shultz told him to mind
his own business. More recently, Gabriel Hauge of Manufacturers Hanover
Trust received a similar rebuff on suggesting the benefits of private bank-
IMF cofinancing.

8. See Aronson, *Money and Power*, chap. 3.

9. Ibid., pp. 104-6.

10. Bankers will claim to be the "conscience of the system," but rarely

admit that they could be political actors, even while lobbying for a bill or moving vast sums of money from currency to currency.

11. Private banks chose to lend to wealthier LDCs because they believed they could (1) generate a high rate of return by imposing large front-end fees and wide margins on LDC loans, (2) assure their future role in these potentially prosperous economies, (3) minimize their direct exposure by lending funds deposited with them in the LDCs, while (4) remain relatively safe from defaults since the LDCs would go to almost any length to protect their worldwide creditworthiness.

12. This has not always been true. A decade ago, the idea of perpetually rolling over loans would have been doubted by bankers and attacked by government regulators more quickly.

13. Cross-default clauses were designed to ensure that a nation would meet its obligations and could not default on some loans without destroying its global creditworthiness. Unfortunately, if a nation cannot meet its payments for economic rather than political reasons, the default clause can still throw the nation into default even though the banks do not want that to occur.

14. Interview with Bank of America official, London, September 1974.

15. David O. Beim, "Rescuing the LDCs," *Foreign Affairs*, July 1977, p. 726.

16. *Wall Street Journal*, November 9, 1976, p. 7.

17. Cited in *Barrons*, October 17, 1977, p. 12.

18. *Wall Street Journal*, February 24, 1978, p. 11.

19. Ibid., June 15, 1978, p. 4.

20. See G. A. Costanzo, "Is the Third World a Sound Debtor?" *New York Times* editorial, April 18, 1977; and Harold van B. Cleveland and Bruce Brittain, "Are the LDCs in over Their Heads?" *Foreign Affairs*, July 1977, pp. 732-50.

21. *Wall Street Journal*, November 5, 1976.

22. See Henry J. Bittermann, *The Refunding of International Debt* (Durham, N.C.: Duke University Press, 1973), pp. 160-64.

23. Morgan Guaranty Trust Company, *World Financial Markets*, June 1977, p. 7.

24. Jane D'Arista provided figures and analytic advice on the Indonesian case.

25. *Wall Street Journal*, November 5, 1976, p. 16.

26. See "Indonesia: The Deal with Rappaport Lifts the Pertamina Cloud at Last," *Euromoney*, October 1977, p. 103.

27. Wells Fargo Bank, "Report in Support of a U.S. $200,000,000 Acceptance Facility for Petrol Ofisi Unconditionally Guaranteed by the Republic of Turkey," November 1976, p. 47.

28. See Bittermann, *Refunding of International Debt*, pp. 139-42.

29. Wells Fargo, "Report," Table 38, p. 47.

30. "The Euromarket's Biggest Problem," *Euromoney*, March 1978, p. 32; and Country Exposure Lending Survey, June 8, 1978.

31. "The Euromarket's Biggest Problem," *Euromoney*, March 1978, p. 32.

32. "The Sick Men of the Euromarkets," *Euromoney*, March 1978, p. 10.

33. "The Euromarket's Biggest Problem," *Euromoney*, March 1978, p. 33.

34. Ibid.

35. Cited in Karin Lissakers, *International Debt, the Banks, and U.S. Foreign Policy*, staff report prepared for U.S. Congress, Senate, Committee on Foreign Relations, Subcommittee on Foreign Economic Policy, 95th Cong., 1st sess. (Washington, D.C.: U.S. Government Printing Office, 1977), p. 51.

36. See W. Ladd Hollist, "Brazil's Debt-Burdened Recession," (chap. 7) in this volume.

37. Figures supplied by Brian G. Crowe (chap. 2) in this volume and in the Country Exposure Lending Survey, June 8, 1978.

38. Lissakers, *International Debt*, p. 54.

39. See Bittermann, *Refunding of International Debt*, pp. 118-28, 207-11.

40. Lissakers, *International Debt*, p. 61.

41. "Bankers Wince as LDCs Prepay Their Loans," *Business Week*, February 27, 1978, pp. 45-46.

42. The cross-default clauses are retained because no banker with money committed wants to be left out of discussions when even a single loan begins to sour. Small banks with minimal exposure in a nation or large banks that find themselves without much exposure frequently refuse to roll over debts, forcing banks with large, complex exposures to assume the burden.

43. See Brian Crowe's article (chap. 2) in this volume.

44. There is some question whether Mexico's energy supplies can be tapped, developed, and brought to market at low prices. Should OPEC collapse and oil prices drop substantially, Mexican oil as well as expensive developments in the North Sea and elsewhere could become uneconomical to pursue in the short- and medium-term.

45. *Wall Street Journal*, June 13, 1977, p. 8.

46. "Brazil: The Lenders and the Borrowers," *Euromoney*, June 1976, p. 48.

47. "Should International Banks Continue to Lend to Brazil?" *Euro-*

money, May 1976, p. 16.

48. Conversation with officer of Wells Fargo Bank.

49. Most bankers are well aware of their dilemma and argue about how best to proceed. They want to continue lending to LDCs because it is profitable and because they have few other options. They are also terrified of the consequences if a major borrower were unable or refused to meet commitments.

50. See the review of the problem of excess bank liquidity and the prospects for the future in the *Banker*, August 1978, pp. 43-51.

51. Given past experience, it might also be possible for a nation to follow a cyclical pattern comprised of allowing new investment and loans, nationalizing those loans, changing government leaders, apologizing for the "rash" actions of the previous leaders and making partial compensation, and then beginning the process once again.

52. Indeed, Brazil and Mexico, as noted elsewhere, opposed the general debt-forgiveness plans proposed by the Group of 77.

53. The only real exception has been in the socialist nations of Eastern Europe. But even there, the concern over North Korean defaults to European and Japanese banks and the buildup of Polish debt has caused a slowing of lending to some nations. If these nations were subject to IMF provisions, lending might be pursued at an even faster rate.

54. On November 1, 1978, President Carter announced dramatic measures designed to strengthen the dollar in the world economy. Although central bank supporters chafed at the president's announcing changes in the discount rate, the markets responded favorably. The dollar improved almost 10 percent against strong currencies within a matter of days. Apparently, the failure of President Carter's energy plan to strengthen the dollar and the similar fate that awaited his call for voluntary wage and price guidelines convinced him to take the risk of recession and "act like a Republican." Until his dramatic message, U.S. policymakers were divided on the proper role of the dollar. Many felt that the United States should run a balance-of-payments deficit to subsidize the monetary system and the developing nations. The banks, however, were unwilling to accept that solution as long as Japan and Germany continued to run huge surpluses. At this writing, it appears that, unless continued government resolve leads to almost monthly improvement in U.S. economic performance, the dollar will continue to remain suspect. Note, however, that in the first half of 1979 Japan has gone into deficit.

12
The IMF, Commercial Banks, and Third World Debts

Charles Lipson

In October 1973, the world price of oil quadrupled and balance-of-payments accountants everywhere began reaching for red ink. The effect was swift and striking. In the three years before the oil embargo, the aggregate, current account deficit for *all* deficit countries amounted to $14.9 billion a year. In the three years after the embargo, the figure was five times as high. Between 1974 and 1976, no less than $220 billion was required for balance-of-payments financing.[1]

The massive sums were largely supplied by banks and private capital markets. According to Treasury Department figures, the IMF supplied $15 billion, other official lenders another $40 billion, and private, market-oriented institutions the remaining 75 percent, nearly $170 billion.[2] The banks' crucial role in financing the unprecedented deficits suggests a profound parallel to the oil embargo itself. There, too, private firms—in this case, transnational oil companies—allocated scarce supplies without effective state direction.[3]

The banks embarked upon this crucial role because oil producers, who wanted to invest their huge surpluses safely and profitably, lacked adequate financial institutions to do the job themselves. For the time being at least, OPEC economies simply could not absorb enough imports to offset their vastly increased exports. Their limited absorptive capacity was powerfully illustrated by the parade of merchant ships stranded in the Persian Gulf, waiting for months to unload their cargoes. Not only did OPEC's leaders face this temporary ceiling on imports, their undeveloped banking systems lacked the expertise to recycle their surpluses into long-term foreign investments. Thus, it was impossible for Saudi Arabia, Kuwait, and the Arab Emirates to bypass the Western banking system entirely and invest abroad directly. The sums were far too large, the foreign investment climate too remote and unfamiliar. Moreover, Arab investors could expect substantial political resistance if their direct foreign investments grew too fast or too visibly.

Into this breach stepped the American and European commercial banks. They offered secure, highly liquid investments for OPEC depositors, even if sometimes at less-than-prime deposit rates. The banks then lent the petrodollars to oil-deficit borrowers, especially in higher-income underdeveloped states. The effect was to interpose commercial banks between surplus and deficit states, between liquidity-conscious depositors and high-risk borrowers.

Such large-scale international lending was not entirely new to big U.S. commercial banks, but they had come to it rather recently. Through the mid-1960s, their foreign loans were mostly trade credits: secure, short-term, self-liquidating. Not until the late 1960s did they begin providing substantial loans for development and balance-of-payment purposes. As the banks' corporate customers became full-scale, multinational enterprises demanding worldwide financial services, money center banks expanded their international networks and aggressively sought their business. Despite U.S. restraints over capital exports in effect until 1974, banks were able to supply investment funds by tapping the fast-growing Euromarkets.[4] By the early 1970s, the largest U.S., European, and Japanese banks were firmly established offshore from London to Singapore. The sharp growth in world trade and the redirection of concessionary aid to the least developed countries also translated into new foreign markets for commercial banks. They were well positioned to profit from the subsequent dislocation in international payments.

The dislocations did not spring solely from oil costs. The ensuing recession-with-inflation also had a serious impact on the financial requirements of underdeveloped countries since it depressed export markets and raised the costs of non–oil-exporting developing countries; deficits increased by about $20 billion a year, half of it attributable to higher oil costs.[5]

Underdeveloped importers, reluctant at first to undertake wrenching adjustments, relied on foreign loans to cushion the blow. Between 1973 and 1977, their borrowing expanded rapidly; their external debt jumped from $75 billion to $160 billion.[6] Most of that new money was lent by commercial banks. Although the International Monetary Fund opened a special lending facility and other official donors upped their aid, private lenders dominated the balance-of-payments financing for all but the poorest countries.[7]

1. Optimism over Debt Service

The enormous buildup of commercial debt and the attendant risks are analyzed elsewhere in this volume. Although some of the sovereign borrowers are in serious trouble, talk about widespread default or substantial losses is wildly exaggerated.[8] One reason most foreign debts are sound is that the nominal debt has risen much faster than export prices. Between 1973 and 1976, debt service payments of non–oil-exporting LDCs grew by 75 percent but merchandise exports rose by nearly the same amount (70 percent), so debt ratios hardly changed.[9] Alternatively, one can deflate nominal debt by changes in export prices, which have doubled over the same period. In real terms, then, the stock of external debt (calculated in 1972 dollars) is up only 15 percent since 1972. By the same token, debt service has increased only slightly in constant dollars, from about $7 billion in 1972 to a projected $9 billion (in 1972 dollars) in 1978.[10]

Since debt service ratios are a weak measure,[11] it is useful to examine several other features of the newly acquired debt. To begin, it is highly concentrated in the largest, faster-growing economies. Ten states in Latin America and East Asia account for over three-quarters of all such lending. The poorest countries, with less than $280 per-capita gross national product (GNP) account for only 5 percent of all LDC private debts.[12] They have faced more drastic contraction and still slower growth, their external financing dependent on whatever official aid dribbled out.

Not only are commercial borrowers relatively more developed, they have not squandered all their funds trying to postpone current account adjustment. For example, after the initial shock wore off, they began adding to reserves. In 1976, non-oil underdeveloped countries added approximately $12 billion to their reserve assets.[13] About half these new reserves were accumulated by Argentina, Brazil, Mexico, the Philippines, and South Korea—the largest commercial borrowers. In fact, of the $14.2 billion these countries borrowed in 1976, 38 percent went into reserve accumulation.[14] Henry Wallich, who watches these matters from the Federal Reserve Board, notes that the largest borrowers continued to build their reserves in 1977.[15]

Some of the borrowed funds are also going to finance industrial growth and diversification, which have continued in middle- and higher-income underdeveloped countries despite the oil price increase. The pace has been slower, naturally, but real growth has not been choked off by the adjustment process. For countries with per-capita incomes ranging from $100 to $2,000, output grew at 7.4 percent in the five years *before* the oil crisis. That figure dropped by about one-third after the price increase. Estimates for 1974-1978 indicate that output is growing at about 5.4 percent. Moreover, assuming recovery continues in the advanced capitalist states, the World Bank estimates that middle-income LDCs will resume 6 to 7 percent growth in the near future.[16]

These are not the only strong points in the banks' loan portfolios. Many of the loans are to branches and subsidiaries of multinational firms. Still others have a guarantee from the lender's home government. Finally, in a serious pinch, the G-10 central banks have agreed (via the offices of the Bank for International Settlements) that each will act as a "lender of last resort" for its own banks.[17] So far, the pinch has not come. Banks' loss ratios on foreign loans are only one-half that of their domestic lending.[18]

The banks' anxiety about balance-of-payments financing is also likely to diminish as current account deficits shrink. The OPEC surplus—the source of so many counterpart deficits—is declining as their industrialization programs proceed. Morgan Guaranty's senior international economist Rimmer de Vries forecasts an OPEC surplus of only $50 to $60 billion between 1978 and 1981, one-third the size of the last four years. With the OECD countries nearly in balance, de Vries projects only $60 to $70 billion in current account deficits for non-oil-exporting underdeveloped nations over the next four years.[19] Even if his figures are optimistic—the 1978 current account deficit may hit $30 billion—it seems likely that developing countries will require substantially less current account financing from all sources, including banks.[20]

Why, then, all the fuss about international lending? One reason is that many underdeveloped states either do not have access to commercial credit or find the repayment burdens onerous. UNCTAD has voiced these concerns in its call for generalized debt relief. The same demands were laid on the table at the Paris CIEC conference.[21] The advanced capitalist states, led by the United States, rejected these demands for several reasons, most of them adding up to "sanctity of contracts." The United States and most other official donors refuse to treat their debts as development aid. Although willing to grant debt relief in extreme cases, they refuse to undertake across-the-board reforms or debt consolidation. They refuse even to discuss private debts. Their position gets some quiet support from major borrowers like Mexico and Brazil, who understand that prospective relief for commercial debts would instantly shut off their access to private capital markets. In any event, the likelihood of generalized, virtually automatic debt relief is nil.

But even if Third World debts are relatively secure and are unlikely to be rescheduled en masse, there are still serious obstacles to smooth debt servicing over the next few years. Export earnings must remain high if the loans are to be repaid on time. That implies continued access to advanced markets, reasonable terms of trade, and, most significantly, no major recession in the United States or Europe. An economic slowdown or renewed protectionism would hit LDC exporters with special force. Protectionism would probably focus on state-subsidized industries and labor-intensive manufactures like footwear and textiles, which represent an increasing share of underdeveloped nations' exports.

Even if the exports remain buoyant, underdeveloped borrowers will face heavy repayments in the late 1970s and early 1980s. The grace period on postembargo loans is running out. The loans are coming due, and cash-flow problems are bound to crop up. Some countries will certainly require roll-over loans, either to bridge downturns in earnings or to relieve bunched-up repayment schedules. Unless there is a global recession, however, the banks and the IMF can manage these roll-overs without dramatic institutional reforms.

But if these aggregate figures do not look apocalyptic, neither do they tell the whole story. They conceal considerable variation among borrowers and uneven exposures among banks. As in the past, some borrowers, saddled with too much debt and too few prospects, will face possible default. As more loans come due, such crises will happen more often. But even this more turbulent future will not threaten the general security of foreign debt. However, debt crises are likely to develop in individual states with distinctive, if not unique, problems such as a collapse in copper prices or overly expansive macroeconomic policies.

2. Managing Debt Crises

So far this discussion has concentrated on the financial soundness of sovereign borrowers. But the security of foreign debt is a question that stretches beyond these narrow calculations. The economic capacity to repay loans does not ensure a willingness to do so, especially when debt service entails domestic political and economic repression. And repression *is* sometimes required if the debts are to be paid. Current consumption and investment may have to be depressed and foreign exchange diverted. Such conservative economic policies often have well-entrenched supporters, but enforcing them on the whole country is not a happy task. Compliance is not voluntary.

Why, then, do so many states, with such diverse political structures, continue to service their debts in spite of the political and social costs? The answer lies in the *political coherence of international finance*, a system that revolves around the IMF. The network of multilateral banks, private lenders, and advanced capitalist states can consolidate and refinance debts in crises and can powerfully sanction borrowers in default. This coherent framework of economic sanctions has important consequences. The promise of sanctions, together with the borrowers' continuing need for international financial services, effectively translates the *capacity* to service debts into the *willingness* to bear the costs.

The effectiveness of these sanctions is underscored in a World Bank study of debt renegotiations. The World Bank concluded that creditor cooperation has made default prohibitively costly to borrowers. "As creditor countries' cooperation has increased through their participation in international institutions, aid consortia, and consultative groups, 'rules of the game' have emerged in the field of international finance. One such rule is that default by a debtor country is now excluded as a means of adjusting financial obligations to debt servicing capacity."[22]

Unilateral default has been replaced by debt reconsolidation, primarily by rescheduling and refinancing. Rescheduling of official debts typically postpones the timetable for repayment without extending any new loans. Refinancing, by contrast, substitutes new credits for maturing obligations. Used mainly by private lenders, it avoids (at least hypothetically) the implication that debt agreements have not been honored. For debtors, refinancing operations push back the day of reckoning; for creditors, they permit old loans to be repaid on schedule and uphold the sanctity of contracts.

Of course, most external debt is repaid or re-lent by mutual choice. In fact, of the many billions lent by governments, international organizations, and commercial banks between 1956 and 1977, only $8.7 billion has been rescheduled.[23] In recent years, the volume of debts rescheduled has increased somewhat, but the number of reschedulings has actually declined. No principal has cancelled since World War II, and only twice has any interest been forgiven.[24] Moreover, the repeated reschedulings of some debtors often indicate that the creditors held the debtors on short leashes, maintaining close surveillance over their economic programs and progress, and not that the rescheduling failed.[25]

The agent of surveillance is the IMF, which plays a crucial and multifaceted role in the debt negotiations. Typically, a troubled debtor negotiates a standby loan from the IMF. The Fund, in turn, demands changes in economic policy as a lending condition (so-called conditionality) and sets performance criteria. To hold the borrower to its promises, the IMF provides credit not in a lump sum, but in several phases as the borrower adapts to IMF guidelines. The Fund's conditions are almost a stock formula. Devaluation is usually mandated along with efforts to curb imports (without protective tariffs), promote exports, and induce new foreign investments. Limits are placed on both domestic credit expansion and new, medium-term foreign debt. Many IMF programs limit the state's internal borrowing, cut public subsidies, and even require tax restructuring.[26]

These stern conditions and the IMF's proven ability to monitor them form the basis for debt renegotiation. Both official and private lenders accept the IMF agreement as a sign that the debtor intends to act forcefully to reduce or eliminate external deficits. They renegotiate their own claims on that condition. Richard Hill, chairman of the First National Bank of Boston, offers a particularly clear appraisal of the IMF's role: "Sophisticated borrowers and lenders increasingly look to the Fund to set standards for economic stabilization and adjustment ... conditional credit from the Fund is increasingly viewed as an 'international certificate of approval,' which enhances the ability of a country to borrow in the private market place."[27] That seal of approval is accepted by other lenders because it rests on the IMF's conservative, highly professional standards as well as their unique access to confidential information. Increasingly, private lenders consider it a precondition for debt renegotiation. They thus join official lenders, who have long taken that position.

The renegotiations themselves have become fairly standard. The debtor approaches the IMF or a major creditor seeking to rearrange its debts, usually to postpone immediate repayment and secure new financing. Official lenders then convene an informal creditor club to negotiate any new arrangements and apportion the burdens among themselves. Assuming an IMF standby agreement is reached, the creditors make a complete inventory of external debts and gather other relevant economic data. The terms of the new arrangements are set out in a multilateral accord between the debtor and participating creditors. The multilateral agreement is not legally binding—it is called an Agreed Minute—but its recommendations form the basis of subsequent bilateral agreements to reschedule and refinance.[28]

The most important convention of the creditor clubs is their burden-sharing arrangement. The fundamental principle is that creditors should be treated equally. Thus, large lenders undertake a proportionately larger share of refinancing and receive the lion's share of repayments. Through a most-favored-nation (MFN) clause, this principle of nondiscrimination is even extended to nonparticipants like the Soviet Union. The MFN clause assures all creditors that their funds will not be diverted to some specially favored creditor. It does not eliminate serious bargaining over burden-sharing (nondiscrimination is a difficult concept in almost every context), but it does minimize the problems. It effectively forecloses side deals in which small creditors settle on easy terms, revive their trade and financial ties, and permit the debtor to hold out for better terms from larger creditors.[29] On the whole, these arrangements have satisfied creditors, who agree that the clubs are effective.[30]

The clubs do not include private creditors, but they do profoundly affect them. Typically, the private creditors collect into protective associations, striking their own refinancing agreements to parallel the official ones, as in the recent examples of Chile and Zaire.[31] Such agreements may be formally linked to creditor-club arrangements, and even required by them. Undersecretary of State Richard Cooper notes that "on occasion, rescheduling of official debt is made contingent on debtor country arrangement to seek to renegotiate debt owed to private creditors."[32] As the World Bank observed in 1969, private debt may be protected by inclusion in the formal bilateral agreements, even if the lender's home government had never guaranteed the credit.[33] If these arrangements for private creditors appear effective, it is also worth stressing that they are still rather new. Most reschedulings have not involved significant private debts, and the banks still have limited experience in these renegotiations.[34]

The pitfalls of inexperience are amply illustrated in the Peruvian case, analyzed by Barbara Stallings in chapter 9 of this

volume. The banks lent to Peru even after it rejected IMF financing, and, as a result, were drawn deeply and visibly into Peruvian politics as they tried to oversee their investment. They confronted continual problems in organizing themselves as lenders
and faced substantial sovereign resistance. The banks learned
their lesson. They cannot impose conditionality. The IMF must.

That note is sounded repeatedly when bankers discuss the
IMF. "In the future," says Frederick Heldring of the Philadelphia Bank, "the IMF . . . will increasingly have to provide this
leadership and discipline role, because only an institution like
the IMF can do so. A commercial bank, generally speaking, cannot really play that role. In banking parlance, I would say that
certain aspects of the vital 'syndicate leadership' role—the
analogy is not perfect—ought to be played by the IMF."[35] Says
Morgan Guaranty's James Nash, "Clearly, *the best way to an
increase in conditionality is via the IMF.*"[36]

Increasingly, banks are acting on that belief. Nash testified
that the 1978 bank negotiations with Peru and Turkey hinged
on their acceptance of IMF conditional adjustment programs.
"Peru and Turkey," he says, "are both countries with little
choice but to go to [the] Fund to maintain their creditworthiness."[37] Thus, the Fund has become the pivot of public
and private debt renegotiation.

3. New Tasks for the Fund

Creditors are naturally trying to strengthen the IMF's pivotal
role. Ironically, the most forceful advocates are the U.S. commercial banks, the same banks that so vigorously objected to a
strong IMF at its inception.[38] Albert Fishlow, who has an eye
for both irony and historical analogy, likens the banks' position
to that of the railroads in the late nineteenth century. The railroads pushed for the Interstate Commerce Commission, he says,
"hoping its regulations would shore up their shaky oli-
gopoly."[39] The banks—to continue the analogy—would like to
see a somewhat stronger IMF, better funded and able to provide
a larger share of balance-of-payments financing. They also advocate closer cooperation between public and private financial
institutions. They want the IMF to continue organizing commer-

cial lenders in debt crises, and they want it to play an even stronger role in supervising deficit countries' finances. Moreover, they would like to see the Fund's resources expanded, permitting it to lend more for balance-of-payments financing as bank lending in that area slows down. The last point is important because the security of existing loans depends on continuing inflows of foreign capital. The banks doubt they can supply that capital in sufficient quantities, and they want the IMF to step in.[40]

Over the past year, the Fund has moved in that direction, if only modestly. It increased its quotas, which had been drawn down, and initiated the $10.5 billion Witteveen Facility. Another general increase in quotas is planned. These are small increments, however, compared to the global scale of balance-of-payments adjustments. New bank lending to non–oil-exporting underdeveloped nations, for instance, could equal $30 billion between 1977 and 1980.[41] If it does, the Fund's new resources would act largely to supplement private financing and undergird its security by ensuring conditionality.

The commercial lenders, attentive to asset management, would especially like access to the IMF's detailed country analyses and the data on which they are based. This is strongly opposed by the developing country borrowers, who gave that information with the promise of confidentiality. They expect to see that promise kept. They raised the issue pointedly at the 1977 IMF/IBRD annual meetings and carried the day. But even though complete disclosure is unlikely, both the Fund and the World Bank will probably provide more and better information to private, nonguaranteed debt in their statistical compilations.

Private lenders, meanwhile, are turning to several other sources for still more information. The OECD, the Bank of England, and the Bank for International Settlements already provide credit information, and major central banks have asked the BIS to compile more-detailed information on debts.[42] There are also several efforts under way to provide checklists of questions for commercial loans, permitting banks to standardize their practices on a voluntary basis.

Complementing this growing exchange of information is an effort to coordinate public and private lending. Several forms of mutual financing are possible. Parallel financing, for instance, involves separate negotiations and loan contracts but makes private credit contingent on meeting public lending conditions. As this discussion of debt renegotiations indicates, parallel financing is already here. Some public lenders have gone even further, directly linking their loans to private ones through cross-default clauses. The U.S. Export-Import Bank pioneered these cofinancing arrangements in 1970. In 1976, the World Bank adopted cofinancing, joining sixteen commercial lenders to finance a Brazilian steel mill. In the next eighteen months, the World Bank helped underwrite over $340 million in cofinanced Euroloans. The program has become a regular feature of the World Bank and will continue to expand.[43] As far as the World Bank is concerned, it multiplies their developmental resources. As far as the private banks are concerned, the cross-default clauses mean virtually risk-free lending since no one has ever defaulted on the World Bank or even required refinancing. The IMF, meanwhile, is considering its own plan to insure some of the risks of private lending.[44]

There is a limit to these arrangements, however. If expanded dramatically, they would threaten the autonomy of both private and public lenders.[45] This issue was raised in 1977 when Gabriel Hauge, chairman of Manufacturers Hanover Trust, suggested a formal connection between commercial banks and the IMF. His proposal met a chorus of objections from his colleagues and Fund officials. The basic reason was that neither private banks nor the Fund wanted to subordinate their objectives or shift their lending criteria. Rimmer de Vries, for instance, excluded the possibility of joint financing and cited private banks' distinctive responsibilities:

> While the Fund is responsible to its member governments, banks have important responsibilities to their depositors and shareholders. Both should remain independent in their lending decisions. In some critical cases, the existence of a standby agreement with the Fund still may not be a sufficient reason for banks to extend new credit.[46]

But even if the style of cooperation between the Fund and commercial banks is still being debated, it is clear that cooperation will increase. That can only dampen the risks of private foreign lending.

The growing cooperation between the Fund and large commercial banks hinges on the IMF's crucial role in providing liquidity and discipline in debt crises. The question of IMF discipline has been analyzed often, but its relationship to the provision of liquidity is obscure and frequently misunderstood. IMF loans seldom solve debt crises in themselves. Rather, they have a *multiplier effect*, inducing major refinancing by private lenders. Hence, even a small IMF conditional loan can often resolve a debt crisis when combined with private financing. By the same token, the IMF's threat to deny a conditional loan unless certain conditions are met is an implicit threat to shut off private financing as well. It is because the loans themselves are massive that the Fund can effectively impose its conditions on borrowers. The lenders, in turn, voluntarily provide refinancing in most cases to secure their existing claims.

IMF loans stimulate such refinancing for several reasons. First, by providing direct credit, IMF loans partially relieve the immediate liquidity crisis, making the prospective borrower more creditworthy. Second, the IMF constrains private lenders from pursuing beggar-thy-fellow-banker policies. Its loans may contain provisions on debt service and new debt acquisition, both designed to assure equality of treatment among lenders. Moreover, by providing the broad political framework for refinancing, the IMF-sponsored debt negotiations minimize individual banks' incentives for declaring default or pursuing go-it-alone strategies. Finally, the Fund's conditional lending procedures encourage parallel refinancing because the Fund's own standards are trusted by private banks. The IMF, with its access to confidential economic data, is in an unmatched position to judge a borrower's short- and long-term creditworthiness. That judgment, especially in the higher-credit tranches, follows the standards of traditional bank lending, not those of concessional development finance. Commercial bankers would, of course, prefer to evaluate all the economic data themselves, and they continue to seek it from the IMF and the debtor countries. But, in the absence of full disclosure, the IMF's evaluation is a reasonable surrogate.

These basic features of the IMF's role in debt crises will probably change little over the next five years. Recent increases in IMF resources, plus a prospective 50 percent increase in its quotas, should ensure the Fund a continuing direct role in balance-of-payments financing. Parallel private lending will continue to reinforce that direct role. As a World Bank report recently observed, "The enlargement of IMF facilities now envisaged should help to avert any serious disruption of private flows arising out of isolated liquidity problems."[47]

Sustaining these flows will doubtless forge closer cooperation between the IMF and commercial lenders, and may even include some contractual arrangements for joint lending. It already has brought a sustained, if low-key, effort by commercial banks to better institutionalize their relations with the Fund. For the moment, that effort has centered on an improved exchange of credit information. But it holds out the longer-term prospect of formal IMF loan guarantees for private banks and joint financing arrangements.

Today, the Fund's role in minimizing private lending risks is an informal one, centering on its role in debt renegotiations and its supervision of repayment plans. And yet, that informal role is crucial to the political structure of world debt. Although the IMF's financial resources are dwarfed by the Euromarkets, its capacity to impose political and economic conditions on borrowers is unequaled. And, after the banks' experience in Peru, they are fully aware of what that means. Private lenders have discovered what their official counterparts learned in the 1950s and 1960s: the IMF is uniquely placed to supervise critical debt problems. To the banks, with over $90 billion in outstanding loans to non–oil-exporting underdeveloped countries, that is a very reassuring prospect.

Notes

1. U.S., Congress, House, Committee on Banking, Finance, and Urban Affairs, *Hearings on U.S. Participation in the Supplementary Financing Facility of the International Monetary Fund* (hereafter referred to as *IMF Hearings*), 95th Cong., 1st sess., 1977, p. 8. See Table 1 in Brian G. Crowe's

article (chap. 2) in this volume.

2. *IMF Hearings*, p. 12.

3. Robert B. Stobaugh, "The Oil Companies in the Crisis," in *The Oil Crisis*, ed. Raymond Vernon (New York: W. W. Norton, 1976).

4. David C. Beek, "Commercial Bank Lending to the Developing Countries," *Federal Reserve Bank of New York Quarterly Review*, Summer 1977, pp. 2-3. For an excellent case study of American banks' expansion into the principal Euromoney Center, see Janet Kelly, *Bankers and Borders: The Case of American Banks in Britain* (Cambridge, Mass.: Ballinger, 1977).

5. Beek, "Commercial Bank Lending," p. 4.

6. See Table 2 in Brian G. Crowe's article (chap. 2) in this volume.

7. Ibid.

8. For one such forecast of widespread debt crises, see Cheryl Payer, "Third World Debt Problems: The New Wave of Defaults," *Monthly Review*, September 1976, pp. 1-22.

9. U.S., Congress, Senate, Committee on Banking, Housing, and Urban Affairs, *Hearings on International Debt*, 95th Cong., 1st sess., 1977, p. 62.

10. *IMF Hearings*, p. 173.

11. Not included in the debt service ratio are several vital aspects of debt servicing capacity, among them export potential and prospective economic growth.

12. *IMF Survey*, June 5, 1978, p. 173.

13. *IMF Annual Report*, 1977, p. 21.

14. *OECD Economic Outlook*, July 1977, Table 32, p. 82.

15. U.S., Congress, Senate, *Hearings on International Debt*, p. 82.

16. Adalbert Krieger Vasena, "Spelling Out the World Bank's Approach to Cofinancing," *Euromoney*, August 1977, p. 54.

17. Foreign banking subsidiaries, which are distinct legal entities incorporated abroad, have an ambiguous status under these arrangements.

18. *IMF Hearings*, p. 78.

19. Rimmer de Vries, "The International Debt Situation," *World Financial Markets*, June 1977, pp. 6-7.

20. Speech by IMF Managing Director H. Johannes Witteveen, *IMF Survey*, May 8, 1978, p. 139.

21. For a discussion of the CIEC conference, including demands on debt questions, see Jahangir Amuzegar, "A Requiem for the North-South Conference," *Foreign Affairs*, October 1977, pp. 136-59. For a rare argument that official donors should treat at least some of their debts as development aid, see Peter B. Kenen, "Debt Relief as Development Assistance," in *The New International Economic Order: The North-South Debt*, ed. Jagdish N. Bhagwati (Cambridge: MIT Press, 1977).

22. IBRD, "Multilateral Debt Renegotiations: 1956-1968," prepared by Patrick B. de Fontenay (unpublished, April 11, 1969), p. 39.

23. *Euromoney,* November 1977, p. 81.

24. IMF, Office of the Secretary, "Multilateral Debt Renegotiations—Experience of Fund Members" (unpublished, August 6, 1971), p. 13.

25. Robert N. Bee, "Lessons from Debt Reschedulings in the Past," *Euromoney,* April 1977, pp. 34-35.

26. "The Sick Men of the Euromarkets," *Euromoney,* March 1978, p. 10; IMF, "Multilateral Debt Renegotiations—Experience of Fund Members," p. 25.

27. U.S., Congress, Senate, *Hearings on International Debt,* p. 127.

28. Christopher Prout, "Finance for Developing Countries: An Essay," in *International Monetary Relations,* Vol. 2 of *International Economic Relations of the Western World, 1959-1971,* ed. Andrew Shonfield (London: Oxford University Press, 1976), pp. 389-401.

29. Ibid., p. 401.

30. See Brian G. Crowe's detailed assessment (chap. 2) in this volume.

31. U.S., Congress, Senate, *Hearings on International Debt,* p. 66.

32. Ibid.

33. IBRD, "Multilateral Debt Renegotiations: 1956-1968," p. 29.

34. W. H. Bruce Brittain, "Developing Countries' External Debt and the Private Banks," *Banca Nazionale del Lavoro Quarterly Review,* December 1977, p. 366; U.S., Congress, Senate, *Hearings on International Debt,* p. 82.

35. *IMF Hearings,* p. 142.

36. Ibid., p. 218; emphasis in the original.

37. Ibid., p. 217.

38. Alfred E. Eckes, Jr., *A Search for Solvency: Bretton Woods and the International Monetary System* (Austin: University of Texas Press, 1975).

39. Albert Fishlow, "Debt Remains a Problem," *Foreign Policy* 30, Spring 1978, pp. 139-40. For a detailed argument on corporate oligopolies and state regulation at the turn of the century, see Gabriel Kolko, *The Triumph of Conservatism: A Reinterpretation of American History, 1900-1916* (New York: Free Press of Glencoe, 1963).

40. U.S., Congress, Senate, *Hearings on International Debt,* p. 167; Marina v. N. Whitman, "Bridging the Gap," *Foreign Policy* 30, Spring 1978, p. 149; M. M. Ahmad, "The Developing Countries and Access to Capital Markets," *Finance and Development,* December 1976, p. 26.

41. *IMF Hearings,* p. 221.

42. *Euromoney*, March 1978, pp. 11-13; Henry C. Wallich, "Oil and Debt: the Risks of International Lending," *World Economy*, October 1977, p. 48.

43. Adalbert Krieger Vasena, "Spelling Out the World Bank's Approach," p. 57; Roger A. Hornstein, "Cofinancing of Bank and IDA Projects," *Finance and Development*, June 1977, pp. 40-43.

44. Xenophon Zolotas, "A Proposal for a New Fund to Insure against Euromarket Defaults," *Euromoney*, April 1978.

45. For a discussion of corporate autonomy and public policy, see Charles Lipson, "The Development of Expropriation Insurance: The Role of Corporate Preferences and State Initiatives," *International Organization*, Spring 1978, pp. 351-75.

46. Rimmer de Vries, *World Financial Markets*, June 1977, p. 12.

47. World Bank, Development Policy Staff, *Prospects for Developing Countries, 1978-85*, November 1977, p. 53.

Selected Bibliography

William E. Westermeyer

Adler, John. "The External Debt Problem." In *The World Bank Group, Multilateral Aid and the 1970s*, edited by J. P. Lewis and I. Kapur, pp. 111-22. Toronto: Lexington Books, 1973.

Ahmad, M. M. "The Developing Countries and Access to Capital Markets." *Finance and Development*, December 1976.

Alter, Gerald M. "The Servicing of Foreign Capital Inflows by Under-developed Countries." In *Economic Development for Latin America*, edited by H. S. Ellis. New York: St. Martin's Press, 1961.

AmEx Bank Review. Various Issues. London: AmEx Bank Limited.

Anderson, Roger E. "Lending to Less Developed Countries: Evaluating the Risk." Speech before the American Bankers Association International Monetary Conference, Tokyo, May 24, 1977. Chicago: Continental Illinois Corporation, 1977.

Areskoug, Kaj. *External Public Borrowing: Its Role in Economic Development*. New York: Praeger Publishers, 1969.

Aronson, Jonathan David. *Money and Power: Banks and the World Monetary System*. Beverly Hills, Calif.: Sage Publications, 1978.

Atlantic Council Working Group on the International Monetary System. *The International Monetary System: Progress and Prospects*. Boulder, Colo.: Westview Press, 1977.

Avromovic, Dragoslav. *Economic Growth and External Debt*. Baltimore: Johns Hopkins Press, 1966.

Avromovic, Dragoslav, and Gulhati, Ravi. *Debt Servicing Problems of Low-Income Countries, 1956-1958*. Baltimore: Johns Hopkins Press, 1964.

Bank for International Settlements. "UNCTAD Ends Preparatory Talks on Debt Problems." Press Review No. 246, December 20, 1977.

"Bank-IMF Links Over-Exaggerated?" *Journal of Commerce*, November 3, 1977.

"Bankers Feel Pressure to Keep Recycling." *Business Week*, January 30, 1978.

Bee, Robert. "Lessons from Debt Reschedulings in the Past." *Euromoney*, April 1977.

Beek, David C. "Commercial Bank Lending to Developing Countries." *Federal Reserve Bank of New York Quarterly Review*, Summer 1977.

Beim, David O. "Rescuing the LDCs." *Foreign Affairs*, July 1977.

Belliveau, Nancy. "Heading Off Zaire's Default." *Institutional Investor*, March 1977.

Bench, Robert R. "How the U.S. Comptroller of the Currency Analyzes Country Risk." *Euromoney*, August 1977.

Bergsten, C. Fred. Speech before the Chicago Council on Foreign Relations. Mimeographed. Washington, D.C.: U.S. Department of the Treasury, April 22, 1977.

——. "Remarks of the Assistant Secretary of the Treasury for International Affairs before the Subcommittee on Taxation and Debt Management of the Senate Finance Committee." Washington, D.C.: U.S. Department of the Treasury, January 23, 1978.

Bhagwati, Jagdish N. "Amount and Sharing of Aid." In *Assisting Developing Countries—Problems of Debts, Burden-Sharing, Jobs, and Trade*. Overseas Development Council Studies, 1. New York: Praeger Publishers, 1972.

Bittermann, Henry J. *The Refunding of International Debt*. Durham, N.C.: Duke University Press, 1973.

Brackenridge, A. Bruce. "Country Exposure, Country Limits, and Lending to LDCs." *Journal of Commercial Bank Lending*, July 1977.

Brittain, W. H. Bruce. "Developing Countries' External Debt and the Private Banks." *Banca Nazionale del Lavoro Quarterly Review*, December 1977.

Burns, Arthur F. "The Need for Order in International Finance." Address before the Columbia University Graduate School of Business, April 12, 1977. *Federal Reserve Bank of Richmond Economic Review*, July/August 1977.

Chenery, Hollis B., and Sprout, Alan M. "Foreign Assistance and Economic Development." *American Economic Review*, September 1966.

Citibank. "LDC Default—Shadow Without Substance." *Monthly Economic Letter*, November 1976.

Cleveland, Harold van B., and Brittain, W. H. Bruce. "Are the LDCs in over Their Heads?" *Foreign Affairs*, July 1977.

Cline, William R. "Oil Prices and the Terms of Trade of Non-Petroleum-Exporting Developing Countries." Mimeographed. Brookings Inflation Project Working Paper. Washington, D.C.: Brookings Institution,

January 1977.

Cohen, Jerome B. "Awash on a Sea of Debt—Banks and LDCs." *The Bankers Magazine*, Summer 1977.

Cohen, N. P. "Econometric Debt Early Warning Systems." Consultant's Paper for U.S. Department of the Treasury, August 30, 1976.

Cooper, Richard N. "International Debt: Current Issues and Implications." Statement before the Subcommittee on International Finance of the Senate Committee on Banking, Housing, and Urban Affairs. Washington, D.C.: U.S. Department of State, August 29, 1977.

Corea, Gamani. "The Debt Problem of Developing Countries." *Journal of Development Planning*, April 1976.

Costanzo, G. A. "Is the Third World a Sound Debtor?" Editorial, *New York Times*, April 18, 1977.

Crittenden, Ann. "Coordination Urged in World Banking." *New York Times*, November 17, 1977.

Davis, Steven I. "How Risky is International Lending?" *Harvard Business Review*, January/February 1977.

"Debt Service Is Seen Slicing Export Income of Poorest Nations." *Wall Street Journal*, December 12, 977.

Dhonte, Pierre. "Describing External Debt Situations: A Roll-Over Approach." IMF Staff Papers, March 1975.

Domar, Evsey D. "The Effect of Foreign Investment on the Balance of Payments." *American Economic Review*, September 1950.

Farnsworth, Clyde H. "Unguaranteed Loans to Poorer Countries by U.S. Banks Listed." *New York Times*, January 17, 1978.

Feder, Gershon. "Economic Growth, Foreign Loans, and Debt Servicing Capacity of Developing Countries." Mimeographed. July 1977.

Feder, Gershon, and Just, Richard E. *Optimal International Borrowing and Creditworthiness Control.* Department of Agriculture and Resource Economics, Working Paper No. 20. Berkeley: University of California, 1977.

———. "A Study of Debt Servicing Capacity Applying Logit Analysis." *Journal of Development Economics*, March 1977.

Feis, Herbert. *Europe, the World's Banker: An Account of European Foreign Investment and the Connection of World Finance with Diplomacy before the War.* New Haven, Conn.: Yale University Press, 1930.

"Financing the LDCs: The Role of the Euro-Markets." *Euromoney*, November 1977.

Finch, David. "Investment Service of Under-Developed Countries." IMF Staff Papers, September 1951.

Fishlow, Albert. "Debt Remains a Problem." *Foreign Policy* No. 30, Spring 1978.

Flanders, M. June. *The Demand for International Reserves*. Princeton Studies in International Finance, Department of Economics. Princeton, N.J.: Princeton University, April 1971.

Frank, Charles R. Jr. *Debt and Terms of Aid*. Overseas Development Council Monograph Series No. 1. Washington, D.C.: Overseas Development Council, 1970.

Frank, Charles R., Jr., and Cline, William R. *Debt Servicing and Foreign Assistance: An Analysis of Problems and Prospects in Less Developed Countries*. AID Discussion Paper No. 19. Washington, D.C.: AID, Office of Policy and Program Coordination, June 1969.

——. "Measurement of Debt Servicing Capacity: An Application of Discriminant Analysis." *Journal of International Economics*, August 1971.

Frenkel, Jacob A., and Johnson, Harry G. "The Monetary Approach to the Balance of Payments—Essential Concepts and Historical Origin." In *The Monetary Approach to the Balance of Payments*, edited by Jacob Frenkel and Harry G. Johnson, pp. 21-45. Toronto: University of Toronto Press, 1976.

Friedman, Irving S. *The Emerging Role of Private Banks in the Developing World*. New York: Citicorp, 1977.

——. "Country Risk: The Lessons of Zaire." *The Banker*, February 1978.

Ganoe, Charles S. "Problem Loans to Less Developed Countries." Speech to the 1977 Financial Conference. New York: The Conference Board, February 15, 1977.

Garg, Ramesh C. "Debt Problems of Developing Countries." *Intereconomics*, March/April 1977.

Goodman, Stephen. "How the Big U.S. Banks Really Evaluate Sovereign Risks." *Euromoney*, February 1977.

Griffin, Keith. "Foreign Capital, Domestic Savings, and Economic Development." *Bulletin of the Oxford University Institute of Economics and Statistics*, May 1970.

Grinols, Earl, and Bhagwati, Jagdish. "Foreign Capital, Savings, and Dependence." *Review of Economics and Statistics*, November 1976.

Guitian, Manuel. "Credit versus Money as an Instrument of Control." IMF Staff Papers, November 1973.

Gulhati, Ravi I. "The 'Need' for Foreign Resources, Absorptive Capacity, and Debt Servicing Capacity." In *Capital Movements and Economic Development*, edited by John H. Adler, pp. 240-67. New York: St. Martin's Press, 1967.

Haley, John C. "A Hard Look at Lending Abroad." *Business in Brief*. New York: Chase Manhattan Bank, April 1977.

Hanley, Thomas H. *United States Multinational Banking: Current and Prospective Strategies*. New York: Salomon Brothers, June 1976.

Haq, Mahbub ul. *The Third World and the International Economic Order.* ODC Paper No. 22. Washington, D.C.: Overseas Development Council, 1976.

Harrington, Michael. "A Bill to Encourage the Development of Appropriate Stabilization Programs by the International Monetary Fund." HR 10318. Referred to the Committee on Banking, Finance, and Urban Affairs, December 15, 1977.

"Heimann Calls the Shots for Overseas Lending." *The Economist*, January 14, 1978.

Hirschman, Albert O., and Bird, Richard M. "Foreign Aid—A Critique and a Proposal." Princeton Studies in International Finance No. 69, Department of Economics. Princeton, N.J.: Princeton University, July 1968.

Holsen, John, and Waelbroeck, Jean. "LDC Balance of Payments Policies and the International Monetary System." Staff Working Paper No. 226. Washington, D.C.: World Bank, February 1976.

———. "The Less Developed Countries and the International Monetary Mechanism." *American Economic Review*, May 1976.

Hornstein, Roger A. "Cofinancing of Bank and IDA Projects." *Finance and Development*, June 1977.

Hughes, Helen. "The External Debt of Developing Countries." *Finance and Development*, December 1977.

Hunt, Shane J. "Evaluating Direct Foreign Investment in Latin America." In *Latin America in the 1970s*, edited by Luisi R. Einandi, pp. 127-46. Rand Corporation, R-1067-DOS, December 1972.

"International Development Cooperation Act of 1973." *Congressional Record*. January 25, 1978, pp. S-407-S-432.

International Monetary Fund. *International Financial Statistics.* Washington, D.C. Various issues.

———. "Multilateral Debt Renegotiations—Experience of Fund Members." Washington, D.C., August 6, 1971.

———. *IMF Survey*, September 6, 1976.

———. "Avoidance and Resolution of Debt Servicing Difficulties." Washington, D.C., September 23, 1976.

———. *IMF Survey, Supplement on International Lending*, June 6, 1977.

———. "Debt Problems of Developing Countries." United Nations, General Assembly Resolution 32/178. *United Nations General Assembly—Thirty-Second Session*, SM/78/10, January 10, 1978.

International Monetary Fund/International Bank for Reconstruction and Development. "Debt." In *Salient Points of Governors Statements of 1977 Annual Meetings.* Washington, D.C., December 1977.

———. Development Committee. *Provisional Record of the Ninth Meeting of the Development Committee.* DC/77-19. Washington, D.C., December 12, 1977.

Irvine, Reed J.; Maroni, Yves; and Lee, Henry F. "How to Borrow Successfully." *Columbia Journal of World Business*, January/February 1970.

Islam, Nural. "The External Debt Problem of the Developing Countries with Special Reference to the Least Developed." In *A World Divided: The Less Developed Countries in the International Economy*, edited by G. K. Helleiner, pp. 225-47. New York: Cambridge University Press, 1976.

Jenks, Leland H. *The Migration of British Capital to 1875*. New York: Knopf, 1927.

Johnson, Harry G. "The Transfer Problem and Exchange Stability." *Journal of Political Economy*, June 1956.

———. "Towards a General Theory of the Balance of Payments." In *International Trade and Economic Growth: Studies in Pure Theory*, edited by Harry G. Johnson, pp. 153-68. Cambridge, Mass.: Harvard University Press, 1961.

———. "The Monetary Approach to Balance-of-Payments Theory." In *Further Essays in Monetary Theory*, edited by Harry G. Johnson. London: George Allen & Unwin, 1972.

Katz, S. Stanley. "A Secondary Market for LDC Debt: Alternative to Rescheduling." Washington, D.C.: U.S. Department of Commerce, February 12, 1977.

Kenen, P. B. "Debt Relief as Development Assistance." In *The New International Economic Order: The North-South Debate*, edited by Jagdish N. Bhagwati, pp. 50-77. Cambridge, Mass.: M.I.T. Press, 1977.

Kindleberger, Charles P. "Less Developed Countries and the International Capital Market." In *Industrial Organization and Economic Development, Essays in Honor of Edward S. Mason*, edited by Jesse W. Markham and G. F. Papanek, pp. 337-49. Boston: Houghton-Mifflin, 1970.

———. "Debt Situation of Developing Countries in Historical Perspective." Paper for a symposium at the Export-Import Bank, April 21, 1977.

King, Benjamin B. *Notes on the Mechanics of Growth and Debt*. World Bank Staff Occasional Papers No. 6. Baltimore: Johns Hopkins Press, 1968.

Krassowski, Andrzej. *Development and the Debt Trap: Economic Planning and External Borrowing in Ghana*. London: Croom Helm, in cooperation with the Overseas Development Institute, 1974.

Krebs, Paul. "The Private Capital Markets and Developing Countries." *Euromoney*, August 1975.

Krueger, Anne O. "Balance-of-Payments Theory." *Journal of Economic*

Literature, March 1969.

Lake, Anthony. "The United States and the Third World: Economic Issues." Speech before the Annual Meeting of the African Studies Association and the Latin American Studies Association. Washington, D.C.: U.S. Department of State, November 5, 1977.

Lal, Deepak. "When Is Foreign Borrowing Desirable?" *Bulletin of the Oxford University Institute of Economics and Statistics*, August 1971.

Landes, David S. *Bankers and Pashas, International Finance and Economic Imperialism in Egypt*. Cambridge, Mass.: Harvard University Press, 1958.

Latour, Pierre. "Euromarkets Wait for LDCs' Credits to be Repaid." *Euromoney*, October 1975.

"LDC International Borrowing on Uptrend." *Economic Intelligence Weekly Review*. Langley, Va.: Central Intelligence Agency, December 1, 1977.

Leipziger, Danny, ed. *The International Monetary Systems and the Developing Nations*. Washington, D.C.: U.S. Agency for International Development, Bureau for Program and Policy Coordination, 1976.

Lisman, Bruce. "Loans to LDCs: Who Owes What to Whom?" New York: Drexel, Burnham, Lambert Newsletter, April 20, 1977.

Lissakers, Karin. *International Debt, the Banks, and U.S. Foreign Policy*, A Staff Report prepared for U.S., Congress, Senate, Committee on Foreign Relations, Subcommittee on Foreign Economic Policy. Washington, D.C.: U.S. Government Printing Office, 1977.

Loser, Claudio M. "External Debt Management and Balance of Payments Policies." IMF Staff Papers, March 1977.

Machlup, Fritz. "The Transfer Problem Revisited." In *International Payments, Debts, and Gold*, edited by Fritz Machlup, 2d. ed., pp. 433-46. New York: New York University Press, 1976.

McKinnon, Ronald I. *Money, Capital, and Economic Development*. Washington, D.C.: Brookings Institution, 1973.

Meguid, Abdel. "The United Nations 1978 Initiative: The Conference on Technical Cooperation among Developing Countries." Speech before the Washington, D.C., Chapter of the Society for International Development, January 17, 1978.

Mikesell, Raymond F. "The Capacity to Service Foreign Investment." In *U.S. Private and Government Investment Abroad*, edited by Raymond F. Mikesell, pp. 377-406. Eugene, Ore.: University of Oregon Books, 1962.

———. "Capital Absorptive Capacity as a Limitation on Lending for Economic Development." In *U.S. Private and Government Investment Abroad*, edited by Raymond F. Mikesell, pp. 360-77. Eugene, Ore.:

University of Oregon Books, 1962.

Miller, Judith. "Limits Formally Proposed on Bank Lending Overseas." *New York Times*, January 9, 1978.

Mintz, Ilse. *Deterioration in the Quality of Foreign Bonds Issued in the United States, 1920-1930.* New York: National Bureau of Economic Research, 1951.

Mohammed, Azizali F., and Saccomanni, Fabrizio. "Short-Term Banking and Euro-Currency Credits to Developing Countries." IMF Staff Papers, November 1973.

Morgan Guaranty Trust Company. "Trends in International Lending." *World Financial Markets*, December 1976.

———. "The International Debt Situation." *World Financial Markets*, June 1977.

———. "International Credit Markets." *World Financial Markets*, December 1977.

Mullaney, Thomas E. "Witteveen Goal: Enlarging Funding Facilities of IMF." *New York Times*, January 20, 1978.

Müller, Ronald. "Poverty is the Product." *Foreign Policy* No. 13., Winter 1973-1974.

Mundell, Robert A. "The Appropriate Use of Monetary and Fiscal Policy for Internal and External Stability." IMF Staff Papers, March 1962.

National Advisory Council on International Monetary and Financial Policies. *International Finance.* Annual Report to the President and to the Congress, July 1, 1975 to June 30, 1976. Washington, D.C.: U.S. Government Printing Office, January 1977.

Nelson, Benjamin J. *The Idea of Usury; From Brotherhood to Universal Otherhood.* Princeton, N.J.: Princeton University Press, 1949.

O'Brien, Richard. "Assessing the Credit Risks of the Developing Countries." *Euromoney*, October 1975.

Ohlin, Goran. *Aid and Indebtedness.* Paris: Organization for Economic Cooperation and Development, 1966.

———. "Debts, Development, and Default." In *A World Divided: The Less Developed Countries in the International Economy*, edited by G. K. Helleiner, pp. 207-23. New York; Cambridge University Press, 1976.

Organization for Economic Cooperation and Development. *Debt Problems of the Developing Countries.* Paris OECD, 1974.

———. Development Advisory Committee. *Development Cooperation: 1975 Review.* Paris, 1975.

———. *Development Cooperation: 1976 Review.* Paris, 1976.

———. Development Assistance Committee. *Development Assistance 1968 Review.* Paris, 1968.

———. *Development Assistance 1970 Review*, Paris, 1970.

Papanek, Gustav F. "The Effect of Aid and Other Resource Transfers on Savings and Growth in Less Developed Countries." *The Economic Journal*, September 1972.

Payer, Cheryl. *The Debt Trap*. New York: Monthly Review Press, 1975.

——. "Will the Government Have to Bail Out the Banks?" *Bankers Magazine*, Spring 1977.

Pearson Commission. *Partners in Development*. Report of the Commission on International Development. New York: Praeger Publishers, 1969.

Platt, D. C. M. *Latin America and British Trade, 1806-1914*. London: Adam and Charles Black, 1972.

"Poor Countries Owe Their Souls to U.S. Banks." *Dollars and Sense* No. 31., November 1977.

Prebisch, Raul. *Towards a New Trade Policy for Development*. Report of the Secretary General of the United Nations Conference on Trade and Development. New York: United Nations, 1964.

Prout, Christopher. "Finance for Developing Countries: An Essay." In *International Monetary Relations*, vol. 2 of *International Economic Relations of the Western World, 1959-1971*, edited by Andrew Shonfield, pp. 360-404. London: Oxford University Press, 1976.

Reddaway, William B.; Potter, S. J.; and Taylor, C. T. *Effects of UK Direct Investment Overseas: Final Report*. London: Cambridge University Press, 1968.

Rothschild, Emma. "Banks: The Coming Crisis." *New York Review of Books*, May 27, 1976.

——. "Banks: The Politics of Debt." *New York Review of Books*, June 24, 1976.

Safarian, A. E. "Perspectives on Foreign Direct Investment from the Viewpoint of a Capital Receiving Country." *Journal of Finance*, May 1973.

Sargen, Nicholas. "Commercial Bank Lending to Developing Countries." *Federal Reserve Bank of San Fransisco Economic Review*, Spring 1976.

"The Secondary Banking Crisis and the Bank of England's Support Operations." *Bank of England Quarterly Bulletin*, June 1978.

Sewell, John W., and Staff of the Overseas Development Council. *The United States and World Development, Agenda 1977*. New York: Praeger Publishers, 1977.

Shapiro, Harvey D. "Monitoring: Are Banks Biting Off More Than They Can Chew?" *Institutional Investor*, October 1976.

"The Sick Men of the Euromarkets." *Euromoney*, March 1978.

Simonis, Udo E. "Some Considerations on the External Public Debt of LDCs." *Intereconomics* No. 7/8, Summer 1977.

Smith, Gordon W. *The External Debt Prospects of the Non-Oil-Exporting Developing Countries*. New International Economic Order Series.

Washington, D.C.: Overseas Development Council, 1977.

Soesastro, Hadi. "Assessing Debt Servicing Capacity of Developing Countries and Implications for Policy: A Survey." Rand Paper Series, P-6060. Santa Monica, Calif.: Rand Corp., December 1977.

Solomon, Robert. "A Perspective on the Debt of Developing Countries." *Brookings Papers on Economic Activity.* Washington, D.C.: Brookings Institution, 1977.

Spitaeller, Erich. "A Survey of Recent Quantitative Studies of Long-Term Capital Movements." IMF Staff Papers, March 1971.

Strange, Susan. "Debts, Defaulters, and Development." *International Affairs*, July 1967.

"U.N. Official Asks an Easing of Debt for Poor Countries." *Wall Street Journal*, January 24, 1978.

United Nations. *Export Credits and Development Financing.* E/4274(ST/ECA/95). New York, 1966.

United Nations Conference on Trade and Development. *Debt Problems of Developing Countries.* Report of the ad hoc Group of Govermmental Experts on Its Third Session. Geneva, February 25–March 7, 1975.

——. "Manila Declaration and Programme of Action." TD/195. Geneva, February 12, 1976.

——. *Selected Issues Relating to the Establishment of Common Norms in Future Debt Reorganizations.* TD/AC.2/9. Geneva, October 31, 1977.

——. Secretariat. *International Financial Cooperation for Development.* TD/188. Geneva, December 29, 1975. *Supplement.* TD/188/Suppl. Geneva, February 13, 1976.

——. "Trade Prospects and Capital Requirements of Developing Countries, 1976-1980." Mimeographed. Geneva, March 17, 1976.

——. "World Economic Outlook, 1976-1977." Mimeographed. Geneva, February 1976.

——. Trade and Development Board. "Report of the Intergovernmental Group of Experts on the External Indebtedness of Developing Countries." Geneva, July 18-22, 1977.

U.S., Congress, House, Committee on Banking, Finance, and Urban Affairs, Subcommittee on Financial Institutions Supervision, Regulation, and Insurance. *Hearings on International Banking Operations.* March 23-24, April 5-6, 1977. Washington, D.C.: U.S. Government Printing Office, 1977.

U.S., Department of State. "Group B Resolution on Debt." Nairobi 5299. Washington, D.C., May 24, 1976.

——. "Proposals Submitted by the G-19 Problems of Indebtedness of Developing Countries in the Financial Affairs Commission." OECD P26985. Washington, D.C., September 16, 1976.

——. "32 UNGA, Second Committee on Debt." USUN N5674. Washington, D.C., December 15, 1977.

——. "International Debt: Current Issues and Implications." In *Statement*. Washington, D.C., August 29, 1977.

U.S., Department of State, and Agency for International Development. *Developing Countries' Debt and U.S. Foreign Assistance: A Case Study*. Report to the Congress. Washington, D.C.: U.S. Department of State, December 1973.

U.S., Department of the Treasury. *Report on External Debt of Developing Countries and on Debt of Developing Countries and on Debt Relief Provided by the United States*. Submitted to Congress. Washington, D.C., January 1976, January 1977, January 1978.

——. "The Debt Issue in the Post-CIEC Era." Briefing for the U.S. Delegation to the IMF/World Bank Annual Meetings. Washington, D.C., September 21, 1977.

——. "The IBRD Capital Increase." Briefing for the U.S. Delegation to the IMF/World Bank Annual Meetings. Washington, D.C., September 21, 1977.

van Agtmael, Antoine W. "Evaluating the Risks of Lending to Developing Countries." *Euromoney*, April 1976.

Vasena, Adalbert Krieger. "Spelling Out the World Bank's Approach to Co-Financing." *Euromoney*, August 1977.

Wachtel, Howard M. *The New Gnomes: Multinational Banks in the Third World*. Washington, D.C.: Transnational Institute, 1977.

Wall, David. *The Charity of Nations*. New York: Basic Books, 1973.

Wallich, Henry C. "Oil and Debt: The Risks of International Lending." *World Economy*, October 1977.

——. "The Critical Information Gap." *Euromoney*, November 1977.

——. "How Much Private Bank Lending Is Enough?" Paper prepared for Export-Import Bank Symposium on Developing-Country Debt. Mimeographed. Washington, D.C.: Federal Reserve Board, 1977.

——. "International Lending and the Euromarkets." Remarks at the 1978 Euromarkets Conference sponsored by the *Financial Times. Financial Times*, May 9, 1978.

Watson, Paul M. "Debt and the Developing Countries: New Problems and New Actors." Development Paper No. 26. Washington, D.C.: Overseas Development Council, 1978.

Weinert, Robert S. "Why the Banks Did It." *Foreign Policy* No. 30, Spring 1978.

Weisskopf, Thomas E. "The Impact of Foreign Capital Inflow on Domestic Savings in Underdeveloped Countries." *Journal of International Economics*, February 1972.

Wellons, Philip A. *Borrowing by Developing Countries on the Eurocurrency Market.* Paris: Organization for Economic Cooperation and Development, 1977.

Williamson, John. "International Debt and Indexation." Address before the National Economists Club. Washington, D.C., November 12, 1977.

Winkler, Max. *Foreign Bonds, An Autopsy: A Study of Defaults and Repudiations of Government Obligations.* Philadelphia: Roland Swain, 1933.

World Bank. *Annual Reports.* Various years.

———. "Suppliers' Credits from Internationalized to Developing Countries." Washington, D.C., 1967.

———. *World Debt Tables.* Doc. No. EC-167/76. Washington, D.C., 1975. Doc. No. EC-167/76. Washington, D.C., 1976.

———. Development Policy Staff. *Prospects for Developing Countries: 1977-85.* Washington, D.C., September 1976.

Yeager, Leland B. *International Monetary Relations: Theory, History, and Policy.* 2d. ed. New York: Harper and Row, 1976.

Index

Accumulation, 152, 154, 176, 191
Acheampong, I. K., 264, 267, 272, 273
Adelman, Irma, 214n
Adjustment, 29, 32, 46, 48, 79, 319, 320, 326, 327
Afghanistan, 31, 200
African debt, 66, 72, 74, 75, 76, 91
African Development, 209
Agency for International Development (AID) (U.S.), 52, 229, 231, 247
Agriculture, 136, 138, 141, 145, 187n
Ahmad, M. M., 332n
Aid, 32, 45, 51, 53, 58, 79, 82, 94, 126, 138, 159, 211, 219, 243, 319, 321; bilateral, 12, 18, 210, 219, 225; multilateral, 55, 210, 283; OPEC, 19; U.S., 12, 34, 82, 113, 225, 235, 321
Aid consortia, 14, 20, 40, 42-43, 54n, 323
Algeria, 53n, 68, 99n, 244
Aliber, Robert Z., 97n, 101n
Allende, Salvador, 129, 130, 256, 257, 258, 266, 267, 269-272, 280n
Allende regime (Chile), 269
American Express, 199, 299
Amuzegar, Jahangir, 331n
Anderson, Charles, 129, 155n
Angolan Civil War, 290-291
Argentina, 16, 20, 72, 76, 196, 199, 203, 268, 269, 271, 320; debt 13, 31, 67, 77, 198, 200; debt renego-

tiations (1956, 1962, 1965), 13, 38-39
Aronson, Jonathan D., 214n, 222, 312n
Arrears, 37, 256, 262, 265, 291, 292, 298, 306
Asheshov, Nicholas, 250n, 251n
Asian debt, 66, 75, 91
Asian Development Bank, 209
Assets, 106, 108, 109, 111, 113, 114, 117-119, 121, 139, 140, 144, 146, 150, 153, 154
Assistance. See Aid
Austerity measures, 48, 166, 195, 199, 202-206, 209, 212, 247, 254, 272. See also under individual countries
Australia, 269
Authoritarian practices, 203, 204, 247
Avromovic, Dragoslav, 11, 25n

Baer, Werner, 137, 155n
Balance of payments, xvi, 28, 32, 41-44, 48-51, 59, 64, 79, 81, 92, 103, 111-117, 144, 146, 150, 162, 186, 191, 194, 197, 201, 257, 310, 317, 318. See also under individual countries
Bangladesh, 31, 39n, 54n, 200
Bank(s), 9, 18, 24, 42, 46, 57-58, 103, 107-109, 130-136, 145, 152, 174, 184, 191-195, 203-206, 225, 326-330; Arab, 85; assets, loans, 19, 47, 59, 74, 106-108, 114, 115; European, 220, 262, 284, 289-290, 318;

Japanese, 73, 99n, 220, 289-290, 294, 318; large, 62, 65, 74-77, 132, 220, 221, 285; liabilities, deposits, 62, 63, 89, 105-107, 108, 115, 117; neutrality, 132-136, 141, 155, 238; small, 76, 77, 80, 100n, 132, 220, 221, 234, 236, 285; U.S., 61-62, 66-80, 85, 89-93, 95n, 96n, 97n, 176, 191-195, 198, 208, 212, 246, 262, 283, 289-290, 294, 297, 300, 301, 303, 310, 318, 322, 326

Bankers Trust, 65, 193, 236, 238

Bank for International Settlements (BIS), 20, 21, 59, 73, 89, 292, 320, 327

Bank influence, power, 202, 204, 284-288, 305-311

Bank of America, 98n, 192, 193, 235

Bank of England, 10, 110, 111, 116, 327

Bankruptcy, 9-10, 69, 132, 161, 197, 202, 205-207, 210, 212, 246

Bargaining power, leverage, 44, 47, 134, 195, 211, 212, 219, 221, 222, 226, 248, 254, 255, 262, 265, 266, 268, 271, 273-275, 287, 289, 299, 308

Barnet, Richard J., 213n

Barriers, 131, 133, 136, 168, 204

Barúa Casteñeda, Luis, 232, 240

Basic human needs, *xv*, 185, 186, 307, 309

Bauer, Raymond, 312n

Bee, Robert, 276n, 332n

Beek, David C., 94n, 97n, 99n, 331n

Beim, David O., 212n, 313n

Belaúnde Terry, Fernando, 227

Belgium, 270, 272, 292

Belliveau, Nancy, 250n, 276n

Bennett, Robert A., 97n

Bergsten, C. Fred, 245

Berne Union of Credit Insurers, 13, 21

Beveridge, Andrew A., 192, 212n

Bittermann, Henry, 275n, 276n, 278n, 313n, 314n

Bleichroder, Gerson von, 17

Blumenthal, Erwin, 292

Blumenthal, W. Michael, 100n, 104, 113, 206

Bollinger, Bill, 250n, 251n

Bonds, 16-17, 60, 61, 100n, 209, 283.

See also Eurobond market

Bonelli, Regis, 173, 176, 187n, 188n

Brazil, 20, 24, 50, 72, 74, 127, 129, 137, 138, 166, 167, 171-186, 196, 203, 222, 248, 256, 258-262, 267, 271, 272, 275, 302-304, 308, 309, 321; agriculture, 173, 178, 179; austerity measures, 198, 259-261; balance of payments, 167, 175, 176, 198, 203, 256, 259, 300; coffee, 258, 259, 300; consumption, 174, 176, 183, 186; debt, 13, 31, 33, 65, 67, 68, 127, 171, 172, 176, 177, 183, 198, 201, 259-262, 272; debt renegotiations (1955, 1961, 1964), 13, 38-40, 47, 184, 256, 259-262, 264, 272, 300; debt service, 177, 180, 184, 300, 301; devaluation, 177, 184, 260; exports, 99n, 172, 175 177, 178, 181, 183, 184, 186, 256, 259, 300; foreign exchange, 177, 186, 262; growth, 166, 167, 171-185, 259, 300; IMF, 259-261, 300; imports, 172, 174, 175, 181, 183, 260; income, 171, 179; inflation, 171, 176, 179-180, 198, 256, 259-262; policy, 171-174, 177, 180-181, 185, 260, 261; prices, 175, 177, 180, 181, 258; production, 171-173, 183; reserves, 171, 320

Bretton Woods monetary system, *xvi*, 103

Bribery. *See* Corruption

Brimmer, Andrew F., 96n

Britain, 22, 59, 68, 118, 248, 270, 292; forgiveness, 219; Ghana, 263-265, 268, 272; IMF, 64, 248; policy, 13, 15, 16, 17, 248

Brittain, W. H. Bruce, 313n, 332n

Bunching of debt, 30, 70, 255, 322

Burns, Arthur, 64, 96n, 97n, 101n, 239

Cambodia, 38-39

Canada, 12, 39, 59, 192, 219, 269, 270, 292

Capital, 63, 65-69, 83, 127, 136-142, 154, 158, 161, 166, 167, 174, 177, 178, 182, 186, 191, 196, 203-206, 211-212; accumulation, 158, 160,

176; flows, 36, 76, 85, 88, 89, 94, 141, 203, 212, *see also* flows of funds; formation, 83, 158, 160, 231; gains, 139, 140, 144; goods, 8, 13, 138, 176, 179; internationalization of, 186, 194, 196; markets, 116-117, 153, 186, 192, 225, 229, 275, 305, 311, 321; return on, 13, 136, 138, 166

Capitalism, 120, 127, 191, 194, 195, 197, 234, 248

Cardosa, Fernando Henrique, 187n

Carpenter, Robert, 155n

Carrion, Juan Manuel, 213n

Carter, James E., 207, 315n

Carter administration, 207, 242, 280n

Case-by-case approach, 24, 33, 34, 41, 49, 50, 52, 207

Cash flow, 105-110, 115-116, 118, 307, 322

Castro, Fidel, 259, 260

Cavanaugh, John J., 96n

Caves, Richard E., 151, 156n

Cayman Islands, 76

Central American Common Market, 154

Central banks, 9, 88, 92, 103, 106-109, 116-119, 132, 145, 195, 201, 208, 209, 320, 327

Central Intelligence Agency (CIA), 269

Cerro, 227

Certificates of Deposit (CDs), 62, 93, 96n, 107, 117

Charter Bank Corporation (Irving Trust), 193

Chase Manhattan Bank, 65, 98n, 193, 227, 229, 235, 244, 249n, 251n

Chemical Bank, 65, 98n, 193

Chick, Victoria, 114, 122n

Chile, 76, 127, 129, 130, 137-138, 143, 164, 165, 167, 196, 199, 203, 223, 255-257, 266-271, 272, 275, 325; balance of payments, 256, 266-270, 280n; copper, 258, 267-270, 280n; debt, 31, 33, 47, 67, 77, 198, 266-271, 276n; debt renegotiations (1965, 1972, 1974, 1975), 37-39, 47, 257, 266-272; exports, 266-268; growth, 165, 167, 267, 269; IMF, 268, 270; imports, 256, 268, inflation, 143, 165, 256, 266-271; na-

tionalization, expropriation, 265, 267-270; policy, 129, 165, 256, 267, 268, 270, 272, 280n

China, People's Republic of, *xviii*, 16, 98n, 269

Christian Democratic Party (Chile), 267

Citibank, 98n, 193, 203, 235, 244, 292, 293, 294, 296

Class, 203, 204, 309; lower, 179, 209, 226, 248, 256, 306, 309; upper, 174, 176, 179, 181, 209, 259, 306

Clausen, A. W., 312n

Cleveland, Harold van B., 313n

Cline, William R., 187n

Cofinancing, 81, 245, 251n, 312n, 328, 330. *See also* Joint financing

Colombia, 14, 31, 76, 129, 198

Colon, Hernandez, 165

Commercial paper, 62, 221

Commodity Credit Corporation (U.S.), 33, 39

Competition, 82, 83, 131-133, 153, 161, 163, 168, 220, 221, 285, 287

Comptroller of the Currency, 26n, 64-65

Concessional terms. *See* Terms, soft

Conditionality, 41, 43, 45, 53, 195, 326. *See also* International Monetary Fund, conditionality

Conference on International Economic Cooperation (CIEC), 23-24, 125, 302, 321

Confidence, 15, 18, 49, 62, 63, 80, 82, 84, 205, 219, 262, 304

Confluence of interest, 41-42

Congress (U.S.), 34, 42, 52, 64, 79, 81, 82

Congressional Budget Office, 99n

Connally, John, 267

Consumer goods, 162, 171-175, 178, 179

Consumption, 8, 27, 29, 83, 155, 166, 174, 176, 186, 205, 206

Continental Illinois, 193, 236, 238

Contract, 34, 110, 134, 255, 258, 264, 274, 307, 320, 323

Controls, 62, 114, 127, 157, 159, 162-167, 285. *See also* Exchange market, controls

Cooper, Richard, 325

Copper, 136-139, 196, 228, 229, 232, 233, 258, 267-270, 289, 290
Corredor, Jaime, 155n
Corruption, 161, 163, 256, 265, 266
Costa Rica, 200
Costanzo, G. A., 137
Country risk, 46, 195, 226
Credit, 93, 132, 133, 134, 154; creation, 3, 8-9, 11, 12, 14, 17, 18, 100n, 108, 201; crunch/squeeze, 61, 93, 100n, 144, 192, 198, 200, 204; standards, 61, 220; structure, 10, 17, 20, 122, 301
Creditor club, 4, 13, 20, 33, 34, 40-45, 47, 50, 54n, 219, 258, 288-289, 291, 324-325, 329
Creditworthiness, 30, 42, 48, 50, 63, 64, 72, 144, 195, 196, 246, 254, 267, 288, 296, 326
Cross-default clause, 21, 26n, 301, 313n, 314n, 317, 318, 328
Cuba, 260, 269, 274
Currency, 84, 88, 89, 101n, 105, 109, 114, 116, 117, 119; appreciation, 118, 119, 121; depreciation, 105, 115-116, 118; international, 103, 110, 111, 113, 114, 116; key, 103, 105, 106, 109, 117, 118, 119, 121

Dahl, Frederick R., 96n
D'Arista, Jane, 4, 96n
Debt, xv, 8-11, 33, 34, 126, 151, 161, 166, 191, 195, 275n, 313n, 319; absorptive capacity, 36, 49; cancellation/forgiveness, 23, 49, 253, 308, 311, 323; consolidation, 37, 50, 321, 322; crisis, 11, 17, 18, 32, 35-40, 48, 191, 197, 198, 201, 202, 205, 206, 211, 257, 322, 327, 329; management, 35, 43, 52, 60, 71, 83, 195, 205; moratorium, 23, 205, 207, 242, 261, 274; peonage, 127, 196-202; refinancing, 37, 47, 70, 71, 107, 184, 246, 253, 288, 322, 323, 325, 329; relief, 33, 37, 40-45, 49-53, 253-258, 321; renegotiation, 4, 24, 35, 37, 40-47, 184, 253-258, 277n, 284, 288, 289, 305, 307, 323-325, 328-330; repayment,

13, 18, 27, 46, 52, 69, 71, 127, 196, 204, 205, 253, 255, 306, 307, 322, 323; repudiation, 255, 262-265, 267, 274, 283, 288, 300; rescheduling, 24, 37, 40-45, 49, 70, 71, 73, 184, 202, 204, 205, 246, 253, 288, 289, 323, 325; service, 18, 19, 29-36, 40-46, 49, 53, 58, 59, 70, 78, 79, 83, 84, 115, 151, 161, 186, 199, 202, 206, 210, 247, 258, 274, 284, 288, 295, 306, 312, 319, 321, 322, 329, 331n; trap, 14, 197. See also under individual countries
Default, 7, 10, 12, 14, 15, 17, 20-23, 34, 40, 53, 64, 70, 84, 194, 198, 202, 206-210, 211, 234, 246, 248, 254, 272, 283, 284, 288, 291, 293, 298, 300, 301, 307, 319, 322, 323, 329
Deficit financing, 64, 81, 85, 171, 177, 180
Deflation, 28, 113, 205
de Fontenay, Patrick, 277n, 332n
Demand, 32, 52, 57-62, 109, 117, 120, 168, 174, 175, 182
Demand deposits, 106-109
Demirel regime (Turkey), 299
Democracy, 140, 164, 247, 260
Denmark, 270
Denoon, David, 276n, 278n
Dependence, xv, 108, 127, 162, 172, 180, 182-184, 187n, 191, 197, 200, 202, 204, 254, 273, 275
Depression, 64, 113, 208, 211, 283
Devaluation, 12, 104, 324
Development, 3, 45, 46, 50, 51, 53, 57, 58, 81, 83, 125-127, 134-137, 151, 157-163, 167-169, 172, 177, 194, 199, 203, 274, 287; deficit-financed, 81, 172, 174, 225; planning/strategy, 30, 49, 73, 81, 127, 159-162, 185, 207, 284
de Vries, Rimmer, 320-321, 328, 331n, 333n
DeWitt, R. Peter, 127, 214n
Dexter, Lewis A., 312n
Dhonte, Pierre, 255, 276n
Dickens, Charles, 9
Direct investment. See Foreign investment; Investment

Distribution, 50, 71, 78, 81, 127-130,
135-137, 141, 155, 169, 304, 306
Dollars, 88-92, 94, 104, 110-121,
121n, 310; denominated in, 84,
103-104, 110, 201; devaluation of,
283, 286
Drago Doctrine, 17
Durant, Will and Ariel, 157, 169n

Eastern Europe, 66, 69, 72, 75, 78, 86,
269, 304
Ecevit regime (Turkey), 299
Eckes, Alfred E., 332n
Economic growth. *See* Growth
Economic performance, 11, 43, 44, 50,
51, 53, 79, 309; strength, 11, 14,
27; theory, 104, 166, 200
Ecuador, 53n, 99n, 166, 188n, 200
Efficiency, 135, 142, 153, 163, 168,
285
Egypt, 15, 31, 33, 206; debt renegotia-
tion (1971), 38-39
Einhorn, Jessica, 249n
Employment, 82, 99n, 129, 137, 161
Entrepreneurship, 131, 136, 140, 141,
184, 197
Equity, 142, 168, 180, 186
Esseks, J. D., 278n
Ethiopia, 200
Eurobond market, 100n, 221, 283.
See also Bonds
Eurocurrency, credits/loans, 58-60, 70,
72-81, 87-94, 94n, 101n, 201,
288, 328; market, xvi, 4, 18, 19,
61, 72, 87-94, 101n, 192, 210,
229, 231, 232, 283, 285, 286,
305, 318
Eurodollars, 89, 91, 93, 117, 201, 202,
221. *See also* Petrodollars; Organiza-
tion of Petroleum Exporting Coun-
tries, surpluses
Europe, 12, 50, 83, 112, 269
Exchange market, 84, 116-117, 310;
controls, 165, 167, 195, 211
Export credit, 11, 36, 257, 265
Export Credit Guarantee Department
(U.K.), 13
Export-Import Bank (U.S.), 33, 34, 39,
78, 82, 83, 209, 229, 231, 245,
251n, 267, 270, 292, 300, 328
Exports, 29, 36, 59, 71, 79, 83, 99n,

111, 136, 144, 150, 162, 167,
168, 205, 209, 255, 257, 258,
327. *See also* under individual
countries
Export subsidies, 83, 162, 191
Extractive industries, 138, 141, 273,
311

Factor endowments, 130, 141, 273, 311
Feder, Gershon, 276n
Federal funds, 93, 100n
Federal Reserve, 107, 113, 114, 208
Federal Reserve Board, 64, 69, 73,
92-93, 239
Fees, 63, 71, 73, 245
Feinberg, Richard, 251n
Feis, Herbert, 15-17, 25n, 312n
Fernandez Maldonado, Jorge, 233
Fertilizer, 59, 171, 183
Financial aspects of economy, 104,
106; crisis/crash, 105, 115; flows:
see Flows of funds; Credit flows;
instruments, 109, 116, 120, 121
First National Bank of Boston, 193
First National Bank of Chicago, 193
Fishlow, Albert, 69, 97n, 99n, 100n,
326, 332n
Fitzgerald, E.V.K., 249n
Flows of funds, 61, 62, 73, 81, 109,
126, 130, 136, 141, 143-153, 178,
196; analysis, 143, 145-154
Food, 59, 178, 179, 269
Foreign aid. *See* Aid
Foreign Assistance Act (U.S.), 33, 34,
52
Foreign exchange, 58, 69, 88, 99n,
144, 151, 162, 220; earnings, 18,
30, 36, 84, 144, 186, 199, 311
Foreign investment, 84, 88, 111, 113,
117, 121, 159, 165, 172, 178, 182,
184, 185, 195, 211, 327, see also
Investment; direct, 12, 58, 81,
174, 180, 184; in U.S., 12, 88, 89;
U.S., 12, 92, 113, 121
Forward cover, 89, 93
France, 15, 17, 59, 269, 272, 292
Franklin National Bank crash, 62,
117, 220
Frannsen, Constant, 202
Fraser, Leon, 283, 312n
Frei, Eduardo, 266

Frei regime (Chile), 257, 267
Friedman, Irving S., 95n, 100n, 195, 213n, 291, 292

Geisel regime (Brazil), 177, 180
George, Henry, 163, 168n
Germany, 85, 86, 91, 264, 270, 292, 310
Ghana, 31n, 222, 255, 256, 258, 262-266, 267, 271, 272, 279n; austerity measures, 262, 264; balance of payments, 256, 264, 265, 275, 279n; Britain, 263-265, 268, 272; cocoa, 264, 275, 278n, 279n; debt, 40, 262-266, 274-275; debt moratorium, 262, 263, 265; debt renegotiations (1966, 1968, 1970, 1974), 11, 37-39, 54n, 262-266, 271, 274, 279n; debt service, 256, 263; devaluation, 264, 265; exports, 263, 275; IMF, 257, 262-264; imports, 256, 264, 265, 279n; policy, 262, 264, 266; price, 258, 264, 265
Glab, Edward, Jr., 276n, 280n
Glassock, C. B., 155n
Gold, 100, 110-117, 119; standard, 110, 116, 119
Gomes, Serevo, 180-181
Goods and services, 109, 111, 144, 185, 186
Goulart, Joao, 260, 261
Goulart regime (Brazil), 174, 261, 272
Grace, W. R. & Co., 227
Gravel, Charles G., 215n
Greene, James, 249n, 279n
Greene Agreement, 231, 249n
Gross Domestic Product (GDP), 143, 154, 164
Gross National Product (GNP), 58, 79, 94n, 198
Group of 77, 49, 50, 51, 52, 55n, 254
Group of 10, 66, 75, 78, 86, 91, 98n
Growth, 8-11, 18, 24, 43, 58, 59, 62, 70, 72, 78, 79, 81, 83-84, 126, 127, 130, 136-142, 150-154, 162, 166-169, 186, 196, 197, 200, 320. *See also* under individual countries

Guarantees, 33, 73, 76, 78, 97n, 98n, 265; government, 19, 47, 82, 84, 245, 320
Guatemala, 17

Hague Convention (1907), 17
Hanley, Thomas H., 96n
Haq, Mahbub ul, 275n
Hauge, Gabriel, 312n, 328
Heckscher, Eli, 137, 155n
Heldring, Frederick, 100n, 326
Herstatt collapse, 21, 62, 220, 289
Hickenlooper Amendment, 229, 235
Hill, Richard, 324
Hollist, W. Ladd, 127
Hong Kong, 196
House Committee on Appropriations, 82-83
House Committee on Banking, Housing, and Urban Affairs, 74
Human rights, 203, 243, 270-271; Carter policy on, 243, 280n
Hunt, Shane, 249n
Hymer, Stephen, 138, 155n

Ibanez, Gaston, 240
IMF. *See* International Monetary Fund
Imports, 59, 64, 70, 79, 83, 111, 113, 114, 116, 144, 145, 151, 153, 154, 162, 167, 168, 183, 186, 202, 205. *See also* under individual countries
Import substitution, 79, 154, 159, 162, 163, 173, 174, 182
Impoverishment, 127, 128, 306, 309, 311; of U.S. 103-104
Incentives, 143, 160-168, 181, 198, 232
Income, 24, 62, 111, 113, 138-141, 144, 151, 158, 160, 169, 194, 204; distribution, 132, 135, 154, 168, 169, 204
India, 13-14, 50, 281n, 302; debt and debt renegotiations (1968, 1971, 1972, 1973, 1974, 1975, 1976, 1977), 13-14, 31, 33, 37-40, 42, 54n, 55n, 271
Indonesia, 53n, 69, 99n, 222, 293-296, 302, 304; balance of payments, 293, 295, 296; central bank, 295, 296; debt, 68, 200, 257, 293-296;

debt renegotiations (1966, 1967, 1968, 1970), 11, 37-39, 44-45, 54n, 266, 271, 276n, 277n, 293-296; IMF, 293, 296; World Bank, 293
Industrialization, 79, 171, 173, 177-183, 196-197
Inequity, *xv*, 171, 203, 204, 206
Infrastructure, 142, 158, 159, 203, 289
Innovation, 141, 154
Instability, 13, 85, 88, 127, 128, 309; political, 11, 119, 158, 202
Insurance, 9-11, 20, 22, 23, 145, 328
Inter-American Development Bank (IDB), 209, 229, 245, 247, 268, 270
Interbank market, 62, 63, 80, 84; placements, 76, 98n, 100n, 121n, 207, 221
Interest, payments, 33, 37, 63, 110; rates, 37, 89, 93, 99n, 116, 130, 134, 153, 199, 200, 202, 235, 257
Interest Equalization Tax (U.S.), 283
Intermediaries, 1, 130; financial, 92, 126, 129, 133, 138. *See also* Banks
Intermediation, 130-135, 145, 152, 154
International Development Agency (IDA), 264
International Financial Corporation (IFC), 16
International Labor Organization (ILO), 185
International Monetary Fund (IMF), *xvii*, 14, 16, 21-23, 35, 40, 41, 43-45, 48, 49, 53, 64, 80-82, 91, 92, 100n, 125, 195, 198, 199, 204, 206-208, 210, 211, 221-223, 226, 244-246, 248, 259, 260, 297, 308, 309, 311, 317, 322-324, 326-330, *see also* under individual countries; conditionality, 46-49, 324, 326, 329, 330; quotas, 64, 81, 327, 330; standby agreements, 41, 43, 206, 207; Witteveen facility (oil facility), 22, 64, 81, 208, 209, 327
International monetary system, *xv*, 52, 85, 94, 103, 104, 109, 110, 118-121, 202, 206-208

International organizations, 23, 71, 200, 205, 209, 238, 244, 267, 274
International Petroleum Company (Exxon), 227, 228, 249n
International Telephone and Telegraph (ITT), 227, 268
Investment, 8, 27, 29, 58, 85, 88, 92, 116, 132, 137, 138, 139, 141-146, 148-154, 164, 167, 176, 191, 318; income, 101n, 113, 116, 117, 154, *see also* Foreign investment
Iran, 53n, 99n, 293
Iraq, 53n, 298
Israel, 210
Italy, 39, 59, 248, 292; debt, 65, 68; IMF, 64, 248
Ivory Coast, 31, 200

Jamaica, 31, 200
Japan, 15-16, 61, 83, 85, 86, 91, 99n, 118, 125, 219, 292, 310; surplus, 32, 85, 119
Javits, Jacob, 96n
Javits amendment, 52
Joint financing, 328, 330. *See also* Co-financing
Just, Richard, 276n

Karaken, John H., 97n
Kaufman, Henry, 110, 121n, 122n
Kelly, Janet, 331n
Kenen, Peter B., 99n, 331n
Kennecott Copper Company, 269
Kennedy administration, 260
Keynes, John Maynard, 109, 122n
Kindleberger, Charles P., 283, 312n
Kissinger, Henry, 92
Kolko, Gabriel, 332n
Korea. *See* South Korea
Kubitschek regime (Brazil), 173, 259, 272
Kuczynski, Michael, 249n
Kuwait, 53n, 318

Labor, 131, 136, 138-141, 158, 167, 194-197, 210
Laffer, Arthur B., 126, 127
Land, 131, 167
Latin America, 12, 13, 19, 66, 72, 75, 76, 86, 126, 129, 130, 134, 143, 153, 260, 269, 304

Latour, Pierre, 94n, 215n
Law of the sea, 125
Least developed nations, 22, 33, 49, 50-52, 219, 254, 308, 318, 319
Lee, Teng-Hui, 151, 156n
Leff, Nathaniel, 277n
Leibestein, Harvey, 169n
Leiva, Gustavo, 156n
Lender of last resort, 9, 320
Lend-Lease, 12
Lerner symmetry theorem, 167
Leverage. *See* Bargaining power
Levine, David I., 187n, 188n
Levine, Robert M., 99n
Lewis, W. Arthur, 99n
Liability management, 62
Libby, Ronald T., 278n
Liberia, 76
Libya, 53n
Licensing, 232, 256
Lipper, Kenneth, 96n, 99n
Lipson, Charles, 223, 333n
Liquidity, 61, 62, 70, 82, 100n, 130, 131, 136, 174, 201, 202, 221, 229, 284, 286, 287, 289, 303, 305-308, 318, 328, 330
Lisakers, Karin, 96n, 212n, 213n, 249n, 314n
Loan(s): balance of payments, 69, 317, 319, 320, 326, 327, 330; demand, 62, 221, 229, 243, 284, 287, 306; limits, 65, 72, 300
Lobbying, 285
Lomé Convention, 22
Losses, 46, 69, 132, 144
Lowenthal, Abraham, 249n

McKinnon, Ronald I., 156n
Malan, Pedro S., 173, 176, 187n, 188n
Malaysia, 31, 67, 77, 200
Manila Declaration, 49-50, 55n, 125, 302
Manufacturers Hanover Trust, 65, 98n, 193, 235-236, 249n
Manufacturing industries, 141, 145, 152, 153, 174, 311
Marcona Mining Company, 234-235
Margins, 61, 63, 93, 130-135, 300, 303
Market: access, 83; forces, 141, 142; imperfections, 132; performance, 157

Marshall Plan, 12, 83
Marx, Karl, 191
Maturity, 33, 37, 61, 72, 73, 76, 134, 200, 246, 287, 297, 303, 304; structure, 70, 71, 200
Mensah, J. H., 263-264, 278n
Merchandise expenditures, 112-114
Mexico, 20, 24, 50, 72, 74, 76, 129, 143, 198, 244, 248, 269, 271, 300, 302, 303, 304, 308, 320, 321; debt, 31, 65, 67, 68, 77, 198, 199, 201, 299, 300, 303; devaluation, 64, 143, 300; IMF, 199; oil, 199, 303; policy, 199, 303
Military, expenditures/spending, 111-113, 196, 228, 233, 241; intervention/conflict, 195, 254, 271; rule, 164, 171; seizure of power, 174, 227, 257, 261, 264, 266, 270
Miller, G. William, 201
Mineroperú, 231
Mining, 136, 139, 153, 195, 234-235, 267, 292
Minsky, Hyman P., 4, 121n, 122n, 312n
Miossi, Alfred, 238
Mitchell, Parren J., 96n
Money, 106-110, 115; supply, 89, 106, 129
Monopoly, 114, 131-133, 136, 154, 161, 163
Morales Bermúdez, Francisco, 232, 233, 236, 240, 242, 250n
Morales regime (Peru), 233, 241, 243, 247
Moran, Theodore H., 281n
Morgan, Dan, 214n
Morgan Guaranty Trust, 65, 98n, 193, 226, 293-296
Morley, Morris, 213n, 214n
Morocco, 15, 31, 71-72
Morris, Cynthia Taft, 214n
Most-favored nation (MFN), 40, 277n, 325
Most seriously affected (MSA) nation. *See* Least developed nations
Movimento Democrático Brasileiro (MDB), 181
Müller, Ronald E., 83, 100n, 213n
Multilateral agencies. *See* International organizations

Multinational corporations/enterprises, 25n, 62, 76, 78, 114, 125, 138, 181, 191, 197, 203, 205, 221, 273, 309, 317

Nacional Financiera (Mexico), 303
Nash, James, 326
Nassau, 76
National Advisory Council (NAC), 33
National Liberation Council (NLC) (Ghana), 262, 272
National Redemption Council (NRC) (Ghana), 264-266
Nelson, Richard R., 169n
Netherlands, 270, 292
New International Economic Order (NIEO), 125, 219, 288, 308-311
New York City debt, 21, 96n, 105, 115
Nigeria, 14, 53n
Nixon, Richard M., 267, 280n, 284
Nkrumah, Kwame, 256, 257, 272
Nkrumah regime (Ghana), 262, 265
Nondiscrimination, 34, 40, 325
North Korea default, 315n
Norway, 270
Nossiter, Bernard D., 214n

O'Conner, Harvey, 155n
Odell, John S., 222
Official Development Assistnce (ODA), 35, 43, 55n. *See also* Aid
Ohlin, Goran, 276n, 277n
Oil, 114, 136, 139, 171, 181, 183, 196, 261, 298; embargo, *xvi*, 317; price and price rise, 19, 27, 36, 59, 60, 62, 97n, 125, 175, 181, 183, 191, 192, 194, 231, 284, 290, 317, 318, 320
Open market operations, 108, 119
Opportunity costs, 130, 131, 140
Organization for Economic Cooperation and Development (OECD), 19, 28, 40, 59, 60, 62, 94n, 327
Organization for European Economic Cooperation (OEEC), 297
Organization of American States (OAS), 143, 155n, 237
Organization of Petroleum Exporting Countries (OPEC), 28, 72, 78, 84-86, 92, 99n, 125, 153, 219,

221, 274, 293, 310; aid, 19; deposits, 74, 80, 85; investments, 85, 88, 318; members, 53n, 229; surpluses, 27, 32, 52, 60, 85, 97n, 317-318, 320-321. *See also* Petrodollars, recycling
Overseas Private Investment Corporation (OPIC) (U.S.), 23, 83
Ownership, 197, 204

Packenham, Robert A., 182, 187n, 188n, 189n
Pakistan, 14, 50, 72-74, 98n, 281n, 302n; debt/debt renegotiations (1972, 1973, 1974), 14, 31, 33, 37-40, 42, 54n, 55n, 72-74, 271, 277n
Palmerston Memorandum (1848), 16
Panama, 31
Paraguay, 200
Parallel financing. *See* Cofinancing
Payer, Cheryl, 213n, 214n, 276n, 277n, 331n
Penetration, 182, 196
Pertamina, 257, 295-296
Peru, 46, 76, 143, 144, 166, 194, 203, 206, 222, 226-248, 255, 297, 298, 302, 325-326; anchovies, 232, 233, 235; austerity measures, 233, 236, 238, 239, 240; balance of payments, 226, 228, 231-233, 238-240; banks monitor economy, 206, 226, 227, 232-237, 241-244, 307, 326, 330; budget, 228, 231, 234, 235, 239-242; central bank, 240; copper, 228, 229, 232, 235, 249n, 251n; debt, 40, 67, 68, 77, 198, 199, 226, 229, 230, 234, 241; debt renegotiations (1968, 1969, 1978), 38-39, 226, 233, 234, 243; debt service, 228, 230, 238; economy, 227-236; exports, 228, 230-233, 241; fish as food, 228, 232, 233, 236, 237, 240, 242; foreign investment, 227, 229, 235, 237; growth, 227, 230, 232, 236, 237, 240; IMF, 226, 227, 233, 235, 238-243, 250n; imports, 228, 231-233, 240-243; inflation, 143, 228, 230-232, 235, 239, 241, 242; nationalization, 227, 231, 234; oil, 228, 229, 234-235; pipeline, 233, 249n-250n;

prices, 231, 232, 234, 239, 240, 242; production, 227, 232, 235, 240; reform, 227, 231; taxes, 228, 232, 235, 240; unemployment, 227-228, 230-233, 237, 241, 242; wages, 228, 230, 231, 233, 237, 240, 241; World Bank, 229, 232
Pescaperú, 231, 235
Petras, James F., 127, 213n, 214n, 280n
Petrobras, 181, 304
Petrodollars, 229, 318; recycling, xvi, 60-61, 80, 84, 221, 284
Petroleum. *See* Oil
Petroperu, 228, 231, 240
Philippines, 76, 99n, 210, 320; debt, 31, 67, 77, 198-200
Phillips, Chester Arthur, 122n
Piazza, Walter, 240, 241
Pinochet regime (Chile), 266, 270, 271, 273
Planning, 126, 130, 141-144, 153-155, 159, 232-233, 247, 263, 304
Poland, 38-39, 68, 315n
Policy intrusion, 111-113
Politics, 141, 238; domestic, 272-275
Ponzi finance, 115
Pool, Ithiel, 312n
Popular Christian Party (Peru), 243
Popular Unity government (Chile), 129, 267, 269, 270, 274
Portuguese default, 15
Potter, S. J., 25n
Pound. *See* Sterling
Poverty, 48, 127, 157, 158, 168, 172, 289, 308
Power, 103, 114, 133, 137, 203, 204, 237, 248, 254, 273
Prepaid loans, 300
Pressure groups, 129
Price, 20, 73, 114, 116-118, 137, 139, 144, 163, 183, 204, 212, 319; stability, 135, 154; volatility, 139, 191
Price-specie flow analysis, 104, 113-114
Pricing, 99n, 131, 153, 257
Privatization, 211, 225-226, 243-248
Production, 79, 129, 136, 139, 141, 158, 163, 172, 174-177, 181,

191, 194, 205; capacity, 173, 176, 180, 182, 184, 186; structure, 171, 173, 176, 177, 184, 185
Productivity, 157, 161
Profit, 17, 23, 62, 63, 70, 114, 132, 134, 138, 144, 151, 153, 154, 157, 194, 201, 204, 208, 210, 221, 225, 226, 258; bank, 21, 81, 84, 133, 220, 225-226, 243, 247, 248, 287, 288, 300, 304, 306; maximization of, 136, 138-139; repatriation of, 166, 197, 211, 261
Programmade de Integração Social (PIS) (Brazil), 185
Protectionism, 79, 82, 83, 153, 154, 167, 197, 310, 321
Prout, Christopher, 14, 25n, 278n, 332n
Public Law 480 (U.S.), 33, 52, 262
Puerto Rico, 127, 159, 164, 165, 197
Purchasing power, 118, 180, 227, 242

Qatar, 53n
Quadros, Janio, 259, 260
Quadros regime (Brazil), 174
Quijano, Anibal, 149n

Rampersand, Frank B., 155n
Rappaport, Bruce, 296
Real Estate Investment Trusts (REITs), 10, 21, 62, 69
Recession, 27, 28, 52, 62, 89, 105, 113, 114, 118, 171, 175-177, 196-198, 202, 221, 225, 318, 321, 322
Recovery, 12, 44, 70, 79, 83-84, 97n, 197, 320
Reddaway, W. B., 25n
Reddaway report, 12
Refinancing. *See* Debt, refinancing
Reform, 134, 135, 141, 155, 164, 165
Regional development banks, 40
Regulations. *See* Controls
Regulatory authorities, 21, 62, 64, 70, 107
Reich, Cary, 251n
Reich, Peter, 188n
Reksten, 21

Renegotiation. *See* Debt, renegotiation
Rent, 126, 141, 142, 152, 155; economic, 130, 131, 136-145, 154; generation of, 136-138, 140-142, 144, 145, 151, 153, 154; innovation (Schumpeterian), 136-139 142, 152, 154; intermediation, 131, 133, 134; natural resources (Ricardian), 136-140, 144, 151, 153, 154; protection (Bain), 136-139, 152, 154; surplus, 174, 186
Repayment. *See* Debt, repayment
Repayment period, 37, 199
Repression, 171, 181, 197, 203, 206, 242, 243, 247, 248, 270, 322. *See also* Violence
Repudiation. *See* Debt, repudiation
Rescheduling. *See* Debt, rescheduling
Reserve requirements, 93, 107, 108, 134, 201, 221
Reserves, 43, 60, 61, 69, 88, 92, 108, 111, 254, 286, 320
Resource, 137, 140, 141, 142, 162, 195, 196; allocation, 132, 133, 136, 153, 157, 159; transfers, 41, 43, 45, 49-51, 135, 153
Retroactive Terms Adjustment (RTA), 51, 52
Reuss, Henry S., 101n
Reynolds, Clark W., 126, 127, 155n, 156n
Risk, 9-10, 14, 23, 46, 61, 131, 136, 139, 195, 209, 273, 318, 330; dispersion, 14, 46, 130, 198, 236, 300, 304
Rockefeller, John D., 139
Roett, Riordan, 187n, 188n
Roll-over, 65, 69, 73, 243, 255, 303, 304, 313n, 322
Romero-Barcelo, Carlos, 165
Rothschild, Emma, 214n
Run on a currency, 117-118, 120
Russia. *See* USSR

Safety net proposal, 82, 92. *See also* International Monetary Fund
Sanford, Jonathan E., 279n
Santistevan, Carlos, 240
Sargen, Nicholas, 26n, 94n
Saudi Arabia, 53n, 318

Savings, 83, 107, 126, 127, 129, 135, 138, 139, 142, 143, 146, 148-152, 160, 161, 164, 166, 167, 185, 186, 194; foreign, 126, 142, 143, 144; rates/ratio, 154, 158
Sayers, R. S., 103, 116, 121n
Schattschneider, E. E., 312n
Schultz, T. Paul, 169n
Scott, Walter, 9
Sectors, 143, 145, 146, 151-154, 162, 174, 177, 179, 186
Securities and Exchange Commission (SEC) (U.S.), 70
Security, 134, 152, 180-181; East-West, 125; political, 120
Security analyst, 63
Security Pacific National Bank, 193
Senate Committee on Foreign Relations, 192, 209; subcommittee on MNCs, 192
Shapiro, Harvey D., 250n, 251n
Shultz, George, 312n
Sideroperú, 231
Sierra Leone, 38-39
Sigmund, Paul E., 279n
Silva Ruete, Javier, 251n
Singapore, 200
Skidmore, Thomas E., 185, 189n, 277n
Slater, Walker, 21
Slighton, Robert L., 169n
Smith, Gordon W., 214n, 275n
Social: accounting, 126, 141, 143, 151; unrest, 78, 144, 303, 306
Socialism, 167, 259
Socialist nations, *xviii*, 8, 60. *See also* USSR; Eastern Europe
Solarz amendment, 52
Solomon, Anthony, 64
Solomon, Robert, 60, 94n, 95n, 97n, 99n, 100n
Sources and uses of funds, 62, 91, 130, 146-148
South Africa, 68
Southern Peru Copper Company, 234-235
South Korea, 20, 67, 72, 76, 99n, 196, 210, 320; debt, 31, 33, 77, 198, 200
Soviet Union. *See* USSR

Spain, 15, 68
Special Drawing Rights (SDRs), 92
Spellman, Lewis, 155n
Spread. *See* Margins
Sri Lanka, 200
Stability, 80, 195, 246; economic, 84,
   210; political, 28, 205, 210
Stabilization, 48, 49, 70, 144, 236,
   324; programs, 48, 53, 73, 78,
   205, 233-235, 247. *See also* Auster-
   ity measures
Stagflation, 83, 176, 202
Stallings, Barbara, 222, 251n, 325
Standard of living, 180, 186, 188n,
   199, 201, 248
Standard Oil (Exxon), 227, 229, 249
State Department (U.S.), 63, 245, 268
Sterling, 12, 110, 111, 116
Stern, Fritz, 26n
Stobaugh, Robert B., 331n
Stocks, 62, 63, 120
Strange, Susan, 3, 25n
Strikes, 206, 239, 241, 242, 247,
   261, 269
Structural change, 32, 48, 129, 130,
   133, 134, 154, 236
Structures, 187n; asset, 133, 135;
   economic, 130, 172, 181, 204;
   liability, 133, 135; political, 181,
   195, 203-206; social, 172, 181,
   195, 203-206. *See also* Production,
   structure
Subsidy, 135, 153, 161, 163, 211
Sudan, 14, 15, 31, 200
Suharto, 293
Sukarno, 293
Suppliers' Credit, 11, 18, 36, 58, 256,
   257, 263, 265, 278n
Supply, 136, 137, 168
Surplus capacity, 82, 137, 140
Sweden, 137-138, 219, 270
Sweezy, Paul M., 213n
Swiss National Bank, 88
Syndications, 63, 285, 289, 291,
   295, 304
Syria, 31

Taiwan, 20, 76, 88-89, 99n, 151,
   196, 210; debt, 31, 67, 68, 77, 198,
   200

Tanzania, 31
Tariffs, 114, 162, 165, 167, 168, 206,
   212
Tax, 93, 126, 127, 140-142, 153, 154,
   161-163, 166-168; income, 165,
   168; luxury/excise, 114, 159, 162,
   164, 168; progressive, 157, 159,
   161, 168; rates, 159-161, 164,
   165; yield, 157, 161, 166, 167
Taylor, C. T., 25n
Terms, 70, 255, 264, 271, 294, 303;
   hard, 40, 226, 262-264, 268,
   270; of trade, 79, 104, 159, 191,
   197, 258, 276n-277n, 321; soft, 30,
   33, 37, 38n, 42, 45, 50, 53, 196,
   257, 263, 272, 294
Term transformation, 134, 135, 153
Thailand, 76, 99n; debt, 31, 67, 77,
   198, 200
Tobin, James, 169n
Tobin Report for Puerto Rico, 159-
   161, 169n
Trade, 13, 20, 79, 84, 92, 106, 167,
   318; balance, 12, 20, 113, 117, 162,
   168; free, 83, 168
Transfer of technology, 125
Transfer pricing, 132
Transnational enterprise. *See* Multinational corporations
Treasury Department (U.S.), 34, 63,
   91, 95n, 245, 317; securities, 88,
   89, 91, 120
Triffin, Robert, 208
Tugwell, Franklin, 281n
Tunisia, 14, 31
Turkey, 17, 46, 69, 222, 296-299,
   302, 308, 326; austerity measures,
   299; balance of payments, 297,
   298; central bank, 299; debt, 296-
   299; debt renegotiations (1959,
   1965, 1972, 1978), 38-40, 47, 200,
   296-299; economy, 297-299
Tyson, Brady, 180, 188n

Unemployment, 158, 161, 168, 212
United Arab Emirates, 53n, 318
United Arab Republic, 11
United Kingdom. *See* Britain
United Nations, 11, 49
United Nations Conference on Trade

and Development (UNCTAD), 11, 32, 45, 49, 51, 125, 321
United States, 12, 14, 22, 33, 34, 39, 49, 61-63, 76, 79, 85, 91, 92, 103-104, 112, 115, 117, 119, 120, 137, 192, 207, 210, 242, 257, 269, 292, 303, 308; as a bank, 104, 121; balance of payments, 15, 85, 87, 91, 92, 111-112, 114, 120, 283; debt policy, 4, 33-35, 42, 43, 47, 52, 88; economy, 82, 84, 89, 93, 94, 103, 104, 211, 284, 310; policy, 27, 82, 93-94, 103-104, 120, 161, 267, 310, 318; trade, 82, 85, 88, 89, 94, 119, 120, 211
Urban, 186, 203
Uruguay, 200, 268
USSR, *xviii*, 68, 86, 98n, 241, 250n, 262, 265, 269, 274, 325

Value, 106, 109, 110
Value added, 154, 179
Vasena, Adalbert Krieger, 331n, 333n
Velasco Alvarado, Juan, 227
Velasco Alvarado regime (Peru), 227, 229, 232, 236, 244
Venezuela, 15, 18, 53n, 99n
Venture capital, 134, 154
Vernon, Raymond, 281n
Viner, Jacob, 109
Violence, 181, 203, 206, 241, 242. *See also* Repression
Voluntary Foreign Credit Restraint guidelines (VFCR) (U.S.), 283
Vulnerability, 82, 144, 172, 182-184, 187n, 273

Wachtel, Howard M., 213n, 214n
Wages, 159, 161, 163, 185, 205, 206, 247; freeze, 144, 204; minimum, 159, 161, 163, 185, 231

Wall, David, 276n
Wallich, Henry C., 61, 64, 70, 95n, 320, 333n
Wanniski, Jude, 169n
Watson, Paul M., 95n
Wealth, 103, 135, 137, 153
Weinert, Robert, 60-61, 95n
Weinstein, Franklin B., 280n
Welfare, 10, 11, 20, 22, 137, 185, 203
Wellons, Philip A., 26n, 98n, 99n, 188n, 192, 212n, 214n, 276n
Wells Fargo Bank, 236
West Germany. *See* Germany
Whitman, Marina von N., 97n, 99n, 100n, 332n
Wilkie, James W., 187n-188n
Witteveen, H. Johannes, 48
Witteveen facility. *See* International Monetary Fund, Witteveen facility
World Bank, *xviii*, 11, 13, 14, 16, 21-23, 26n, 37, 40, 42, 59, 125, 198, 200, 209, 210, 226, 245-247, 265, 268-270, 320, 323, 325, 327, 328
World Health Organization (WHO), 180

Yugoslavia, 38-39

Zaire, 46, 115, 194-196, 203, 222, 255, 289-293, 297, 298, 302, 304, 308, 325; aid, 293; austerity measures, 195-196, 291; central bank, 195, 291, 293; civil war, 206, 290, 292; copper, 289, 290; debt, 31, 47, 195-196, 200, 257, 271, 272, 289-293; debt renegotiation (1976, 1977), 38-39, 289-293; economy, 195, 290-292; IMF, 195, 291-293
Zambia, 31, 200
Zolotas, Xenophon, 333n